"As a candidate, Barack Obama
that he'd provide the desperately
empire and national security state that we so fervently desired.
Instead, as Jeremy Kuzmarov lays out in this extraordinary book,
Obama doubled down on most of Bush and Cheney's hawkish,
confrontational, and surveillance-obsessed policies and helped
pave the way for the current nightmare of Trumpian warmongering
and perversity. In ways no one else has done, Kuzmarov punctures
Obama's phony liberal and humanitarian veneer and skillfully
deconstructs the carefully crafted Obama creation myth, while laying
bare the rot at the base of the Democratic Party and its decades
of bipartisan, empire-affirming, militaristic policies, dating back
to Woodrow Wilson and Harry Truman and culminating with the
centrist troika of Obama, Clinton, and Biden."

—PETER KUZNICK,
co-author with Oliver Stone of
The Untold History of the United States

"Kuzmarov's latest is not just a disturbing look at Obama's
disastrous interventions abroad, it is a devastatingly clinical analysis
of the cynical thinking that defines the Democratic Party's foreign
policy consensus – and of the public relations tactics the party's
leadership applies to sell it to their liberal base. As such, it is a
critical guidebook to the 2020 primary field."

—MAX BLUMENTHAL
author of *The Management of Savagery* and
The 51 Day War: Ruin and Resistance in Gaza

"This important book is an urgent reminder that the forever wars
of the United States are a bipartisan affair; in this in-depth study of
the Obama presidency, Jeremy Kuzmarov documents the continued
imperial domination policies and actions."

—ROXANNE DUNBAR-ORTIZ
author of *An Indigenous Peoples' History of the United States*

"For all those liberals who have romanticized Barack Obama as an
enlightened leader of the people, Jeremy Kuzmarov busts through
such myths with a well-documented book showing Obama for what
he was and is — the kind face of US imperial aggression. This is a

must-read for anyone believing that simply getting rid of Trump and returning to 'normal' is a way forward."

—DAN KOVALIK
author of *The Plot to Overthrow Venezuela*

"Written in muckraker fashion, Kuzmarov's *Obama's Unending Wars* is a bombshell blowing the progressive camo off the Obama presidency."

—JERRY LEMBCKE
author of *The Spitting Image: Myth, Memory, and the Legacy of Vietnam*

"Kuzmarov's impeccable and extensive research reveals the reality of Barack Obama's eight presidential years favoring the economic and military-warring interests of the rich. Obama, the drone president, stood for seven aggressive wars, more than any other US president. The author peals the imperial white mask off the black skin in an analogy to Frantz Fanon's classic work. Racism, colonization and contemporary neo-colonialization have distorted the psyches of all colors of peoples. Obama's black Kenyan roots allowed him to do the white man's bidding throughout Africa, and many other nations. While George Bush founded the US African Command (AFRICOM), in 2007, it was Obama, who set about implementing military (and economic) domination to 53 African governments. Kuzmarov shows how many white progressives, who, in their anxiety to reject any racist appearance, embraced this warmongering president. Obama also convinced most African-Americans to give him leeway to do them justice, which he never did."

—RON RIDENOUR
author of *The Russian Peace Threat*

OBAMA'S UNENDING WARS

Fronting the Foreign Policy of the Permanent Warfare State

---

by

JEREMY KUZMAROV

Clarity Press, Inc

© 2019 Jeremy Kuzmarov
ISBN: 978-1-949762-00-6
EBOOK ISBN: 978-1-949762-01-3
In-house editor: Diana G. Collier
Cover: R. Jordan P. Santos

Library of Congress Cataloging-in-Publication Data

Names: Kuzmarov, Jeremy, 1979- author.
Title: Obama's unending wars: fronting the foreign
  policy of the permanent warfare state / Jeremy Kuzmarov.
Description: Atlanta, GA : Clarity Press, Inc., [2019] | Includes
  bibliographical references and index.
Identifiers: LCCN 2019016447 (print) | LCCN 2019020079 (ebook) | ISBN
  9781949762013 | ISBN 9781949762006 (alk. paper) | ISBN 9781949763013
  (ebook)
Subjects: LCSH: Obama, Barack. | United States--Foreign
relations--2009-2017.
  | United States--Military policy--History--21st century. | United
  States--Politics and government--2009-2017. | Militarism--United
  States--History--21st century. | Politics and war--United
  States--History--21st century. | Political leadership--United
  States--History--21st century.
Classification: LCC E907 (ebook) | LCC E907 .K89 2019 (print) | DDC
    327.73009/051--dc23
  LC record available at https://lccn.loc.gov/2019016447

Clarity Press, Inc.
2625 Piedmont Rd. NE, Ste. 56
Atlanta, GA. 30324 , USA
http://www.claritypress.com

TABLE OF CONTENTS

Dedication:
*To the memory of Fred Branfman, 1943-2014
a man of peace and compassion*

FOREWORD

Obama: Imperialism's Second Wind

Glen Ford

Barack Obama may go down in presidential history as the most effective—and deceptive—imperialist of them all.

U.S. empire is deeply indebted to Obama, both as commander-in-chief and savior of the finance capitalist class. In late September 2008, just weeks before voters made him the first Black president of the United States, candidate Obama rescued the Lords of Capital from the consequences of the catastrophic meltdown of their own making. On Monday, September 29, despite Treasury Secretary Henry Paulson's warnings of looming Armageddon, the outgoing Bush administration's $700 billion Wall Street bailout bill came up 13 votes short in the House. One third of Democrats and two thirds of Republicans rejected legislation to save the banks by buying up worthless securities. The crisis had rendered Republican presidential candidate Sen. John McCain incapable of coherent speech, leaving the salvage of Wall Street to Obama. He quickly went to work on the holdouts, who constituted a 21 to 18 majority in the Congressional Black Caucus. By Friday, Obama's intervention had convinced all but eight Black Democrats to cough up hundreds of billions in "cash for trash"—the first act in Obama's 8-year mission to make the banks too big to fail.

American empire was also in need of rescue. Obama would be U.S. imperialism's "second wind"—or, in Paul Street's words, "the emperor's new clothes"—a tanned and polished "Son of Africa" who would make the continent the starting point of a global military offensive and New Cold War.

It was the last thing that most of his bedazzled American supporters expected from their young Black prince. The nation and world were weary of George W. Bush's blustering and bumbling "cowboy" imperialism. Certainly, the Iraqi people were desperate to be rid of the occupier that had laid waste to their nation, once the most developed in the Arab world. Polls showed U.S. public support for the war had risen from 62 percent right after the March, 2003 invasion to 79 percent when Bush declared "Mission Accomplished" in May -- proof that Americans love nothing more than a short war they think they've won. But in fact, the Iraqi war of resistance had just begun, and would ultimately result in most of the country's ethnic, religious and political factions demanding a U.S. exit.

By the spring of 2004, Moqtada al-Sadr's Shiite Muslim militia rose in armed revolt against the occupation regime, seizing Shiite cities and at times collaborating with fighters holding Sunni cities, most notably Fallujah. Americans, in and out of uniform, were shocked. They had been told the U.S. had waged war against Saddam Hussein, in part, to rescue the Shiite majority from his rule. But Hussein was dead, as were thousands of U.S. soldiers, and the Shiites were demanding an American withdrawal. Ayatollah Sistani threatened to put millions of Iraqis in the streets if the U.S. didn't negotiate an exit.

In the imperial homeland, support for the war shrank to about half the public. By 2007, it was clear to most military commanders that the U.S. was incapable of pacifying Iraq – despite America's near-infinite capacity to kill and destroy. As the U.S. election season approached, the Bush administration agreed to withdraw from Iraqi cities by June 30, 2009—when a new U.S. president would be in office—and to pull out all U.S. combat forces by December 31, 2011.

Iraqi infrastructure and institutions had been devastated, with hundreds of thousands dead, yet no one could deny that the U.S. had lost the war, which had never been about weapons of mass destruction or Baath Party oppression of Shiite Muslims or the ridiculous claim that Saddam Hussein was allied with

Islamist jihadists, his worst enemies. The invasion of Iraq was a cold blooded aggression—recognized as "illegal" even by the compliant UN chief Kofi Annan—dictated by the imperatives of empire.

Hell-bent on war from its first day in office, the Bush-Cheney regime ignored European allies who cautioned that Washington's fixation with Iraq threatened to destabilize the Middle East and the whole world order. But the great U.S. crime against Iraq is only fathomable if it is understood that Washington's *purpose* was to disrupt a world order that was moving inexorably towards multi-polarity. With every passing day, the global chessboard was becoming less favorable to sole superpower supremacy. If there was to be a "New American Century," the chessboard would have to be smashed and all the pieces realigned to restore U.S. advantage. The Bush Administration believed that Iraq was the place to the smash the board, reorder a shocked and awed world, and start the game again.

The clock was ticking—then, as now—on global U.S. hegemony. The nation that had emerged from World War Two producing fully half the finished goods on Earth accounted for only 28 percent of global manufacturing in 2000, as capitalist investors shifted the actual production of things to the Global South. The Chinese command economy welcomed the sea change. China would overtake the U.S. in manufacturing by 2010, but it was already clear where the world was heading when George Bush and his neocon advisors took power. Before 1850 and stretching back millennia, China had been the center of the world economy, a position it was about to reclaim, thus posing an existential threat to U.S. supremacy. China would have to be contained.

Russia, too. Free of the drunken U.S. lackey Yeltsin, in July of 2001 the Russian Federation signed a treaty of friendship and cooperation with China and joined the Shanghai Cooperation Organization, linking the world's most populous nation and its largest with the former Soviet republics of Kazakhstan, Kyrgyzstan, Tajikistan and Uzbekistan.

Back then, nobody predicted that a New Silk Road would

emerge from this alliance, but U.S. strategic planners understood their mission: to alter the politico-military game board on the Eurasian land mass. The pieces must be rearranged to empower the U.S.—either in league with its allies, or alone—to block China's access to energy and trade, and otherwise strangle the emerging Sino-Russian alliance, at will. Otherwise, the Middle Kingdom would once again be the center of the Earth, in league with the planet's biggest land mass.

The attack on Iraq was supposed to be just the beginning of an "enduring" U.S. presence on the Asian mainland. In the year leading up to the invasion, U.S. imperial planners bragged openly that Iraq was to be a power-projection base for deep American penetration of Central Asia, and that the former Soviet "stans" —with their vast resources—would soon be brought into the U.S. orbit. It was a foregone conclusion that the Americans would quickly smash Iraq's no longer formidable military. With supreme imperial arrogance, the U.S. disbanded the defeated Iraqi army and outlawed the multi-million member Baath Party, giving these men and women no option but to wage war against the occupation. Five years later, George Bush signed the agreement to leave the country.

The U.S. emerged from Iraq far weaker than it went in. U.S. public opinion had turned decisively against large scale deployment of U.S. forces in the region, thus rendering the imperial superpower incapable of using its huge land army as an offensive weapon in Asia. And China and Russia had grown closer than ever, overcoming centuries of mutual fear and hostility to collaborate in the building of an interdependent, multi-polar world. Against the advice of its allies, Washington had rolled the dice in Iraq, and lost. Not since the U.S. was evicted from Vietnam had the superpower been brought so low.

The U.S. was militarily embarrassed and politically discredited. Catastrophically, the war had failed to solve the empire's existential dilemma: the rapid rise of China and its deepening alliance with Russia. A new cycle of violence was necessary, but that required a new face of imperial leadership—and a different skin.

"What I am opposed to is a dumb war. What I am opposed to is a rash war," U.S. Senate candidate Barack Obama told anti-war activists in Chicago, on October 2, 2002. The speech was later endlessly cited to validate Obama as the 2008 "peace" candidate, but by 2004 he was no longer sure he would have voted against war, had he had the chance. "What would I have done? I don't know," said Obama. But in his yearly reports to the Chicago Council on Global Affairs, Obama was unswerving in his commitment to the maintenance of U.S. empire. "We must always reserve the right to strike unilaterally at terrorists wherever they may exist," he told the corporate conclave in 2007, affirming the U.S. exceptionalist birthright.

Endless warfare is only "dumb" when you lose, as Bush had done. Obama would wrap his wars in "humanitarian" colors, claiming moral legitimacy while sidestepping international law. "In military parlance, legitimacy is a force multiplier," said presidential candidate Obama, showing off his fluency in military-speak.

Obama's audition as the new face of empire was a hit, igniting the nation's first billion dollar presidential campaign and a thumping repudiation of the warmongering Republican, John McCain. Despite Obama's protestations that he only opposed "dumb" and "rash" wars, in a thoroughly racialized society the candidate's blackness was perceived as inherently progressive and war-averse. People of color around the globe, especially of African descent, were as ecstatic as the million-strong revelers that packed the Washington Mall for the First Black President's inauguration. Euphoric Norwegians awarded him a Nobel Peace Prize -- for nothing besides his perceived essence and the symbolism of his presence. Fidel Castro called Obama "intelligent, refined, and even-handed." Venezuela's Hugo Chavez hoped that, "as a black man about to become president of the United States," Obama would "take his place in history" by ending the embargo against Cuba."

But the "new day" was a mass illusion. In real, historical time, capitalism was in its late stages and the U.S. empire faced imminent eclipse by the rising powers of the East. A 2010 McKinsey report showed the world economic center of gravity already situated at a point in Russia, pulled inexorably away from the Euro-American North Atlantic towards the hyper-economies of China and its neighbors. By 2025, the center of global gravity would be near China's border, not far from the point McKinsey reckoned it was situated in Year 1 A.D. A new world was, indeed, being born—or an old one reawakening from European subjugation. Obama's assignment was the same as Bush, eight years earlier: to halt the rise of a multi-polar planet, by any means necessary.

The new U.S. administration, shed of the Bush-Cheney "cowboy" baggage, chose to mask its military aggressions as "humanitarian interventions," but Obama faced the same existential problem as his predecessor—only now more acute after eight more years of Chinese growth and Russian military resurgence. Obama's must put a military stranglehold on the East, allowing the U.S. to unilaterally deprive China of energy and markets; isolate Russia from Europe and its former sister socialist republics, and roll back the "pink tide" in Latin America while garrisoning all of Africa with U.S. troops and bases. A multi-polar economic world may have been born, but it would still have one master: the United States, which reserves the right to change other people's governments at will.

All this would have to be accomplished without resort to America's huge and astronomically expensive land army, since the U.S. public would not permit "another Iraq." Peace Prize winner Obama marshaled tens of thousands of Islamic jihadists, armed and financed by the U.S. or its allies and coordinated by U.S. special forces and the CIA, for the assaults on Libya and Syria. The head-choppers won in Libya, with the help of round-the-clock NATO bombing, but have been pushed into pockets in Syria with the help of Russia, Iran and Lebanese Shiite militias, at a cost of half a million lives. Despite the corporate media's attempts to suppress the truth of U.S. collaboration with al-Qaida and its offshoots, U.S. imperialism's jihadist strategy has been exposed, rendering that gruesome weapon -- Barack Obama's most shameful, hideous legacy -- far less useful for future regime change campaigns. That means imperialism is running out of cannon fodder.

Like Bush, Obama failed to turn back the clock on U.S. imperial decline. It is America's mission impossible, but one that can get us all killed in the attempt. Humanity will remain in peril until U.S. rulers finally accept the verdict of history.

Jeremy Kuzmarov guides us masterfully through Obama's tenure at the helm of the imperial state as it doggedly resisted decline. Awesomely talented, Obama's greatest strength lay outside himself, in the wishful perceptions of his various audiences, foreign and domestic. Africa opened its arms to her "son," only to be set aflame and recolonized with remarkable rapidity. The Arab world allowed itself to be wooed by the polished, handsome man with the middle name Hussein—and was soon under siege by Obama's Islamist legions. Obama "reset" relations with Russia, then dialed them back to a New Cold War, and answered China's offer of "win-win" relations with a military "pivot." Kuzmarov brings clarity to the turbulent geopolitics of the Obama era and shows us how the worldview of the First Black President was profoundly shaped by his forbearers in the imperial rogue's gallery. Like other "liberal" U.S. presidents, Obama was a more effective champion of war and austerity than his crude and repugnant Republican opposite numbers who, as Kuzmarov explains, "tend to be more truthful in their aspirations to dominate the world and earn profits in whatever ways, thus making them easier to mobilize against." The empire is right now searching for a "new Obama" to pull off yet another global beguilement—which makes this book indispensible.

PREFACE

This book essentially is a story of how money has corrupted politics and perverted American foreign policy. When candidates are beholden to arms merchants, crooks and billionaires, they will adopt a policy that is antithetical to national and human interests. Court intellectuals may try to spin it that the United States is intervening militarily for humanitarian purposes, but the contradictions are so egregious and actual consequences so horrific, it is incredible that so many people have bought into the façade. Barack Obama is a political genius but not in a positive way. Using identity politics and liberal guilt about race to his advantage, he crafted a narrative about himself that was misleading and hypnotized liberals into believing that he was pragmatic and a do-gooder even as he escalated bombing, drone strikes, and secret wars. Obama had been known by his poker-playing buddies back in the Illinois State House as an effective bluffer because he was very strategic and smooth about it.[1] This is what differentiates him from conservative presidents such as George W. Bush and Donald Trump whose lack of intellectual sophistication and guile have made them easier to mobilize against.

In writing this book, I have tried to read every book written about Obama. This includes many conservative critiques. Some of these, embodying what the historian Richard Hofstadter termed the "paranoid style in American politics," assumed Obama was a socialist alien implant on America. Mixed with the bad, I often found some good information and probing scrutiny into Obama's background and qualifications for the presidency lacking among liberal authors who adopted a defensive posture in his regard. An example of the latter is Harvard University Professor James Kloppenberg's book, *Reading Obama,*[2] which attributes to Obama phantom intellectual influences and fails to recognize how Obama often bends or distorts the truth. According to one critic, the book "might as well be a biography of Kim Il-Sung on sale at Pyongyang airport."[3] Kloppenberg refuses to acknowledge Obama's actual lukewarm commitment to social reform, deep corporate ties and the regressive features of his thought, including his positioning himself in the archetype of "reformed" radical reminiscent of the professional anti-communists of the McCarthy era.

David J. Garrow's 1300+ page tome *Rising Star* is more critical about Obama's background than Kloppenberg and an excellent resource for researchers. However, for all the interviews he conducted, Garrow fails to probe into certain aspects of Obama's background or milieu of supporters and his critique of Obama's foreign policy draws exclusively on the assessment of newspaper columnists who attack his foreign policy for not being militaristic enough.[4] Ta Ne-Hisi Coates in his award winning book *We Were Eight Years in Power* presents Obama as an heir to Malcolm X., which ignores X's fiery and prescient denunciations of American imperialism and Obama's political conservatism, which Coates himself acknowledges.[5] Some other black intellectuals such as Peniel Joseph want to root Obama in the black radical tradition and depict him as a fulfilment of the Black Power movement whose leaders Obama in fact criticized and spirit he often betrayed.[6]

I have written this book in order to provide a comprehensive assessment that provides a critical perspective on Obama's foreign policy which is lacking among most previous books. Garrow and Kloppenberg and other authors like Morton Keller in a study published by Oxford University Press efface certain kinds of analysis, and rely exclusively on mainstream media sources, ignoring alternative and international media and many critical books about Obama, including by conservative authors. Keller calls foreign policy isolationists "delusional" and considers Obama's policy in Libya as "successful leading from behind," which is counter to Obama's own assessment (Obama called Libya a "shit show" in 2016).[7] A number of journalists have done important work in showing the inner working and deliberation of the Obama administration. However, I ask these questions: Would it have been so difficult to track down people affected by U.S. foreign policy to provide a more rounded assessment? Afghan civilians or Pakistanis targeted by drone strikes? Libyans who lived through the Operation Odyssey Dawn, Okinawans or residents of Jeju-do? Or Eastern Ukrainians, Russians who might like Putin, Africans living under the shadow of AFRICOM, Yemenis or Latin Americans? With limited resources, I have myself tried to capture a broader perspective and hope future historians will do the same.

Endnotes

1   Sasha Abramsky, *Inside Obama's Brain* (New York: Penguin, 2012), 85.

2   James Kloppenberg, *Reading Obama: Dreams, Hope, and the American Political Tradition* (Princeton: Princeton University Press, 2012).

3   Chris Bray, "Party of None," *The Baffler*, July 2012.

4   David J. Garrow, *Rising Star: The Making of Barack Obama* (New York: William Morrow, 2017).

5   Ta Nehisi Coates, *We Were Eight Years in Power: An American Tragedy* (New York: One World Publishers, 2017). On X, see Manning Marable, *Malcolm X: A Life of Reinvention* (New York: Penguin, 2011).

6   Peniel Joseph, *Dark Days, Bright Nights: From Black Power to Obama* (New York: Basic Books, 2010).

7   Morton Keller, *Obama's Time: A History* (New York: Oxford University Press, 2015).

INTRODUCTION

On December 6, 2016, President Barack H. Obama II delivered his final speech on counter-terrorism before a cheering throng of U.S. troops at MacDill Air Force base in Tampa, Florida. Obama started by thanking the soldiers for their extraordinary service over the last eight years and stated that he was feeling sentimental since this was going to be the last "Hail to the Chief" of his watch. He went on to convey his pride that as a result of the Global War on Terror, Al-Qaeda was now a shadow of its former self; the troop surge had denied Al-Qaeda a safe haven in Afghanistan and allowed girls to go to school there, and the U.S. military had worked to dislodge ISIL [Islamic State in the Levant] terrorists from Syria and Libya. The loudest applause came when Obama stated that he would become the first President of the United States to serve two full terms during a time of war.[1]

Passing unnoticed in much of the media, Obama's latter observation showed the significance of his presidency in institutionalizing a permanent warfare state. In 2016, the U.S. dropped 26,171 tons of bombs in seven countries (Pakistan, Afghanistan, Libya, Yemen, Iraq, Syria, Somalia), equivalent to nearly three bombs every hour, 24 hours a day. Special Forces could be found in 138 countries, a jump of 130 percent from the previous Bush administration. Obama further brokered more arms sales than any other president since the Second World War, with a 54% increase over Bush, sanctioned more entities, and authorized over 10 times more drone strikes.[2] More money was allocated for war-related initiatives under Obama than under Bush ($866 billion to $811 billion) and more bombs were dropped (100,000 tons to 70,000). Obama's defense budgets also outstripped those of Bush by an average of $18.7 billion per year and his base budgets exceeded those of Bush during his two terms by $816.7 billion.[3]

Obama was himself a gifted orator who had an ability to make people of different political outlooks feel like his views were aligned with their own. His convictions were predominantly conservative in his respect for tradition and belief that the world could only be changed very, very slowly. People who worked with him described him as "cold," "calm," "calculating," "opaque," "very corporate" and one who had always possessed "delusions of grandeur."[4] Journalist Evelyn Pringle referred to him as a "political psychopath" because of his association with the Illinois combine, the state's crooked businessmen and politicians, and his willingness to do whatever it took to win, including accepting donations from corrupt figures.[5] According to political analyst Chris Hedges, Obama was marketed effectively as a brand "designed to make us feel good about ourselves." At times he sounded like a progressive, however, "like all branded products spun from the manipulative world of corporate advertising," he "duped the public into doing and supporting a lot of things that were not in its interest."[6] This included extending Bush's imperial wars and the empire of military bases along with unprecedented domestic surveillance.

One of Obama's primary financial sponsors was Henry Crown & Company, which owns twenty percent of General Dynamics (GD), manufacturer of the Trident rocket, Stryker troop carrier, bunker buster bombs, LAV-25 amphibious armored vehicle, Abrams tank, and nuclear-powered submarines and naval destroyers.[7] During Obama's presidency, General Dynamics bought out 11 firms specializing in satellites, geospatial intelligence, surveillance, and reconnaissance and amassed contracts from sixteen intelligence agencies after investing $10 million in annual lobbying. Paying $4 million to settle a lawsuit for defrauding the government, its revenues shot up to over $30 billion in 2016, a three-fold increase from 2000.[8] The Crown family's net worth was estimated at $8.8 billion, double from when Obama first took office, and they rose in the *Forbes* rankings to 27th richest family in America.[9]

During the 2008 election, Obama received more money than military icon John McCain from General Dynamics as well as from Raytheon and Lockheed Martin.[10] A voracious consumer of intelligence, Obama's trademark was to move war into the shadows, a light footprint approach designed to expand U.S. power covertly.[11] In a meeting over Afghanistan, he told CIA Director Leon Panetta that the CIA would "get everything it wanted."[12] *The New York Times* reported that "in the 67 years since the CIA was founded, few presidents have had as close a bond with their intelligence chiefs as Mr. Obama forged with Mr. [John] Brennan," an architect of the CIA's extraordinary rendition program and former CIA station chief in Saudi Arabia. Obama's worldview meshed so closely with this "unsentimental intel warrior" and "terrorist hunter" that Obama "found himself finishing Brennan's sentences."[13] An anonymous Cabinet member explained that "presidents tend to be smitten with the instruments of the intelligence community [but] Obama was more smitten than most – this has been an intelligence presidency in a way we haven't seen maybe since Eisenhower."[14]

The consequences could be seen in expanded financing of the CIA's paramilitary forces, suppression of evidence about CIA torture, refusal to pursue a criminal case against the CIA's money laundering bank (HSBC), eavesdropping even of a U.S. Congressman (Dennis Kucinich), and prosecution of whistleblowers under the Espionage Act.[15] Not by happenstance, the Crowns were among the prime beneficiaries. General Dynamics embraced "every intelligence driven style of warfare," developing small target and identification systems and equipment that could intercept insurgents' cell phone and lab-top communications and computer software used for cyber and psychological warfare.[16]

Ideological rationalization for military intervention in the Obama era was provided by Samantha Power, an adviser on the National Security Council and U.S. envoy to the UN, in her Pulitzer Prize winning book, *A Problem from Hell: America in the Age of Genocide* (2002) which claimed that America failed to prevent genocides in the past when it had a moral responsibility to do so. Even if lacking perfect information, a president must have a "bias towards belief" that massacres are imminent, justifying pre-emptive war.[17] Senator Obama is alleged to have hired Power – the founding executive director of Harvard University's Carr Center for Human Rights – as an aide after reading her book. In 2011, Obama ordered a presidential study directive which stated that preventing mass atrocities and genocide was a "core national security interest and moral responsibility of the United States.... history has taught us that our pursuit of a world where states do not systematically slaughter civilians will not come to fruition without concerted and coordinated effort."[18] These comments derive directly from Power who provided America's ruling class with a useable past which misrepresented many aspects of history and affirmed belief in American exceptionalism. Her book lionized a war propagandist, Henry Morgenthau Sr., the U.S. ambassador to Turkey during World War I who misled the public about the Turkish atrocities towards the Armenians, and ignored instances where the U.S. facilitated mass atrocities, including at the nation's founding when the "age of genocide" really began.[19]

Dubbed the "femme fatale of the humanitarian assistance world" (attractive and athletic, she once posed for *Men's Vogue*), Power was predictably selective in her concern for human rights during her time in Washington. Like her colleagues Hillary Clinton and Susan Rice, she fixated on the plight of Afghan women and Syrian refugees from the Bashir al-Assad regime, while ignoring the victims of U.S. sponsored violence such as the Israeli assault on Gaza, Rwandan occupation of North Kivu, the Saudi attack on Yemen, the Ugandan occupation of South Sudan and the Ukrainian military assault on its eastern provinces. Unmoved by abuses in America's carceral state, Power further promoted a new Cold War with Russia, pledged $100 million in support of a French neocolonial venture in the Central Africa Republic (CAR) and backed war in Afghanistan, Syria, Sudan and other countries to "save the natives" without considering whether they wanted outside intervention or whether the U.S. was in fact a source of their misery.[20]

Power is a fitting symbol of the hollowness of Obama's commitment to human rights and his use of the concept to expand the warfare state. The Joint Strategic Operations Command (JSOC) under his watch came to run a global assassination campaign that John Nagl, counterinsurgency adviser to General David Petraeus, termed an "almost industrial scale counter-terrorism killing machine."[21] The Pentagon spent over $480 billion to produce "an armada of fantastical new aerospace weapons...from the stratosphere to the exosphere worthy of [the 1920s sci-fi comic strip] Buck Rogers," as historian Alfred W. McCoy put it. Their aim was to "patrol the entire planet ceaselessly via a triple canopy aerospace shied that would reach from sky to space and be replaced by an armada of drones with lethal missiles and Argus-eyed censors monitored through an electronic matrix controlled by robots."[22]

Reminiscent of the cult of Camelot, scholarly appraisals of Obama's foreign policy have been predominantly enthusiastic, despite its imperial quality. University of Texas historian Jeremi Suri, for example, praises Obama for offering a liberal internationalist vision – emphasizing multilateralism, negotiation and disarmament – after eight years of neoconservative militarism under President George W. Bush. Suri writes that "Obama's vision was progressive and pragmatic, focused on American leadership through democratic alliances and common law that would underpin legitimate force. He worked vigorously to build alliances and negotiations. He sought to tame war with law and where possible end American military conflicts. As a good lawyer, he sought to nurture careful procedures for assessing targets, collateral damage and regional reverberations."[23] Such claims are undercut by the fact that Obama violated the U.S. constitution and sowed regional instability in invading and bombing seven Muslim countries, and ordered the assassination of terrorist suspects without due process.[24]

Characteristic of the political landscape, most scholarly criticism of Obama's foreign policy has come from the right. For example, a University of Chicago Ph.D., Ann Pierce, claims in her book, *A Perilous Path: The Misguided Foreign Policy of Barack Obama, Hillary Clinton and John Kerry* that Obama "remained idle" and "mute" with regard to Syria and compromised with some of the world's worst human rights abusers, most notably North Korea, Iran and Russia. Invoking misguided appeasement analogies to World War II, Pierce writes that "if we do not take the lead, those who hate democracy will. Under Obama, Clinton, and Kerry they have."[25]

Alfred McCoy, a brilliant scholar whose work has otherwise exposed CIA criminal activity, asserts that Obama revealed himself as "one of those rare grand masters with an ability to go beyond mere foreign policy and play the Great Game of Geopolitics." "Let's give credit where credit is due," McCoy writes, "Obama moved step by step to repair the damage caused by a plethora of Washington foreign policy debacles, old and new, and then maneuvered sometimes deftly, sometimes less so, to rebuild America's fading global influence."[26] Acknowledging a ruthless side, McCoy places Obama in an elite category of visionary empire builders along with Zbigniew Brzezinski, who contributed to the defeat of the Soviet empire by bogging it down in Afghanistan, and Elihu Root, a Secretary of State and War who modernized the military and promoted the advancement of international law.

If Obama stands among these alleged giants, however, this should be considered cause for dismay. Brzezinski, after all, was an extreme Russophobe who, parroting Lenin, characterized peace activism during the Vietnam War as an "infantile disorder" and contributed to the growth of al-Qaeda. His Machiavellian schemes were so unpopular he was loudly booed by delegates at the 1980 Democratic Party Convention.[27] Brzezinski's colleague, Cyrus Vance, referred to him as "pure evil."[28] Root was architect of the bloody suppression of an anticolonial revolt in the Philippines and author of the Platt amendment enabling military interference in Cuba. Employed as an attorney for Boss Tweed, head of the corrupt Tammany Hall political machine, and the Havermeyer Sugar Trust, he considered labor unrest a "war of poverty on wealth" and championed intervention in World War I, which resulted in the death of 100,000 Americans.[29]

Obama gets high marks by the professoriate for his pivot to Asia policy even though it trampled on indigenous rights and "changed the atmosphere of U.S.-China relations from cooperation to confrontation for the first time since Richard Nixon's visit in 1972," according to historian Chi Wang.[30] Obama is also credited for showing military restraint in Syria when he orchestrated one of the CIA's largest operations in support of jihadists there, and dropped over 12,000 bombs in 2016 alone, based on the pretext that Syrian leader Bashir al-Assad had waged chemical gas attacks on his own people (as of this writing, the UN was pursuing further investigation into this).[31]

Obama's reputation as a grand chess-master[32] is further belied by the fact that the U.S. continued to lose political influence under his stewardship in the Middle East and Southeast Asia, where a 2015 RAND Corporation study observed a "progressively receding frontier of U.S. dominance."[33] In sub-Saharan Africa, China built soccer stadiums and roads as Team Obama was busy building drone bases, arming dictators and chasing third-grade bandits such as Joseph Kony whom it could not even capture. Harsh sanctions combined with support for a coup in Ukraine meanwhile prompted effective Russian counter-moves, including the return to Russia of Crimea, and greater regional integration and strategic alliance with China.[34]

The Obama administration is estimated to have added as much as $10 trillion to the U.S. national debt, the largest total of any president in history; he oversaw the debt to GDP ratio increase from 64.8% to 104.7% and a balance of payments deficit of $463 billion in 2015.[35] China's ownership of over one trillion of the U.S. debt helped to shift the economic balance in its favor as the

U.S. dollar began losing its appeal as a global currency exchange, further undercutting the claim that Obama was a deft manager of empire.[36] His administration wasted taxpayer money on billion-dollar boondoggles like Lockheed Martin's F-35 fighter jet, which military analyst Pierre Sprey called "an inherently terrible airplane," while adversaries like Russia began to develop greater electronic and cyberwarfare capabilities and long-range missiles capable of threatening U.S. military bases.[37]

Obama alienated traditional allies because of pervasive eavesdropping and espionage. With military spending consuming over forty percent of the budget, austerity policies championed by Wall Street resulted in extensive cutbacks in public services, including in education, thereby weakening American society. The institutionalization of militaristic values was also manifest in the repeal of the Posse Comitatus Act prohibiting the use of the military in civilian policing, development of paramilitary police and an epidemic of mass shootings.[38]

Obama's Unending Wars provides the first comprehensive critical history of the foreign policy of Barrack Hussein Obama, America's forty-fourth president—the drone king who bombed seven Muslim countries, backtracked on a pledge to reduce America's nuclear arsenal, and helped fuel a new Cold War with Russia. During his years in office, Obama also sponsored a coup in Honduras, contributed to the recolonization of Africa, perpetuated the failed War on Drugs, and sold billions of dollars of arms to Saudi Arabia, assisting it in crushing pro-democracy demonstrators in Bahrain and invading Yemen.

While any Democratic Party president would have faced peril in confronting the Pentagon which had carried out a slow coup d'état over the decades, Obama was in many ways the most perfect spokesman for the military-industrial complex. Who else but this articulate constitutional law professor could respond to winning the Nobel Peace Prize with a pro-war speech while ramping up drone assassinations and still retain the support of liberal-progressives? Had a white conservative compiled the same record, the streets of American cities might have been filled with protestors, but instead, with the exception of Occupy Wall Street, they were as quiet as a schoolyard playground in summer.

The first two chapters of this book provide an overview of Obama's background and the tradition of liberal internationalism which underlay his approach to foreign policy. The book then proceeds to dissect Obama's foreign policies in different regions of the world. Many liberals and night-time TV hosts revere Obama and look back at his presidency with nostalgia because of the embarrassing behavior of Donald J. Trump. In doing so, they overlook the many destructive facets of his presidency that set the groundwork for the Trump nightmare. Ilhan Omar (D-MN) told *Politico* that: "We can't be only upset with Trump. ... His policies are bad, but many of the people who came before him [Obama] also had really bad policies. They just were more polished than he was... We don't want anybody to get away with murder because they are polished. We want to recognize the actual policies that are behind the pretty face and the smile."[39]

What was striking about Obama was indeed his ability to provide a liberal and humanitarian veneer to policies that were consistent with those of past imperial statesmen, and to maintain his reputation despite presiding over horrendous disasters. His forerunner in this respect was Woodrow Wilson, with whom Obama had a great deal in common. Both were like hypnotists who successfully manipulated public opinion with the assistance of elaborate propaganda campaigns that were supported by media pundits and Ivy League intellectuals. Prior to Obama's ascension, the Pentagon had been successful in coopting the human rights movement of the 1960s by developing new technologies like drones and smart bombs that required less manpower and gave the illusion of being surgically precise and hence rendering war more "humane." In making use of these tools and cultivating linkages with humanist icons like Nelson Mandela and Martin Luther King Jr., Obama was able to isolate the antiwar movement and convert liberals into supporters of military intervention.

Code Pink founder Medea Benjamin lamented in 2013 that she and her group had "been protesting Obama's foreign policy for years now, but we can't get the same numbers because the people who would've been yelling and screaming about this stuff under Bush are quiet under Obama."[40]

First Lady Michelle Obama assisted her husband effectively through her initiative to support military families and enlist American academic institutions and scientists in combating Post-Traumatic Stress Disorder (PTSD) and Traumatic Brain Injury (TBI). This initiative fed into a discourse that urged support and sympathy for military veterans for the price they were paying, clouding their actual role as agents enforcing American imperialism and overshadowing any concern for the ravaging effects of the wars on the subject societies. The critiques of antiwar veterans, who were stigmatized as having been physically or psychologically damaged from war, was marginalized; instead, the wounded veteran became a metaphor for an aggrieved nation.[41]

In a 1960 study, *The Rising American Empire,* on the expansionist impulses of the founding fathers, historian Richard Van Alstyne noted that in side-stepping terms that would even hint at aggression or imperial domination, American foreign policy "developed a vocabulary all its own," which "took refuge in abstract formulae and idealistic clichés that explain nothing. The assumption is always that American diplomacy is different, purer morally than the diplomacy of other powers."[42] Obama carried on this tradition so magnificently that he was awarded a Nobel Peace Prize. He will go down in history as the first black president, but if we scrutinize his policies, they do not reflect much improvement over his predecessors. More than anything, he embodies the limitation of the American two-party system in an age of corporate-rule and the obfuscation of the left's current brand of identity politics.

Endnotes

1   Barack Obama, "Remarks by the President on the Administration's Approach to Counter-Terrorism," MacDill Air Force Base, Tampa, Florida, December 06, 2016, https://obamawhitehouse.archives. gov/the-press-office/2016/12/06/remarks-president-administrations-

approach-counterterrorism

2   Medea Benjamin, "America Dropped 26, 171 Bombs in 2016: What a Bloody End to Obama's Reign," *The Guardian*, January 9, 2013; William D. Hartung, "The Obama Administration Has Brokered More Weapons Sales Than Any Other Administration Since World War II," *The Nation Magazine*, July 26, 2016; Mike Stone "U.S. Arms Exports Boom Under Obama, Sees Continuity with Trump," *Reuters*, November 9, 2016. In 2010 and 2011, the U.S. accounted for a monopolistic 70% of all weapons sold in the world.

3   Edward Delman, "Obama Promised to End America's Wars – Has He?" *The Atlantic*, March 30, 2016; Fred Kaplan, "Obama's Whopping New Military Budget," *Slate*, February 9, 2016; Nicolas J S Davies, "Obama's Bombing Legacy," *Consortium News*, January 18, 2017.

4   Richard Miniter, *Leading From Behind: The Reluctant President and the Advisors Who Decide for Him* (New York: St. Martin's Press, 2012), 16; Larissa MacFarquhar, "The Conciliator: Where is Barack Obama Coming From?" *New Yorker*, May 7, 2007; Edward Klein, *The Amateur: Barack Obama in the White House* (Washington, D.C.: Regnery, 2012), 3; Wayne Madsen, *The Manufacturing of a President* (self-published, 2012); David Remnick, *The Bridge: The Life and Rise of Barack Obama*, rev ed. (New York: Vintage, 2011).

5   Evelyn Pringle, "Barack Obama – The Wizard of Oz," *Countercurrent*, March 28, 2008; John Kass, "In Combine, Cash is King, Corruption is Bipartisan," *The Chicago Tribune*, March 23, 2008. These corrupt figures include Tony Rezko (discussed in chapter 1), Aiham Alsammarae, who was imprisoned for stealing millions of dollars from the Coalition Provisional Authority (CPA) in Iraq while Electricity Minister, and Alex Giannoulis, the Illinois State Treasurer whose family's bank loaned money to organized crime figures.

6   Chris Hedges, "Buying Brand Obama," in *The World as it Is: Dispatches on the Myth of Human Progress* (New York: The Nation Books, 2010).

7   "Obama was the Candidate of the War Lobby Funded by the Crown Family," *Global Research News*, September 5, 2013; Nicolas J.S. Davies, "Investing in Weapons, War, and Obama," *Z Magazine*, April 17, 2012; Webster G. Tarpley, *Barack H. Obama: The Unauthorized Biography* (Joshua Tree, CA: Progressive Press, 2008), 364.

8   Davies, "Investing in Weapons, War and Obama;" General Dynamic, Annual Report, 2016, https://www.gd.com/sites/default/files/2016-GD-Annual-Report.pdf.

9   "Crown Family Profile," https://www.forbes.com/profile/crown/#1223a6116044

10   https://www.opensecrets.org/orgs/toprecips.php?id=D000000175&ty

pe=P&sort=A&cycle=2008. One of Obama's top all-time fundraisers, Larry Duncan, had made a fortune as a Lockheed lobbyist.

11   Nick Turse, *The Changing Face of Empire: Special Ops, Drones, Spies, Proxy Fighters, Secret Bases, and Cyberwarfare* (Chicago: Haymarket Books, 2012); David Sanger, *Confront and Conceal: Obama's Secret Wars and Surprising Use of American Power* (New York: Broadway, 2012), xviii.

12   Leon Panetta, *Worthy Fights: A Memoir Of Leadership in War and Peace* (New York: Penguin Press, 2014), 252.

13   Daniel Klaidman, *Kill or Capture: The War On Terror and The Soul of the Obama Presidency* (Boston: Houghton Mifflin, 2012), 22, 23, 52.

14   David J. Garrow, *Rising Star: The Making of Barack Obama* (New York: William Morrow, 2017), 1072, 1073; Philip Giraldi, "Let's Investigate John Brennan," Ron Paul Institute, March 27, 2018; Alfred W. McCoy, *Torture and Impunity: The U.S. Doctrine of Coercive Interrogation* (Madison: University of Wisconsin Press, 2012).

15   Wayne Madsen, *The Manufacturing of a President. Jerome Corsi, Killing the Deep State: The Fight to Save President Trump (Florida: Humanix Books, 2018), 166; Klaidman, Kill or Capture, 121.Obama's choice as White House Council, Greg Craig, had tellingly represented Richard Helms, the keeper of the CIAs secrets; his Vice President Joe Biden, had ordered a halt to Congressional restrictions on the CIA in the 1970s. See also, Joe Concha, "Dennis Kucinich on Trump's Wiretap Charge: It Happened to Me," The Hill, March 14, 2017.*

16   Dana Priest and William M. Arkin, "National Security Inc," *Washington Post*, July 20, 2010.

17   Samantha Power, *"A Problem From Hell:" America in the Age of Genocide* (New York: Basic Books, 2002).

18   "Presidential Study Directive on Mass Atrocities," The White House, Office of the Press Secretary, August 04, 2011, https://obamawhitehouse. archives.gov/the-press-office/2011/08/04/presidential-study-directive-mass-atrocities.

19   Jeremy Kuzmarov, "The Responsibility of Intellectuals Redux: Humanitarian Intervention and the Liberal Embrace of War in the Age of Clinton, Bush and Obama," *The Asia-Pacific Journal*, Vol. 11, Issue 24, No. 1, June 16, 2014; Ward Churchill, *A Little Matter of Genocide: Holocaust Denial in the Americas, 1492 to the Present* (San Francisco: City Light Publishers, 2001). Morgenthau acknowledged his ghost-written memoirs were designed to facilitate U.S. military intervention.

20   Evan Osnos, "In the Land of the Possible: Samantha Power Has the President's Ear – To What End?" *The New Yorker*, December 22 & 29, 2014; Tara McKelvey, "Libya War: Samantha Power and the Case for Liberal Interventionism," *The Daily Beast*, March 22, 2011; Edward

S. Herman, "Double Standards and Hypocrisy Running Wild," *Z Magazine*, August 19, 2013; Max Blumenthal, "Samantha Power, Obama's Atrocity Enabler," *Alternet*, October 27, 2014.

21   Turse, *The Changing Face of Empire*, 13.

22   Alfred W. McCoy, *In the Shadows of the American Century: The Rise and Decline of U.S. Global Power* (Chicago: Haymarket Books, 2017), 183.

23   Jeremi Suri, "Liberal Internationalism, Law and the First African-American President," In *The Presidency of Barack Obama: A First Historical Assessment*, ed. Julian Zelizer (Princeton University Press, 2018), 195, 197.

24   "Obama's Covert Drone War in Numbers: Ten Times More Strikes than Bush," *Bureau of Investigative Journalism*, January 17, 2017; *Living Under the Drones: Death, Injury and Trauma to Civilians From U.S. Drone Practices in Pakistan* (Stanford and NYU Law Schools, September, 2012). This important report is not cited in Suri's article.

25   Ann Pierce, *A Perilous Path: The Misguided Foreign Policy of Barack Obama, Hillary Clinton and John Kerry* (Post Hill Press, 2016). See also Robert G. Kaufman, *Dangerous Doctrine: How Obama's Grand Strategy Weakened America* (University Press of Kentucky, 2016).

26   McCoy, *In the Shadows of the American Century*, 203; Alfred W. McCoy, "Barack Obama is a Foreign Policy Grandmaster," *The Nation*, September 15, 2015.

27   Zbigniew Brzezinski, *Between Two Ages: America in the Technetronic Society* (New York: Praeger, 1982); Tarpley, *Barack H. Obama*, 69.

28   Douglas Brinkley, "The Lives They Lived," *The New York Times*, December 29, 2002.

29   Ferdinand Lundberg characterized Root as a devious "janizary to the economic royalists" directly implicated in corrupt financial dealings. *America's 60 Families* (New York: Vanguard Press, 1937), 64, 65. Founder of the Council on Foreign Relations, Root was colonial overseer of Puerto Rico and wrote the treaty facilitating U.S. control of the Panama Canal.

30   David Shambaugh, "President Obama's Asia Scorecard: The Obama Administration Deserves High Marks for Its Asia Policy," *The Wilson Quarterly*, Winter 2016; Chi Wang, *Obama's Challenge to China* (London: Ashgate, 2015), 292.

31   Seymour Hersh, *The Killing of Osama Bin Laden* (London: Verso, 2016); Harriet Agerholm, "Map Shows Where President Barack Obama Dropped his 20,000 Bombs," *The Independent*, January 19, 2017. Second Report of the Organization for the prohibition of Chemical weapons, UN Joint Investigative mechanism, June 10, 2016, which determined that Assad's forces dropped barrel bombs with chlorine gas though specified the possibility that the bombs hit toxic

32

chemicals on the ground. ISIS forces also used chemical weapons in Marea in August 2015.

32   See Francis Kornegay, "The Grandmaster Logic Behind Obama's Audacious Foreign Policy," *The Wilson Quarterly*, Winter 2016.

33   Eric Heginbotham et al., *The U.S.-China Military Scorecard: Forces, Geography, and the Evolving Balance of Power, 1996-2017* (Santa Monica: RAND Corporation, 2015), xxx, xxxi.

34   See Natylie Baldwin and Kermit Heartsong, *Ukraine: Zbig's Grand Chessboard & How the West Was Checkmated* (San Francisco: Next Revelation Press, 2015), 336; Glenn Diesen, *Russia's Geoeconomic Strategy for a Greater Eurasia* (New York: Routeledge, 2018).

35   Kimberley Amadeo, "National Debt Under Obama: How Much Did Obama Add to the Nation's Debt," *The Balance*, May 29, 2018; Diesen, *Russia's Geoeconomic Strategy for a Greater Eurasia*, 39; Jude Woodward, *The US vs China: Asia's New Cold War?* (Manchester: Manchester University Press, 2017), 249. Unfunded U.S. liabilities exceeded $100 trillion.

36   Kimberley Amadeo, "U.S. Debt to China. How Much Does it Own?" *The Balance*, May 30, 2018.

37   Sprey quoted in Michael P. Hughes, "What Went Wrong with the F-35, Lockheed Martin's Joint Strike Fighter?" *Scientific American*, June 14, 2017; Andrei Martyanov, *Losing Military Supremacy: The Myopia of American Strategic Planning* (Atlanta: Clarity Press, 2018).

38   Patrick J. Buchanan, "On a Fast Track to National Ruin," *Tulsa World*, May 13, 2015; Radley Balko, *The Rise of the Warrior Cop: The Militarization of America's Police Forces* (New York: Public Affairs, 2014); Alfred W. McCoy, "Imperial Illusions: Information Infrastructure and the Future of U.S. Global Power," In *Endless Empire: Spain's Retreat, Europe's Eclipse, America's Decline*, ed. Alfred W. McCoy, Joseph M. Fradera and Stephen Jacobson (Madison: The University of Wisconsin Press, 2012), 360-386.

39   Tim Alberta, "The Democrats Dilemma: What Ilhan Omar and Dean Phillips Tell Us About the Future of the Democratic Party," *Politico*, March 8, 2019.

40   Daniel Martin, "Whither the Antiwar Movement?" *The American Conservative*, December 15, 2017. See also Michael T. Heaney and Fabio Rojas, *Party in the Street: The Antiwar Movement and the Democratic Party after 9/11* (New York: Cambridge University Press, 2015).

41   "First Lady Michelle Obama Announces Major Coordinated Effort by America's Academic Institutions to Combat PTSD & TBI," The White House, January 11, 2012; Jerry Lembcke, *PTSD: Diagnosis and Identity in Post-Empire America* (Boston: Lexington Books, 2015).

42   Richard Van Alstyne, *The Rising American Empire* (New York: W.W. Norton, 1960), 6, 7.

Chapter 1

IN WOODROW WILSON'S SHADOW

OBAMA AND THE LIBERAL INTERNATIONALIST TRADITION

"From Palestine through Iraq, Obama has acted as just
another steward of the American empire, pursuing the same
aims as his predecessors, with the same means but with
more emollient rhetoric....Historically, the model for the
current variant of imperial presidency is Woodrow Wilson,
no less pious a Christian, whose every second word was
peace, democracy, or self-determination, while his armies
invaded Mexico, occupied Haiti, and attacked Russia [yes,
Russia!], and his treaties handed one colony after another to
his partners in war. Obama is a hand-me-down version of the
same, without even Fourteen Points to betray."
—Tariq Ali, *The Obama Syndrome.*

While many commentators have tried to look deeply
into Obama's past to uncover the motives behind his action, it is
equally fruitful to look into the traditions of American politics and
history which Obama followed. Regardless of his skin color and
mixed parentage, Obama is a product of the American political

tradition, which as historian Richard Hofstadter pointed out, never strays too far from the center or rocks the boat very much. Even the most liberal-leaning presidents, with the exception of Franklin D. Roosevelt during the Great Depression, predominantly favored big business and wealthy class interests and supported an aggressive foreign policy.[1]

Richard Pettigrew, a North Dakotan Senator from 1889-1899, wrote in his memoirs that the ten presidents with whom he was acquainted were "not brainy men. They were not men of robust character. They were pliable men, safe men, conservative men. Many of them were useable men, who served faithfully the business interests that stood behind them."[2] Obama fits this archetype. He holds much in common with Thomas Jefferson, immortal author of the Declaration of Independence and hallowed liberal, who according to historian David Brion Davis had "an extraordinary capacity to sound like an enlightened reformer while upholding the interests of the planter class."[3]

As a quintessential liberal internationalist, Obama also has much in common with Woodrow Wilson. Both came from an academic background and were brilliant orators skilled in "camouflaging their settled opinion," as Pettigrew wrote of Wilson, and winning over liberals while functioning essentially as Tories. Pettigrew had accurately predicted before Wilson's election that he would "undertake some reforms [and] rail about the bosses [and] talk about purity but he is absolutely owned by the great moneyed interests of the country who paid the expenses of his campaign."[4] So too, of course, was Obama.

Wilson's greatest gift to his benefactors was his effectiveness in framing military intervention as a moral crusade. In a dramatic speech on April 2, 1917 announcing the sending of U.S. combat forces into the Great War, Wilson emphasized his "profound sense of the solemn and even tragical character of the step he was taking" and yearning for a lasting international framework [the League of Nations] capable of "vindicating principles of freedom and justice in the life of the world as against selfish and autocratic power [Germany]."[5]

Germany never declared war or attacked the U.S., while Britain and France were also autocratic in their colonial domains, and Wilson had secretly prepared for war six months in advance.[6] Wilson's presidency nevertheless established the framework of U.S. foreign policy for the next century in championing military intervention to purportedly advance human rights and democracy and open world trade. Historian Tony Smith notes that the Alliance for Progress, Carter's human rights policy, Reagan's freedom crusade, and Bush's bringing democracy to Iraq were all influenced by Wilson as was President Obama's promotion of just war doctrine even as he accepted the Nobel Peace prize.[7]

This chapter will compare Obama and Wilson, both of whom functioned as the greatest frontmen for military interests in American history. Both were shrewd in their understanding of power and where it lies and tailored their policies accordingly. They believed in executive authority and relied on close advisers of Machiavellian outlook; in the case of Wilson, Colonel Edward M. House, a wealthy Texas kingmaker who orchestrated a secret agreement with Great Britain to facilitate U.S. intervention in the Great War; and for Obama, Valerie Jarrett, a member of the Illinois Combine who according to a West Wing staffer, "pretty much ran the government" through much of his presidency.[8]

Who Paid the Piper?

Wilson's campaign received large financial donations from Jacob H. Schiff, senior partner of the Wall Street investment firm Kuhn, Loeb & Co., and Bernard Baruch, a Wall Street speculator and member of New York's War Preparedness Committee who came to head the War Industries Board. Wilson's chief fundraiser and informal adviser, Cleveland H. Dodge, was scion of the Dodge copper and munitions fortune and a director of the National City Bank and Winchester Arms Company. A Princeton classmate of Wilson (class of 1879), he gave over $50,000 to Wilson's presidential campaigns and $75,000 to New Jersey boss James Smith Jr. to secure Wilson's position as Governor. During the

Mexican revolution, Dodge illegally smuggled a million cartridge rounds to Venustiano Carranza and profited from government purchases of copper during the Great War which caused a spike in prices. Chairing the "survivors of the victims of the Lusitania Funds," he pressed for intervention after Germany sank the *Lusitania* which illegally carried his munitions.[9]

Dodge's ruthlessness towards organized labor was apparent when he brought in gunmen from the underworld and shipped machine guns and rifles to the sheriff to suppress a strike in July 1917 at the Phelps-Dodge copper mine in Bisbee, Arizona where 1,200 miners were demanding a greater share of war profits (a 10 cent raise) and basic safety regulations. The Citizen's Protective League helped herd the miners into cattle cars owned by a Phelps Dodge subsidiary which, without food or water in 112-degree heat, took them to desert internment camps in Columbus, New Mexico. A member of the radical Industrial Workers of the World (IWW) union who resisted was killed. Dodge had previously been indicted for fraudulently taking over government lands with rich minerals, though he was saved when the Attorney General, James C. McReynolds, had the case dismissed, leading to Reynolds' appointment by Wilson to the Supreme Court (Wilson also exonerated Dodge-Phelps for the Bisbee deportations).[10]

One of Obama's earliest and top donors, Penny Pritzker, was similarly protected from investigation into her family's white-collar crime—notably massive tax evasion schemes and promotion of toxic high risk, subprime mortgages that contributed to the 2008 financial crash. In 2011, the Federal Deposit Insurance Corporation (FDIC) discounted a balance of $144 million from a $460 million fine Pritzker had been assessed for illegal bank and loan shark operations at the failed Hinsdale, Illinois Superior Bank while depositors, who were still owed $10.3 million, lost their savings. The FDIC subsequently helped Pritzker— who served on Obama's council of economic advisers and as Commerce Secretary and had her lawyer Tom Donilon appointed as Deputy National Security adviser— buy another failed bank in Birmingham, Alabama.[11]

Besides benefitting from crony capitalism, the Pritzkers had in common with Dodge a connection to organized crime as a leading depositor in the Bahamas based Castle Bank, a CIA outfit founded by the CIA's mob liaison, Paul Helliwell, that specialized in off-shoring money. They further shared a history as war profiteers—the Pritzkers set up a Hyatt hotel on Mount Scopus in Israeli occupied East Jerusalem following the 1967 six-day war—and were also anti-union, having intimidated workers and replaced Latina room cleaners holding the highest rate of injury of any chain with non-union subcontractors after a strike in their Boston Hyatt hotels.[12]

Obama's other top benefactor, the Crown Family, once hired mafia-connected lawyer Sidney Korshak to intervene when the Teamsters would not allow family patriarch Henry's non-union trucks to have access to his gravel pits in Indiana. His company, Material Services Corporation (MSC), was one of the government's largest Second World War contractors but was sued for over $1 million by the Office of Price Administration for price-gouging. In 1962, its successor General Dynamics, in which Crown remained the largest investor, was target of a major influence peddling investigation by the Senate Governmental Operations Committee after being awarded a $7 billion Pentagon contract for TFX fighter bombers (later F-111) that was quashed after John F. Kennedy's assassination.[13]

Henry's son Lester, who opposed the 1987 Intermediate-Range Nuclear Forces (INF) Treaty with Russia outlawing mid-and short-range nuclear missiles, admitted to paying $23,000 in bribes in 1972 to Illinois legislators to secure favorable legislation (only the legislators were sent to prison), and was investigated again in 1984 for expense padding, contract fraud, stock manipulation and bribery.[14] *Fortune Magazine* reported that General Dynamics was "to many American newspaper readers the symbol of waste and corruption in military spending."[15] In 2013, Lester's son, James, was the target of a Congressional and criminal probe as chairman of the J.P. Morgan Chase & Company's risk committee. Its chief investment officer roiled world credit markets and misled investors after losing $6.2 billion through high-risk credit derivative trades that were unknown to regulators.[16]

The Crown family, which had once owned the Empire State Building, gave at least $863,636 to Obama between 1990 and 2012 and raised $3,205,233 between 2007 and 2012 while paying $135,000 for his inauguration. Susan Crown, Lester's daughter, sat on the Board of Northern Trust, which gave Obama a sweetheart loan for purchase of a $1.65 million Georgian revival mansion in Hyde Park replete with a thousand bottle wine cellar. James Crown, who had managing stakes in the Chicago Bulls, New York Yankees, Maytag and Rockefeller Center and was a director of General Dynamics and Sara Lee Corp. which operated in 50 countries, was Obama's fundraising chair in his campaign for State Senate.[17]

Ms. Pritzker served in that role in Obama's campaign for president. She and her husband donated at least $290,258 and helped Obama raise over a half a billion dollars, including from the Wall Street investment banking firm Goldman Sachs, Lehman Brothers, Microsoft, Kaiser Permanente, Pfizer, General Electric, J.P. Morgan, and defense contractor Booz Allen Hamilton. George Soros, a frontman for the Rothschild banking dynasty with ties to U.S. intelligence, once convicted of insider trading, raised $60,000 for the 2004 Senate campaign and gave $250,000 for the inauguration. The Carlyle Group, a private equity firm which invested in defense contractors, gave $110,083 in 2008. Its managing director (Julius Genachowski) worked with Obama on the *Harvard Law Review*.[18]

The Democratic Party by this time had become reliant on corporate donations because of the decline of organized labor after years of right-wing attack, whereas in Wilson's time, organized labor had not yet become as influential as in the period of FDR's New Deal.[19] Both leaders' policies should be viewed in this context.

Wilsonian Idealism: Rhetoric versus Reality

Wilsonian internationalism drew on the deeper American

tradition of manifest destiny in which military conquests were always presented as having a humanitarian rationale. James Madison, for example, justified the invasion of Canada in 1812 as responding to British depredations, and colonial Virginians exaggerated the autocratic features of native chief Powhatan and the splendor in which he lived in order to justify the takeover of his people's land. Historian Edmund S. Morgan wrote that "the settlers considered themselves on par with the Romans who had converted the 'primitive' Britons into civilized Roman subjects. Although they hoped for profits by extracting the resources, theirs was a patriotic enterprise that would bring civility and Christianity to the savages of the North."[20]

Professor Wilson in his writings celebrated the role of the settlers in civilizing a "virgin continent," and said it was the Americans' duty to "help undeveloped people, still in the childhood of their natural growth." He applauded the Spanish American Philippines War and creation of an overseas empire because in his view the closing of the frontier required the U.S. to look abroad.[21] Wilson's friends said that he was an armchair militarist who romanticized the army and the navy. He carried Rudyard Kipling's poem "the White Man's Burden" in his wallet for years and had "regretted he was not free to enlist in the armed forces and fight—read each day's news with the eagerness of a boy."[22] This is not unlike Obama who, by his own account, had grown up admiring military culture, surrounded by military bases in Hawaii, and embellished the military exploits of his Great Uncle in World War II.[23]

Wilson campaigned as a pacifist in the 1916 election under the slogan that he "kept us out of war" but committed U.S. troops to the Great War just three months later. Peace activists and a handful of antiwar Senators were among those to point out that Wilson's language provided a cover for special interests who stood to profit from war. In Eastern Oklahoma, radical farmers hung posters in 1917 that called for rebellion against a "rich man's war [and] poor man's fight. If you don't go, J.P. Morgan is lost. Speculation is the only cause of the war now."[24]

The farmers' analysis was confirmed in a 1934 Congress-ional committee led by Senator Joseph Nye (R-ND) which detailed the origins of what future President Dwight Eisenhower called the military-industrial complex, or dependence of the U.S. economy on war. It concluded that "if the United States did not enter the war, the Allies would have been defeated which would have led to a serious financial situation and widespread default on the [allied] loans [made by Morgan]. The entire financial structure of the allies would have collapsed, possibly carrying with them their American banking group."[25]

Literary critic Randolph Bourne called out Wilson and his intellectual boosters (Walter Lippmann, John Dewey) for believing that the war technique could be used "without trailing along with it mob-fanaticism" and "injustices and hatreds" which were "bound up with it."[26] The Committee on Public Information (CPI), a propaganda agency headed by a Madison Avenue executive, helped whip up hysteria against Germany by broadcasting lurid atrocity stories in the context of its invasion of Belgium. Correspondent Irvin Cobb estimated that only about 10 percent were true.[27]

Henry Kissinger in his 2014 book *World Order* referred to Wilson as a "prophet" whose "greatness must be measured by the degree to which he rallied the tradition of American exceptionalism" and "harnessed American idealism" in the service of "great foreign policy undertakings."[28] However, Wilson's foreign policies were a failure in his own time; 70 percent of Americans thought they were mistaken. The Senate rejected U.S. membership in the League of Nations-a world parliament that would prevent future wars—and a harsh peace imposed on Germany fueled the rise of Nazism and led directly to World War II. Dalton's Trumbo's 1939 novel *Johnny Got His Gun* spotlighted the plight of Joe Bonham, a doughboy who so innocently marched off to war like many others and returned home a mere stump of man with no legs or arms, blind and deaf, with no jaw, mouth or tongue (he was fed through a tube in his stomach). Thinking back to the good times he had with his girlfriend and father, he laments how he had become swept up with all the war propaganda drummed up about Germany and how everybody wanted "the tar kicked out of them." But now, sitting in a vegetated state, he recognized that:

> Joe, this [was] no war for you. This thing wasn't any of your business. What do you care about making the world safe for democracy? All you wanted to do Joe was to live. You were born and raised in the good healthy country of Colorado and you had no more to do with Germany or England or France or even Washington, D.C. than you had to do with the man on the moon. It wasn't your fight Joe. You never really knew what the fight was all about.[29]

Bonham goes on to state that there have

> always [been] people willing to sacrifice somebody else's life. They're plenty loud and they talk all the time. You can find them in churches and schools and newspapers and legislatures and congress. They sound wonderful. Death before dishonor. This ground sanctified by blood. These men who died so gloriously. They shall not have died in vain. Our noble dead.

Bonham asks, though:

> But what do the dead [whom in essence he speaks for] say? All the guys who died all the five million or seven million or ten million who went out and died to make the world safe for democracy to make the world safe

for words without meaning, how did they feel as they watched the blood pump out into the mud? How did they feel when the gas hit their lungs and began eating them all away?[30]

The answer:

rather than thinking about these noble principles in their last minutes, the majority had died crying in their minds like little babies; yearning for the face of a friend. They died whimpering for the voice of a mother, a father, a wife, a child. They died with their hearts sick for one more look at the place where they were born; 'please god just one more look.'[31]

Bonham's ruminations display the hollow shell underlying Wilson's rhetoric and terrible human costs of war. A companion volume—General Smedley Butler's *War is a Racket* (1935) juxtaposed pictures of hideously disfigured soldiers and victims of chemical gas attacks with the enormous profits of the DuPont Corporation and Bethlehem Steel. Butler wrote that for a "very few, the [war] racket, like bootlegging and other underworld rackets, brings fancy profits, but the cost of the operation is always transferred to the people—who do not profit."[32]

The New Merchants of Death

An updated version of these classic texts could be written for the Bush-Obama age. It would record the thoughts of a crippled Afghan war veteran who served in Kandahar following Obama's troop surge, and juxtapose an image of Libya's lynched President, the incinerated bodies of drone victims and Gazan and Yemeni children with the majestic beachfront mansion of Neal Blue, the CEO of General Atomics, chief manufacturer of the Predator drone, or the 3,400 square foot condominium of Lester Crown atop Chicago's Water Tower Place and the family's $5 million limestone mansion in Winnetka, Illinois.[33]

Producing surveillance and targeting technology used in the drone war along with Abrams tanks and nuclear submarines, the Crowns' company, General Dynamics, earned over $31 billion in revenues in 2016 and $4.3 billion in profits, up from $3.6 billion in 2008.[34] In comparison, Raytheon, which made precision weapons, electronic warfare jammers, naval systems, tomahawk cruise missiles used to incinerate people in Libya and air surveillance radars, recorded net sales of $24 billion in 2016, while Lockheed Martin, which produced Black Hawk helicopters and the F-35 jet, recorded over $5 billion in profit.[35]

To put these contemporary totals in perspective, DuPont earned $58 million per year during the Great War, or $1.117 billion in 2018 dollars accounting for inflation, and Bethlehem Steel $49 million, or around $1 billion in today's dollars. Science Applications International Corporation (SAIC-also known as "NSA-West"), on whose board Defense Secretary Robert Gates sat, earned $4.3 billion in revenues in 2016, while DynCorp, which received major contracts for police training and troop support in Afghanistan, reported a revenue of $1.8 billion after donating a quarter of a million dollars to the Democratic Party.[36]

Might Makes Right:
The True Meaning of Wilsonian Internationalism

Wilson's impressive oratory supporting the rights of people to self-determination did not extend to those at the "lowest stage of civilization," Noam Chomsky writes. Vietnamese leader Ho Chi Minh was rebuffed when seeking Wilson's support for the anti-colonial struggle against France. In Haiti, the Wilson administration imposed a new constitution that enabled U.S. corporations to take over its economy and then sent in the Marines to hunt nationalist "rebels like pigs" as Smedley Butler, who commanded the force, put it. Reinstituting a system of forced labor prevalent under French rule, the Marines executed the nationalist leader, Charlemagne Peralte, and circulated photos of his body which backfired when he appeared to resemble Christ strung up on the cross.[37]

The true meaning of Wilsonian internationalism was further evident during the Mexican revolution, when Wilson ordered the shelling and occupation of the Port of Vera Cruz to block German arms shipments to Victoriano Huerta, who was installed in place of Standard Oil's proxy. Wilson subsequently tried to coopt Venustiano Carranza, who was favored by the National City Bank and by Cleveland Dodge, who owned big Mexican copper properties, and again sent in the Marines to suppress the radical "Pancho" Villa.[38]

After Russia's Bolshevik revolution, Wilson secretly sent 13,000 U.S. troops alongside 100,000 British, French, Canadians, Italians, Romanians, Greeks, Poles, and 100,000 Japanese in support of counter-revolutionary generals, shipping arms clandestinely through the former Russian ambassador. Commanding General William S. Graves expressed "doubt if history will record in the past century a more flagrant case of flouting the well-known and approved practice in states in their international relations and using instead of the accepted principles of international law, the principle of might makes right."[39]

When the U.S. Senate issued a resolution on June 23, 1919 requesting Wilson to inform them of the reasons for sending and maintaining U.S. troops in Siberia, Wilson responded that the purpose was to "save Czech armies which were threatened with destruction by hostile armies," protect the Trans-Siberian railway, and to "steady any efforts of the Russians' self defense" and promote "law and order."[40] This was a blatant lie; U.S. soldiers were involved in counter-revolutionary operations and allied with former czarist officers who committed atrocities that a military intelligence operative said would have been considered "shameful in the Middle Ages."[41] Lt. John Cudahy of the 339th army regiment and later U.S. ambassador to Luxemburg, characterized Wilson's war as a "freebooters excursion, depraved and lawless. A felonious undertaking for it had not the sanction of the American people."[42] Wilsonian internationalism takes on a new meaning if we consider these comments.

An Heir to the Wilsonian Tradition

Obama cast himself as an important heir to the Wilsonian tradition in his 2006 campaign book, *The Audacity of Hope*, which left unmentioned the huge gap between Wilson's rhetoric and action. Obama marveled at Wilson's leadership in the First World War, writing that Wilson "avoided American involvement until the repeated sinking of American vessels by German U-boats and the imminent collapse of the European continent made neutrality untenable.... When the war was over, America had emerged as the world's dominant power whose prosperity Wilson now understood to be linked to peace and prosperity in faraway lands."[43]

This interpretation of history is wrong on many levels including its insinuation that American intervention was purely defensive and responsive to German U-boat attacks and that the war bred wide prosperity and ushered in peace and prosperity in faraway lands.[44] Distinguished from previous statesmen who made decisions based on real politick and commercial interests, Obama's Wilson embodied a high moralism in his goal of "making the world safe for democracy." This didn't involve just winning a war, but "encouraging the self-determination of all people and providing the world a legal framework that could help avoid future conflicts." Obama continued:

> As part of the Treaty of Versailles, which detailed the terms of the German surrender, Wilson proposed a League of Nations to mediate conflicts between nations along with an international court and a set of international laws that would bind not just the weak but also the strong. "This is the time of all others when democracy should prove its purity and its spiritual power to prevail," Wilson said, "It

is surely the manifest destiny of the United
States to lead in the attempt to make this spirit
prevail."

Unfortunately, according to Obama, Wilson's grand vision
was stymied by conservative obstructionists in Congress led
by Henry Cabot Lodge who considered the League of Nations
an encroachment on American sovereignty and a constraint on
American policy. For the next twenty-two years, Obama wrote,

> America turned reluctantly inward and stood
> idly by as Italy, Japan and Germany built up
> their military machines. The Senate became
> a hotbed of isolationism and ignored the
> president's appeals as Hitler's armies marched
> across Europe. Not until the bombing of Pearl
> Harbor would America realize its terrible
> mistake. In the aftermath of World War II, the
> United Stated had a chance to properly apply
> the lessons from the past and stood strong in
> the face of the threat of Soviet totalitarianism.[45]

This analysis falsely claims that the rise of fascism resulted from
American isolationism and obscures the hideous nature of the First
World War and punitive nature of the Treaty imposed on Germany
at Versailles, which fueled its desire for revenge. Failing to point
out how FDR's naval build-up in the Pacific Seas and blockade
provoked Japan's military leaders in the 1930s, Obama further
reinforces a triumphalist view of the Cold War that obscures how
aggressive American behavior dating to Wilson's invasion of
Russia helped cause its outbreak, and how the Soviet threat was
constantly exaggerated.[46]

In a speech, "The World Beyond Iraq," given on March
19, 2008 in Fayetville, North Carolina, Obama compared himself
to Wilson who had told Congress that it was a "fearful thing to
lead this great peaceful people into war... but the right is more

precious than peace."[47] "The World Beyond Iraq" foreshadowed Obama's Nobel Prize winning address, given just months into his presidency, which referenced conservative theologian Reinhold Neibuhr's 1939 essay "Why the Christian Church is Not Pacifist." In advocating for war against evil, Obama stated:

> As someone who stands here as a direct consequence of Dr. [Martin Luther] King's life work, I am living testimony to the moral force of non-violence. I know there's nothing weak – nothing passive – nothing naïve – in the creed and lives of Gandhi and King. But as a head of state sworn to protect and defend my nation, I cannot be guided by their examples alone. I face the world as it is and cannot stand idle in the face of threats to the American people. For make no mistake: Evil does exist in the world. A non-violent movement could not have halted Hitler's armies. Negotiations cannot convince al Qaeda's leaders to lay down their arms. To say that force may someday be necessary is not a call to cynicism – it is a recognition of history, the imperfections of man and the limits of reason.[48]

Here Obama sounded quite like Wilson who justified the Spanish-American Philippines War by declaring that "when men take up arms to set other men free, there is something sacred and holy in the warfare. I will not 'cry' peace as long as there is sin and wrong in the world."[49] Then as now, American military interventions killed many innocents, however, and resulted in the adoption of unsavory methods such as the water torture that were both sinful and wrong. The U.S. furthermore allied with vicious elements that included al-Qaeda affiliates.[50] If evil exists in this world, Obama put America on its side.

Obama's Nobel speech included a plaudit to Wilson. He stated that

a quarter century after the United States Senate
rejected the League of Nations – an idea for
which Woodrow Wilson received this prize [in
1919] – America led the world in constructing
an architecture to keep the peace: a Marshall
Plan and a United Nations, mechanisms to
govern the waging of war, treaties to protect
human rights, prevent genocide, restrict the
most dangerous to weapons."[51]

However, the U.S. did not keep the peace. It carried out well over
50 military interventions and regime change operations during the
Cold War, sponsored death squads and mass killings, and bombed
countries back to the stone age.[52]

Obama the Interventionist

Obama made liberals believe he was one of them by
acknowledging limits to American power and claiming to want
to battle the foreign policy establishment, or "blob," as aide Ben
Rhodes termed it. Obama's speeches, however, also showed
his commitment to American global military supremacy. On
the campaign trail, Obama declared that his foreign policy was
"actually a return to the traditional bipartisan realistic policy of
George Bush's father, of John F. Kennedy, of, in some ways,
Ronald Reagan."[53] One of Obama's chief foreign policy advisers,
Zbigniew Brzezinski, was founder of the Rockefeller financed
Trilateral Commission, which championed the use of surrogate
forces to re-establish American world primacy after Vietnam, and
strove to return to the days when "Truman, Acheson, Forrestal,
Marshall, Harriman, and Lovett could unite on a policy of global
intervention and domestic militarism as our common purpose, with
no interference from the undisciplined rabble [1960s activists],"
as Noam Chomsky wrote.[54]

Neoconservative Robert Kagan penned a column in the
Washington Post titled "Obama the Interventionist" that praised
him for "embracing cold war language" and "describing the

United States as a leader of the free world. Obama talks about rogue nations, hostile dictators, muscular alliances, and mounting a strong nuclear deterrent. He talks about how we need to seize the American moment. We must begin the world anew. This is realism? That's left liberal foreign policy? Ask Noam Chomsky the next time you see him."[55] Many liberals, nevertheless, had been seduced by Obama and did not want to oppose the nation's first black president. When Obama threatened to bomb Syria in 2013, many African Americans supported the initiative, more so even than whites. Black writer Cornel West stated that the "black prophetic tradition had lapsed into a coma."[56] Not even Wilson could achieve such a feat.

The Liberal Internationalist Tradition and Libya

Obama's nod to the liberal internationalist tradition, in all of its Orwellian manifestations, was probably best exemplified in the rhetoric used to sell war in Libya. Like Wilson's war in Russia, this intervention was waged without Congressional sanction or vote, which Obama claimed was not needed because the U.S. was not at war and Libya never threatened it with attack. Obama asserted in February 2011 that the U.S. strongly supported the "universal rights of the Libyan people, including the right of assembly, free speech, and the ability of the Libyan people to determine their own destiny," which he said, "could not be denied through violence or suppression."[57] However as we shall see in chapter 3, by arming sectarian and Islamic rebels, bombing the country and blocking peace overtures, the U. S and its allies were denying the ability of the Libyan people to determine their own destiny through violence. And their actions effectively turned it into a failed state.

In March 2011, Obama explained the decision to join France and Great Britain in launching air and missile strikes to oust the Libyan leader, Muammar Qaddafi, in neo-Wilsonian terms centered on the responsibility to protect. He stated that:

if not for our intervention, the democratic
impulses that are dawning across the region
would be eclipsed as oppressive leaders
conclude that violence is the best strategy
to cling to power.... So while I will never
minimize the costs involved in military
action, I am confident that a failure to act in
Libya would have carried a far greater price
for Americans. To brush aside America's
responsibility as a leader and more profoundly
our responsibility to our fellow human beings
under such circumstances would have been a
betrayal of who we are. Some nations may be
able to turn a blind eye to atrocities in other
countries. The United States of America is
different.[58]

It was a potent mix of American exceptionalism with emphasis
on humanitarian imperatives, which masked the economic and
geopolitical motives underlying the war and its brutal reality.
Later it was acknowledged that Secretary of State Hillary Clinton
had exaggerated Qaddafi's atrocities in the suppression of
demonstrations by ten times, and that false rumors were spread -
as had been done with Germany during the Great War. The rumors
included that Qaddafi was giving his soldiers Viagra to induce
rape when human rights groups found no evidence of rapes.[59]

After Qaddafi's brutal murder on October 20, Obama
gushed that it was a "momentous day in the history of Libya. The
dark shadow of tyranny has been lifted and the Libyan people now
have a great responsibility to build a more inclusive society."[60]
However, Libya in reality became enmeshed in internecine warlord
feuds as the progressive features of Qaddafi's rule—including
free public housing and investment of Libya's oil wealth in its
economy and in African development—were undermined, and
jihadist terrorists carried out gruesome atrocities.

The Libyan intervention provides a stunning example of

the contradictions of the Wilsonian tradition embraced by Obama, which has left the world a blood-soaked legacy. It has much in common with the First World War in that it was packaged as part of a human rights crusade to spread democracy and good governance but was underlain by hidden agendas, including a desire to access Libya's oil and to expand AFRICOM, one of ten combatant commands of the American Armed Forces responsible for military operations in Africa.

Liberal intellectuals were exceedingly hypocritical in displaying outrage at Qaddafi's alleged atrocities—instances which were exaggerated and taken out of context—while ignoring those of the jihadist rebels and strategic clients across the region such as Saudi Arabia, Bahrain or Rwanda and Uganda. Similarly in World War I, great moral outrage was exhibited towards German atrocities in Belgium when British and French atrocities, including the use of poisonous gases and shooting of prisoners of war, were ignored, as were pre-Soviet Russian atrocities in East Prussia where 866,000 people were driven from their homes, 34,000 buildings were burned and an estimated 1,620 civilians were murdered.[61]

These case studies fit perfectly with Noam Chomsky and Edward S. Herman's propaganda model indicating how the media and intellectual classes serve government interests by fixating on the crimes of official enemies while ignoring those of its allies.[62] The main difference between Libya and World War I was that no U.S or European soldiers were killed in Libya, as by then the Pentagon had developed sophisticated technologies like drones that could shield the American military and public from the human costs of war and thereby defuse the threat of antiwar activism. Obama was thus saved from public condemnation, unlike Wilson—and might live out his post-presidency as a national and international celebrity.

Endnotes

1   See Richard Hofstadter, *The American Political Tradition and the Men Who Made It* (New York: Alfred A. Knopf, 1948).

2   Richard Franklin Pettigrew, *Imperial Washington: The Story of American Public Life From 1870 to 1920* (Chicago: Charles H. Kerr & Company, 1922), 215.

3   Davis quoted in Richard Drinnon *Facing West: The Metaphysics of Indian-Hating & Empire-Building* (Norman: University of Oklahoma Press, 1980), 79, 80.

4   Pettigrew, *Imperial Washington*, 243-245.

5   Woodrow Wilson, *War Messages*, 65th Cong., 1st Sess. Senate Doc. No. 5, Serial No. 7264, Washington, D.C., 1917; pp. 3-8, *passim, https://wwi.lib.byu. edu/index.php/Wilson%27s_War_Message_to_Congress*.

6   C. Hartley Grattan, *Why We Fought* (Indianapolis: Bobbs-Merrill, 1969); Harry Elmer Barnes, *The Genesis of the World War: An Introduction to the Problem of War Guilt* (New York: Alfred A. Knopf, 1929); Ferdinand Lundberg, *America's 60 Families* (New York: The Vanguard Press, 1937), 144.

7   Tony Smith, *Why Wilson Matters: The Origins of Liberal Internationalism and Its Crisis Today* (New Jersey: Princeton University Press, 2017).

8   George Viereck, *The Strangest Friendship in History: Woodrow Wilson and Colonel House,* rev ed. (New York: Praeger, 1976); Richard Miniter, *Leading From Behind: The Reluctant President and the Advisors Who Decide For Him* (New York: St. Martin's, 2012), 19.

9   Lundberg, *America's 60 Families*, 109, 113, 117, 123, 125, 126, 127, 128; A. Scott Berg, *Wilson* (New York: G.P. Putnam & Sons, 2013), 212, 225. Wilson also received large donations from clothing retailer Edward Filene, real estate mogul Henry Morgenthau, and Cyrus McCormack, Head of the International Harvesters Company which had considerable investments in Russia.

10   Lundberg, *America's 60 Families*, 123-128; Thomas A. Sheridan, *Arizona: A History* (Tucson: The University of Arizona Press, 1995), 183, 184; Rob e. Hanson *The Great Bisbee IWW Deportation of July 12, 1917* (Bisbee, AZ: Signature Press, 1989). One miner wrote on a boxcar: "what the little red rooster did to the little red hen was what President Wilson did to the working men."

11   Greg Palast, "Penny's From Heaven," in *Billionaires and Ballot Bandits* (New York: Seven Stories Press, 2012); Dennis Bernstein, "The Privilege of the Pritzkers," *Counterpunch*, May 3, 2014; Suzanna Andrews, "Shattered Dynasty," *Vanity Fair*, May 11, 2003; Chuck Neubauer, "Obama Donors Get Deal, Depositors Get Stiffed Again," *Washington Times*, June 10, 2012.

12   David Moberg, "Three Troubling Things to Know About Pritzker," *In These Times*, May 3, 2013; Gus Russo, *Supermob: How Sidney Korshak and His*

Criminal Associates Became America's Hidden Powerbrokers (New York: Bloomsbury, 2006), 440, 499; Steven Rosenfeld, "Obama Picks Billionaire Tax Evader to Head Commerce Department," *Occupy*, May 8, 2013; Carl Finamore, "National Actions Against Billionaire Pritzker's and the Hyatt Hotel Chain," *Truthdig*, July 19, 2010. Pritzker opposed the employer free choice act expanding union membership.

13   Russo, *Supermob*, 19; Peter Dale Scott, *Deep Politics and the Death of JFK* (Berkeley: University of California Press, 1993), 155. The contract, which was the largest given by any government in history to that point, was awarded by Roswell Gilpatrick, GDs former Special Counsel when Boeing's design was found to have been cheaper and "operationally superior." Crown's attorney Albert Jenner, who represented labor racketeers and figures in organized crime, became a senior staff attorney for the Warren Commission investigating JFKs assassination.

14   Bob Tamarkin, "The Ordeal of Lester Crown," *New York Times*, December 7, 1986; Margaret Carroll, "Crown Jewels*," Chicago Tribune*, February 3, 1988. Lester allegedly fired a ski instructor at his Aspen resort for trying to form a union.

15   Philip Mattera, "General Dynamics: Corporate Rap Sheet," *Corporate Research Project*, https://www.corp-research.org/general-dynamics.

16   U.S. Senate, Permanent Subcommittee on Investigations, Committee on Homeland Security and Governmental Affairs, "J.P. Morgan Chase Whale Trades: A Case History of Derivatives, Risks and Abuses," Majority and Minority Staff Report, Carl Levin and John McCain, March 13, 2013; "J.P. Morgan Director Retire After 'Whale" Debacle," *Reuters*, July 20, 2013. J.P. Morgan was forced to pay $920 million in fines for what was considered "manipulative conduct" in violation of the Dodd-Frank Act and other laws.

17   Webster Griffin Tarpley, *Barack J. Obama: The Unauthorized Biography* (Joshua Tree, CA: Progressive Press, 2008), 302; www.opensecrets.com; "Obama's Top Fundraisers," *New York Times*, September 13, 2012. The Crowns also held ownership in oil and gas companies. Open Secrets lists other members of Henry Crown & Co. as Obama bundlers such as Barbara Manilow who raised $100,000.

18   Ken Silverstein, "Barack Obama Inc." *Harper's Magazine*, November 2006, 33; Peter Schweizer, *Secret Empires: How the American Political Class Hides Corruption and Enriches Family and Friends* (New York: Harper, 2018), 188; Patrick Martin, "Obama Crony Joins Carlyle Group," *World Socialist Web*, January 9, 2014; Tariq Ali. *The Obama Syndrome: Surrender at Home, War Abroad* (London: Verso, 2011). Obama also received major donations from large corporate law and lobbying firms (Kirkland & Ellis, and Skadden, Arps et al.) and got three times more money from banks than John McCain in 2008.

19   See Lance Selfa, *The Democrats: A Critical History* (Chicago: Haymarket, 2012).

20   Edmund S. Morgan, *American Slavery, American Freedom: The Ordeal of Colonial Virginia* (New York: W.W. Norton, 1975), 47; Roger Peace, "The War of 1812," United States Foreign Policy, History and Resource Guide, www. peacehistory-usfp.org.

21   Woodrow Wilson, *A History of the American People*, Vol. 5 (New York: Harper & Brothers, 1901), 278; John Milton Cooper Jr. *Woodrow Wilson: A Biography* (New York: Alfred A. Knopf, 2009), 76.

22   Cooper Jr. *Woodrow Wilson*, 75, 76.

23   Barack Obama, *The Audacity of Hope: Thoughts on Reclaiming the American Dream* (New York: Crown, 2006), 31; David Maraniss, "Obama's Military Connection," *Washington Post*, May 4, 2012; "Spiegel Interview with Obama's Great Uncle," *Der Spiegel*, May 26, 2009;.

24   In Michael Kazin, *War Against the War: The American Fight for Peace, 1914-1918* (New York: Simon & Schuster, 2018), 207.

25   Munitions Industry, Report on Existing Legislation, Special Commission on Investigation of the Munitions Industry; John Kenneth Turner, *Shall It Be Again?* (New York: B.W. Huebsch Inc., 1922); Paul A.C. Koistinen, *Planning War, Pursuing Peace: The Political Economy of American Warfare, 1930-1939* (Lawrence: University Press of Kansas, 1998), 254.

26   Randolph S. Bourne, "Twilight of the Idols," in *War and the Intellectuals: Collected Essays 1915-1919*, ed. Carl Resek (Indianapolis: Hacket Publishing, 1964), 53, 54, 60.

27   Philip Knightly, *The First Casualty: From the Crimea to Vietnam: The War Correspondent as Hero, Propogandist, and Myth Maker* (New York: Harcourt, Brace Jovanovich, 1975), 120.

28   Henry Kissinger, *World Order* (New York: Penguin Books, 2015).

29   Dalton Trumbo, *Johnny Got His Gun* (New York: Bantam Books, 1939), 24.

30   Ibid., 116, 117.

31   Ibid., 116, 117.

32   Smedley Butler, *War is a Racket: The Antiwar Classic by America's Most Decorated Soldier* (Los Angeles: Feral House, 2003), 26, 27, 28; H.C. Engelbrecht and Frank Hanighen, *Merchants of Death* (New York: Dodd & Mead, 1934), 176, 177, 178; Paul Koistinen, *Mobilizing for Modern War: The Political Economy of American Warfare, 1865-1919* (Lawrence: University of Kansas Press, 1997), 263.

33   James Risen, *Pay Any Price: Greed, Power and Endless War* (New York: Mariner Books, 2015); Dennis Rodkin, "All in the Crown Family – Winnetka," *Chicago Real Estate*, February 8, 2010.

34   General Dynamics, 2016 Annual Report, https://www.gd.com/sites/default/ files/2016-GD-Annual-Report.pdf; General Dynamics, Annual Report, 2010, http://investorrelations.gd.com/~/media/Files/G/General-Dynamics-IR/ documents/annual-reports/2010AR.pdf; Bruce Gagnon, "Crazy Horse Back

on the War Path," in *The Military Industrial Complex at Fifty*, ed. David Swanson (David Swanson, 2011), 218, 219.

35   Raytheon, 2016, Annual Report, Engineering a Safer World, file:///C:/Users/jeremy-kuzmarov/Downloads/2016_RTN_AR_Full.pdf; 2016 Annual Report, Lockheed Martin, http://www.annualreports.com/HostedData/AnnualReportArchive/l/NYSE_LMT_2016.pdf.

36   https://www.opensecrets.org/pacs/lookup2.php?strID=C00409979.

37   Noam Chomsky, *Year 501: The Conquest Continues* (Boston: South End Press, 1993), 202, 203; Hans Schmidt, *The United States Occupation of Haiti* (New Jersey: Rutgers University Press, 1971).

38   Lundberg, *America's 60 Families*, 123-126; Lloyd C. Gardner, *Imperial America: American Foreign Policy Since 1898* (New York: Harcourt, Brace Jovanovich, 1976), 73.

39   William S. Graves, *America's Siberian Adventure 1918-1920* (New York: Peter Smith, 1941), 348.

40   "Message of the U.S. President of the United States in Response to a Resolution of the Senate agreed to June 23, 1919 – Inform the Senate of the Reasons for Sending U.S. soldiers to and maintain them in Siberia," White House, July 22, 1919, M917, Military Intelligence Division, Roll 1, RG 395, NACP, American Expeditionary Forces in Siberia, National Archives, College Park Maryland.

41   Summary of the Staff of the Commander-in chief of the Russian Allied Armies Operating Against the Bolsheviks, October 27, 1918, RG 395, U.S. Army Overseas Operations, Historical Files of the Expeditionary Forces in Siberia, 1918-1920, M917, National Archives, College Park Maryland; Jeremy Kuzmarov and John Marciano, *The Russians are Coming, Again: The First Cold War as Tragedy, the Second as Farce* (New York: Monthly Review Press, 2018), ch. 1.

42   John Cudahy, *Archangel: The American War with Russia* (Chicago: A.C. McClurg & Co., 1924), 29, 30.

43   Obama, *The Audacity of Hope*, 282.

44   Burton Yale Pines, *America's Greatest Blunder: The Fateful Decision to Enter World War One* (New York: RSD Press, 2013).

45   Obama, *The Audacity of Hope*, 283-285.

46   Kuzmarov and Marciano, *The Russians Are Coming, Again*; *Perpetual War For Perpetual Peace: A Critical Examination of the Foreign Policy of Franklin Delano Roosevelt and Its Aftermath*, ed. Harry Elmer Barnes (Ostara Publications, 2013; 1953).

47   Barack Obama, foreign policy speech, "The World Beyond Iraq," March 19, 2008, Fayeteville, North Carolina in David Olive, *An American Story – The Speeches of Barack Obama* (ECW Press, 2008), 272.

48   "Nobel Lecture by Barack H. Obama, Oslo, December 10, 2009, https://www.nobelprize.org/nobel_prizes/peace/laureates/2009/obama-lecture_en.html

49   Quoted in William Appleman Williams, *The Tragedy of American Diplomacy*, rev ed. (New York: W.W. Norton & Co., 1972), 69.

50   See chapters four and nine. On U.S. misbehavior in the Philippines, see Paul Kramer, *The Blood of Government* (Chapel Hill: University of North Carolina Press, 2006).

51   "Nobel Lecture by Barack H. Obama, Oslo, December 10, 2009. Obama went on to say that "in many ways, these efforts succeeded.... [even though some terrible wars were fought], the Cold War ended with jubilant crowds dismantling a wall."

52   See William Blum, *Killing Hope: U.S. Military and CIA Interventions Since World War II* (Monroe, ME: Common Courage Press, 1998).

53   Morton Keller, *Obama's Time: A History* (New York: Oxford University Press, 2015), 156; Webster G. Tarpley, *Obama: The Postmodern Coup* (Joshua Tree, CA: Progressive Press, 2008), 228. Samantha Power told *Rolling Stone* in 2007 that Obama sees that you "have to grasp the limits of American power in order to transcend them." In Sasha Abramsky, *Inside Obama's Brain* (New York: Penguin, 2012), 79.

54   Webster G. Tarpley, *Barack H. Obama.*

55   Robert Kagan, "Obama - The Interventionist," *Washington Post*, April 29, 2007.

56   Glen Ford, "Black America More Pro-War than Ever," *Black Agenda Report*, September 2013. A *Washington Post*/ABC poll conducted between August 28 and September 1, 2013 showed 40 percent of African Americans supported President Obama's threats of airstrikes against Syria—two points more than whites and nine percent more than Hispanics.

57   Smith, *Why Wilson Matters*, 255.

58   Smith, *Why Wilson Matters,* 256.

59   *The Illegal War on Libya*, ed. Cynthia McKinney (Atlanta: Clarity Press, 2012); Jo Becker and Scott Shane, "Hillary Clinton, 'Smart Power,' and a Dictator's Fall," *New York Times*, February 27, 2016; Patrick Cockburn, "Lies, damn lies, and reports of battlefield atrocities," *The Independent*, June 19, 2011.

60   "Remarks by the President on the Death of Muammar Qaddafi," The White House, Office of the Press Secretary, October 20, 2011.

61   *The Illegal War on Libya*, ed. McKinney; Thomas Fleming, *The Illusion of Victory: America in World War I* (New York: Basic Books, 2003); Jim MacGregor and Gerry Docherty, *Prolonging the Agony: How the Anglo-American Establishment Deliberately Extended World War I by Three-and-a-Half Years* (Walterville, OR: Trine Day Press, 2018), 48.

62   Noam Chomsky and Edward S. Herman, *Manufacturing Consent: The Political Economy of the Mass Media* (New York: Pantheon Books, 1989).

Chapter 2

A TISSUE OF LIES
THE FALSE MARKETING OF
BRAND OBAMA

In September 2017, Jeanette Taylor, the education director of the Kenwood Oakland Community Organization, confronted ex-President Obama via Skype about the impact of his presidential library which threatened to raise property values and displace residents on Chicago's South Side Woodlawn neighborhood, next to Obama's old haunting ground at the University of Chicago. "The library is a great idea, but what about a community benefits agreement [CBA]?" Taylor asked Obama, referring to a contract between a developer and community organizations that requires investments in, or hiring from, a neighborhood where a project is built. "The first time investment comes to black communities, the first to get kicked out is low-income and working-class people. Why wouldn't you sign a CBA to protect us?" Obama responded by reminding Taylor of his background as a community organizer. He then said that he "knew the neighborhood," and that "the minute you start saying 'well we're thinking about signing something that will determine who's getting jobs and contacts, and this and that...next thing I know, I've got 20 organizations coming out of the woodwork.'" This condescending response infuriated Taylor, who told journalist Edward McClelland that "he had a lot of nerve saying that. He has forgotten who he is. He forgot the community got him where he is."[1]

This exchange with Ms. Taylor revealed a great deal about Obama's moral character and willingness to slough off the black community which sustained support for him and his political rise to fame. Historian David J. Garrow describes Obama in his 2017 biography as a man who long ago had become a "vessel [that] was hollow at its core." He noted how disappointed and betrayed many of Obama's former friends felt by a president who "doesn't feel indebted to people (to quote a former close assistant) and who spent inordinate time on the golf course and celebrity hobnobbing."[2]

Garrow further quotes Al Sharp, executive director of Protestants for the Common Good, who stated that as state senator Obama was "so very pragmatic" that "he," in Garrow's words, "was unwilling to fight to the good fight." Legal aid veteran Linda Mills further recalled that "[state senator] Barack 'sponsored a number of bills I wrote,' but 'I stopped seeking him out as a chief sponsor early on' because Barack was 'disengaged' rather than actively pushing the bills. 'He was never involved in the legislation,' and on many days Barack was simply 'unavailable. Golfing, playing basketball. He was just out to lunch so often.'" Mills added that Obama could be "exasperatingly rude at times with Senators and lobbyists. On the floor, he would put his hands-on people as though they were his subjects. It was the most patronizing and condescending body language I'd ever seen."[3]

All these recollections are important and help place in context Obama's actions as president, including in the realm of foreign policy. Historian Thomas C. Reeves pointed out in a study of John F. Kennedy that Americans value high moral and intellectual integrity in their presidents; something Obama has often lacked.[4] A genuinely progressive leader and man of sincerity could never get before the American public and justify with a straight face sending thousands of young men to fight a war deep down everyone knew could never be won, order the assassination of people thousands of miles away when they had never been charged with a crime in court, or quietly recolonize the African continent while purporting to follow in the legacy of Martin Luther King Jr. and Nelson Mandela. Obama's political genius lay in his ability to create an identity that endeared him to liberals. This identity was entirely constructed, however, and based on effective marketing. Obama waffled on policy positions based on political expediency and rivaled Richard M. Nixon in his use of executive power. If Donald J. Trump is a con man who hoodwinked America, as his attorney Michael Cohen testified before Congress, Obama is better at it, as relatively few have accused him of this. And it all started with his 1995 memoir *Dreams from My Father*.

False Advertising: *Dreams from My Father*

Published prior to his becoming a senator when he was only thirty-three, Obama's memoir would transform an affable young man of respectable achievement into an icon of multiculturalism and globalization. It made him into an ideal front-man for U.S. foreign policy since he appeared sensitive to cultural differences, worldly and committed to social change. Obama was especially perfect for an age when diversity was being celebrated as an exemplification of American progress, marginalizing critiques of capitalism and American imperialism. While his role-model example would have positive effect, it also gave the (false) impression that America's racial inequalities had been resolved, and sidelined the African American struggle.

Initially a modest commercial success, *Dreams from My Father* became a best-seller after Obama gave his breakout speech before the Democratic Party National Convention in Boston in 2004.[5] The book, with its successor, *The Audacity of Hope: Thoughts on Reclaiming the American Dream* (2006), can be compared to John F. Kennedy's 1956 ghost-written book, *Profiles in Courage*, which took a "young whippersnapper" who "never said a word of importance in the Senate and never did a thing," as his vice president Lyndon B. Johnson noted, and "somehow created an image of himself as a shining intellectual, a youthful leader who could change the face of the country."[6]

Whereas Kennedy had gifted writers like Theodore Sorenson and the historian Arthur Schlesinger Jr. assisting him, Obama's collaborators remain a source of speculation.[7] *Dreams from My Father* follows Obama's quest to find out about his African heritage, to come to terms with his mixed-race background, and to make a difference as a community organizer. On the surface, it is a gripping coming of age tale. However, critical scrutiny reveals that it is largely a work of "historical fiction" as David Garrow describes it. Various names are changed, dates are wrong such as the date when his father left his mother, and certain facts about Obama's life from what we know are embellished or made up.

The book depicts Obama as growing up with an anguished racial identity when his home state of Hawaii was one of the most racially tolerant states. His closest friends and classmates from that period do not recall him ever expressing consternation about his race and note that he was absent from discussions by the handful of black students who said they struggled with their race. (Obama's friend Keith Kakugawa told *The Chicago Tribune* that the idea that his biggest struggle was with race is "bull"). Obama claimed that he had experienced his racial awakening at age nine when he saw a *Life Magazine* article in the American embassy in Jakarta about a man who suffered when he tried to bleach his skin white. This article, as confirmed by *Life*'s editors, never existed.[8]

Another misleading aspect of *Dreams from My Father* is its insinuation that Obama was a political radical as a college student, an image that became central to his identity, projected in *The Audacity of Hope* as a reformed, matured radical. While Obama did give a speech protesting apartheid at Occidental College, the head of the black student association, Louis Hook, said that Obama "wasn't an especially active member of the group."[9] At Columbia, which he attended in the 1982-1983 school year, Obama was a ghost. The director of the black students' association, Mark Attich, said he was shocked to learn that Obama had claimed he was involved with the group.[10]

As for his stint as a community organizer, Obama was paid almost twice the amount he claimed in the book and embellished his role in organizing residents in the Altgeld Gardens housing project on Chicago's South side against environmental hazards, failing to mention Hazel Johnson, a tireless community activist who was the major driver of the campaign. Obama also demeaned residents, claiming that they had pounded on a government official's limousine, pressed their faces against the tinted glass and cursed at him, when there is no evidence they had done so.[11]

Biographer G. Webster Tarpley points out that Obama failed to acknowledge that he had been employed by The Gamaliel Foundation, a satellite of his mother's old employer, the Ford Foundation, whose underlying aim was to avert class solidarity and the revival of Martin Luther King Jr.'s inter-racial poor people's movement, which would challenge corporate power. Corporate foundations employed organizers like Obama to focus on parochial neighborhood concerns which would divert activist energies and divide different neighborhoods or racial and ethnic groups from one another—a strategy of divide and rule.[12] Later on, many residents of Altgeld Gardens, including Hazel's daughter, Cheryl, felt that Obama had used them for a "line on his cv." He never once came back to visit during his presidency as he had promised or followed-up on his earlier work.[13]

Dreams' conservative politics become apparent in a passage where Obama recalls attending a lecture by Black Power icon, Stokely Carmichael (Kwame Touré), in the early 1980s in which Carmichael, appearing with the "eyes of a madman or a saint," upbraids a woman for her "bourgeois tendency" after she questions his plan to "establish economic ties between Harlem and Africa that would circumvent capitalist imperialism." Clinching the negative portrayal, Obama refers to two women selling Marxist literature down the hall, whom he says call each other "Stalinist pig" and "reformist bitch." Obama editorializes that the "movement had died years ago, shattered into a thousand fragments" and that "even those with the best of intentions could end up further and further removed from the struggles of those they purported to serve. Or just plain crazy."[14]

So much for the movement, then. But for a purported progressive, if not continuing to fight valiantly against the current for social justice causes in a new era marred by rising social inequality and revanchist militarism, as many of the 1960s veterans did, then what?

Strategically casting himself in *Dreams from My Father* as an heir to the early 1960s organizing tradition, Obama underplays the significance of his employment for a Manhattan-based consulting house to multi-national corporations, Business International Corporation (BIC), after his graduation from Columbia. According to former employees, Obama's job was to edit newsletters on business conditions in countries around the world. Headed by a close friend of former vice president Hubert Humphrey, BIC had functioned as a CIA front with a subspecialty in recruiting left-wing organizers to use as assets, and in infiltrating foreign labor unions with the goal of promoting disruptions in targeted economies.[15] An activist with the Students for a Democratic Society (SDS) described Business International as the guys who wrote the Alliance for Progress (Marshall Plan for Latin America). "They're the left-wing of the ruling class."[16]

BIC's director, Orville Freeman Jr., was a former Governor of Minnesota involved with Humphrey in the purge of suspected communists in the Farmer-Labor party. Omitting mention of the company's CIA connection, Obama wrote that when he worked at BIC he was "like a spy behind enemy lines."[17] This comment reinforces the overarching narrative of his story in which the liberal hero eschews Christ's temptation by giving up the perks associated with work for corporate America, goes out instead to do God's work organizing the poor and dispossessed then discovers that he can better effect change by infiltrating the halls of power.

Per *Dreams*, young Obama eschews another dangerous temptation when he gives up his relationships with a white woman from a wealthy family, Genevieve Cook, who allegedly disparaged blacks after watching a play written by a black playwright. He then marries Michelle, an upwardly mobile African-American woman from a more modest family. In actuality, however, Cook denied seeing any plays by a black playwright or making disparaging remarks—which Obama later acknowledged to be true.[18]

False Advertising II: Obama's Family Background

Obama's 2008 presidential campaign manager David Axelrod specialized in using personal stories to market political candidates and he knew he had a winner in Obama. *Dreams from My Father* centers on Obama's journey to uncover his African heritage and learn more about his estranged father who had pursued advanced degrees in the U.S. so he could help his country, though fell into despair after his political mentor, Tom Mboya, is assassinated in an inter-tribal feud. Abandoned by both his father and mother, Obama is raised by his grandparents from his mother's side—Stanley Armor Dunham ("Gramps") and Madelyn Dunham (Grandma "Toot")—who reflect the traditional values of the frontier and America's "Greatest Generation," as journalist Tom Brokaw coined them. Both are hardworking and patriotic and overcome their racial prejudice in raising young Barry. Stanley was a World War II veteran and furniture salesman and Toot was Rosie the Riveter, working at a Boeing plant in Wichita, Kansas to support the war effort.

Obama depicts his mother, Stanley Ann Dunham, as a free-spirited hippie who pursues a career as an anthropologist in Indonesia, where she worked tirelessly to help poor craftsmen and women. She had broken every racial taboo by falling in love with and marrying a son of Africa and then an Indonesian colonel. True to her 1960s values, she grew estranged from the latter when he became an oil executive, resenting the dinner conversation at the elite social club she brought him to where Texas and Louisiana businessmen boasted about the "palms they had greased" to obtain off-shore drilling rights and their wives complained about the "Indonesian help." Repudiating these "Ugly Americans," Ann was one to roll up her sleeves, and go out in the field to interact with real Indonesians and to help boost local craft industries through providing microfinancing credits and loans.[19]

The story Obama tells in *Dreams from My Father* and *The Audacity of Hope* was crucial to his election victories and captured the American public in a way no previous president in recent memory has. But was Obama telling the truth, or was it false marketing? Readers can be the judge, but there is considerable evidence to suggest the latter. Obama Sr., for example, is alleged to have come to study at the University of Hawaii as part of a State Department or CIA sponsored exchange, and met Ann in a Russian language class in the fall semester of 1960 where they fell in love, got married in Maui, and had Barack. However, Obama Sr. and Ann never lived together, no friends or relatives attended their wedding, and Ann quickly relocated to Seattle while Obama Sr. launched into his senior year at the University of Hawaii. Even more suspicious is that Stanley Dunham was part of a group photo taken with Obama Sr. on his departure from Hawaii. This would suggest that Dunham was no mere furniture salesman but a coordinator of the exchange.[20] Dunham had served with the 9th Air Force Division in the Second World War and was pictured in a military uniform with no insignia, which suggests an intelligence unit. Another photo featured his daughter, Ann, with the insignia of an elite school in Lebanon on her shirt in the 1950s where Stanley may have worked.[21]

Film-maker Joel Gilbert suggests that Obama's real father was Frank Marshall Davis, an African American journalist, sexually libertine poet, political radical and a target of Grandpa Dunham's surveillance. Gilbert was told by Obama's friend Keith Kakugawa that Ann had had the affair with Davis because she was angry that the family had to move to Hawaii away from her high-school friends who were all attending the University of Washington. Ann became pregnant and to hide the truth, Dunham paid Obama Sr. to marry Ann, giving him an opportunity to extend his visa and attend Harvard.[22]

Barack eventually found out the truth about his family. In *Dreams from My Father*, he wrote that the visits to "Frank's" house "always left me feeling vaguely uncomfortable as if I were witnessing some complicated, unspoken transaction between the two men, a transaction I couldn't understand."[23] Obama paid tribute to his real father in the 1981 poem published in the Occidental College Literary Journal called "Pop" which attributes to him features that resemble Davis, and references Pop's poetry, written before his mother died. Barack Sr. was not a poet and though Stanley dabbled in poetry, Barry called him "Gramps" and his mother committed suicide before his eighth birthday.[24]

Obama's depiction of his mother Ann as a free-spirited hippie is also problematic and contradicted by her curriculum vitae. She worked as a consultant for major bastions of the American political establishment in Indonesia such as USAID, the Asia Foundation, Development Alternatives Inc., the Ford Foundation, and the World Bank which all pursued the objective of integrating Indonesia into the world capitalist economy and undermining its then socialist tendency. The microfinancing projects Ann worked on were designed to "tether third world masses to the mentality of finance capitalism."[25] Dunham's boss at USAID, Dr. Gordon Donald Jr. whom she followed to Pakistan, where she lived out of the swanky Hilton hotel in Lahore, was identified as a CIA agent. Another boss, Peter Geithner, was the future Treasury Secretary Timothy Geithner's father.[26]

Ann's employers were deeply complicit in the anti-communist pogroms carried out by Indonesian General Suharto after he came to power in a CIA backed coup d'état in 1965 that ousted the Socialist President Ahmed Sukarno. The latter had taken measures to nationalize key industries and resources in Indonesia. The American embassy was ecstatic at the coup and considered it as a great victory for the United States in the Cold War. After killing and imprisoning well over a million people, Suharto would open Indonesia up to foreign economic exploitation and permit the clear-cutting of Indonesia's forests. The Indonesian military went on to invade West Papua and East Timor with further American backing, crushing the independence aspirations of their peoples.[27]

Though Ann had come of age politically during the 1960s she was described by her academic mentor, Alice Dewey, not as a new leftist critical of U.S. imperialism, but as a "garden variety

Democrat." Her dissertation argued that Indonesian villagers were dynamic and could produce greater wealth if they had access to market incentives and capital.[28] Socially liberal like her son, she had studied Marxism and knew multiple languages including Russian, all of which made her a "CIA recruiter's wet dream."[29] A considerable amount of Ann's anthropological and consulting field work was carried out in Java, which provided a hotbed of support for the Indonesian Community Party (PKI). Members of the Javanese women's association and labor federation were staunch supporters of Sukarno and the PKI. The CIA at this time employed anthropologists and development workers as undercover agents to gather information on villagers' political affiliations, in which Ann, according to Dewey, had taken an interest. While her recruitment as an agent has never been openly acknowledged, she was among the few U.S. government employees with the language skills and access to fulfill this role effectively. Development projects in the region were explicitly designed to pry villagers away from the PKI orbit, and Ann's work would have contributed to this.[30]

In March 1965, Ann had married an Indonesian Lieutenant Colonel, Lolo Soetoro, whom she met at the University of Hawaii's East-West Center, a "kinder, gentler version" of the infamous "School of the Americas" and "cover for a training program in which Southeast Asians were brought to Hawaii and trained to go back.... to create agent nets," as U.S. Information Service (USIS) Director Frank Scotten described it.[31] A friend of Ann's told her biographer that the marriage to Lolo was not real. This suggests that Ann may have been acting as a female "honeypot" for the CIA whose job was to recruit assets and help them to obtain U.S. citizenship. There was no wedding and the couple never lived together in Honolulu although they did have a daughter together, Maya.[32] Heralding from an aristocratic family which lost out in Sukarno's land reform, Soetoro was recalled in July 1965 before General Suharto's right-wing coup. Working as an army geographer in Java and Papua New Guinea, Soetoro went on to become an executive at Mobil Oil and its liaison to Suharto, whose economic policies Ann Dunham praised.

Obama's claim in *The Audacity of Hope* that his mother

did not know about mass killings before she went to Indonesia because the newspapers did not report on it is unlikely because the killings were reported on favorably in the *New York Times* and mainstream publications.[33] There remains much in Obama's family history that did not come to light in his depiction of it. Besides the aforementioned, he did not disclose that as Vice President of the Bank of Hawaii, his Grandma Toot would have handled escrow accounts used to pay American Cold War clients in Indonesia, Taiwan, Philippines, South Korea, and elsewhere through CIA proprieties.[34]

Obama's family background generally exemplifies the wide reach of the American Empire, which his supporters did not want to dwell upon, and he covered up. It helps place in context many of his actions as president, and likely, his cynicism. To the extent that Obama had a worldview that was not attached to political calculation, it derived not just from his family, but from the elite academic institutions he attended. The professor of a class he took on state socialism at Columbia acknowledged that the syllabus did not "present a flattering portrayal of political and social life in these now-thankfully defunct systems."[35] Obama also took a seminar on U.S. foreign policy that featured proponents of liberal internationalism like Joseph Nye and Ernest May, who wrote a book defending Wilson's decisions in the First World War. At Harvard Law, though exposed to critical legal studies, Obama was drawn to the courses of a libertarian professor and wrote about the progressive potential of "market forces."[36]

Reformed Radical

Obama's first public expression of his views on foreign policy ironically was in "Breaking the War Mentality," an article he wrote in 1983 for Columbia University's *Sundial Magazine* which provided a positive profile of local antiwar groups. Referencing "American puppet dictators" Obama conveyed concern that the public's distance from the costs of war "made resisting it a difficult task," though he believed America "could be pulled off the dead-end track" and "twisted logic of which we are a part."[37]

What a different tone state Senator Obama struck nineteen years later when he spoke at an antiwar rally in Chicago where he specified that he was not against all wars, only ill-conceived ones like that against Iraq. Before his speech, he turned to the women who invited him, and referring to anti-war anthems "Blowin' in the Wind," "Where Have all the Flowers Gone," and "Give Peace a Chance," asked "couldn't they think of something else to play?"[38] Carl Davidson, a Vietnam protest leader who helped organize the rally, said that Obama's position on Iraq subsequently began to morph. Davidson said Obama began saying "we have to find a 'smart path' to victory and not Bush's dumb path.... [I]n dealing with Iran, we had to leave on the table bombing their nuclear sites. For this, a lot of antiwar activists started calling him 'Barack O'bomb 'em.'"[39]

After election to the U.S. Senate, Obama opposed legislation to withdraw troops from Iraq, and in *The Audacity of Hope*, openly denounced his supposed youthful radicalism. Obama wrote:

> rejection of authority [in the allegedly radical period of his youth] spilled into self-indulgence and self-destructiveness, and by the time I enrolled in college, I'd begin to see how any challenge to convention harbored within it the possibilities of its own excesses and its own orthodoxy. I started to re-examine my assumptions, and recalled the values my mother and grandparents had taught me. In this slow, fitful process or starting out what I believed, I began silently registering the point in dorm room conversation when my college friends and I stopped thinking and slipped into cant: the point at which the denunciations of Capitalism or American imperialism came too easily, and the freedom from the constraints of monogamy or religions was proclaimed

without fully understanding the value of such
constraints, and the role of the victim was
too readily embraced as a means of shedding
responsibility, or asserting entitlement, or
claiming moral superiority over those not so
victimized.[40]

These carefully crafted comments appear to be disingenuous
in light of the fact that his "Breaking the War Mentality" piece
was written at the end, and not beginning of his college career
as indicated, and there is no evidence Obama partook in radical
political activity in high school or much in college—which would
make sense, as a child brought up by Stanley Dunham. The
passage serves to place Obama as an archetype of the "reformed
radical" whose maturation leads him to outgrow the juvenile
doctrines of the political left, to rebuke his former comrades and
to affirm what are articulated as mainstream American values. It
was an echo of plutocratic interests' use, during the McCarthy
era, of reformed radicals such as former *Time Magazine* editor
Whittaker Chambers and philosophy professor Sidney Hook, who
were called to testify against their ex-comrades before the House
on un-American Activities Committee (HUAC). Following the
demise of the 1960s movements, critiques by ex-Students for a
Democratic Society (SDS) radicals like David Horowitz, were
similarly adopted to discredit generations of activists.[41]

Obama's Neoliberalism and the Chicago Way

Obama followed in this regressive American tradition
in his carefully orchestrated rise to political fame. Many people
on the left including those celebrating his 2008 election in Grant
Park believed Obama was one of them. However, his neoliberalist
orientation was evident from his time in the Illinois Senate
(from 1995-2004) where he got into a fistfight with a member
of the Black Caucus after voting with the Republican Governor
in favor of budget cuts that led to the closure of the only child

welfare office on Chicago's west side.[42] Earning a 75 percent rating from the Illinois Chamber of Commerce, higher than most other Democrats, Obama aimed to create jobs by bringing more private equity and venture capital to the state, and promoted bills facilitating the privatization of public housing while helping to obtain subsidies for political benefactors and clients whose buildings were rat infested, overrun by sewage, and in violation of city codes.[43]

On the good side, Obama advocated expanding health insurance coverage for the poor and funding for day care, helped pass tax breaks for working people and measures to bar discrimination against gays, and a bill to require videotaping police interrogations in homicide cases by securing police support. On the other hand, Obama supported military-style boot camps for first time juvenile offenders, loan guarantees for new coal-fired power plants with no means of controlling carbon emissions, and betrayed a promise to Maytag machinists that he'd work to protect their jobs when their Illinois plants were moved to Mexico (Lester Crown was on Maytag's Board).[44]

Obama was the kind of legislator who was too busy to meet with community activists but had time for golf outings with the state's top gambling lobbyist who gave him $10,500, and convinced him to change his position on a gambling bill.[45] He would frequently vote "present" on controversial bills or along lines dictated by powerful House Speaker Mike Madigan. His record was predominantly mediocre until given credit for a flurry of legislation by Senate Speaker Emil Jones in a ploy to burnish his image for higher office.[46] Characterized by Chicago gossip columnist Kevin DuJan as a "dirty politician," Obama reduced the state health facilities planning board while chairing the Senate Health and Human Services Committee, giving campaign donors on the board greater influence over voting outcomes [which could enrich their employers].[47]

Obama's aggressive fundraising resembled Governor Rod Blagojevich (2003-2009) who wound up in prison.[48] To win his first campaign, Obama had an aide comb through signatures compiled by his opponent and mentor, Alice Palmer, to find errors so she would be excluded from the Democratic Party primary (she needed 757 to run). Congressman Bobby Rush, a former Black Panther, said that Obama "betrayed Alice and... her faction of the progressives [who] represented a challenge to the white liberal elites."[49] Obama's benefactors included millionaire black investors given a stake in managing state pension funds and city powerbrokers who were in direct contradiction to Martin Luther King Jr's adage that one could "not talk about ending the slums without first saying profit must be taken out of slums."[50]

Tony Rezko, Obama's earliest supporter and a top fundraiser, participated in a scheme that allowed Obama to purchase his Hyde Park mansion for below market value as a form of kickback. Rezko was sued by the city of Chicago for failing to provide heat to residents in his dilapidated housing projects, 17 of which were foreclosed. Rezko was a client of the law firm, Davis, Miner, Barnhill & Galland, where Obama worked. Though Obama claimed never to have done any political favors, journalist Tim Novak uncovered letters Obama wrote to city and state officials helping Rezko to secure more than $14 million in taxpayer subsidies and loans to build low-income housing facilities and supporting his bid to manage them. Obama continued to take Rezko's money even after constituents notified him that Rezko was ripping them off and Rezko was under indictment for bribery and fraud (he was sentenced to ten years in prison).[51]

Reverend Arthur Brazier was another Obama benefactor against whom King's adage might have been aimed. He failed to provide heat and running water to his tenants and evicted them into the cold. Obama's lawyering allowed him to escape with a mere $50 fine. Valerie Jarrett meanwhile received tax subsidies while CEO of Habitat Co. which owned and managed apartment complexes that faced demolition after they were considered uninhabitable. In 2004, a sport utility vehicle driven by a woman trying to buy drugs struck a building Habitat managed, actually causing it to collapse. Locals subsequently gathered to rally against then U.S. Senate candidate, Obama.[52]

Obama's strong corporate ties were evident in his connection with Exelon Corporation, the nation's largest nuclear power plant operator, which raised over $227,000 for his campaigns and was directed by one of his earliest supporters, black millionaire John Rogers Jr. Represented by Sidley & Austin where Obama did his law internship, Exelon was formerly called Commonwealth Edison and owned by Thomas Ayers, the father of Weatherman terrorist Bill Ayers, who sat on various foundation boards with Obama. As a U.S. senator Obama opposed giving loan guarantees for power plant generators to develop new energy projects, and after initial support, backed off on supporting a bill that would force them to report radioactive leaks.[53] Senator Obama also opposed a bill to cap interest rates on credit cards at 30 percent and to reform mining laws when one of his key advisers was a Nevada based lobbyist in the employ of mining companies. He voted for bills to build a fence along the Mexican border and to expand NSA surveillance. Obama in addition obtained $1.3 billion for High Explosive Air Burst technology funding for General Dynamics and tripled federal earmarks to his wife's employer, the University of Chicago Hospital.[54] This was all consistent not only with neoliberalism but with the Chicago Way of using government to reward one's family and friends.

Sell-Out of Blacks

African Americans were ecstatic to finally have a black man in the White House but in hindsight would have preferred one who represented their interests as a community. Obama's reduction of non-defense discretionary spending to its "lowest levels since Dwight Eisenhower" adversely affected blacks including in the cuts to food stamps and other social programs (his "Grand Bargain" with the GOP proposed even worse cuts but failed).[55] In the first year of his presidency, Obama cut $73 million for historically black colleges and $150 million overall. Though his Affordable Care Act cut uninsured health-care rates in the black community by a third, his program to buy toxic bank assets excluded subprime borrowers who were mostly black.[56]

Only 1.7 percent of small business administration loans went to blacks compared with 8 percent under Bush, and he appointed only one black to his Cabinet. Obama also failed to stand up for black residents of Flint, Michigan after their water was poisoned in a scheme by the Republican governor's business associates, going so far as to drink the water in front of them. In addition, he extended the provision of military weaponry to police prone to brutality against blacks, and supported broader police asset forfeiture powers, which resulted in the disproportionate seizure of black property, often for unfair reasons.[57]

Obama's famous Philadelphia speech on race, "A More Perfect Union," given in March 2008, sought to strike "balance" by finding moral equivalence in black anger over slavery and economic discrimination, which he depicted as often counter-productive, and white resentment against affirmative action and perceptions of black entitlement. Obama stated that "when [whites]... in an era of stagnant wages and rising global competition... are told to bus their children to a school across town; when they hear an African-American is getting an advantage in landing a good job or a spot in a good college because of an injustice that they themselves never committed; when they're told that their fears about crime in urban neighborhoods are somehow prejudiced, resentment builds over time."[58] This analysis is problematic because African-Americans experienced far greater levels of discrimination. Another shortcoming of the supposedly epic speech was the failure to discuss the rise of what author Michelle Alexander termed, "The New Jim Crow," or mass incarceration of blacks owing to racial profiling and discriminatory drug laws.[59]

As president, Obama made only tepid efforts to confront these latter problems. When he did pass a law reducing disparities in crack-cocaine sentencing, he made sure it was not applied retroactively, thus keeping many blacks unjustly locked up.[60] Black median income decreased during his presidency by 10.9 percent to $33,500 compared to a 3.6 drop for whites to $58,000, black unemployment reached a twenty-seven-year high, and the number of black children living in poverty eclipsed those of whites for the first time since the census began collecting data in 1974.[61] Tef Poe, a St. Louis hip hop artist wrote an open letter to Obama excoriating his statement on the August 2014 Ferguson, Missouri protests in which he refused to condemn the police killing of an unarmed black teenager and "completely played into racist connotations that we are violent, uneducated, welfare recipient looters. Your remarks in support of the National Guard attacks upon us and our community devoured our dignity."[62]

Obama set an important precedent for his career at Harvard Law School when he made a bargain with the anti-black, conservative Federalist Society that he would promote their viewpoint in exchange for being named as the first black president of the *Harvard Law Review*. When Malcolm X's eldest daughter came to speak, Obama was nowhere to be seen.[63] Black community leaders on Chicago's South Side perceived him to be self-absorbed and a "white man in a black face," as state Senator Donne Trotter put it. "You just have to look at his supporters. Who pushed him to get where he is so fast? It's these individuals in Hyde Park, who don't always have the best interests of the community in mind."[64]

Congressman Bobby Rush called Obama a "lackey of the white elites" and said he went to Harvard and "became an educated fool." He noted that the strut that he walked with as president came from the street, but was part of an act since he had not walked in this way when he first met him.[65] Lu Palmer, a radio talk show host and chairman of the Black Independent Political Organization, compared Obama to Mel Reynolds, a promising but hubristic young black politician who veered to the right after being appointed to the House Ways and Means committee, and went from a Rhodes Scholarship to Congress to prison after he was convicted of having sex with an underage campaign staffer. "When Obama first hit town, my recollection is that he came here running some voter registration drive," Palmer said. "He came to our office and tried to get us involved, and we were turned off then. We sent him running. We didn't like his arrogance, his air."[66]

According to Paul McKinley, a black Republican Congressional candidate in Illinois' 2nd district, Obama did not understand that many blacks did not want to integrate with whites but rather wanted to strengthen their community. Backed by the finance, insurance and real-estate (FIRE) industries, he did little during his tenure in the State legislature to help his constituents fight discrimination in hiring practices in mostly white-owned construction firms and by the Democratic Party machine, or promote opportunities for ex-offenders and black business ownership.[67]

A number of his supporters got rich on a $1.6 billion demolition program which destroyed 25,000 low income apartments, thrusting many blacks into homelessness.[68] Michelle Obama meanwhile oversaw an illegal "patient dumping" scheme as vice-president for community outreach at the University of Chicago hospital, which redirected uninsured patients, many poor blacks, to substandard clinics, leading to at least one death.[69]

The Obamas embody the myth, first exposed in E. Franklin Frazier's classic 1957 book *Black Bourgeoisie*, that individual personal advancement was synonymous with a collective community development.[70] Obama was quick to distance himself from the black radical tradition as embodied by his Pastor Reverend Jeremiah Wright who long preached a gospel that championed social justice, condemned racism and imperialism, and instilled in his parishioners the beauty of blackness.[71] In his "A Perfect Union" speech, Obama said that Wright "expressed a profoundly distorted view of this country - a view that sees white racism as endemic, and that elevates what is wrong with America above all that we know is right with America; a view that sees the conflicts in the Middle East as rooted primarily in the actions of stalwart allies like Israel, instead of emanating from the perverse and hateful ideologies of radical Islam."[72] Here Obama was cleverly positioning himself not only as a moderate on race and adversary of the so-called "anti-American left," but also as a champion of Israel and the War on Terror.

Obama depicted Wright much like Frank Marshall

Davis in his book *Dreams from My Father* as an archetype of the angry black man of the 1960s, a relic from the past who carried "memories and baggage from that time."[73] In this vein, Obama rejected political support from Louis Farrakhan, the controversial head of the Nation of Islam who led the 1995 million man march in Washington, D.C., a day of atonement for the crimes committed against black people.[74] Obama also opposed reparations for the injustices of slavery and Jim Crow even though his mentor at Harvard Law School, Charles Ogletree championed them.[75]

When protests erupted against the state of Georgia's execution of Troy Davis, a black man whom even one of the jurors in his trial believed was innocent, Obama invoked the trope of states' rights, and failed to stand up for black members of his administration (Van Jones and Shirley Sherrod) when they were forced to resign after unfair right-wing attacks.[76] The Reverend Jesse Jackson stated in 2015 that while facing historic and unfair opposition, Obama had "failed miserably in leveraging the full force of federal agencies to target systemic and historical inequities that keep blacks in the U.S. behind whites in employment, opportunity and wealth."[77]

Jackson was a protégé of Martin Luther King Jr. who was among those to weep when Obama won the 2008 election, though criticized him during the campaign for "talking down to black people," particularly in his suggestion that African-American fathers needed to take more responsibility for their children - a point made frequently by disgraced entertainer Bill Cosby.[78] According to people who knew him, Barack's psychology was like Booker T. Washington: he had internalized a belief in black inferiority and thought himself superior because of his education and lifestyle.[79] Professor Keeanga-Yamahtta Taylor points out that Obama's vision of American exceptionalism was sustained by writing off black poverty as a product of personal irresponsibility and cultural backwardness.[80] Lecturing blacks but never whites on their alleged shortcomings, he allowed himself to be used to create the façade of a post-racial and post-colonial society and affirm belief in the reality of the American dream. Senator

Harry Reid (D-NV) said that he liked Obama because he did not speak in the "negro dialect"—a comment which helps explain why he emerged as the chosen one alongside his predominantly conservative policy positions.[81]

After Obama's historic 2008 election victory, Obama's campaign manager David Axelrod said that he had made a "conscious decision to hold the victory rally in Grant Park," because they "wanted to do something that would systematically overcome the damage that had been done to American idealism forty years before—there, in Memphis, and in Los Angeles."[82] He was referring to the assassination of Martin Luther King Jr. in Memphis and Bobby Kennedy in L.A. and the brutal suppression of the antiwar riots outside the Democratic convention in Chicago after the nomination of pro-war candidate Hubert Humphrey in 1968 in the same election cycle. Axelrod's calculated gesture was designed to cast Obama as forged in the 1960s' revolution but now older and wiser, per his campaign message of national unity and healing from the lingering divisions and wounds of that era. Nonetheless, Obama proved to be a polarizing president, partly for reasons that were out of his control—namely, the residue of racism in the country that resulted in a resurgent white supremacist backlash directed against him, and the political acumen of right-wing moguls like the Koch Brothers—but also for reasons that were of his own making.

Very quickly, he betrayed his progressive base who failed all along to see him for what he was: the latest in a long breed of cynical and calculating political operatives who rode the wave of liberal guilt over the history of slavery and Jim Crow to personal fame and glory. Obama never really was an heir of the 1960s and its organizing tradition, as he had falsely packaged himself, but a social climber and neoliberal who was eager to disassociate himself from the "radical left" and would sell himself to the highest bidder. His status as a civil rights icon was undercut by many of his policies and aloofness from the plight of the black underclass. Obama's yearning for peace was also a mirage and only apparent when he thought it might benefit him politically.

Axelrod's specialty was in using personal stories to market political candidates and he knew he had a winner, even if the story Obama told was only at best half true. Obama's propensity to use people for his own ends was best embodied in how he discarded his African relatives who had been used as key props in his life story that helped catapult him into power. When his half-brother Malik, whom Obama had spent time with in Kenya, contacted him for his assistance in giving a proper burial to his Aunt Zeituni who was featured in *Dreams from My Father*, Obama gave Malik the cold shoulder and refused to provide him a penny. When Muammar Qaddafi subsequently tried to broker a peace agreement through Malik to avert the bloodshed in Libya, Obama again ignored his half-brother, who now wants nothing to do with him.[83] This story can stand as a metaphor for Obama's career, in which a friendly appearance was but a deceptive front.

Endnotes

1   Edward McClelland, "Meet the Community Organizers Fighting Against… Barack Obama," *Politico*, February 28, 2018.

2   David J. Garrow, *Rising Star: The Making of Barack Obama* (London: William & Morrow, 2017), 1067.

3   Garrow, *Rising Star*, 731, 732.

4   See Thomas C. Reeves, *A Question of Character: A Life of John F. Kennedy* (New York: Forum, 1997). Kennedy displayed many similarities to Obama in his cold and calculating nature, moral obtuseness and superficiality, and effectiveness in creating a cult of personality that grew to gigantic proportions after his assassination.

5   Barack Obama, *Dreams from My Father: A Story of Race and Inheritance* (New York: Three Rivers Press, 1995).

6   Reeves, *A Question of Character*, 136.

7   Jack Cashill in *Deconstructing Obama: The Life, Loves and Letters of the First Post-Modern President* (New York: Threshold Editions, 2011) compares *Dreams* with other of Obama's writings and finds a marked contrast in quality and style, indicating that it was ghost-written. Obama claims to have written *The Audacity of Hope* in the late-night hours during his first year in the Senate but on page 325 describes a hectic schedule which would have made this

impossible. In the acknowledgment he thanks Samantha Power for reviewing the proofs as if they were her own, which may indicate she played a direct role in the writing. Garrow emphasizes that Obama's Harvard classmate Rob Fisher played an important role in writing *Dreams*.

8   Kirsten Scharnberg and Kim Barker, "The Not So Simple Story of Barack Obama's Youth," *Chicago Tribune*, March 25, 2007; G. Webster Tarpley, *Barack H. Obama: The Unauthorized Biography* (Los Angeles: The Progressive Press, 2008). When Obama was told there was no article, he said maybe he had seen it in *Ebony*. However, a search of *Ebony*'s archives found no such article in it either.

9   David Remnick, *The Bridge: The Life and Rise of Barack Obama*, rev ed. (New York: Vintage, 2011), 102, 104. Caroline Boss, a leftist student leader at Occidental said Obama did not go to meetings of various groups very often and was "mainly an observer."

10   Garrow, *Rising Star*, 160; David Maraniss, *Barack Obama: The Story* (New York: Simon & Schuster, 2013), 436.

11   Peter Wallstein, "Fellow Activists Say Obama's Memoir Has Too Many I's," *Los Angeles Times*, February 19, 2007; Tarpley, *Barack H. Obama*, 64; Obama, *Dreams from My Father*, 245.

12   Tarpley, *Barack H. Obama*, 62. Money for Obama also came from the Woods Fund, a foundation created by the reactionary Woods family, who owned coal mines.

13   William Wan, "At the Housing Project Where Obama Began His Career, Residents Are Filled with Pride – and Frustration," *Washington Post*, January 8, 2017.

14   Obama, *Dreams from My Father*, 139, 140.

15   Wayne Madsen, *The Manufacturing of a President: The CIAs Insertion of Barack Obama Into the White House* (self-published, 2012), 309; Mondo Frazier, *The Secret Life of Barack Hussein Obama* (New York: Threshold Editions, 2010).

16   James Kunen, *The Strawberry Statement: Notes of a Revolutionary* (New York: Avon Books, 1970), 112. Kunen noted how Business International favored Eugene McCarthy as an antidote to the fascism of George C. Wallace in the 1968 election. He said that they offered to pay to launch protests they could presumably then coopt and were with the SDS on black and student control and the removal of Columbia University President Grayson Kirk. However, they differed on the question of imperialism, believing that the U.S. has the technology the world needs, and ought to have some control over where it goes and for what.

17   Obama, *Dreams from My Father*, 135; Remnick *The Bridge*, 102; Garrow, *Rising Star*.

18   David Maraniss, "Becoming Obama," *Vanity Fair*, May 2, 2012. Obama also

exaggerated Cook's families' wealth.

19   Obama, *Dreams from My Father* and *The Audacity of Hope* (New York: Crown Publishers, 2006), 47 as well as public speeches. See also William J. Lederer and Eugene Burdick, *The Ugly American* (New York: W.W. Norton, 1999).

20   Garrow, *Rising Star*, 50, 51, 53; Madsen, *The Manufacturing of a President*, 17, 18, 35. Obama Sr's never told his classmates about his alleged wife and child whom he did not bother to visit in Seattle on his way to Harvard and he never asked about them when back in Kenya.

21   Madsen, *The Manufacturing of a President*; Joel Gilbert, *Dreams from My Real Father* (2012). An FBI file existed on Armor but was mysteriously destroyed in 1997. Proficient in French, Stanley is suspected of working in domestic surveillance on B-52 production at the Boeing plant in Seattle, Washington, and in Hawaii. Obama's great uncle, Charles Payne, was in naval intelligence in World War II, helped liberate the Buchenwald concentration camp and served in the U.S. military occupation of Austria. His great-uncle, Ralph Dunham, was also allegedly in military intelligence.

22   Gilbert, *Dreams from My Real Father* (2012); author interview with Joel Gilbert, January 10, 2019. In order for ten-year old Barry to attend Punahou, Stan tracked down the Kenyan and brought him to Hawaii for two weeks where he did not stay with the family.

23   Obama, *Dreams from My Father*, 77.

24   Pop is available at: https://genius.com/Barack-obama-pop-annotated; Maraniss, *Barack Obama*, 382; Garrow, *Rising Star*, 86; Jack Cashill, "Just Who is Obama's 'Pop'?" *World Net Daily*, February 18, 2010. None of Barack's other poems show such depth leading researchers to suspect Davis may be the author.

25   Madsen, *The Manufacturing of a President*; Tarpley, *Barack H. Obama*, 28.

26   Madsen, *The Manufacturing of a President*; Janny Scott, *A Singular Woman: The Untold Story of Barack Obama's Mother* (Riverhead Books, 2012). On the Ford Foundation's operations in Indonesia and its promotion of U.S. national interests, see John Bresnan, *At Home Abroad: A Memoir of the Ford Foundation in Indonesia, 1953-1973* (Jakarta: Equinox Publishing, 2006).

27   See George Mc.T Kahin and Audrey Kahin, *Subversion as Foreign Policy: The Secret Eisenhower-Dulles Debacle in Indonesia* (New York: The New Press, 195); Bradley R. Simpson, *Economists with Guns: Authoritarian Development and U.S.-Indonesian Relations, 1960-1968* (Palo Alto: Stanford University Press, 2010); Peter Dale Scott, *"North American Universities and the 1965 Indonesian Massacre: Indonesian Guilt and Western Responsibility," The Asia-Pacific Journal*, Vol. 12, Issue 50, No. 2, December, 15, 2014; Peter Dale Scott, *"Still Uninvestigated After 50 Years: Did the U.S. Help Incite the 1965 Indonesia Massacre?", The Asia-Pacific Journal*, Vol. 13, Issue 31, No. 2, August 3, 2015.

28   Scott, *A Singular Woman*; S. Ann Dunham, *Surviving the Odds: Village Industry*

in Indonesia (Duke University Press, 2009).

29   Scott, *A Singular Woman*; Frazier, *The Secret Life of Barack Hussein Obama*, 113.

30   Madsen, *The Manufacturing of a President*; Remnick, *The Bridge*, 86-88.

31   The latter quote is from USIA Director Frank Scotten; in Douglas Valentine, *The CIA as Organized Crime: How Illegal Operations Corrupt America and the World* (Atlanta: Clarity Press, 2017), 118, 119. The marriage with Lolo ended in divorce in 1974.

32   Scott, *A Singular Woman*, 214. Madsen, *The Manufacturing of a President*, 47; Garrow, *Rising Star*, 61.

33   Obama significantly underplayed Lolo's army rank in *The Audacity of Hope*, 273-275; Angelo M. Codevila, "The Chosen One," *Claremont Review of Books*, Summer 2011, 52-58; Madsen, *The Manufacturing of a President*, 51, 136; 146.

34   Madsen, *The Manufacturing of a President*.

35   Garrow, *Rising Star*, 155; Remnick, *The Bridge*. The Professor of the state socialist course, Andrew G. Walder, assigned Alex Nove's *Stalinism and After*, a survey of Soviet history that focused on how deadly Soviet rule had proven for the regime's many victims, including early Bolsheviks, and Milovan Djilas' *The New Class*, written by a Yugoslav dissident which showed how party apparatchiks had become all powerful exploiters and masters. The second half focused on problems like bureaucratization, corruption and social stratification and inequality behind the Iron Curtain. Ignored were some of the major achievements like providing free health care and housing, dramatic increases in literacy, improved living standards and industrial productivity and the growth of a powerful military that could defeat the Nazis.

36   Garrow, *Rising Star*, 146. May's book *The World War and American Intervention, 1914-1917* (Cambridge, MA: Harvard University Press, 1959) suggested that Wilson was justified in defending America's prestige and honor in lieu of German submarine attacks by force of arms.

37   Barack Obama, "Breaking the War Mentality," *Sundial*, March 10, 1983, http://www.columbia.edu/cu/computinghistory/obama-sundial.pdf;   Maraniss, *Barack Obama*, 461, 462; Remnick, *The Bridge*, 116.

38   David Maraniss, "Obama's Military Connection," *Washington Post*, May 4, 2012, Remnick, *The Bridge*, 345.

39   Adam Turl, "Is Obama Different? Liberals Pin Their Hopes on a 'Good Democrat,'" *Socialist Workers*, February 2, 2007.

40   Barack Obama, *The Audacity of Hope: Thoughts on Reclaiming the American Dream* (New York: Crown Publishers, 2006), 30, 31.

41   See David Horowitz, *Destructive Generation: Second Thoughts About the Sixties*, rev ed. (New York: Encounter Books, 2005).

42   Rickey Hendon, *Black Enough/White Enough: The Obama Dilemma* (Chicago: Third World Press, 2009), 29-35.

43   Binyamin Applebaum, "Grim Proving Ground for Obama's Housing Policy," *Boston Globe*, June 27, 2008; David Freddoso, *The Case Against Barack Obama* (Washington, D.C.: Regnery, 2008), 219; Martin DuPuis and Keith Bochelman, *Barack Obama: The New Face of American Politics* (Westport, CT: Praeger, 2008), 8. Obama's boss, Allison Davis at Davis, Miner, Barnhill & Galland law firm, received more than $100 million in subsidies and loans to renovate and build more than 1,500 apartments including a North side building which flowed with raw sewage. The President's "first friend" Martin Nesbitt oversaw the disastrous transition to privatized management as Chairman of the Chicago Housing Authority before becoming Vice President of Pritzker Realty.

44   Tarpley, *Barack H. Obama*, 303; Garrow, *Rising Star*, 607, 631, 633, 730, 732; David Mendell, "Obama's Record, a Plus, a Minus," *The Chicago Tribune*, October 8, 2004; Edward Spannaus, "Obama Fires the Maytag Repairman," *Lyndon Larouche Publication*, August 8, 2008; Bob Secter, "Obama's Fundraising, Rhetoric Collide," *Chicago Tribune*, February 1, 2008. Obama promoted gun control and death penalty reform, though voted to strengthen criminal penalties for drug dealers and did little on school reform and spoke in favor of charter schools. He helped pass welfare reform that forced welfare recipients into low-wage work and supported a campaign finance law that "forced few changes in the real-world relationship between cash and politics," according to an Illinois political scientist.

45   Richard Pollack, "The Myth of Obama as State Senate Reformer," *Washington Examiner*, September 19, 2012.

46   Edward McClelland, *Young Obama: Chicago and the Making of a Black President* (New York: Bloomsbury, 2010); Fredosso, *The Case Against Barack Obama*.

47   Larry Bell, "Obama Kick-Back Cronyism – Part 2: Illinois Health and Human Disservices," *Forbes* Magazine, November 2, 2011; James Kimberley et al. "Hospital Board Flouts Its Rules," *The Chicago Tribune*, July 14, 2004; DuJan quoted in Jerome Corsi, "Claim: Obama Hid 'Gay life' to Become President;" *World Daily Net*, September 11, 2012. The planning board decided on new building contracts for hospitals. It included Dr. Michael Malek, who gave $10,000 to Obama and was on staff at Joliet's Provena St. Joseph Medical Center, which had opposed pending applications to build new hospitals in the southwest suburbs, Dr. Fortunee Massuda, a podiatrist who gave $2,000 to Obama, and Dr. Imad Almanaseer, who gave $3,000 to Obama and invested in bundler Tony Rezko's fast food business and bought an apartment from Rezko.

48   Jeff Coen and John Chase, *Golden: How Rod Blagojevich Talked Himself Out of the Governor's Office and Into Prison* (Chicago: Chicago Review Press, 2012).

49   Remnick, *The Bridge*, 316. Palmer endorsed Hillary Clinton in 2008 and Danny Davis who ran against Rahm Emmanuel for Mayor in 2011.

50   King quoted from a 1966 speech he gave to his staff in Michael Eric Dyson, *I May Not Get There with You: The True Martin Luther King Jr.* (New York: Simon & Schuster, 2000), 87.

51   Evelyn Pringle, "Barack Obama – Operation Board Games for Slum Lords," *Countercurrents*, April 7, 2008; Tim Novak, "Obama's Letters For Rezko – As a State Senator, He Went to Bat for Now Indicted Developer's Deal," *Chicago Sun Times*, June 13, 2007; Tim Novak, "Broken Promises, Broken Homes," *Chicago Sun-Times*, April 24, 2007; Tim Novak, "Obama and His Rezko Ties," *Chicago Sun-Times*, April 23, 2007, 22; Jerome Corsi, *The Obama Nation: Leftist Politics and the Cult of Personality* (New York: Threshold, 2008), 160, 162. Obama also wrote a letter supporting New Kenwood LLC's proposal to build 97 unit apartments. The company was founded by Rezko and Allison Davis. Obama's Senate office entered into negotiations with one of Rezko's companies further to lobby the U.S. government to push through a $50 million contract to train Iraqi security personnel at a site in Chicago.

52   Remnick, *The Bridge*, 214; Tarpley, *Barack H. Obama*, 172; Christopher Drew and Mike McIntire, "After 2000 Loss, Obama Built Donor Network From Roots Up," *New York Times*, April 3, 2007; Applebaum, "Grim Proving Ground for Obama's Housing Policy;" "For the Slumlord's Defense, Barack Obama Esq," *Washington Examiner*, September 19, 2012; Larry Bell, "Obama Kick-Back Cronyism: Stimulating Green Energy the Chicago Way," *Forbes*, October 25, 2011.

53   Ken Silverstein, "Barack Obama Inc," *Harper's Magazine*, November, 2006, 37, 38; Mike McIntire, "Nuclear Leaks and Responses Tested Obama in Senate," *New York Times*, February 3, 2008; Tarpley, *Barack H. Obama*, 139. Roger D. Hodge, *The Mendacity of Hope: Barack Obama and the Betrayal of American Liberalism* (New York: HarperCollins, 2010), 24-26.

54   Matt Gonzalez, "The Obama Craze," *Counterpunch*, February 29, 2008; Michelle Malkin, *Culture of Corruption: Obama and His team of Tax Cheats, Crooks and Cronies* (Washington, D.C.: Regnery, 2009), 62; Evelyn Pringle, "Curtain Time for Barack Obama," *Countercurrents*, May 15, 2008.

55   "Obama's 'Fiscal Grand Bargain' is a Great Betrayal to America's Most Vulnerable," *The Conversation*, December 5, 2012; Ned Resnikoff, "President Obama Signs $8.7 Billion Food Stamps Cut Into Law," *CNBC*, February 7, 2014; Doug Stranglin, "47 Million Hit by Food Stamp Cuts Starting Today," *USA Today*, November 4, 2013; Shamus Cook, "Austerity USA," *Counterpunch*, February 25, 2013.

56   Glen Ford, "First Black President Cuts Funds for Black Higher Education," *Black Agenda Report*, May 13, 2009; Matt Bruenig and Ryan Cooper, "How Obama Destroyed Black Wealth," *Jacobin*, December 7, 2017.

57   Ibid., Michael Eric Dyson, *The Black Presidency: Barack Obama and the Politics of Race in America* (Boston: Houghton Mifflin, 2016), 166;

Radley Balko, "7 Ways the Obama Administration Has Accelerated Police Militarization," *The Huffington Post*, December 6, 2017; Nathaniel Cary and Mike Ellis, "65% of cash seized by SC police comes from black men. Experts blame racism," *The Greenville News*, January 27, 2019.

58   "Transcript: Barack Obama's Speech on Race," *National Public Radio*, March 18, 2008, https://www.npr.org/templates/story/story.php?storyId=88478467.

59   Michelle Alexander, *The New Jim Crow: Mass Incarceration in the Age of Colorblindness* (New York: The New Press, 2010).

60   Paul Street, "Posing as the Great Emancipator: Obama's Prison-Posturing is Nothing New," *Black Agenda Report*, August 12, 2015; Margaret Kimberley, "Freedom Rider: Obama Fights to Keeps Black People in Jail," *Black Agenda Report*, July 31, 2013.

61   Eileen Patten and Jens Krogstad, "Black Child Poverty Rate Hold Steady Even as Other Groups See Decline," *Pew Research*, July 14, 2015; Tavis Smiley, *The Covenant with Black America – Ten Years Later* (Hay Books, 2016); Dyson, *The Black Presidency*, 165; Keeanga-Yamahtta Taylor, *From #Black Lives Matter to Black Liberation* (Chicago: Haymarket Books, 2016), 11.

62   Taylor, *From #Black Lives Matter to Black Liberation*, 136.

63   Author interview with Dr. Randy Short, a student at Harvard Divinity School when Obama was at the law school. September 25, 2018; David Mendell, *Obama From Promise to Power* (New York: Harper Collins, 2007), 91; PBS, https://www.youtube.com/watch?v=s5m6YFBcixo&feature=related. Three members of the Federalist society were promoted to the editorial board and only one black and progressive views were marginalized under Obama's leadership.

64   McLelland, *Young Obama;* Ted Kleine, "Is Bobby Rush in Trouble?" *Chicago Reader*, March 16, 2000.

65   Kleine, "Is Bobby Rush in Trouble;" Remnick, *The Bridge*, 316, 317.

66   Kleine, "Is Bobby Rush in Trouble;" Janny Scott, "In 2000, a Streetwise Veteran Schooled a Young Obama," *New York Times*, September 9, 2007.

67   Author interview with Paul McKinley, Chicago, Illinois, January 6, 2018; Bradford Richardson, "Obama Defends Gentrification Ahead of Presidential Library Construction," *Washington Times*, February 28. 2018.

68   Alison Kilkenny, "How Obama and Valerie Jarrett Helped Launch Their Political Careers in an Outrageous Urban Renewal Scheme," *Alternet*, January 25, 2013.

69   Richard Miniter, *Leading From Behind: The Reluctant President and the Advisers Who Decide for Him* (New York: St. Martin's Press, 2013), 21; Tarpley, *Barack H. Obama*, 143, 166.

70   See E. Franklin Frazier, *Black Bourgeoisie* (New York: The New Press, 1957).

71   S. Eudora Smith, "The Liberation of Reverend Wright," *The Nation*, April 17, 2008; Glen Ford, "Angela Davis Has Lost Her Mind Over Obama," *Black Agenda Report*, March 28, 2012.

72   "Transcript: Barack Obama's Speech on Race," *National Public Radio*, March 18, 2008, https://www.npr.org/templates/story/story.php?storyId=88478467; Dyson, *The Black Presidency*, 87.

73   Dyson, *The Black Presidency*, 87, 110. This negative depiction accorded with popular cultural portrayals. See Kristen Hoerl, *The Bad Sixties: Hollywood Memories of the Counterculture, Antiwar, and Black Power Movements* (Jackson: University Press of Mississippi, 2018).

74   "Obama Rejects Farrakhan's Support," *UPI*, February 26, 2008; Arthur Magida, *Prophet of Rage: A Life of Louis Farrakhan and his Nation* (New York: Basic Books, 1997).

75   "Barack Obama Explains Why He Doesn't Think Reparations to Black People are Practical," *The Atlantic*, December 21, 2016.

76   Taylor, *From #Black Lives Matter to Black Liberation*, 144, 145; Dyson, *The Black Presidency*, 157, 158.

77   Terry Shropshire, "Rev. Jesse Jackson Slams President Obama For Failing Black People," *Atlantic Daily World*, August 7, 2015.

78   Suzanne Goldberg, "U.S. Elections 2008: 'I Want to Cut His Nuts Off' – Jackson Gaffe Turns Focus on Obama's Move to the Right," *The Guardian*, July 10, 2008.

79   Author Live interview with Dr. Randy Short, and Paul McKinley who knew Obama.

80   Taylor, *#From Black lives Matter to Black Liberation*, 25. Obama suggested that welfare policies sapped black initiative and that the best way to end black poverty was to discourage black teenagers from having babies out of wedlock.

81   Dyson, *The Black Presidency*, 76; Mendell, *Obama*; Mclelland, *Young Obama*, 153, 182; Kleine, "Is Bobby Rush in Trouble?" Joe Biden said Obama was the first "mainstream African American who is articulate and bright and clean and a nice-looking guy."

82   Quoted in Tom Hayden, *The Long Sixties: From 1960 to Barack Obama* (Boulder, CO: Paradigm Publishers, 2009), V1.

83   Joel Gilbert Interview with Malik Obama, https://www.youtube.com/watch?v=eRKVunuTGDQ. Obama skipped Aunt Zeituni's funeral because he was golfing. See Jason Horowitz, "Amid Politics, Obama Drifted Away From Kin," New York Times, April 22, 214.

Chapter 3

BLACK SKIN, WHITE MASKS

BARACK OBAMA
AND THE RECOLONIZATION
OF AFRICA

Late one morning in September 2009, Saleh Ali Saleh, a boyish-looking thirty-year old held partly responsible for the bombing of the U.S. embassy in East Africa in 1998 and attacks on tourists in Kenya, stopped for breakfast while driving through a fishing village 150 miles south of Mogadishu. Suddenly, helicopter gunships swooped from the sky and began firing on him and his companions, leaving him dead within twenty minutes. The targeted assassination had been coordinated several hundred miles away at Camp Lemonier in the neighboring East African state of Djibouti, a French colony until 1977, which housed the central base in Africa of the U.S. Africa Command (AFRICOM), headquartered in Stuttgart.

Set up in 2003 on a rundown French legionnaires' base, the U.S. base at Djibouti was part of an archipelago of outposts that housed over 2000 U.S. military personnel. It was expanded in the Obama years from 88 to 500 acres as the Army Corps of engineers undertook "the biggest active military project in the entire world," according to U.S. ambassador Tom Kelly. The U.S. ran commando, intelligence and drone operations from Camp Lemonier, coordinated training of other African militaries, and under Obama built a naval pier and established a major surveillance center at Oblock, a fishing port at the mouth of the Babel Mandeh straits, where it could monitor access to the Suez. The main base also has a covert compound dedicated to special operations.[1]

Djibouti was a powerful focal point for the militarization of Africa during the Obama years. The country was ruled by a despot, Ismael Omar Guellah. Propped up by $70 million in annual U.S. aid, Guellah was welcomed as a guest in the Obama White House. While Obama had condemned other strongmen on the continent, notably Robert Mugabe who had seized land from white farmers, not so Guellah, whose security forces jailed and tortured political opponents and journalists and gunned down peaceful demonstrators while allowing draconian child labor and female genital mutilation practices.[2]

In May 2014, Presidents Obama and Guelleh agreed on a 20-year extension of the American lease, at $70 million a year in rent—about double what it was paying before. Despite injections of foreign capital and infrastructural development around the base, the trickle-down effect for the local population was extremely limited as the International Monetary Fund (IMF) admitted. Most locals lived in abject poverty and were left to sit around without jobs chewing khat, an amphetamine-like substance which yellowed their teeth. Describing the country as a "hot hell box in the armpit of Africa," U.S. military personnel rarely left the base other than to enjoy the local nightlife and cavort with local prostitutes. They lived a life of luxury, eating at a chic café on the base, watching films in a state-of-the-art theatre, playing ping pong and x-box in the game room and exercising in a well-kept gym or playing soccer on a well-manicured field.[3]

In a return to the memes of the age of colonialism, Obama and his team were masters at packaging foreign intervention in a humanitarian guise, broadcasting their concern about the spread of terrorism and human rights violations by Boko Haram militants and the heterodox Christian Lords' Resistance Army (LRA) commanders who used child soldiers, and about female genital mutilation, gay rights and the rape of women. These humanitarian concerns were often raised to support military intervention and were selectively applied. Underlying them was a desire to tap into Africa's rich mineral and oil wealth to counter militarily the growing Chinese economic engagement on the continent.

In *Black Skin, White Masks* (1952), psychologist Frantz Fanon had warned about the deep psychological effects of colonialism and how it would yield a breed of post-independence leaders in Africa who were submissive to white Western interests and willing to keep their own people subordinate not just because they were cynically out for themselves but because they believed in their own inferiority.[4] Barack Obama claimed to have read and discussed Fanon; if so and despite that, his policies in Africa reflected his submission to the white power structure and military industrial complex in a manner that would have saddened but not surprised Fanon. Rather than demonstrating or providing any insight on the inequities and skewing of the global economy as it concerned Africa, Obama often patronized Africans like he did African-Americans, blaming them for their problems. He promoted the colonialist assumption that America and its institutions were superior, a goal towards which the Africans needed to strive, and that the U.S. was best equipped to save them from "genocide" or other atrocities, while burying the West's complicity in these very crimes. Obama thus in many respects embodied Fanon's worst fears.

When Obama was first elected, much of Africa was gripped with Obamamania. Obama was greeted like a rock star by adoring fans and featured on t-shirts and photographs alongside African luminaries like Nelson Mandela and Patrice Lumumba. The Cinderella syndrome wore off quickly, however. In the eight years of his presidency, Obama doubled funding for AFRICOM, which AFRICOM officials themselves had admitted was set up to "preserve the free flow of natural resources from Africa to the global market."[5] He increased financing for human terrain teams, or anthropologists who were embedded with AFRICOM to conduct ethnographic studies designed to take advantage of inter-tribal conflicts.[6] Obama also hired shady mercenary firms with connection to past colonial operations and rolled out the red carpet for autocrats like President Bongo Ondimba of Gabon who inherited the country's presidency from his father, Omar Bongo, in a process akin to a monarchical secession.[7]

South African commentator Ade Keye emphasized that Obama did not even come close to fulfilling the "unrealistic expectation among Africans that he would act as a messiah." Obama rather "continued several of Bush's most egregious policies," such as the extraordinary rendition programs, supported autocratic regimes in oil rich nations, and dispatched drone strikes to Somalia and Mali that killed innocent civilians as AFRICOM-trained forces roamed Africa in search of "mad mullahs."[8]

Obama's UN ambassador and National Security adviser, Susan Rice, displayed a particularly "unsettling sympathy for African despots." She supported an invasion of Congo by strongman Paul Kagame of Rwanda, who had been one of her clients when she worked for a Pentagon-linked private intelligence consulting firm, and showered praise on Ethiopian dictator Meles Zenawi who set up a U.S. training base at Camp Hurso as he dismantled the rule of law, carried out ethnic cleansing and silenced political opponents.[9] The construction of a huge U.S. embassy in Swaziland stands as a symbol of the imperialist character of Obama's foreign policy. The size of five rugby fields, it had a three-story high fence shield that gave the impression it was used for intelligence gathering. The country at the time was led by King Mswati III, an absolute monarch in the style of Louis XIV.[10]

Obama had written eloquently about his African family and roots in his first political memoir and went to many of the right stops on the continent, visiting for example the famous "door of no return" on Gorée Island off the coast of Dakar, Senegal through which slaves were led out to waiting ships at the Cape

Coast castle. At times, he used highly personalized language, telling a massive audience in Cairo, Egypt about his grandfather who was a cook for the British in Kenya, but was called "boy" by his employers despite his status as a respected community elder. Obama stated that he "had the blood of Africa within me and my family's own story encompasses both the tragedies and triumphs of the larger African story."[11]

In South Africa, Obama visited with Nelson Mandela's family and acclaimed the great anti-apartheid leader for "inspiring the world including me."[12] Then in Ghana, Obama earned cheers when he declared that the 21st century would be shaped "by what happens not just in Rome, or Moscow, but what happens in Accra as well."[13] This was followed up, though, with a message of tough love, in which he told Ghanaians and other Africans to "take responsibility for their future," exclaiming that Africa did not "need strong leaders but strong institutions;" that "no country was going to create wealth if its leaders exploited the economy to enrich themselves;" and that "for all its previous sins, the West [was] not responsible for the destruction of the Zimbabwean economy over the last decade or wars in which children were enlisted as combatants."[14]

However, the West indeed bore some responsibility for the destruction of Zimbabwe's economy via its imposition of structural adjustment, financial liberalization, debt servicing and sanctions that were politically motivated, and Obama resumed arms sales to countries that used child soldiers.[15] Western banks also accepted dirty money, Western mining conglomerates orchestrated corrupt deals, and U.S. and other foreign and mercenary militaries helped prop up corrupt leaders or promoted regime change of those who weren't.[16]

Reminiscent of his blame-the-victim approach towards African Americans, patronizing comments cropped up in other Obama speeches in which he told Africans to "stop blaming colonialism and Western oppression for the continent's problems."[17] This message absolved the West of its sins by consigning them to the past—even as the Obama administration continued to adopt policies that helped foment conflict and resulted in the ongoing exploitation of the continent's resources by multi-national corporations. In 2010, oil and mineral exports from Africa were worth $333 billion, dwarfing by over seven times the amount of aid that flowed into the continent. Five years later, African countries received $162 billion in loans, half of which was paid in interest on debt, while $203 billion was taken out, either through multinationals repatriating profits and illegally moving money into tax havens, or by costs imposed by the rest of the world through climate change adaptation and mitigation. This led to an annual financial deficit of $41.3bn.[18]

In 2006, Senator Obama set a precedent for his presidency by traveling to Kenya and providing cover for an attempt to undermine President Mwae Kibaki who had cut the poverty rate and raised economic growth after allying with China. Obama campaigned and helped bundle money for Raila Odinga, an ethnic Luo and nephew of Obama's reputed father (making him Barack's cousin). In the contested 2007 election, Odinga's campaign slogans were the same as Obama's. Allied with Muslim radicals, Odinga helped stir ethnic conflict against the Kikuyu that left hundreds of people dead. Odinga was appointed Prime Minister in a power-sharing arrangement designed to quell the violence as the U.S. consolidated control over military bases at Camp Simba and Manda Bay.[19]

In a throwback to the classic era of colonialism, President Obama's development policies emphasized creating private sector investment opportunities rather than promoting land reform, public sector growth, labor rights, and wealth redistribution. The African Growth and Opportunity Act (AGOA) granting trading preferences to thirty-nine countries, reinforced export-based economies, placing heavy emphasis on primary commodities including, especially, oil and gas and the import of U.S. capital goods. Most of the jobs created were low wage. In East Africa, Obama backed American firms such as Bechtel and GE which were investing in a massive transport pipeline which threatened the displacement of farmers and ecological degradation.[20]

Obama's agricultural policy promoted genetic engineering and chemical intensive agriculture at the urging of the Bill & Melinda Gates Foundation, DuPont and Monsanto, whose former executives served in his administration. The Power Africa initiative relied heavily on private sector investment to try to increase access to affordable electricity, meeting only five percent of its goal.[21] Its largest private patron was billionaire investor Tony Elumelu of Heirs Holdings, who pledged $2.5 billion for mainly oil and gas projects.[22] Citigroup and Goldman Sachs were additional financial sponsors and supported microfinance loan projects targeting female entrepreneurs.

A primary function of development assistance was to subsidize U.S. businesses including top political donors— the Chicago Way. American exports and imports to Africa not coincidentally increased along with foreign direct investment which jumped from $43.6 billion in 2009 to $57 billion in 2011.[23] Mo Ibrahim, a Sudanese-born cellphone tycoon, told the *New York Times* that Africans would have appreciated it if Obama had tried to compel U.S. companies to pay their local taxes as many had used legal techniques to dodge them, hence depriving the African people of vital tax revenues that could be used for public works.[24]

Obama's public health initiatives promoting population control re-invoked legacies of colonialism in their underlying implication that people of color were overpopulating the earth. Heavy priority was placed on promoting Depo Provera, a contraceptive drug made by Pfizer (which gave $138,291 to Obama in the 2012 election and stood to gain $36 billion in sales) and pushed by the Gates foundation. Depo Provera, which was at one time banned in the U.S., brought adverse side effects locals were not warned about, including a link to cervical cancer and easier transmission of HIV/AIDS. The Obama administration all-the-while administered deep cuts ($200 million in 2016) to the Global AIDS budget.[25] When an Ebola virus epidemic broke out in Sierra Leone and Liberia under mysterious circumstances, Obama deployed 3,000 AFRICOM troops, replicating a tradition of colonialist powers imposing militarization and control in the name of public health. A 25-bed U.S. military field hospital treated foreign health workers only, repeating another colonialist pattern.[26]

Obama's military "pivot" to Africa was broadly designed to counter the growing influence of China, whose trade with Africa eclipsed $200 billion in 2013, and whose imports of oil and minerals and export of electronics and textiles was twice that of the U.S.[27] China's interactions with Africa went back over a thousand years and had always been more positive than those of the West which had ruined the continent through the slave trade, colonialism and neocolonialism.[28] The U.S. once again offered militarization and brutal IMF austerity while China won hearts and minds, despite poor labor standards, by offering interest free-loans, and building infrastructure, roads, hospitals, football stadiums and dams. Melvin Foote, the founder of a charitable NGO, told the *Guardian* newspaper that whenever he traveled to Africa, he was told that "America is losing influence and respect in Africa. Africans say – why do we need the United States? When I travel around Africa, I've seen airports; all kinds of things that are really impressive built by China, that you have to say the U.S. refused to build."[29]

Somalia

American military operations relied heavily on private contractors as a means of avoiding any political fall-out. In Somalia, in violation of a UN arms embargo, Obama's State Department contracted with Prescott Support Co. and RAM Air Services to provide clandestine arms shipments to the Somali and Puntland intelligence services in its fight against the Islamic nationalist group, Al-Shabaab, and with DynCorp and Bancroft Global Development, whose 40-man team of military advisers helped to "turn a bush army into an urban fighting force." Bancroft's founder, Michael Stock, a great grandson of a partner in the legendary banking firm Kuhn, Loeb & Co., had invested in a luxury hotel sprawled across 11 acres of rocky white beach.

Spotted by journalists drawing up battle plans, the preppy Stock envisioned that Bancroft's operations would help guide Somalia towards peace, hence turning his investment into a big money maker.[30]

Stock's most prized employee was Richard Rouget, a former big game hunter convicted in a South African court of illegally recruiting mercenaries in Ivory Coast's civil war where he fought for Laurent Gbagbo. Rouget had also been the right hand man of Bob Denard, a notorious agent of French colonialism who backed four coups in the Comoros and was suspected of involvement in the murder of African National Congress (ANC) leaders Godfrey Motsepe and Dulcie September.[31] Johnnie Carson, the top State Department official for Africa, stated that the U.S. did not want a visible military presence because of Somalia's history as a graveyard for American missions—notably during the Black Hawk Down episode in 1993 when Somali militiamen killed 18 American service members.[32] The presence of figures like Rouget was nonetheless conspicuous.

American strategic interests centered on controlling the major international shipping routes that lay off Somalia's coast and through the Gulf of Aden.[33] The country was further thought to have the world's most underexploited oil and gas reserves and provided a secret military base 70 kilometers south of Mogadishu and enabled construction of two underground rendition facilities, including a hole where suspects were tortured beneath the president's palace.[34] Somalia experienced brief stability under the Islamic Courts Union (ICU) until American-backed Ethiopian invasions in 2006 and 2011 plunged the country into renewed civil war. A CIA-allied warlord, Indha Adde, who acquired the moniker the "butcher," stated: "America knows war, they are war masters. They are teachers, great teachers."[35]

America's adversary, Al-Shabaab, tried to depict itself as an heir of Islamic nationalist fighters in Somalian history who had fought outside powers. It was supported by youth who felt their elders had betrayed the country and some clan elders. While succeeding in infiltrating the highest levels of the government, Al-

Shabaab alienated Somalis by its excessive violence and embrace
of the Wahhabist strand of Islam which emerged after the collapse
of the Siad Barre regime in 1991 when many practiced a mystical
form of Sufi Islam.[36]

The Obama administration sent in commando teams to
hunt down Al-Shabaab's leaders who had bounties placed on their
heads, prompting Al-Shabaab to place a bounty of ten camels on
Obama. Drone strikes began in June 2011 as the U.S. equipped the
African Union Mission in Somalia (AMISOM), an African Union
(AU) force consisting primarily of Ugandan and Burundian troops
who worked in collaboration with Somalian government troops,
described in the *New York Times* as "ineffective, disorganized
and corrupt; a composite of independent militias loyal to senior
government officials and military officers who profit from the
business of war."[37]

AMISOM forces were accused of indiscriminate shelling
of civilians and gang rape of girls as young as twelve.[38] They
supported a President (Hassan Sheikh Mohamud) who conspired
with a U.S. law firm (Shulman Rogers) to steal overseas assets
that had been recovered by the Somali central bank and was
considered the most corrupt in the nation's history.[39] In 2016,
the Pentagon admitted to conducting thirteen ground raids and
air strikes in Somalia, one of which killed over a dozen Somali
government soldiers, its ostensible partners. The U.S. military had
been "duped by clan rivals" and "fed bad intelligence," hardly
surprising in a country whose politics and culture they barely
understood.[40]

The main beneficiary of American missteps was Al-
Shabaab, which obtained American weapons on the black market
from disgruntled AMISOM troops and amassed handsome
profits from the illicit charcoal trade in collusion with American-
trained Kenyan defense forces who had invaded Somalia when
terrorist attacks extended to their soil.[41] One activist reflected
popular sentiment when he suggested that Somalis "did not want
ANY foreign invaders and intervention" including Americans,
"Ugandans, Burundians (AMISOM) who are criminals (also did

crimes in Congo) and have killed thousands of innocent Somalis" [following the Ethiopian invasions of 2006 and 2011]. "The best solution," he said, was to "apologize to the Somali people, pay reparations for all the people killed, and leave Somalia to the Somali people."[42]

Uganda

This idea of leaving Somalia to the Somalians and Africa to the Africans was anathema to the Obamians who saw themselves, in true American narcissistic fashion, as the only ones capable of saving the continent. Yet the regimes they invested in were among the most brutal. A case in point was that of Yoweri Museveni of Uganda which received over $500 million in annual foreign aid. Museveni first came to power in 1986 after fighting a bush war against Socialist Milton Obote (President of Uganda 1966-1971; 1980-1985), and had been heralded by the Clinton administration, along with Rwandan Tutsi president Paul Kagame, as part of the "new face of democracy" in Africa. A quarter century later, however, a record number of journalists had been jailed, elections had been rigged, corruption was rampant, democracy uprisings were crushed, and political opponents tortured or murdered.[43] With its advanced health-care system falling into disarray, Ugandans died from preventable famine as foreign aid money was siphoned off to pay political bribes. The country earned more money from the export of mercenaries than from its staple crop, coffee.[44]

In 2011, the Obama administration deployed 150 Special Forces and provided tilt rotor aircraft capable of vertical take-off and landing and surveillance drones as part of a $780 million package to aid in the hunt for Joseph Kony, a warlord estimated to have abducted 20,000 children to use as soldiers, servants and sex slaves. The Acholi Religious Leaders Peace Initiative raised immediate concern about the U.S. intervention and called for a peaceful resolution of the conflict through diplomacy, which the Obama administration never attempted.[45]

The Kony campaign was supported by an odd mix of

conservatives and liberal interventionists like Susan Rice and her successor as U.S. ambassador to the UN, Samantha Power, who spoke before Invisible Children, an evangelical Non-Governmental Organization (NGO) which promoted *Kony 2012*, a crude propaganda film broadcasting images of Kony's crimes.[46] In portraying Kony as the embodiment of evil, Power left out the fact that the Ugandan military too had a long record of human rights abuses including the deployment of child soldiers.

Political scientist Adam Branch details in *Displacing Human Rights: War and Intervention in Northern Uganda* how the northern-based Acholi people, from where Kony sprang, had backed the regime of Milton Obote and were in turn assaulted by Museveni's army. According to one bishop, it "behaved worse towards the Acholi than Idi Amin [a notoriously brutal leader in the 1970s]."[47] Villages were shelled, cattle stolen, civilians burnt alive, shot and deliberately infected with HIV. Over a million civilians were driven into displaced persons camps which held the highest mortality rates of anywhere in the world.[48]

For years, Museveni justified the war against Kony as needed to retain control over the North, which sat atop oil and gold. Thwarting peace efforts numerous times (1985, 1992, 1994 and 2003), Museveni maintained a crisis environment that enabled the government to "justify measures that would be unacceptable in different circumstances" and allowed it to "silence political dissidents, including vocal members of the Acholi population in parliament accused of being 'friends of the terrorists.'"[49]

American Special Forces were deployed from military bases in Entebbe and Obo in the Central African Republic (CAR) where Kony was allegedly based, as well as Dungu in Eastern Congo and South Nzara in South Sudan, bases whose existence were all justified by the campaign. The Americans placed bounties on the heads of Kony and other LRA commanders. They worked alongside Muslim insurgents, the Seleka, who had overthrown the CAR government and engaged in smuggling operations and human rights violations "on an unprecedented scale," according to Amnesty International.[50]

The Special Forces also teamed up with Executive Outcomes (EO), a private mercenary outfit created by veterans of the apartheid war in South Africa, which was contracted by Shannon Sedgwick Davis, a wealthy Texas philanthropist and founder of the Bridgewater charitable foundation, an arm of a multi-million-dollar hedge fund, which financed Invisible Children. In October 2013, *The New Yorker* reported that Ms. Davis, who has CIA written all over her sleeve, forged close relations with Ugandan army General Edward Katumba Wamala. According to Human Rights Watch, Wamala was trained at the U.S. Army War College and headed Ugandan military operations in Eastern Congo which resulted in significant atrocities along with the looting of at least $10 billion in mineral wealth.[51] While Obama's policy had been packaged as being driven by humanitarian concern, in actuality it supported some of the region's worst killers.

Rwanda and Congo

The crème de la crème in this department was Rwandan dictator Paul Kagame, who has been compared to Idi Amin and Adolph Hitler by Central Africans, though depicted in the Western media as Rwanda's Abraham Lincoln. Director of Uganda's feared intelligence service under Museveni in the 1980s known for inflicting brutal torture on regime opponents, Kagame received $15 million in security assistance and $196 million in annual aid during Obama's presidency.[52] Oklahoma Senator James Inhofe said the United States "does not have a better friend than Kagame."[53] This friend was suspected of murdering four heads of state (Juvenal Habayrimana, Cyprien Ntrimanda, Joseph Mobutu and Laurent Kabila), hunting down and killing scores of regime opponents, carrying out ethnic cleansing and terrorist operations including placing bombs in minibuses and hotels, and starting three wars of aggression.[54]

Trained in low intensity warfare and psychological operations including the art of deception at the army war college at Ft. Leavenworth, Kagame had led the Rwandan Patriotic Front

(RPF) invasion of Rwanda from exile in Uganda in October 1990 with CIA agent Roger Winter, having been groomed by the British to overthrow the French-supported government of Juvenal Habyarimana. Investigators determined that this "fair haired boy of the CIA and British MI-6" as FBI agent Jim Lyons characterized him, orchestrated the shooting down of Habyarimana's plane in April 1994, which triggered mass killings by Hutu and Tutsi extremists. Kagame personally oversaw the massacre of Hutu civilians at Byumba soccer stadium and set up an efficient system for incinerating bodies through use of acid and outdoor crematoria reminiscent of the Nazis.[55]

In 1996 and then again in 1998, the Rwandan Patriotic Front (RPF) invaded Congo alongside the Ugandans with Clinton administration backing, installing Laurent Kabila and then a puppet, Hyppolite Kanambe (alias Joseph Kabila) after Laurent Kabila had revoked western mining concessions and was shot by his bodyguard. Kanambe enforced the Rwandan and Ugandan occupation of North Kivu province and provided western multinational corporations access to Congo's mineral wealth, including coltan, cobalt, uranium, gold and diamonds as well as tantalum capacitators which are important for aerospace military technologies such as smart bombs and on-bound navigation in drones.[56]

To sustain an alleged economic miracle, Kagame opened Rwanda to foreign businessmen like Clinton Foundation donor Howard Buffet, Warren's son, who invested $500 million to "transform" the country's agriculture "into a more productive, high-value, and market-oriented sector" primarily for export.[57] Despite a glistening capital built with stolen Congolese loot and high ranking on the World Bank's "ease for doing business index," Rwanda was the second poorest country in East Africa with a per capita income of $697.3. Its per capita GDP ranked 197th out of 213 countries, below Zimbabwe.[58] Obama, however, never moralized about a leadership failure here, marking his singling out Zimbabwean leader Robert Mugabe for criticism as purely political (Mugabe's crimes in crushing his ethnic and political rivals were minor in comparison to those of Kagame).[59]

Samantha Power was among those to praise Kagame for "his epic scale of achievement."[60] In April 2010, after Kagame was sued by Habyarimana's widow while visiting Oklahoma to give a commencement address, the Obama administration filed a Suggestion of Immunity on Kagame's behalf, making it difficult to prosecute him.[61] Susan Rice subsequently tried to suppress a 2012 UN report, which found that Rwanda financed the M23 militia, which was responsible for murder, rape, pillage and using child-soldiers in Congo. Obama in response cut $200,000 from a Rwandan military academy. Military aid continued, however, and security assistance was increased to $7 million in 2014 as M23 Commander Laurent Nkunda continued to recruit in Rwanda.[62]

In 2013, Secretary of State John Kerry appointed former Senator Russell Feingold (D-WI) as a special envoy to the Great Lakes. Feingold had supported Obama's military action against Joseph Kony while a member of the Senate Foreign Relations Committee on African Affairs. He called for political dialogue and accountability for human rights abusers but renewed U.S. commitment to Rwanda, which he considered a valued "friend and ally." Then he threatened military action against the Hutu-dominated FDLR (Democratic Forces for the Liberation of Congo), which he blamed for destabilizing the region and provoking Rwanda, when the group had been mercilessly hunted down by Rwandese militias and the Congolese army.[63] *Politico Magazine* featured a photo of Feingold gorilla watching on safari, crediting him with ending a war. In reality, the progressive hero was providing political cover for Rwanda's brutal occupation of North Kivu, plunder and genocide.[64]

According to journalist Keith Harmon Snow, the Pentagon ran a military intelligence fusion cell in northeast Congo with the UN peacekeeping force, headed by an ex-Marine named "Tom" with backing from Rwandan troops, whose task was to oversee the plunder of strategic minerals essential for U.S. military stockpiles.[65] Obama had rolled out the red carpet during an African leaders' conference for Congo's president Hyppolite Kanambe who provided cover for these operations, turning a blind eye to his electoral fraud, wide-scale looting and to the massacre of anti-regime protestors.[66]

Known by Congolese as "le petit Rwandais," Kanambe was a quisling of Rwandan origin. His father, Adrien Christophe Kanambe, was a Tutsi leader of an anti-Mobutist group in Tanzania who served as head of state from 1997-2001, and was killed by Laurent Kabila after he had been accused of disloyalty. Hyppolite was then adopted by Kabila who married his widowed mother but could not take care of him because he had too many other wives and kids. After working as a taxi driver, Kanambe was taken under the wing of his uncle, RPF chief of staff James Kabarebe, and was then installed in power by Kagame after presiding over the massacre of Hutu in Rwanda in the late 1990s.

The Congolese army under his command had integrated thousands of Rwandan and Ugandan Tutsi. It committed legions of atrocities against Hutu and Mai Mai soldiers and their supporters fighting for the liberation of Kivu. Kanambe's security forces also detained and tortured trade union organizers and murdered human rights activists like Floribert Chebeya, the president of the NGO Voice for the Voiceless, priests such as Cardinal Frederic Etsou, the Pope's representative in the Congo, and members of Laurent Kabila's family who threatened to expose his secrets, including Laurent's outspoken younger sister Esperance. At least forty-five assassinations were carried out by Dr. Jean Pierre Tumba-Longo, who used special poisons to kill victims like General Mbuza Mabe, who had kicked Rwandan troops out of Kivu and threatened to pursue them back into Rwanda.[67]

In spite of Congo's atrocious human rights record, the Obama administration provided Kanambe with an estimated $193 million in security assistance over eight years, training Congolese military forces in psychological warfare and other counterinsurgency methods. The recipients included Congo's 391st battalion who raped close to one hundred women and more than thirty girls and shot a fourteen-year old boy in the village of Kalungu near Goma during the M23 militia's seizure of the town.[68] In turn, Kanambe provided the U.S. with, inter alia, an intelligence fusion cell in Kisangani to oversee regional security, meaning "U.S. and Israeli access to Congo's gold, diamonds, uranium, platinum and coltan," as a report to the CIA-connected intelligence firm STATFOR framed it.[69]

A primary goal of the military campaigns was to clear North Kivu of its people in order to pave the way for Rwandan annexation and plunder by Western mining companies, which bankrolled the Kanambe regime. One of Kanambe's first acts as president had been to fly to America to give back mining concessions to companies that had had them revoked under Laurent Kabila's rule. The Lunden Group, a Canadian mining company with ties to the Clinton Foundation, made billions in DRC copper mines, buying out shares owned by Israeli Dan Gertler, partner of an American hedge-fund Och-Ziff which paid over $100 million to Kanambe in exchange for lucrative mining rights. Secretary of State Clinton subsequently refused to push for the implementation of key provisions of a law she had passed as a Senator to regulate conflict minerals, and directly intervened to restore the license of First Quantum Minerals Limited, which was founded by a Clinton Foundation benefactor.[70]

Maurice Carney, Director of the NGO Friends of the Congo, said that "Kabila [Kanambe] served as a toll-gate for Western corporate interests, sell[ing] off Congo's riches for pennies on the dollar."[71] Kanambe is alleged to have even met with Maurice Templesman, head of the U.S.-based Corporate Council on Africa, a big-time donor to the Democratic Party with a long and dubious history of illicit involvement in Congolese affairs and arms and diamond trading who had been linked to the assassination of Patrice Lumumba.[72]

The Obama administration's policy in Congo reflected a strong degree of continuity from the age of colonialism. Celebrities like Oprah Winfrey reinforced the stereotype of black victimization and savagery, while failing to draw attention to the fact that the atrocities in Congo had been abetted by the West. China all the while emerged as an effective new competitor in the Great Game, which used its ties to Kanambe, who received military training there, to purchase over half of the Tenke Fugurume copper mine, a prized copper asset, for $2.65 billion.[73]

Sudan

China also gained an upper-hand in Sudan despite the State Department helping in 2011 to midwife the new nation of South Sudan, which controlled three quarters of oil production including 350,000 barrels destined mainly for Chinese ports. China had long supported the North, headed by Omar al-Bashir. South Sudan bordered the oil-rich Darfur province, which was made a UN protectorate. Whoever controlled it would potentially be able to sabotage Chinese oil infrastructure there (Zbigniew Brzezinski's plan was to cut off Chinese oil supply from Africa altogether, in the hope that it would force China to encroach on Siberia which would cause a new Sino-Russian rift).[74]

The geopolitical stakes were underplayed by the anti-genocide Save Darfur coalition, which Obama had supported as a Senator when he spoke at a rally on the National Mall with George Clooney and Elie Wiesel.[75] Human rights, however, took a backseat when Obama as president removed sanctions against the North because of its cooperation with the War on Terror, and allowed for continued provision of $425 million in annual security assistance to South Sudan as it descended into civil war between rival leaders, Salva Kiir of the Dinka, who had the backing of Ugandan troops, and Reik Machar of the Nuer, who were targeted in ethnic cleansing operations. By executive decree, Obama even waived application of the Child Soldiers Prevention Act barring military assistance to governments that used child soldiers for what he claimed were "national security" purposes.[76] After President Kiir signed a deal to turn over South Sudan's petroleum resources to China, the deep state began covertly backing Machar, who had overseen the infamous Bor massacre in 1991.[77] Supported by the Khartoum government, Machar had worked as an adviser to Jareh Capital, a New York investment firm specializing in natural resources headed by Hillary Clinton's *eminence grise* for Africa,

Joe Wilson, which had taken out a 400,000 hectare lease (about the size of Vermont) that allowed it to extract uranium and oil.[78]

West Africa

The illusion that American soldiers in West Africa served only in an advisory capacity was dispelled in October 2017 when four Special Forces were ambushed on patrol in the Niger desert and killed by Islamic insurgents.[79] The Obama administration had promoted a military buildup as part of the War on Terror and in an effort to secure mineral resources, including uranium, oil and gas deposits located beneath Lake Chad, and gold which Clinton Foundation donor Barrick Gold had concessions to mine.[80] Niger's President Mahamadou Issoufou, was a former employee of Areva, the French company that dominates Africa's uranium trade, and was accused of human trafficking through Nigeria. His human rights abuses were overlooked because he allowed the U.S. to fly Predator drones from the capital Niamey and construct a $110 million drone base on the edge of the Sahara Desert—in violation of Niger's constitution which required parliamentary approval.[81] A man selling children's textbooks and novels on a busy corner in Niamey told Joe Penney of *The Intercept* that "for us, this [the drone base] is another form of colonization." Jdibril Abarché, president of the Nigerian Human Rights Association, further noted that Niger was "not at a level where it [could] say yes or no to the French or Americans... the Americans don't give orders to our Generals, they give orders to our soldiers."[82]

The American base building spree extended to Cameroon where terrorist suspects who included resisters to the rape of their country were beaten and tortured at a secret military base used for drone surveillance. The Obama administration provided one of the continent's longest serving dictators, Paul Biya, with over $185 million in security assistance and sent Special Forces and Mossad subcontractors to help crush a revolt undertaken in the name of anti-colonial freedom fighter Ruben Um Nyobé.[83] Obama further drew close with Burkino Faso's leader, Blaise Campaoré, who in

1987 murdered Thomas Sankara, Africa's Che Guevara. In return for over $35 million in security assistance, Campaoré brought Burkino Faso firmly into the web of U.S. military and surveillance activities. AFRICOM was permitted to open a surveillance base at Ouagadougou International Airport in a classified program known as Operation Creek Sand and a classified regional intelligence fusion center known as Aztec Archer was also established.[84] Reminiscent of the Cold War, American Special Forces worked with the chief of Campaoré's presidential guard, Gilbert Diendéré, who was accused of massacring protestors and then launching a coup after Campaoré was overthrown in a popular revolution modeled after the Arab Spring.[85]

Black Skin, White Mask

By the end of Obama's presidency, the U.S. was providing military training to almost every country in Africa, including in at least one case (Burundi) without consent from its head of state. The U.S. had amassed over 60 military outposts and was running one and a half military missions per day, a 217 percent increase since AFRICOM was established in 2008. U.S. Army Africa disclosed a 94 percent increase in its activities from 2011 to 2013, including a 436 percent jump in advice and assist operations. Secret teams did everything from teaching Kenyan troops how to use Raven surveillance drones and helping Algerian forces field new mine resistant ambush protected vehicles to training Chadian and Guinean infantrymen and aiding France's ongoing interventions in West and Central Africa.[86]

Contrary to claims about Obama being a deft strategist, American intervention provoked greater military intervention by China, which established its first overseas military base in Djibouti [which was used primarily to protect Chinese cargo ships from pirates]. The resultant terrorist incidents which could include acts of resistance to foreign plunder, increased from 119 in 2001 to around 500 in 2011 and averaged between 144 and 204 per year during Obama's presidency. Piracy also increased by 80 percent in the Gulf of Guinea. Berny Sebe of the University of Birmingham ticks off post-revolutionary Libya, the collapse of Mali, the risk of Boko Haram in Nigeria, the coup in the Central African Republic and violence in Africa's Great Lakes region as evidence of increasing volatility. He wrote that "the continent is certainly more unstable today than it was in the early 2000s when the U.S. started to intervene more directly."[87]

Many militaries the U.S. trained were known as we have seen for human rights abuses. This list of countries impacted includes Morocco, which sustained one of the world's last colonial occupations; Kenya, whose army incited ethnic violence and bombed and shelled populated areas in Somalia; Ivory Coast, whose president Alassane Ouattara oversaw ethnic violence after a fraudulent election; and Mauritania, whose leader Mohamed Ould Abdel Aziz legalized slavery.[88] American advisers further worked with former South African mercenaries to train forces subsidized by Shell Oil who had a record of brutality in the Niger Delta. In a single incident in the war against Boko Haram, a terrorist group that gained notoriety for kidnapping 276 school girls in Chibok, Nigerian security forces destroyed two thousand homes, and killed 183 civilians as ethnic violence increased and the Fulani because of their link to the security forces were subjected to reprisal attacks.[89]

An editorial in the *Cape Argus* by Iqbal Jamat, "The Real Kidnappers are the West," noted that Boko Haram's illegal methods of kidnapping had unfortunately paved the way for an expanded U.S. military presence in the resource rich country as the U.S. had joined with Britain, France and Israel in an effort to locate and rescue the captured girls. "On the surface," Jamat wrote, "the western nations were fulfilling their humanitarian responsibility; however, it is known that Nigeria is one of many African countries which like South Africa had resisted American pressure to allow military bases linked to AFRICOM. Boko Haram's misdeeds in turn now opened Nigeria up to Western hegemony in an obscene replica of the colonial era."

Jamat continued:

China's expanding footprint on the continent needs to be contained and countered. What better way to 'moralise' the West's so called humanitarian intervention than with the slogan 'Bring Back our Girls.' Discredited figures associated with the illegal War on Terror responsible for far worse atrocities [than Boko Haram] that include mass killings, dispossession and major refugee crises cannot by any stretch of the imagination expect us to conceal our scepticism. Boko Haram [has] caused an international outcry and paved the way for the abduction of Africa by the West.[90]

Jamat's editorial resonates with the findings of this chapter which has sought to demonstrate how the Obama administration used fears about terrorism and Chinese encroachment and feigned concern about human rights atrocities as a means of setting up a vast archipelago of military bases while expanding military assistance and training to forces engaged in dirty war operations. Zimbabwe's much-maligned and defiant leader Robert Mugabe, aged 91, earned a standing ovation before the African Union in January 2016 when he lamented how even after colonialism, "the former colonists were still everywhere in Africa.... through NGOs....as spies, pretenders, some say they are here in Africa to assist us, even in armed groups in our territories" effecting regime change. Criticizing whites for "dragging Africans across the ocean as slaves," he said "those blacks might now seem free— particularly Obama. But what is he? A voice made to speak their language, to act their act and not our act."[91]

Mugabe may be a flawed leader, but he was on the mark in his assessment. At the end of the second decade of the 21st century, Africa remained weak, divided, and susceptible to the kind of neocolonial interference he identified. The continent cried out for leaders like Lumumba, Nkrumah, Sankara, Mandela and Nyerere who had promoted unity and pride during the golden age of decolonization. The main heirs of these revolutionaries, alas, had self-destructed or been isolated, or were overthrown and lynched. America's first black president, Obama, had at one time been considered part of the great pantheon and as a continental savior. He proved, however, to be a man with black skin in a white mask. With drones buzzing overhead, and the ghosts of dead Congolese littered about, he duped and deceived Africans in a manner that even Cecil Rhodes would have admired!

Endnotes

1   Christopher Thompson, "What the U.S. Africa Command Does," *Financial Times*, June 18, 2010; Thom Shanker, "Djibouti Outpost Behind Somalia Rescue is Part of New Defense Strategy," *New York Times*, January 26, 2012, A14.

2   U.S. State Department, Djibouti Human Rights Report, 2016, https://www.state.gov/documents/organization/265460n 199 .pdf; Jeffrey Smith, "Washington's Closest Ally on the Horn of Africa Has a Terrible Human Rights Record," *Foreign Policy*, July 11, 2016. Guellah had been appointed in 1999 by his Uncle who ruled since independence in 1977.

3   Thompson, "What the U.S. Africa Command Does;" Katrina Morgan, "Jostling for Djibouti," *Financial Times*, April 1, 2016. For the larger pattern, see David Vine, *Base Nation: How American Military Bases Harm America and the World* (New York: Metropolitan Books, 2015).

4   Frantz Fanon, *Black Skin, White Masks* (New York: Grove Press, 1969).

5   Nick Turse, *Tomorrow's Battlefield: U.S. Proxy Wars and Secret Ops in Africa* (Chicago: Haymarket Books, 2015).

6   Wayne Madsen, "The Toxic Mix of AFRICOM and Human Terrain Ops," *Strategic Culture Foundation*, October 31, 2017.

7   George Klay Kieh Jr. "The Obama Administration's Policy Toward Africa," in *Obama and the World: New Directions in U.S. Foreign Policy*, 2nd ed. ed. Inderjeet Parmar, Linda B. Miller and Mark Ledwidge (New York: Routeledge: 2009).

8   Ada Keye Abadjo, "The Wave of Obamamania in Africa Peters Out," *Business Day Johannesburg*, June 3, 2013, accessed at British National Library, Newsbank database.

9   Salem Solomon, "Susan Rice and Africa's Despots," *New York Times*, December 10, 2012, A27; Keith Harmon Snow, "Ethnic Cleansing in Ethiopia,"

Global Policy Forum, November 4, 2004.

10   Malcolm Rees, "U.S. Setting up Spy Base in Swaziland," *Sunday Johannesburg Times*, July 20, 2014, accessed at British National Library, Newsbank database; Peter Kenworthy, "Swaziland: Uprising in the Slipstream of Africa," in *Africa Awakening: The Emerging Revolution*, ed. Firoze Manji and Sokari Ekine (Capetown: Pambazuka Press, 2012), 156.

11   Peter Baker, "Obama Delivers Call for Change to a Raptured Africa," *New York Times*, July 21, 2009, 1.

12   Michael D. Shear and Rick Lyman, "Unable to Visit Mandela: Honors Legacy," *New York Times,* June 30, 2013, 1.

13   Anakwa Dwamena, "Obama's Disappointing Legacy in Africa," *Johannesburg News*, October 31, 2016, accessed at British National Library, Newsbank database.

14   Baker, "Obama Delivers Call for Change to a Raptured Africa," 1.

15   See eg. Patrick Bond and Masimba Manyanya, *Zimbabwe's Plunge: Exhausted Nationalism, Neoliberalism and the Struggle for Social Justice* (Trenton, NJ: Africa World Press, 2002); Lloyd C. Gardner, *The Killing Machine: The American Presidency in the Age of Drone Warfare* (New York: The New Press, 2013), viii.

16   See eg. Tom Burgis, *The Looting Machine: Warlords, Oligarchs, Corporations, Smugglers, and the Theft of Africa's Wealth* (New York: Public Affairs, 2016).

17   Maeve Shearlaw, "Africa Should Stop Blaming History for Its Economic Problems – Is Obama Right?" *The Guardian*, July 30, 2014.

18   Lee Wengraf, *Extracting Profit: Imperialism, Neoliberalism and the New Scramble for Africa* (Chicago: Haymarket Books, 2018), 136; Karen McVeigh, "World is Plundering Africa's Wealth of Billions of Dollars a Year," *The Guardian*, May 24, 2017.

19   Paula Abeles, "Obama and Odinga: The True Story," *Canada Free Press*, August 8, 2008; "Obama's Kenya Ghosts," *Washington Times*, October 12, 2008; Jerome Corsi, *The Obama Nation: Leftist Politics and the Cult of Personality* (New York: Threshold, 2008), 96, 97, 104. Odinga was allegedly paid $1 million by the CIA.

20   Mark Landler, "Meeting Teams African Leaders and American Investors: Deals are Sought Beyond Resources," *New York Times*, August 6, 2014, A4; Wengraf, *Extracting Profit*, 99, 117-119.

21   Jill Richardson, "How the US Sold Africa to Multinaitonals like Monsanto, Carglil, DuPont, Pepsico and Others," *Alternet*, May 23, 2012; "Powering Africa: President Obama's Plan to Bring Light to Millions," *New York Times*, July 16, 2013, A22; Jacob Dlamini, "A Hyphenated Legacy? Obama's Africa Policy" in *The Presidency of Barack Obama: A First Historical Assessment*, ed. Julian Zelizer (Princeton University Press, 2018).

22   D.A. Barber, "Is Obama's Power Africa Simply Enabling More Climate

Change," *The Huffington Post*, July 18, 2013; Toluse Olorunnipa and Tope Alake, "Obama's Africa Power Plan Falls Short, Leaving Continent in Dark," *Bloomberg News*, September 20, 2016. Part of the reason for the failure was that the Import-Export Bank only provided a fraction of the funding due to political gridlock.

23   Kieh Jr. "The Obama Administration's Policy Toward Africa," in *Obama and the World*, ed. Parmar et al.

24   Mark Landler, "Meeting Teams African Leaders and American Investors: Deals are Sought Beyond Resources," *New York Times*, August 6, 2014, A4.

25   William F. Jasper, "Global Obama Care and World Population Control," *The New American*, January 19, 2010; "Depo Provera: Deadly Reproductive Violence Against Women," The Rebecca Project for Human Rights, http://www.1037thebeat.com/wp-content/uploads/2013/06/DEPO-PROVERA-DEADLY-REPRODUCTIVE-VIOLENCE-Rebecca-Project-for-Human-Rights-June-2013-2.pdf; Sudarsan Raghavan and David Nakamura, "Bush AIDS Policies Shadow Obama in Africa," *Washington Post*, June 30, 2013; Michael Tikili, "Obama's Budget Betrays Presidential Commission on Global AIDS," Health Gap Global Access Project, https://www.healthgap.org/obama_s_budget_betrays_president_s_commitments_on_global_aids.   Bill Gates' father was a eugenicist. Critics felt the promotion of Depo Provera, which was given mainly to black women in the U.S., amounted to forced sterilization. The Israeli and Indian governments banned prescription of Depo Provera, which the head of Obama's Global Health Initiative, Dr. Rajiv Shah was surely aware.

26   Joeva Rock and Foreign Policy in Focus, "Why Are We Sending Soldiers Trained for War To Respond to the Ebola Crisis," *The Nation*, September 25, 2014. Suspicion abounds as to how the human-made virus spread when it was contained through local efforts in Congo and Uganda. See Antoine Roger Lokongo, "Ebola: Who Created This Terrible Virus and Why?" *Pambazuka News*, January 8, 2015.

27   Chris McGreal, "Obama Woos African Leaders to Counter Increased Chinese Influence," *The Guardian*, August 4, 2014.

28   See Basil Davidson, *The Lost Cities of Africa* (Boston: Little & Brown, 1959), 181-191.

29   Damian Whitworth and Michael Evans, "The Secret Front Line: Inside the Heart of the CIA War against Al-Qaeda in Africa," *The Guardian*, June 22, 2010; Turse, *Tomorrow's Battlefield*, 128.

30   Christopher S. Stewart, "A Bet on Peace for War-Torn Somalia," *Wall Street Journal*, May 20, 2013; Colum Lynch, "Is the U.S. Ramping Up a Secret War in Somalia?" *Foreign Policy*, July 23, 2013. Stock was a graduate of Princeton University and only 34.

31   David Axe, "U.S. Hires Shady Mercenary for Somali Proxy War," *Wired*

Magazine, August 11, 2011; Jeffrey Gettleman, Mark Mazzetti and Eric Schmitt, "U.S. Relies on Contractors in Somalia Conflict," *New York Times*, August 11, 2011, A1; James Ferguson, *The World's Most Dangerous Place: Inside the Outlaw State of Somalia* (New York: Da Capo Press, 2013), 33. Bancroft employee Brett Fredericks, 55, a retired member of Delta Force and Iraq War veteran who taught Somali forces in counter-irregular warfare, was shot between the eyes and died. Sean D. Naylor, "Profit and Loss in Somalia," *Wall Street Journal*, January 22, 2015.

32   Gettleman et al. "U.S. Relies on Contractors in Somalia Conflict."

33   Bronwyn E. Bruton and Paul D. Williams, *Counterinsurgency in Somalia: Lessons Learned From the African Union Mission in Somalia, 2007-2013* (Tampa Florida: Joint Special Operations University Press, 2014).

34   Jan Wellmann, "After the Black Hawks Arrived: In Somalia, a History of U.S. Meddling Continues," *Truthout*, February 7, 2016; Jim Armitage, "Soma Oil Lobbies UK for Help in Somalia Despite Serious Fraud Office Inquiry," *The Independent*, January 31, 2016; Danny Fortson, "Former Tory Leader Braves Pirates for Oil – Michael Howard Raises Money from Russian Tycoon to Explore for Oil Off Coast of Somalia," *London Sunday Times*, January 12, 2014. The London-based Sona oil, which received $50 million in financing from a Russian billionaire and was chaired by former Tory leader Sir Michael Howard, made improper payments to Somali officials in the process of becoming the first foreign company to prospect for Somali oil since Exxon Mobil in 1990.

35   Jeremy Scahill, *Dirty Wars: The World is a Battlefield* (New York: The Nation Books, 2013), 201.

36   Hussein Solomon, "Somalia's Al-Shabaab: Clans Versus Islamic Nationalism," *South African Journal of International Affairs*, 21, 3 (2014), 351-366; Dan Joseph and Harun Maruf, *Inside Al-Shabaab* (Bloomington: Indiana University Press, 2018).

37   Human Rights Watch, World Report, 2013; Jeffrey Gettleman and Neil MacFarquhar, "Somali Food Aid Bypasses Needy, UN Study Says," *New York Times*, March 9, 2010, 1; Mark Mazetti and Eric Schmitt, "U.S. Expands Its Drone War into Somalia," *New York Times*, July 2, 2011, A1; Joseph and Maruf, *Inside al-Shabaab*, 227.

38   Bruton and Williams, *Counterinsurgency in Somalia*; David Smith, "AU Troops in Somalia Accused of Gang Rapes," *The Guardian*, September 9, 2014. The troops sexually exploited women seeking medicine for their sick babies at AU military bases and traded food aid for sex.

39   Wellman, "After the Black Hawks Arrived;" Jerome Starkey, Tristan McConnell, "Labor Peer Denies Firm Hid Somali Corruption," *The Financial Times*, July 24, 2014. Mohamud's brother had been accused of trying to steal $420 million from a Swiss bank account set up by Siad Barre and went around Mogadishu buying real estate property with bags of cash.

40   Mark Mazetti, Jeffrey Gettleman and Eric Schmitt, "In Somalia, U.S. Escalates a Shadow War," *New York Times*, October 16, 2016.

41   Helen C. Epstein, *Another Fine Mess: America, Uganda, and the War on Terror* (New York: Columbia Global Reports, 2017), 162; Lynch, "Is the U.S. Ramping Up a Secret War in Somalia?" Joseph and Maruf, *Inside al-Shabaab*, 266, 267.

42   L-Ban, online post, August 12, 2011, http://tachesdhuile.blogspot.com/2011/08/max-boot-is-gonna-learn-us-all-up-about.html

43   Ollive Kobusingye, *The Correct Line? Uganda Under Museveni* (Authorhouse, 2010); Epstein, *Another Fine Mess*; 182; "Uganda's All-You-Can-Eat Corruption Buffet," American Embassy Kampala to Department of Justice, January 5, 2010, https://wikileaks.org/plusd/cables/10KABUL22_a.html. Cerinah Nebanda, a 24-year old MP who spoke out against government abuses was among those thought to have been poisoned by Museveni in December 2012. General David Sejusa reported that "many other prominent Ugandans who had died from mysterious illnesses or in sudden accidents had been deliberately killed on 'orders from on high.'" Francis Ayume, the Attorney General who tried to block Museveni's extension of presidential term-limits, died in a mysterious car crash in which it was claimed his car hit a pothole in the middle of the night, which was miraculously filled by morning. In 2016, Museveni ordered the security forces to storm the royal palace of the Rwenzururu, a traditional kingdom in Western Uganda, leaving over 100 dead.

44   David Garvey Herbert, "Uganda's Top Export: Mercenaries – The African Nation Makes More Money from Military Contractors than Coffee," *Bloomberg Business Week*, May 10, 2016.

45   Dr. Gary K. Busch, "The United States and the Lord's Resistance Army," in Wikileaks, Global Intelligence File, October 19, 2011, https://wikileaks.org/gifiles/docs/12/1278834_-analytical-and-intelligence-comments-re-uganda-reasons-for.html.

46   Invisible Children was part of a network of NGOs including the Enough Project, another possible CIA-front which played on liberal sentimentality for human rights and concern about genocide in order to promote U.S. military intervention.

47   See Adam Branch, *Displacing Human Rights: War and Intervention in Northern Uganda* (New York: Oxford University Press, 2013).

48   Branch, *Displacing Human Rights*; Epstein, *Another Fine Mess*, 67, 86, 91; Ebony Butler, "A Brilliant Genocide," documentary film shown on RT News, https://www.youtube.com/watch?v=8boQaql6Ofc.

49   Branch, *Displacing Human Rights*; Epstein, *Another Fine Mess*, 79.

50   Epstein, *Another Fine Mess*, 128, 129; Craig Whitlock and Thomas Gibbons-Neff, "U.S. Troops Have Turned to Some Unsavory Partners to Help Find Warlord Joseph Kony," *The Washington Post*, September 29, 2015; David

Smith, "Unspeakable Horrors in a Country on the Verge of Genocide," *The Guardian*, November 22, 2013.

51   Elizabeth Rubin, "How a Texas Philanthropist Helped Fund the Hunt for Joseph Kony" *New Yorker*, October 21, 2013; Laura Joyce Davis, "Meet the Mom Who Stopped Joseph Kony," *Christianity Today*, February 10, 2015. EO chairman Eeben Barlow, was former commander of a battalion created by South African Prime-Minister Johannes Vorster to destabilize Angola.

52   See Edward S. Herman and David Peterson, *Enduring Lies: The Rwandan Genocide in the Propaganda System, 20 Years Later* (Evergreen Park, IL: Real News Press, 2014); Yaa-Lengi M. Ngemi, *"Joseph Kabila," Identity Thief, Imposter, and Rwandan Trojan Horse in Congo: Hyppolite Kanambe a.k.a. Joseph Kabila: Rwandan Tutsi and Hitler Paul Kagame's Agent in DRC* [The Evidence] (New York City, 2017); J.E. Murphy, *U.S. Made* (Meadville, PA: Christian Faith Publishing, 2015), 59, 60; Security Assistance Monitor, Rwanda, https://securityassistance.org/data/program/military/Rwanda/2009/2016/all/Global//

53   Inhofe quoted in Anjan Sundaram, "Rwanda: The Darling Tyrant," *Politico*, March/April 2014.

54   See sources from note 52 and Keith Harmon Snow, "Rwanda's Secret War," *Z Magazine*, April 29, 2007; "Rwandans are Cold Ass Mofos," bayless.parsley@stratfor.com to analysts@stratfor.com, Global Intelligence Files, Wikileaks, https://wikileaks.org/gifiles/docs/11/1191753_re-discussion-rwanda-south-africa-rwandans-are-cold-ass-mofo.html; Human Rights Watch, 2013 World Report, 148.

55   Judi Rever, *In Praise of Blood: The Crimes of the Rwandan Patriotic Front* (Toronto: Random House Canada, 2018). 2, 4, 79, 90; 217, 235; Peter Erlinder, *The Accidental Genocide* (International Humanitarian Law Institute, 2013), 336, 337; Robin Philpot, *Rwanda 1994: Colonialism Dies Hard* (Montreal: Baraka Books, 2010); Hazel Cameron, *Britain's Hidden Role in the Rwandan Genocide: The Cat's Paw* (London: Routeledge, 2013), 80. Conferring on him a global citizenship award, Bill Clinton called Kagame among the "greatest leaders of our time."

56   Edward S. Herman and David Peterson, *The Politics of Genocide* (New York: Monthly Review Press, 2011); Wayne Madsen, *Genocide and Covert Operations in Central Africa, 1993-1999* (New York: Edwin Mellen, 1999); Asad Ismi, "The Congo Still Ravaged by U.S. Funded Conflict and Plunder," *Global Research*, Mach 25, 2014.

57   Ann Garrison, "Neocolonial Kleptocracy and Clinton Connections," *Black Agenda Report*, November 22, 2017; Zahra Moloo, "The Problem with Capitalist Philanthropy," *Jacobin*, February 6, 2018..

58   David Himbara, *Kagame's Economic Mirage* (South Carolina: Create Space Independent Publishing, 2016). Youth unemployment or underemployment

topped 40 percent, imports quadrupled exports, and forty-four percent of children under five had stunted growth.

59   For a fair-minded assessment, see Sue Onslow and Martin Plaut, *Robert Mugabe* (Athens: Ohio University Press, 2018). Mugabe supported ethnic/political violence as part of the drive to consolidate the power of his party (ZANU-PF) in the early 1980s Gukurahundi whose death toll is estimated to be around 5,000, a shocking figure but not comparable to Kagame and the RPF's killing spree.

60   Rever, *In Praise of Blood*, 225; Murphy, *U.S. Made*, 96.

61   Himbara, *Kagame's Economic Mirage*, 97.

62   Alexis Arieff, "Democratic Republic of Congo: Background and U.S. Policy," *Congressional Research Services*, February 24, 2014. M23 commander Boscoe Ntganda was later remanded to the International Criminal Court on charges of crimes against humanity.

63   Arieff, "Democratic Republic of Congo;" Chris McGreal, "U.S. Tells Armed Group in DRC to Surrender or Face 'Military Option' – Barack Obama's Special Envoy to Central Africa Issues Warning to FDLR, a Group Formed by Leaders of the Rwandan Genocide," *The Guardian*, August 6, 2014; Snow, "Rwanda's Secret War." Feingold condemned the FDLR for keeping the genocide ideology alive, however, Hutu leaders had been acquitted by the ICC of planning genocide.

64   Stuart Reid, "Did Russ Feingold Just End a War? The Unlikely Story of How the Former Wisconsin Senator Made Peace in Congo," *Politico Magazine*, March 11, 2014.

65   Keith Harmon Snow, "Apocalypse in Central Africa: The Pentagon, Genocide and the War on Terror," *Z Magazine*, December 4, 2010; Keith H. Snow, "Disaster Capitalism's Greatest Carnage of Them All," in *How the US Creates "Sh*thole" Countries*, ed. Cynthia McKinney (Atlanta: Clarity Press, 2018), 201.

66   David Martokso, "Obama Welcomes Congolese Strongman to the U.S." *Daily Mail*, August 4, 2014.

67   Ngemi, *Joseph Kabila, Identity Thief*. See also Human Rights Investigation, Uganda in Eastern DRC: Fueling Political and Ethnic Strufe, March 1, 2001; Keith Harmon Snow, "Gertler's Bling Bank Torch Gang: Israel and the Ongoing Holocaust in Congo," *Dissident Voice*, February 9, 2008.

68   Arieff, "Democratic Republic of Congo: Background and U.S. Policy;" Turse, *Tomorrow's Battlefield*; Keith Harmon Snow, "Western Backed Terrorism in the Congo: Where is General Laurent Nkunda?" *Global Research*, June 9, 2015. For background, see Emizet Francis Kisangani, *Civil Wars in the DRC, 1960-2010* (Boulder, CO: Lynne Riener, 2012).

69   Dr. Gary K. Busch, "The United States and the Lord's Resistance Army," in Wikileaks, Global Intelligence File, October 19, 2011, https://wikileaks.org/

gifiles/docs/12/1278834_-analytical-and-intelligence-comments-re-uganda-reasons-for.html.

70   Stanley Opeyemi, "Why is the West Supporting Joseph Kabila's Rule?" *Foreign Policy Journal*, August 26, 2017;Snow, "Western Backed Terrorism in the Congo," *Global Research*, June 9, 2015; Peter Schweizer, *Clinton Cash: The Untold Story of How and Why Foreign Governments and Businesses Helped Make Bill and Hillary Rich* (New York: Harper & Row, 2016), 117-125. Quantum Minerals received a $1 billion concession for the Lonshi mine through questionable means. The company was founded by Jean-Raymond Boulle, a friend of Bill whose diamonds Hillary had worn at the Arkansas' Governors Ball in the early 1980s.

71   Asad Ismi, "The Congo Still Ravaged by U.S. Funded Conflict and Plunder," *Global Research*, Mach 25, 2014. Keith Harmon Snow referred to Kanambe (Kabila) as a "black gatekeeper for mining cartels run by dynastic families like Templesman, Oppenheimer, Mendell, Forrest, Blattner, Gertler and Steinmetz."

72   Snow, "Apocalypse in Central Africa." Kanambe also gave concessions to Western oil companies, Dominion Energy and Soco International, which moved into the Lake Albertine basin in Kivu to sink new wells. Another beneficiary was Herman Cohen, the former U.S. ambassador to Rwanda and Zaire, whose consulting firm partnered with Kagame to exploit methane in deep water under Lake Kivu on the Congo-Rwanda border

73   Peter Schweizer, *Secret Empires: How the American Political Class Hides Corruption and Enriches Family and Friends* (New York: Harper Collins, 2018), 53.

74   F. William Engdahl, *Target China: How Washington and Wall Street Plan to Cage the Asian Dragon* (San Diego: Progressive Press, 2014), 21, 22.

75   Armin Rosen, "How Obama Went from Calling to Save Darfur to De-Sanctioning Sudan in His Final Days in Office," *Tablet*, January 24, 2017.

76   Mahmood Mamdani, "Who's to Blame in South Sudan," *Boston Review*, June 28, 2016; Global Security Assistance Monitor, South Sudan, https://securityassistance.org/data/program/military/South%20Sudan/2009/2016/all/Global//; Column Lynch, "Inside the White House Fight Over the Slaughter in South Sudan," *Foreign Policy*, January 26, 2015; Nick Turse, "The U.S. is Sponsoring an Army That Recruits Child Soldiers," *The Nation*, May 18, 2015.

77   See Nick Turse, *Next Time They'll Count the Dead: War and Survival in South Sudan* (Chicago: Haymarket Books, 2016); Thomas C. Mountain, "The CIAs Dirty War in South Sudan," *Defend Democracy Press,* September 13, 2016; Thomas C. Mountain, "Obama's War in South Sudan," *Counterpunch*, July 16, 2015. Machar had a white American girl-friend, Becky Hagman.

78   Schweizer, *Clinton Cash*, 137; Lt. Gen. Osman Taj-Asir, Republic of Sudan, 01/09/2014, http://sudanreeves.org/2014/10/22/new-and-exceedingly-accurate-translation-into-e/

79   Rulemini Callimachi et al. "'An Endless War:' Why Four U.S. Soldiers Died in a Remote African Desert," *New York Times*, February 20, 2018.

80   Snow, "Petroleum and Empire in North Africa;" Eric Draitser, "AFRICOM: A Neocolonial Occupation Force?" *Counterpunch*, December 11, 2018; Yadira Soto-Viruet,"The Mineral Industries of Mali and Niger," United States Department of the Interior, U.S. Geological Survey, August 2012, https://minerals.usgs.gov/minerals/pubs/country/2010/myb3-2010-ml-ng.pdf.

81   Niger 2013 Human Rights Report, https://www.state.gov/documents/organization/220356.pdf; Nick Turse, "U.S. Military is Building a $100 Million Drone Base in Africa," *The Intercept*, September 29, 2016; Nick Turse, "The U.S. is Building a Drone Base in Africa That Will Cost More than $280 Million by 2024," *The Intercept*, August 21, 2018.

82   Joe Penney, "Drones in the Sahara," *The Intercept*, February 18, 2018.

83   Nick Turse and Robert Trafford, "Cameroonian Troops Tortured and Killed Prisoners at Base Used for U.S. Drone Surveillance," *The Intercept*, July 20, 2017; Security Assistance Monitor, Cameroon, https://securityassistance.org/data/program/military/Cameroon/2009/2016/all/Global//; Kah Walla, "The Power is Within Us: A Protest Diary From Cameroon," in *Africa Awakening*, ed. Manji and Ekine 107-111; Dionne Searcey, "Atrocities Nudge Cameroon Toward Civil War Ahead of Election," *New York Times*, October 7, 2018.

84   Craig Whitlock, "U.S. Expands Secret Intelligence Operations in Africa," *The Washington Post*, June 13, 2012; Wayne Madsen, *The Manufacturing of a President* (self-published, 2012), 159; Security Assistance Monitor, Burkino Faso, http://securityassistance.org.

85   Joe Penney, "Africa, Latest Theater in America's Endless War," *New York Review of Books*, March 12, 2018; Baba Aye, "Revolution and Counter-Revolution in Burkino Faso," *African Review of Political Economy*, November 25, 2015; Lila Chouli, "People's Revolts in Bukrino Faso," in *Africa Awakening*, ed. Manji and Ekine, 131-145.

86   Turse, *Tomorrow's Battlefield*, 75; Wesley Morgan, "Behind the Secret U.S. War in Africa," *Politico*, July 2, 2018.

87   Turse, *Tomorrow's Battlefield*, 75; Wengraf, *Extracting Profit*, 222.

88   Compare figures compiled by Security Assistance Monitor with Human Rights Watch reports for these and other African countries.

89   Turse, *Tomorrow's Battlefield*; Security Assistance Monitor, Nigeria. The Obama administration provided approximately $100 million in security assistance to Nigeria. William Wallis and Katrina Manson, "Africa's Soldiers of Fortune Join Fight Against Boko Haram," *London Financial Times*, March 26, 2015; Afia Hirsch and John Vidal, "Shell Pays Millions to Nigerian Security Forces Data Finds," *The Guardian*, August 20, 2012, accessed at British National Library, Newsbank database; "Nigeria's Fulanis Say They Are

Being Vilified for Violence," *Voice of America*, July 2, 2018; Mike Smith, *Boko Haram: Inside Nigeria's Unholy War* (London: I.B. Tauris, 2016).

90   Iqbal Jamat, "Real Kidnappers are the West," Capetown, Cape Argus, May 14, 2014, accessed at British National Library, Newsbank database.

91   Peter Fabricius, "Mugabe Rants at Whites, Obama," *Africa*, January 30, 2016.

Chapter 4

THE LIBERALS
HAVE THEIR WAR
THE ILLEGAL ATTACK
ON LIBYA

On March 23, 2011, *New York Times* columnist Maureen Dowd published a column entitled "Fight of the Valkyries," in which she pointed to a gender flip in the Obama administration. The fierce women, Secretary of State Hillary Clinton, U.S. Ambassador to the UN Susan Rice, and National Security Council adviser Samantha Power, urged Obama to "man up against the crazy Qaddafi [the Libyan ruler]" whereas the men in Obama's circle, Generals and the Defense secretary [Robert Gates], were "more reluctant." The dynamic went against Freudian theories and feminists who had pointed to the psychosexual undertone of military terminology, promising a kinder, gentler world if run by women. How odd, Dowd concluded, "to see the diplomats as hawks and the military as doves," and to "see Rush Limbaugh [conservative radio host] and Samantha Power on the same side."[1]

Rice, Hillary Clinton and Power had all come of age politically in the 1990s and claimed to harbor regrets that they did not do more to press the Clinton administration to intervene to halt genocides in Serbia and especially Rwanda in April 1994. In 2001, Power had penned a piece in the *Atlantic Monthly*, "Bystander to Genocide," in which she rebuked the "self-serving caution and flaccid will—and countless missed opportunities to mitigate a colossal crime."[2]

Overwhelming evidence disputes Power's interpretation, however. Far from a bystander to genocide, the U.S. supported the Rwandan Patriotic Front (RPF)'s illegal invasion of Rwanda from Uganda in October 1990, which was opposed by Ambassador Robert Flaten, who called for sanctions on Uganda; and it has helped block Paul Kagame's prosecution for shooting down Prime Minister Juvenal Habyarimana's airplane, the act that triggered the mass killing. The International Criminal Court was unable to corroborate evidence that Hutu hard-liners planned the extermination of Tutsi, undercutting Power's claim that the Clinton administration had evidence in advance of a genocide and should have acted more swiftly. Undersecretary for Global Affairs Timothy Wirth was given instructions to suppress a human rights investigation detailing that many of the killings were carried out by the RPF.[3] Beginning in June 1994, American soldiers were deployed to rebuild and control Kigali's airport and provided military training, satellite surveillance and arms to the RPF as they set up a totalitarian police state and invaded and plundered the Congo.[4]

The myth of non-intervention in Rwanda would be used by Power and the Obama administration to sell the need for it in Libya. The opportunity to right a fictitious historical wrong came in March 2011 when Arab Spring protests erupted against Qaddafi but were repressed. When Qaddafi's armies began marching on Benghazi, the siren call of an impending bloodbath was raised. The liberal community quickly rallied behind military intervention, even though it was engendered in violation of the 1973 War Powers Act and UN Charter. The African Union (AU) came up with a peace agreement that would allow Qaddafi to step down and set up elections. Reflecting a colonialist mindset, Power claimed the AU was acting "foolishly." The implication was that only military intervention could avert the "looming humanitarian catastrophe."[5]

Targeting a Long-Time Foil of the American Empire

The Libyan intervention in particular shows Obama to be the kind of leader Frantz Fanon warned about: a black who served the interests of the white masters and helped legitimize their exploitative practices. Muammar Qaddafi was a long-time foil of the American Empire. Born to a poor family in Sirte which fought against Italian colonial rule, he had come to power in a bloodless 1969 revolution against the Sanussi King Idris, a corrupt U.S. and British ally who gave concessions to Western oil companies in return for military and technical aid. King Idris also allowed a large American military base at Wheelus near Tripoli, along with rights to a naval port, air and ammunition storage facility at Tabruk, a guided missile range in Tripoli, a communications site at Derna, and a radar station and airfield at Benghazi and Cape Misrata. State Department planning documents emphasized Libya's significance as a "southern flank of NATO" and the value of the air base and military facilities for testing the latest military equipment. These were assets the Obama administration wanted to restore.[6]

A Pan-Arab and African supportive of the Palestinian cause, Qaddafi kicked out the U.S. military when he came to power in 1969 and placed Libya's high quality, light sweet crude oil under national control, reinvesting profits in health and education. Life expectancy increased from fifty-four to seventy-one years under his rule, the literacy rate went from six to 88 percent, and homelessness was eliminated. Through its state-owned bank which did not charge interest, Libya also financed an African satellite that slashed communications costs and became a world leader in hydrological engineering due to development of a man-made river that won a major UNESCO award for "remarkable scientific research work on water usage in arid areas."[7]

The late South African journalist Ruth First wrote a book

entitled *Libya: The Elusive Revolution*, which emphasized Qaddafi's top-down approach to social change, although many felt a sense of participation in decision-making it afforded through local councils and Qaddafi's *Green Book* promoted a system of direct democracy.[8] Tribal conflict was also averted through a power-sharing system and women's rights were advanced. Since 2006, Qaddafi had taken on the role of a spiritual guide, deferring on many issues to the elected Prime Minister Al-Baghdadi al Mahmoudi. He possessed a ruthless streak to be sure—imprisoning Idris' nephew for over twenty-five years and torturing and hanging dissidents, many of them Islamists—in part owing to the colonial legacy and as a survival mechanism in the face of constant foreign attack.[9]

The Nixon administration had first considered assassinating Qaddafi right after he first came to power, referring to him in dehumanizing language as a "desert rat" and "international outlaw." Subsequent U.S. leaders called him "subhuman" (President Jimmy Carter), a "deranged and murderous dictator" (CIA Director and Defense Secretary Leon Panetta), a "cancer that had to be removed" (Secretary of State Alexander Haig) and a "barbarian" and "mad dog" (President Ronald Reagan).[10]

In May 1984, the Reagan administration sponsored an attack on Qaddafi's headquarters by the dissident Libyan National Salvation Front and subsequently engaged in provocative maneuvers in the Gulf of Sidra that left thirty Libyan sailors dead. Then, after unproven allegations Qaddafi sent terrorists to strike a West Berlin discotheque, Reagan undertook another assassination attempt, which left up to 100 civilians dead. Qaddafi's 15-month-old adopted daughter was killed and eight of his children and wife were hospitalized after bombs struck his tent and family home. Qaddafi survived because of the malfunction of the laser-guided bombing system and because the attacking planes were forced to abort their mission after Libyan air defenses picking up their movement fired anti-aircraft missiles.[11]

Backed by his team of female war hawks, the Obama administration came back to finish the job and remove the "mad dog" once and for all. Ironically, Qaddafi had expressed pride that a son of Africa had become U.S. president after the 2008 election and believed Obama would break with a foreign policy that had mounted constant threats and "brought poisonous roses upon Libyan children" in the 1980s. Only later, when it was too late, would Qaddafi realize he had been tricked. Qaddafi appears to have written his death warrant in a speech he gave before the UN General Assembly in September, 2009 where he juxtaposed praise for Obama with demand for the return of $777 trillion that had been stolen from Africa by the colonial powers. He further called for investigation into the assassinations of Patrice Lumumba, UN Secretary-General Dag Hammerskjold, John F. Kennedy and Martin Luther King Jr.[12]

Picking up the mantle of Ghanaian leader Kwame Nkrumah, Qaddafi at the time was promoting a Central African Court, Monetary Fund and Bank capable of lessening African dependence on Western financial institutions. He was planning to renationalize significant parts of the oil sector, had spurned a building contract with Bechtel, a San Francisco construction giant, which builds military bases around the world, and had initiated 50 major economic projects with China. Further, Qaddafi was beginning efforts to initiate a new currency with Libya's vast gold and silver holdings that could undercut the French franc and U.S. dollar. He refused to cooperate with the U.S. military's African command (AFRICOM), stating that he preferred it to remain "headquartered in Europe."[13]

In 2006, then-Secretary of State Condoleezza Rice had signed a treaty with Libya requiring Qaddafi to step down from power (which he did), which also required Libya to dismantle its nuclear enrichment program and place reserve funds in the U.S. Federal Reserve and European Central Bank. Another treaty sponsored by John McCain in 2009 required Libya to get rid of half of its existing military and all defensive weapons. This was agreed to on the condition that the U.S. would provide some weaponry and help in its defense if Libya was ever attacked.[14]

Following the outbreak of the rebellion in February 2011, Saif al-Islam Qaddafi, Muammar's son, told Libyans that those urging on the protestors were Libyans who lived in Europe and USA, whose children went to school there and who were comfortable and want [now] to come and rule us and Libya. They want us to kill each other then come, like in Iraq.

Saif emphasized that Libya was different from Tunis or Egypt, that

if there was disturbance it will split to several states. It was three states before 60 years ago. Libya are Tribes not like Egypt. There are no political parties, it is made of tribes. We will have a civil war like in 1936. American Oil Companies played a big part in unifying Libya. Who will [if Qaddafi is removed] manage this oil? How will we divide this oil amongst us? Who will spend on our hospitals? All this oil will be burnt by the Baltagiya (Thugs) they will burn it.

A civil war would also disrupt the $200 billion in development projects currently underway. Three quarters of our people, Saif said:

live in the East in Benghazi, there is no oil there, who will spend on them? Your children will not go to schools or universities. There will be chaos, we will have to leave Libya if we can't share oil. Everyone wants to become a Sheikh and an Emir, we are not Egypt or Tunisia so we are in front of a major challenge.[15]

Saif's analysis proved to be prescient as Libya was indeed thrust into civil war and chaos as well as destitution by the U.S.-

NATO invasion, which was supported by most of the Arab and Western media. Many of Libya's people sided with Qaddafi, holding huge solidarity rallies in Tripoli, as his government had used oil revenues to raise living standards, cut debt and allowed for religious freedom. A small black woman whose son was beheaded by the rebels told Jimmy and Jo Anne Moriarty, a Texas couple who worked in the oil industry and became spokesmen for Libya's tribes, to "tell the world that Muammar Qaddafi saved our country." If Libyans were "shooting other Libyans it is our country, we will deal with it [we don't want you]."[16]

The First Casualty of War is Truth

To drum up support for the illegal intervention, the Obama administration followed an old playbook in spreading atrocity stories; in this case rumors that Qaddafi was giving his soldiers Viagra to carry out rape and was employing black foreign mercenaries. Libya's blacks in fact supported Qaddafi as he was turning towards Africa and supplied them with jobs.[17] The CIA and rebel coalition were the ones employing foreign mercenaries including Arab jihadists who committed atrocities that were blamed on Qaddafi. The CIA set up 29 training centers for the rebels, and sanctioned clandestine arms shipments from the United Arab Emirates (UAE) and Qatar. In March 2011, Obama signed an order designating CIA operatives to the eastern Libyan cities of Derna and Benghazi in preparation for the subversion of the Libyan government.[18] When a U.S. fighter jet crashed near Benghazi, the two rescued pilots admitted they were CIA operatives.[19]

In a speech before the U.S. Army War College nine days after authorizing air strikes, President Obama in Wilsonian fashion claimed he had ordered warships into the Mediterranean in conjunction with European allies in order to "confront Qaddafi's brutal repression" and "stop the killing." According to Obama, Qaddafi was killing and sexually assaulting journalists and shelling towns:

Gaddafi declared that he would show 'no mercy' to his own people. He compared them to rats and threatened to go door to door to inflict punishment. In the past, we had seen him hang civilians in the streets, and kill over a thousand people in a single day. Now, we saw regime forces on the outskirts of the city. We knew that if we waited one more day, Benghazi—a city nearly the size of Charlotte—could suffer a massacre that would have reverberated across the region and stained the conscience of the world. It was not in our national interest to let that happen. I refused to let that happen. And so nine days ago, after consulting the bipartisan leadership of Congress, I authorized military action to stop the killing and enforce UN Security Council Resolution 1973. We struck regime forces approaching Benghazi to save that city and the people within it.[20]

As if scripted by Woodrow Wilson, these comments were clever in emphasizing multilateralism and a humanitarian imperative and necessity of saving civilians from massacre and genocide, which made the war seem like a noble undertaking. On March 17th, the UN Security Council, with China and Russia abstaining, passed a resolution authorizing a no-fly zone in Libya and "all necessary measures" to protect civilians short of occupying ground forces. This gave the UN-authorized "Right to Protect" (R2P) intervention in Libya the veneer of legality, as the U.S. and NATO forces went on to pursue regime change, exceeding their mandate, and targeting pro-Qaddafi forces regardless of whether or not they posed a threat to civilians. Obama never obtained authorization from Congress in violation of the 1973 War Powers resolution, claiming he did not need to do so because the United States was not engaging in an act of war.[21]

Dennis Kucinich (D-OH) called for Obama's impeachment for this serious constitutional abuse. Senator Rand Paul (R-KY) took to the Senate floor to broadcast a quote from Obama in the *Boston Globe* four years earlier when he had said, "the president does not have power under the Constitution to unilaterally authorize military attack in a situation that does not involve stopping an actual or imminent threat to the nation." The House by a 268-145 vote passed a resolution asserting that the president had failed to provide a compelling rationale for bombing.[22]

Obama's claims about America witnessing Qaddafi hanging civilians in the streets and killing over a thousand people in a single day, is at best a half truth. The latter is a reference to the killing of rebellious Islamic prisoners under the orders of Qaddafi's intelligence chief at Abu Salim prison near Tripoli in June 1996. The facts surrounding this incident and number of deaths remain murky and are reliant on information supplied by émigrés who had a motive for exaggerating the scale of the atrocity, which prior to this had not prevented the dubious U.S. rapprochement with Qaddafi. After Qaddafi's ouster, the new governing council claimed to have unearthed mass graves to confirm that over 1,200 people died, but these were determined to have been filled with animal bones![23] Historical parallels can be drawn with the playing up of German atrocities in Belgium by Woodrow Wilson's propaganda agency (The Creel Committee) during the First World War, and invocation of Iraqi leader Saddam Hussein's gassing of the Kurds during the Iran-Iraq War in 1982 when he was an ally of the U.S. as a means of justifying the U.S. invasions of Iraq years later in 1991 and again in 2003.[24]

The revolt in Benghazi—a trigger for national protests—was initiated by families of the victims of the Abu Salim massacre in February 2011 after Qaddafi arrested a lawyer, Fathi Terbil, who had demanded a public inquiry. You tube videos show demonstrators chanting "Muammar is the enemy of Allah" and other Islamist slogans. Police responded by dispersing tear gas and rubber bullets.[25] Afterwards, International Criminal Court (ICC) chief prosecutor Luis Moreno-Ocampo estimated that 500–

700 people were killed across the country by security forces, who also suffered casualties.[26]

Saif al-Islam Qaddafi claimed that armed militia fighters in Benghazi precipitated the crisis by killing children and terrorizing the population and denied the ICC's allegations that he or his father (Muammar Qaddafi) ordered the killing of civilian protesters. Saif told *Russia Today* that his father was not a member of the government or the military and therefore had no authority to give such orders. Saif also said that his father had made recorded calls to General Abdul Fatah Younis, who later defected to the rebel forces, in order to request not to use force against protesters, though Younis responded that protesters were attacking a military site and soldiers were acting in self-defense.[27]

Disregarding this viewpoint, the Obama administration claimed the number of Libyan government victims was ten times higher than it was and falsely accused the Qaddafi regime of genocide. It also failed to disclose that Qaddafi had made an amnesty offer to the rebels. CIA Director Leon Panetta went so far as to accuse Qaddafi of unleashing violent attacks on America in his struggle to maintain power, of which there is no evidence.[28]

Believing that holding back the military would have been "extremely chilling, deadly and a stain on our collective conscience," Samantha Power said she was inspired by the Benghazi protestors "who were taking tremendous risks; coming to the square and reading poetry."[29] This misrepresentation was used as a basis for backing something that was already intended, much like Bush in the buildup to war in Iraq. The protests in Libya were in fact of a different character to those in Tunisia and Egypt, as Saif noted, or to the Occupy Wall Street movement; they were primarily Islamic, regional and sectarian in character and supported restoration of the old Sanussi order, even adopting its flag. They were backed by the CIA, British and French intelligence, and imported jihadists from Chechnya, Algeria and Afghanistan, and were violent from the outset. A female activist lamented that the Islamists "stole our revolution" like they would attempt to do in Syria.[30]

"We Didn't Lose a Single Life:" Operation Odyssey Dawn

According to Italian journalist Franco Bechis, foreign coordination of the uprising began in November 2010 when French soldiers disguised as businessmen were flown into the country under the oversight of Nuri Mesmar, Qaddafi's chief of protocol who sold him out like Brutus did Caesar.[31] The Obama administration spent about $1 billion on Libya's "revolution," and helped NATO with everything from munitions to surveillance aircraft, carrying out roughly 20 percent of the over 26,000 bombing sorties in the seven-month NATO mission that included dropping cluster munitions, phosphorus and Fuel Air Explosives which are outlawed under international law. Rebel commanders were awestruck by precision munitions and rapid communication capability enabling "some guy [to] talk into a radio or push a button and [then like magic] the tank in front goes boom!"[32]

In the opening hours of the campaign, an American submarine, the USS *Florida,* launched 100 cruise missiles against Libyan air defenses, crucially opening an entry corridor for the airstrikes that followed. Predator drones flew overhead for hundreds of hours, chronicling the "pattern of life below" to prepare target selection for B-2 stealth bombers and hellfire and tomahawk missiles with depleted uranium warheads.[33] Vice President Joseph Biden Jr. bragged that "we didn't lose a single life," and that the war served as a "prescription for how to deal with the world as we go forward."[34]

Civilians only loosely linked to Qaddafi's regime were targeted in the bombing. Buildings and homes were hit along with desalinization plants, the man-made river and water pipe infrastructure supplying over 4 million people. The town of Sirte, a Qaddafi stronghold envisioned as the center of united Africa, was reduced to a "ghost town filled with the stench of death," as one eyewitness described it. Qaddafi's home was bombed in another illegal assassination attempt that killed his son and three of his grandsons, adding to the tally of family members already killed by Reagan.[35]

NATO bombing of Ain Zara, South of Tripoli on July 24, 2011 came 100 years to the day that the same target had been hit by two small bombs dropped by an Italian plane, the first bombing in history.[36] Taking a page from Italian air power theorist Giulio Douhet, who argued in a classic 1921 study that air power could shorten conflicts and save lives, Samantha Power had been adamant that U.S. intervention was necessary to halt a bloodbath resulting from Qaddafi's drive on Benghazi. However, Qaddafi had not perpetrated any bloodbaths in any of the cities his forces had recaptured. His Foreign Minister, Khaled Kaim, had asked for a delay of NATO bombing to allow for inspection and was rebuffed.[37] Libyan tanks on the road to Benghazi were bombed not when they were advancing, furthermore, but during their retreat.[38]

The *London Daily Telegraph* reported that a bloodbath took place *when the Sanussi rebels took control of Benghazi*, after which Al Qaeda flags were seen flying over the courthouse. Black African migrants who supported Qaddafi were dragged from apartments, beaten and killed. $900 million dinars ($500 million U.S. dollars) was stolen from the Libya's state owned central bank, as the rebels quickly established a new central bank and oil company. According to the *Telegraph*, "so-called 'revolutionaries' and 'freedom fighters' [were] in fact rampaging gunmen committing atrocities airbrushed from mainstream reports."[39] Among their victims were Tawherga, black-skinned peoples living on the outskirts of Misrata who were subjected to an ethnic cleansing operation. Graffiti on the walls of their abandoned homes read: "abeed," a slur for blacks.[40]

"We Came, We Saw, He Died."

The final rebel assault on Tripoli was led by Qatari Special Forces paid by the CIA and Pakistani ISI mercenaries. Sensing Qaddafi's demise, over a hundred high-level military officers defected to the opposition in May.[41] Qaddafi was subsequently found, with the assistance of U.S. predator drones, hiding in a sewer pipe. The rebels tortured him and allegedly sodomized him with a sword. They then shot him in the head and displayed his body in a meat locker. Hillary Clinton jubilantly told a reporter. "We came, we saw, he died," a twisted play on the words of Julius Caesar following his victory over the King of Bosporus at the Battle of Zela around 47 B.C.[42]

CIA director John Brennan told speechwriter Ben Rhodes that Qaddafi's death "marked a fitting end for one of the biggest rats of the 20th century."[43] No Western leader would ever be characterized in this way. Obama gave his own victory speech only nine days after the first NATO bombs were dropped. He told soldiers at the National Defense University that "because of them…countless lives have been saved."[44] This would have come as news to Faiz Fathi Jfara, who lost five family members including his nine-year-old sister when a laser guided bomb struck his home in Ban Walid, 170 kilometers south of Tripoli or to residents in Majer, southeast of Zliten, where thirty-four people died and thirty were wounded after a laser guided bomb hit two family compounds along with a delegation of relief workers.[45]

Obama's speech had echoes of his predecessor's Mission Accomplished speech as Libya thereafter descended into chaos. Journalist Patrick Cockburn wrote about roaming militias selling crude oil on the black market and sectarian warfare between the Zawiya and Wirshifana tribes just 15 miles from the Prime Minister's office.[46] The brother of one of Osama bin Laden's deputies was put in charge of passport and border control, enabling the flooding of foreign terrorists into the country (heroin and other hard drugs flowed in too). Reminiscent of post-invasion Baghdad, streets were piled high with rubbish. Blackouts lasted up to eight hours with buildings left cratered by bombs.[47] Women's rights were eroded and there were even reports about the revival of slavery. They exemplified the folly of "cruise missile leftists" like Nicholas Kristof who had written in the *New York Times* that "Libya is a reminder that sometimes it is possible to use military tools to advance humanitarian causes."[48]

With Friends Like These….

Libya's first post-invasion Prime Minister, Mahmoud Jibril, a Ph.D. in political science from the University of Pittsburgh, was ironically targeted under an ill-conceived political isolation law adopted by the Obama administration and its allies, which bore eerie resemblance to the de-baathification policy in Iraq. The law prohibited anyone formally tied to the Qaddafi regime from holding office for ten years (Jibril had had an association with Saif al-Islam at one time). The law's definition of complicity was so broad that like in Iraq it banned a vast stratum of technocrats, military officers and union leaders from effectively rebuilding the government and country.[49]

Supported by the Muslim Brotherhood, Libya's first post "liberation" President Mohammed Youssef el-Magarief had been expelled from Libya in 1980 when as ambassador to India he was accused of stealing millions sent to build a mosque.[50] Gen. Khalifa Hiftar, another U.S. favorite, was disowned by Qaddafi after leading an ill-fated invasion of Chad in the 1980s. A senior State Department official considered him a "vigilante" comparable to "white Russians in the Russian civil war." Armed by the United Arab Emirates (UAE), Egypt, Jordan, France, Russia and Saudi Arabia, Hiftar left his comfortable Virginia suburban home where he had resided for three decades at the same time as Obama issued his executive order for the CIA. His forces were subsequently accused of committing unlawful executions, torture, beheadings and bombing schools, and his son of stealing millions from Benghazi's newly-created Central Bank.[51] Joshua Geltzer, Obama's senior director for counterterrorism, stated that U.S. support for Hiftar was one of "those grudging things. You look at him and you say, 'well he's keeping some bad guys at bay though at times with what seemed to be great brutality.'"[52] Where have we heard that before?

Clare Lopez, a former CIA officer, told MailOnline that America "switched sides in the war on terror [in Libya] and knowingly facilitated the provision of weapons to known al-Qaeda militias and figures," including through the UAE.[53] These figures included Abdelhakim Belhadj, long-time leader of the Islamic insurgency against Qaddafi who oversaw the pogroms against the Tawherga. Meeting at one point with bin Laden, Belhadj fought with the Taliban in Afghanistan and against America in Iraq and helped plan the horrific March 2004 train bombing in Madrid.[54]

The American alliance with jihadists against the secular left fit with a pattern dating to the Cold War when Zbigniew Brzezinski and other Ivy League intellectuals envisioned an arc of Islam as a bulwark against Pan-Arab Socialism.[55] The new Grand Mufti, Sheikh Sadeq al-Ghariani, issued fatwas legitimizing polygamy and banning women from marrying foreigners and called on the Ministry of Education to delete passages on democracy and freedom of religion from textbooks. Libya's great patriot Imam, Sheikh Khaled Tantoush, who was against radical Islam, was meanwhile imprisoned and tortured in a Misrata jail for over five years.[56]

In 2012, the Obama administration denied a request from Libyan tribal elders to cleanse the country of Islamic terrorists in return for the departure of U.S.-NATO soldiers.[57] The result was an atrocity laden environment epitomized by incidents such as the February 2015 beheading by ISIS militants of 21 Egyptian oil workers on a beach near Tripoli, destruction and vandalism of Sufi shrines and mosques, assassination of former Qaddafi officials, and shooting of homosexuals.[58]

The New Merchants of Death

The private military industry had been salivating at the prospect of reconstruction contracts following the Operation Odyssey Dawn. The head of the security contractor network based out of Alexandria, Virginia wrote on his blog about the new post-Qaddafi context in which there was an "uptick of activity as foreign oil companies scramble[d] to get back into Libya. This means an increase in demand for risk assessment and security related services.... Keep an eye on who is winning the contracts. Follow the money and find your next job."[59]

British-based G4S, the world's third-largest private employer which provides surveillance equipment to checkpoints and prisons in the Israeli-occupied territory, was one of the bigger winners along with Aegis Security headed by the infamous soldier of fortune Tim Spicer, and Blue Mountain Group, another British firm hired to guard the U.S. temporary mission facility in Benghazi, which also housed a major CIA base (called the "annex"). Equipped mainly with flashlights and batons instead of guns, the Blue Mountain Guards were ill-equipped to deal with the September 11, 2012 insurgent attack that led to the death of U.S. Ambassador J. Christopher Stevens and three other Americans, two of whom were CIA contractors.

An FBI probe into Hillary Clinton's emails uncovered that one of Clinton's top aides, Sidney Blumenthal, a longtime family fixer and $10,000 per month employee of the Clinton Foundation, used his direct access to the then Secretary of State to promote his business interests in Libya. Prior to and during the war, Blumenthal would frequently email Clinton with intelligence information derived from the off-the-books intelligence spy networks that may have encouraged Clinton's strong backing for an expanded U.S. military role in Libya. Blumenthal at one point enthused to Clinton about opportunities for private security firms that could "put America in a central role without being direct battle combatants."[60]

A key firm wanting to get in on the action was Osprey Global Solutions, in which Blumenthal had a financial stake. According to Tyler Drumheller, an ex-CIA agent and Osprey executive, Blumenthal was to receive a finder's fee for helping to secure State Department approval and arrange a contract for training security forces and building a floating hospital and schools in the war-torn country. At one point, Blumenthal even proposed bringing in, as an adviser to the fledgling post-Qaddafi government, a man named Najib Obeida, whom he hoped would then finance Osprey's operations in Libya.

Though the deal eventually fell through, the Blumenthal and Osprey conflict of interest epitomizes how the lure of private contracts and monetary gain could help skew intelligence and push the United States into war. Policymakers like Clinton themselves saw great utility in private contractors who fed them information that would rationalize a hawkish position and help open up opportunities for foreign investors who would line their political coffers come election season.[61]

Blowback

Obama himself showed disinterest in Libya after Qaddafi's overthrow, disbanding the working group to track jihadists. As USAID consultants recommended building up fast-food outlets like McDonald's and Kentucky Fried Chicken, new civil society groups sprang up seeking money from foreign donors headed by Libyans who had spent even less time in Libya than the aid workers. Locals referred to them as "shafras," a mocking reference to the Arabic term for a cell phone's SIM card; the returnees usually had two SIM cards, a Libyan and a foreign one that they switched out—just as Saif al-Islam Qaddafi had warned.[62]

In summer 2013, after protests were crushed by the new authorities, Obama sent Cobra helicopters and Harrier attack jets to pound ISIS-aligned militants flooding Qaddafi's hometown of Sirte. 495 air strikes were launched between August 1st and December 5th, 2014 alone. In its last military operation, the Obama administration unleashed the Northrop Grumman B-2A spirit stealth bomber backed by MQ-9 Reapers armed with hellfire missiles and 500 pound-Paveway laser-guided bombs to destroy an ISIS training camp south of the city.[63]

Libya by this time exemplified the destabilizing consequences of the use of American power, whose fighting machines were now directed against the very enemy it helped unleash. Pete Hoekstra (R-MI), the former head of the House Intelligence Committee, feared that Islamic terrorists had gotten hold of the remnants of Gaddafi's chemical weapons arsenal of sulfur mustard gas.[64] Blowback came with the killing of Ambassador Stevens, a University of California at Berkeley graduate with a "talent for breaking bread with men in camouflage fatigues," according to a profile in *Vanity Fair*. The former Peace Corps volunteer is thought to have run an illicit arms pipeline that provided 50,000 shoulder-fired rockets to jihadist rebels in Syria. With re-election in 2012 hinged on the belief that the War on Terror was successful (Joe Biden famously said: "Osama bin Laden is dead and General Motors is alive"), Obama put out a story that the Benghazi attack was prompted by an internet video defaming the prophet Muhammed, which was not what CIA analysts concluded.[65]

The regional destabilizing effects of the Libyan war were felt in nearby Tunisia, the most stable beneficiary of the Arab Spring, which was stung by the massacre of tourists by gunmen fresh from Islamic State training camps in Libya.[66] Tuareg soldiers who fought for Qaddafi and were targeted in ethnic cleansing operations fled to Mali and took over territory there, which prompted a coup by an American-trained officer. Other parts of the country were seized by an Al-Qaeda affiliate that fought the Tuareg, prompting French intervention, which the Obama administration assisted.[67]

At the end of his presidency, Obama acknowledged the Libyan War to have resulted in a "shit show" though he cowardly tried to blame British Prime Minister David Cameron.[68] The scope of the Libyan calamity is almost immeasurable in human terms. Local estimates place the number of deaths at over 600,000 with countless more displaced. ISIS increased its presence to over 5,000 men by the end of 2015 as Libya became a hub for illicit arms transfers and international terrorism. Over 180,000 Libyans risked their lives to escape to Italy, with thousands perishing along the way in the depths of the Mediterranean. If any outside power benefitted from the Operation Odyssey Dawn, it was Russia, which became a powerbroker in Libya. The concept of democracy was discredited, with one woman in Benghazi asserting that she would "cut off her finger" before "voting in another election."[69]

Obama apologists may claim that the U.S. was dragged into the Libyan War by Britain and France and had no other option.

However, this ignores the precedent set during the 1956 Suez crisis when President Dwight Eisenhower forced the withdrawal of Britain, France and Israel when they invaded Egypt after its President Gamal Abdel Nasser, a hero to Qaddafi, nationalized the Suez Canal.[70] Obama unfortunately did not follow in Eisenhower's footsteps. The war on Libya exposed his weakness as a leader, and true colors as little more than a black frontman for the white "masters of mankind" who worked to divide, conquer and ultimately destroy a defiant African nation.

Endnotes

1   Maureen Dowd, "Fight of the Valkyries," *New York Times,* March 23, 2011.

2   Samantha Power, "Bystanders to Genocide," *The Atlantic Monthly*, September 2001.

3   Peter Erlinder, *The Accidental Genocide* (International Humanitarian Law Institute, 2013); Christopher Black, "The Dallaire Genocide Fax: A Fabrication," December 7, 2005, www.sandersresearch.com; Edward S. Herman and David Peterson, *Enduring Lies: The Rwandan Genocide in the Propaganda System, 20 Years Later* (Evergreen Park, IL: Real News Press, 2014); Judi Rever, *In Praise of Blood: The Crimes of the Rwandan Patriotic Front* (Toronto: Random House Canada, 2018), 96, 97; J.E. Murphy, *U.S. Made* (Meadville, PA: Christian Publishing, 2015), 135, 136. Former UN Secretary Boutros Boutros Ghali believed the U.S. helped orchestrate the shootdown of Habyarimana's plane.

4   Wayne Madsen, *Genocide and Covert Intervention in Congo, 1993-1999* (New York: Edwin Mellen, 1999); David Himbara, *Kagame's Economic Mirage* (South Carolina: Create Space Independent Press, 2016), 85.

5   Frederic Wehrey, *The Burning Shores: Inside the Battle for the New Libya* (New York: Farrar, Straus and Giroux, 2018), 40; Alex de Waal, "The AU and the Libya Conflict of 2011," *World Peace Foundation*, December 19, 2012. Obama also spurned a peace proposal advocated by his Kenyan half-brother Malik.

6   Maximilian Forte, *Slouching Towards Sirte: NATOs War on Libya and Africa* (Montreal: Baraka Books, 2012); Mennen Williams to Governor Harriman, "Libya Military Assistance;" Philip E. Haring to Grant V. McLanahan, "Petroleum Companies," Department of State, RG 59, Records of the Bureau of African Affairs, box 8, Libya; "Base Rights and Other Quid Pro Qu Benefits

to Which Military Assistance Plan [MAP] Contributes;" Joseph Palmer to Mr. Murphy, "Problems Created by British Withdrawal from Libya," January 1957; "Strategic and Political Importance of Libya," RG 59, General Records of the Department of State, Bureau of African Affairs, Box 2, National Archives, College Park Maryland.

7   Stephen I. Danzansky to Colin L. Powell, August 11, 1988, Robert Oakley Papers, National Security Council box 4, Libya, Ronald Reagan Presidential Library, Simi Valley California; Geoff Simmons, *Libya and the West: From Independence to Lockerbie* (London: I.B. Taurus, 2003); William Blum, *Killing Hope: U.S. Military and CIA Interventions Since World War II* (Monroe, ME: Common Courage Press, 1998), 283; Mark Metcalfe, "NATO Bombs the Great Man Made River," in *The Illegal War on Libya*, ed. Cynthia McKinney (Atlanta: Clarity Press, 2012), 56.

8   Ruth First, *Libya: The Elusive Revolution* (New York: Penguin Books, 1975); Paolo Sensini, *Sowing Chaos: Libya in the Wake of Humanitarian Intervention* (Atlanta: Clarity Press, 2016).

9   Interview with Jimmy and Joanne Moriarty, September 28, 2018; George Kaziolis, "A Criminal Silence Over the Libya Mess," *The Africa Report*, April 5, 2012; Wehrey, *The Burning Shores*, 26, 27.

10   Forte, *Slouching Towards Sirte*, 70; Leon Panetta, *Worthy Fights: A Memoir of Leadership in War and Peace* (New York: Penguin Press, 2014), 381.

11   Seymour Hersh, "Target Qaddafi," *New York Times Magazine*, February 22, 1987; Francis Boyle, *Destroying Libya and World Order: The Three-Decade U.S. Campaign to Terminate the Qaddafi Revolution* (Atlanta: Clarity Press, 2013), 73, 74; Nicholas Laham, *The American Bombing of Libya: A Study of the Force of Miscalculation in Reagan Foreign Policy* (Jefferson, NC: McFarland, 2008), 138. At the time, a special commission set up by the German government found "no indication that Libyans placed the bomb" and believed the explosives came from the Syrian embassy. After the fall of the Berlin Wall, prosecutors uncovered Stasi documents that implicated a Lebanese Stasi agent and his German wife and a Libyan agent who worked at the East Berlin embassy. The prosecution was unable to prove though that Colonel Qaddafi was behind the attack – a failure the court blamed on the "limited willingness" of the German and U.S. governments to share intelligence information. Qaddafi told Francis Boyle, a law professor who visited Libya: "who would have thought a superpower would come to a small country like Libya and bomb innocent people sleeping in their homes in the middle of the night?"

12   "Muammar Qaddafi's Speech to the UN General Assembly," In *The Illegal War on Libya*, ed. McKinney, 253-274.

13   Forte, *Slouching Towards Sirte*; Horace Campbell, *Global NATO and the Catastrophic Failure in Libya* (New York: Monthly Review Press, 2012); Peter Dale Scott, "American Power and the Decline of the Petrodollar System," *The*

Asia-Pacific Journal, Vol. 9, Issue 18, May 2, 2011; Sensini, *Sowing Chaos*; Jean Paul Pougala, "The Lies Behind the West's War on Libya," in *African Awakening: The Emerging Revolution*, ed. Firoze Manji and Sokari Ekine (Capetown: Pambazuka Press, 2012), 170, 171; "Libya Fact Sheet, 2011," ronridenour.com. Libya sat atop an ocean of water under the Nubian Sandstone Aquifer System (NSAS) capable of transforming solar power for European consumers.

14   See eg. Joan Polaschik, Charge D'Affaires, U.S. Embassy Tripoli, Department of State, https://wikileaks.org/plusd/cables/09TRIPOLI677_a.html

15   "Saif Qaddafi Speech, February 21, 2011," in email from Hillary Clinton to Oscar Flores, Wikileaks Hillary Clinton email archive, https://www.wikileaks.org/clinton-emails/emailid/24538.

16   Interview with Jimmy and Joanne Moriarty, September 28, 2018.

17   Campbell, *Global NATO and the Catastrophic Failure in Libya*; *The Illegal War in Libya*, ed. McKinney.

18   Interview with Jimmy and Joanne Moriarty, September 28, 2018; Dr. Christof Lehman, "Neocolonialism, Subversion in Africa and Global Conflict," in *The Illegal War on Libya*, ed. McKinney, 203; Mark Hosenball, "Exclusive: Obama Authorizes Secret Help for Libyan Rebels," *Reuters,* March 30, 2011; James Risen, Mark Mazetti and "Michael S. Schmidt, "U.S. Approved Arms" for Libya Rebels Fell Into Jihad's Hands," *New York Times*, December 5, 2012.

19   Mahmood Mamdani, "Libya: Behind the Politics of Humanitarian Intervention," in *African Awakening*, ed. Manji and Ekine 149, 150. CIA Deputy Director Michael Morrell wrote that it "was the policy of the U.S. government to be supportive of the goals of the rebels and we gave them considerable assistance – short of lethal arms." Michael Morrell, with Bill Harlow, *The Great War Of Our Times: The CIAs Fight Against Terrorism – From Al Qa'ida to ISIS* (New York: Twelve, 2015), 191.

20   "The President's Address to the Nation on Libya - As prepared for Delivery, National Defense University, March 28, 2011, hrod17@clintonemail.com > Sent: Monday, March 28, 2011 7:42 PM To: 'sullivanjj@state.gov,' Wikileaks, Hillary Clinton email archive, https://wikileaks.org/clinton-emails/emailid/5660

21   Charlie Savage, *Power Wars: Inside Obama's Post-9/11 Presidency* (Boston: Little Brown & Company, 2015), 636, 637.

22   Savage, *Power Wars*, 631, 638; Peter Hoekstra, *Architects of Disaster: The Destruction of Libya* (New York: The Calamo Press, 2015), 30.

23   Wehrey, *The Burning Shores*, 27; "Libya: June 1996 Killings at Abu Salim Prison," June 27, 2006; https://en.wikipedia.org/wiki/Abu_Salim_prison. The Wikipedia entry notes that human rights watch has been unable to verify the allegations that over 1,200 prisoners were massacred, basing their claim on an interview with an inmate who did not personally witness anyone killed, but

based his calculation on the number of meals he prepared while working in the prison's kitchen. See also Lindsey Hilsum, *Sandstorm* (New York: Penguin, 2012), based on interviews with family members, which corroborates that the estimated number of people killed is unknown and notes that Qaddafi's involvement has not been established. 24.

24   See Jeremy Kuzmarov, Charles Howlett and Roger Peace and Charles Howlett, "United States Participation in World War I," http://peacehistory-usfp.org/united-states-participation-in-world-war-one/

25   Paul Amar and Vijay Prashad, *Dispatches From the Arab Spring: Understanding the New Middle East* (Left Word Books, 2013); Hoekstra, *Architects of Disaster*, 73.

26   Marlise Simons, Neil McFarquhar, "Libya Officials Arrests Sought by Court in Hague," *New York Times*, May 4, 2011.

27   David Smith, "Gaddafi's Son Claims NATO Wants Deal with Libya," *The Guardian*, October 29, 2011; "Al Qathafi Family Not Afraid of UN Resolution, Seif al Islam Says, "*Tripolipost.com*, February 22, 2013; "U.S. Looks on Libya as McDonald's – Gaddafi's Son," *RT*, July 11, 2011.

28   Jo Becker and Scott Shane, "Hillary Clinton, 'Smart Power,' and a Dictator's Fall," *New York Times*, February 27, 2016; Panetta, *Worthy Fights*, 310.

29   Wehrey, *The Burning Shores*, 37, 39; Christopher S. Chivvis, *Toppling Qaddafi: Libya and the Limits of Liberal Intervention* (New York: Cambridge University Press, 2014), 51.

30   Forte, *Slouching Towards Sirte*; Sensini, *Sowing Chaos*; Wehrey, *The Burning Shores*, 53 Hilsum, *Sandstorm*, 34.

31   Charles Abugre, "Libya – the True Costs of War," in *African Awakening*, ed. Manji and Ekine, 298; Wehrey, *The Burning Shores*, 117.

32   John Barry, "America's Secret Libya War," *The Daily Beast*, August 30, 2011; quote taken from Frederic C. Wehry, "The Libyan Experience" in *Precision and Purpose: Air Power in the Libyan Civil War*, ed. Karl P. Mueller (Santa Monica: RAND Corporation, 2015), 50.

33   Barry, "America's Secret Libyan War;" Thom Shanker and Eric Schmitt, "Seeing Limits to 'New' Kind of War in Libya," *The New York Times*, January 10, 2011; Spencer Ackerman, "Libya: The Real U.S. Drone War," *Wired Magazine*, October 20, 2011.

34   Shanker and Schmitt, "Seeing Limits to 'New' Kind of War in Libya."

35   Forte, *Slouching Towards Sirte*, 32; Cynthia McKinney, "Anatomy of a Murder: How NATO Killed Qadaffi Family Members," in *The Illegal War on Libya*, ed. McKinney, 51; C.J. Chivers, "In Strikes on Libya by NATO, an Unspoken Civilian Toll," *New York Times*, December 17, 2011; "Libya Disabled Children's School Hit in NATO Strike," Email sent from Huma Abedin to Hillary Clinton, April 30, 2011, April 29, 2011, https://wikileaks.org/clinton-emails/emailid/28021.

36   Patrick Cockburn, *The Age of Jihad: Islamic State and the Great War for the Middle East* (London: Verso, 2016), 219.

37   Alan Kuperman, "Lessons from Libya: How Not to Intervene," *Harvard Kennedy School Quarterly Journal*, September 2013; Dan Kovalik, *The Plot to Attack Iran: How the CIA and the Deep State Have Conspired to Vilify Iran* (New York: Skyhorse Publishing, 2018), 19. Kaim told Kovalik this.

38   Mamdani, "Libya," in *African Awakening* Manji and Ekine, 153.

39   Wayne Madsen, "Dispatches From Tripoli," in *The Illegal War on Libya*, ed. McKinney, 35; Alex Newman, "Libyan Rebels create Central Bank, Oil Company," *The New American*, March 30, 2011; Peter Dale Scott, "Bosnia, Kosovo, and Now Libya: The Human Costs of Washington's Ongoing Collusion with Terrorists," *The Asia-Pacific Journal*, Vol. 9, Issue 31, August 2011; Washington's Blog and Wayne Madsen, *Unmasking ISIS: The Shocking Truth* (San Diego, CA: Progressive Press, 2016), 37, 38.

40   See Tarik Kafala, "'Cleansed' Libyan Town Spills Its Terrible Secrets," *BBC News*, December 12, 2011. One witness said even the birds fled.

41   "Scores Defect from Qaddafi's Army," *Al Jazeera*, May 30, 2011; Forte, *Slouching Towards Sirte.*

42   Forte, *Slouching Towards Sirte*; Wehrey, *The Burning Shores*, 63. Hilsum, *Sandstorm*, 34.

43   Ben Rhodes, *The World as it Is: A Memoir of the Obama White House* (New York: Random House, 2018), 159.

44   Forte, *Slouching Towards Sirte*, 82.

45   "Unacknowledged Deaths: Civilian Casualties in NATOs Air Campaign in Libya," *Human Rights Watch*, May 13, 2012, https://www.hrw.org/report/2012/05/13/unacknowledged-deaths/civilian-casualties-natos-air-campaign-libya.

46   Forte, *Slouching Towards Sirte*; *The Illegal War on Libya*; ed. McKinney. "Bosnia, Kosovo, and Now Libya;" Patrick Cockburn, "Lawlessness and Ruin in Libya," *Counterpunch*, September 5, 2013.

47   Garikai Chengu, "The Descent of Libya," *Counterpunch*, October 20, 2014; *Escape from Al-Qaeda: The True Story of Jimmy and Joanne Moriarty*, DVD, 2017.

48   Casey Quackenbush, "The Libyan Slave Trade Has Shocked the World: Here's What You Should Know," *Time Magazine*, December 1, 2017.; Kristof quoted in Brian Cloughley, "NATO's Destruction of Libya," *Counterpunch*, December 19, 2014.

49   Jo Becker and Scott Shane, "Hillary Clinton, 'Smart Power,' and a Dictators Fall," *New York Times*, February 27, 2016, A1; Wehrey, *The Burning Shores*, 147.

50   Becker and Shane, "Hillary Clinton, 'Smart Power,' and a Dictators Fall."

51   Wehrey, *The Burning Shores*, 32, 33; Jon Lee Anderson, "The Unraveling: In

a Failing State, an Anti-Islamist General Mounts a Divisive Campaign," *New Yorker Magazine*, February 23, 2015; Abdulkader Assad, "UN Panel of Experts Report Haftar's Son Took Central Bank of Libya's Money in Benghazi," *Libya Observer*, September 13, 2018. Hiftar's forces were also accused of posing for photos with enemy corpses. Later when he gained power, activists and journalists who opposed him were forced to flee the country or disappeared.

52   Wehrey, *The Burning Shores*, 180.

53   Washington's Blog and Madsen, *Unmasking ISIS*, 38.

54   Garikai Chengu, "Libya: From Africa's Wealthiest Democracy under Qaddafi to Terrorist Haven after U.S. Intervention," *Counterpunch,* October 20, 2015; "Abdel Hakim Belhaj to Receive UK Settlement – What About the Tawherga?;" Wehrey, *The Burning Shores*, 58, 59; Hoekstra, *Architects of Disaster*, 11, 77. Senator John McCain called Belhaj a "heroic freedom fighter."

55   See Robert Dreyfuss, *Devils Game: How the United States Helped to Unleash Fundamentalist Islam* (New York: Metropolitan Books, 2005).

56   "The Truth Perspective: Libya Ruined: Jimmy and JoAnne Moriarty Interview Sheikh Khaled Tantoush," *Sott Focus*, February 5, 2017.

57   Interview with Jimmy and Joanne Moriarty, September 2018.

58   Washington's Blog and Madsen, *Unmasking ISIS*, 102; Wehrey, *The Burning Shores*, 233; Hoekstra, *Architects of Destruction*, 90.

59   Jeremy Kuzmarov, "The New Merchants of Death*," Roar Magazine*, December 2016.

60   Kuzmarov, "The New Merchants of Death."

61   Kuzmarov, "The New Merchants of Death;" Fred Burton and Samuel N. Katz, *Under Fire: The Untold Story of The Attack in Benghazi* (New York: St. Martin's Press, 2013), 56.

62   Wehrey, *The Burning Shores*, 68, 72, 73, 87.

63   Tyler Rogeway, "Why the B-2 Stealth Bomber Was Used to Strike ISIS Camps in Libya," *War Zone*, January 19, 2017; "Obama's Covert Drone War in Numbers: Ten Times More Strikes Than Bush," *Bureau of Investigative Journalism*, January 17, 2017.

64   Hoekstra, *Architects of Disaster*.

65   Fred Burton and Samuel M. Katz, "40 Minutes in Benghazi," *Vanity Fair,* July 8, 2013; Jack Cashill, *"You Lie!" The Evasions, Omissions, Fabrications, Frauds. And Outright Falsehoods of Barack Obama* (New York: Broadside Books, 2014), 219, 220; Morrell, *The Great War of Our Time*, 206.

66   Cockburn, *The Age of Jihad,* 210.

67   See Nick Turse, *Tomorrow's Battlefield: US Proxy Wars and Secret Ops in Africa* (Chicago: Haymarket Books, 2015), *Mali, Events of 2015, Human Rights Watch*, https://www.hrw.org/world-report/2016/country-chapters/mali; "Mali Security Forces Disappear 20, Torture Others: Crackdown on People Linked to Countercoup, Journalists," *Human Rights Watch*, July 25,

2012. Revenge terror attacks on the Amenas gas plant in Algeria were carried out by Libyan war veteran Mokhtar Belmokhtar.

68   Jeffrey Goldberg, "The Obama Doctrine: The U.S. President Talks Through His Hardest Decisions About America's Role in the World," *The Atlantic Monthly*, April, 2016.

69   Interview with Moriarty's; Max Blumenthal, T*he Management of Savagery: How America's National Security State Fueled the Rise of Al Qaeda, ISIS and Donald Trump* (London: Verso, 2019), 156; Wehrey, *The Burning Shores*, 266, 272; Hoekstra, *Architects of Disaster*, 86, 87.

70   See David Nichols, *Eisenhower 1956: The President's Year of Crisis – Suez and the Brink of War* (New York: Simon & Schuster, 2012).

Chapter 5

ZEUS THE AVENGER
OBAMA, DRONE WARRIOR
AND ASSASSIN

On May 29, 2012, the *New York Times* ran a front cover story describing how every Tuesday, Obama convened a meeting of top national security advisers in the White House Situation Room, where they poured over mug shots and biographies of presumed terrorists that looked like they came from a "high school yearbook." One official termed them the "macabre baseball cards of unconventional war." With CIA Director John Brennan by his side, Obama gave the final assassination orders. Some were just teenagers like a young girl who looked "less than her seventeen years."[1]

Leaked email conversations between Hillary Clinton and her top aide Cheryl Mills, which reference a briefing by the State Department's press officer Harry Edward, specify that the *Times* article was not the product of a leak, but was rather a "White House press release" designed to portray Obama as a tough guy.[2] It included on the record quotes from top aides who said that Obama was a president who was "quite comfortable with the use of force on behalf of the United States" and that he had described his decision to kill an American cleric in Yemen, Anwar al-Awlaki, as "an easy one."[3]

Prior to publication of the article, there was worry that Obama had looked weak "standing by helplessly as thousands were massacred in Syria; being played by Iran in nuclear negotiations...[and] being treated with contempt by Vladimir Putin, who blocks any action on Syria or Iran and adds [a] personal insult by standing up [to] Obama at the G-8 and NATO summits." Mills told Clinton that the administration "thought that any political problem with foreign policy would be cured with the Osama bin Laden operation. But the administration's attempt to politically exploit the raid's one-year anniversary backfired, earning ridicule and condemnation for its crude appropriation of the heroic acts of others." Thus, Obama's handlers conceived of a new PR campaign, depicting the dear leader as a "steely and solitary drone warrior, dealing death with cool dispatch to the rest of the Al Qaeda depth chart," a new "Zeus the Avenger [marvel comic hero based on Greek God], smiting by lightning strike."[4]

The leaked emails confirm that Obama was a product of the public relations industry and reflect poorly on the character and mentality of a settler colonial society which valued a leader cast in the archetype of a comic book assassin coolly smiting the savage terrorists, reminiscent of Andrew Jackson and the frontier fighters of yesteryear. A February 2012 Washington Post-ABC poll found that eight in ten Americans (83 percent) approved Obama's use of drones. A whopping 59 percent strongly approved the practice—even though Defense Intelligence Agency (DIA) officials warned that drones create more terrorists than they kill. A CNN report found that less than two percent of drone fatalities were high value insurgent leaders.[5] The latter findings did not give Team Obama pause as their concern was with poll numbers and branding the president's image, rather than with ethics or national security.

War Stars: A Brief History of Drones

Obama's championing of drone strikes fits a long historical lineage. The country always excelled at technological development. Dime novels and science fiction stories long celebrated the archetype of the lone inventive genius whose wonder weapons save civilization from communist adversaries or alien hordes. Gen. George Patton wrote in his memoir that "the Americans as a race are the foremost mechanics in the world; America as a nation has the greatest ability for mass production of machines. It therefore behooves us to devise methods of war which exploit our inherent superiority."[6]

Pilotless planes "loaded with death" were first developed by inventor Elmer Sperry during the Great War and became operational in World War II when Joseph Kennedy Jr. was killed bailing out of one that caught fire before it was launched in a covert mission targeting Nazi missile sites. At the end of the conflict, Hap Arnold predicted that "the next war may be fought with airplanes with no men in them at all."[7] During the Vietnam War, the Air Force carried out over three thousand Unmanned Aerial Vehicle (UAV) surveillance missions which transmitted real time visuals used for bomb targeting to a moving jeep serving as a ground station. Some launched air-to-ground munitions including AGM-65 Maverick and Stubby Hobo TV-guided missiles along with 250- and 500-pound bombs, and in the case of the Navy's QH-50 hunter killer model, laser-guided rockets.[8]

After the Vietnam War ended, the U.S. government invested seven hundred million dollars in Remotely Piloted Vehicles (RPVs) which were valued for their ability to perform "high-risk and politically sensitive missions more practically and inexpensively than piloted aircraft."[9] Major Jack Clifton, coordinator of the army RPV program, stated that "we intend to use these birds as an integral part of our artillery.... We're trying to remove the individual as much as possible from the battlefield." He and others envisioned that war in the post-Vietnam era would become a "contest between machines—which do not bleed, die, get addicted to drugs, shoot their officers or refuse to fight," as Robert Barkan, a former Bell Telephone Laboratories engineer wrote in *The New Republic*, referencing the breakdown of the U.S. army in Vietnam. "A pilot flying an RPV bombing run from a swivel chair in an underground control center doesn't look out his cockpit window at the death and destruction below and wonder, 'Why am I doing this?' He doesn't watch the flak coming at him and swear that he'll never fly again. He feels no more compunction than the engineer who designed the machine."[10] The drone was thus the perfect vehicle for perpetuating the American imperial project in an era when a considerable portion of the public either no longer believed in its tenets or wanted to fight for it.

Imperfect Technology

The groundwork for the Global War on Terror was set in the 1990s Balkans Wars when RPVs provided eavesdropping and surveillance functions, probed Serb air defense, identified bombing targets, performed battle damage assessment, served as airborne communication relays and jammed Yugoslav communications.[11] The problematic nature of the technology was evident in the CIA's first drone strike in the War on Terror in February 2002 which killed three Afghans in Tarmek Farm near Kandahar (bin Laden's hideout). One of the victims was thought to be bin Laden since he was identified as a "tall man with a long robe." Later, it was admitted that it was not bin Laden. A Pentagon spokeswoman claimed the "target was [still] appropriate" but acknowledged that "we do not know exactly who it was." Reports later suggested the three individuals were local civilians collecting scrap metal.[12]

Obama's first drone strikes just three days after his inauguration on January 23, 2009, killed between eight and fifteen civilians in Waziristan, including three children and a tribal elder, and wounded a fourteen-year-old boy who lost his left eye and suffered a fractured skull.[13] According to the Bureau of Investigative Journalism, a non-profit organization that seeks to hold people in power accountable for their actions, Obama went on to launch 563 strikes during his presidency, ten times more than the Bush administration, which had launched 57 strikes in eight years. Over eleven hundred civilians were allegedly killed, six times more than the official government claim of sixty-four to one hundred and sixteen.[14] These figures do not include Afghanistan, which experienced over 1,000 drone attacks between 2008 and 2012 alone, along with 36,000 armed drone flights, an average of 25 per day.[15] An odd curiosity is that many of the "high value" targets identified by the U.S. government were reported killed several times over, raising questions about credibility.

Proponents of drone strikes claimed that they could precisely eliminate terrorist commanders operating in rugged terrain and that the U.S. could stop torturing suspected terrorists to get information since their commanders were already dead and thus reduce the number of casualties. Henry Crumpton, the deputy chief of CIA counter-terrorism programs, said weaponized drones were designed "to be as precise as possible to kill bin Laden.... Look at the firebombing of Dresden and compare what we are doing today; public expectations have been raised dramatically and that's good news."[16]

Nonetheless, many civilians were still being killed. In March 2011, two days after Obama paid $2.3 million to secure the release of a CIA contractor who murdered two Pakistani civilians, missile drones struck a bus depot in Datta Khel, North Waziristan, killing 42 civilians and injuring 14 more. A majority were tribal elders and government officials attending a Jirga, or community meeting designed to resolve local disputes. Witness Idris Farid, who suffered a severe leg injury and was left terrified of large noises, recalled that "everything was devastated. There were pieces—body pieces—lying around. Lots of flesh and blood." Afterwards, the shattered community "had to collect body pieces and bones and then bury them, doing their best to identify the pieces and the body parts so that the relatives at the funeral would be satisfied they had the right parts of the body and the right person."[17]

According to *New York Times* journalist David Rhode, who was held hostage in Northern Waziristan between November 2008 and June 2009, life for the local population under the threat of drones was "hell on earth." From the ground, he said, "it is impossible to determine who or what they are tracking as they circle overhead. The buzz of a distant propeller is a constant reminder of imminent death. Drones fire missiles that travel faster than the speed of sound. A drone's victim never hears the missile that kills him."[18]

The lack of precision was apparent in the large number of friendly fire deaths. In April 2011, a Marine Staff Sergeant, Jeremy Smith, 26, and Navy Corpsman, Benjamin Rast, 23, were killed near Sangin, Afghanistan while on their way to rescue Marines pinned down by Taliban gunfire. In June 2014, two drone strikes killed another five U.S. soldiers and one Afghan army officer in Zabul Province. Another drone killed Warren Weinstein, an American hostage on the Pakistani border. When shown a video image of the attack that killed his son, Jerry Smith of Arlington Texas said that all he could make out were blobs in dark shadows: "you couldn't even tell they were human beings," he said, "One-inch blobs."[19] No wonder that in one five month period, as many as 90 percent of drone victims were not the intended targets.[20]

White House Death Cult

Obama seemed to relish in his media-constructed image as Zeus the Avenger, telling aides that: "it turns out I'm really good at killing people."[21] He said he considered drones a "remarkable new tool" in fighting Al-Qaeda. They provided an alternative to military invasions which "lead us to be viewed as occupying armies, unleash a torrent of unintended consequences...result in large numbers of civilian casualties, and ultimately empower those who thrive on violent conflict."[22] In the same speech, Obama claimed that "acts of terrorism against Muslims [by terrorist organization the U.S. was targeting] dwarf[ed] any estimate of civilian casualties from drone strikes."[23] This assessment ignored that drones were found by the DIA to have provoked terrorist acts, and the fact that acts defined as terrorist may be considered by locals as acts of resistance against foreign imperialism and its domestic agents.[24]

Obama's presidency was unique in ushering in a new "death cult" in the White House. Past presidents delegated the act of assassination to the CIA and usually practiced a kind of plausible deniability.[25] The State Department's legal adviser Harold Koh, a critic of Bush's torture policies, was unsettled by the bloodless euphemisms the military used to talk about violent death, including reference to targeted killings as "kinetic strikes" and use of the names of provincial American cities as code for hunted militants. "Killer Koh" as he became known nevertheless developed a legal theory of "elongated imminence" to justify the strikes which he likened to "battered spouse syndrome" in which a wife was justified in attacking her husband if he had engaged in a pattern of beating her, even if the threat was not imminent.[26]

This logic sounded similar to Samantha Power's argument about a president needing to act if mass atrocities *might* be imminent. Both sought to justify pre-emptive military action under a human rights veneer, dispensing with the need to provide evidence before a higher body or court either before or after crimes were committed. Mary Ellen O'Connor, a professor of international law at Notre Dame, found that drone use was illegal beyond the battlefield, (meaning strikes in Pakistan, Yemen and Somalia were illegal). Students at New York University protested Koh's appointment as a visiting professor, accusing him of "crafting and defending what objectively amounts to an illegal and inhumane program of extrajudicial assassination and potential war crimes."[27]

Who Profited and Who Spoke Out?

The main beneficiaries of the inhumane program included companies like General Atomics, Northrop Grumman, and L-3 Communications, in which John Kerry owned $500,000 to one million dollars of stock when he had headed the Senate Foreign Relations committee.[28] The Crowns also profited as General Dynamics produced software, surveillance and sensor technologies to track and select targets and received contracts to provide training at the naval strike and air warfare center in Fallon, Nevada. Operating out of a gleaming new headquarters filled with avant-garde lobby art, bistro meals served on fine china, and an auditorium with upholstered seats equipped with their own lab-top clocking station, the company was a pioneer in naval drones, and the integration of ground combat vehicles with drone technology and launching of GPS-guided munition from Unmanned Aerial Vehicles (UAVs).[29]

Obama's chief of staff, Rahm Emmanuel, who was close with Lester Crown from his time as a fundraiser for Chicago Mayor Richard M. Daley, considered drone strikes important for insulating Obama from charges that he was weak on terror. According to colleagues, Emmanuel kept tabs on the hunt for terrorists "with an avidity that left even some CIA veterans uncomfortable."[30] John Brennan was given the nickname the "grim Irishman" after being entrusted with the task of selecting targets.[31] Dennis Blair, the Director of National Intelligence, was a lone internal dissenter, considering drones "dangerously seductive" as they gave off the "appearance of toughness" with "a low cost and no U.S. casualties" but were "unpopular in other countries," and could yield "long term damage to U.S. interests."[32] Blair was fired in May 2010.

CODEPINK, along with groups like Veterans for Peace and Voices for Creative Nonviolence, spearheaded grassroots efforts to educate the public on the horrors of drone warfare. They organized two Global Drone Summits in Washington, DC; wrote books, articles, and op eds; traveled around the country giving talks at universities, churches, and community centers; disrupted Congressional testimonies by drone czar John Brennan and John Kerry; organized die-ins at the CIA; and carried out acts of civil disobedience at drone bases. While increasing public opposition, the campaign never reached the scale of a mass movement because of the covert nature of Obama's drone killing, which made it harder to mobilize against.[33]

At the right moment, Obama would offer dose of black humor that helped normalize pathological activity as when he threatened to call in a drone strike at the 2010 correspondent's dinner on a teen pop idol, the Jonas Brothers, who expressed interest in dating his daughter.[34] Obama's graceful delivery ("boys don't get any ideas: two words for you: predator drone. You will never see it coming") can be compared with the crude demands of Hillary Clinton to incinerate Wikileaks founder Julian Assange by drone, and her giddiness over the lynching of Muammar Qaddafi, which made her appear to many as an evil witch.

Living under the Drones

Just a few hours before Obama delivered his drone joke, a Bridgeport, Connecticut man, Faisal Shahzad attempted to detonate a car bomb in New York City's Times Square. He stated that one of his main motivations was "the drone strikes in Somalia and Yemen and in Pakistan," which he said, "don't see children, they don't see anybody. They kill women, children, they kill everybody."[35] Obama claimed that before any strike was undertaken, the military took pains to ensure that no civilians would be killed or injured, though the CIA had a policy of considering all military age males as legitimate targets if they were part of a large gathering or had contacts with militants, unless there was intelligence proving otherwise. Thirty people were considered acceptable "collateral damage" on any single strike. Funeral-goers and rescuers were among the victims. Shazad Akhbar, a Pakistani lawyer representing drone victims, said he had a problem with the use of the term militant because those labeled as such "might be Taliban sympathizers but they are not involved in any criminal or terrorist acts.... All men [in certain areas] carry AK-47s and all believe in sharia law. This is part of their culture. Since when can we kill people because of their beliefs?"[36]

In March 2010, drone operators at Creech Air Force base in Las Vegas mistook a group of Afghans saying a morning prayer for Taliban and ordered their incineration, killing twenty-three people, including two toddlers, and severely wounding three more children. An army investigation found the crew's conduct to have been "almost juvenile in their desire to engage the targets," though it then blamed the special operations command for failing to supervise the operation.[37] This incident pointed to another major problem with the drone war, namely that the "pilots" were so far removed from the scene they could easily become trigger happy, as if they were playing a video game. Brandon Bryant likened flying a drone to "playing dungeons and dragons." He came to feel that he had become a dark alter ego of himself and that the dystopian science fiction classic *Ender's Game* about children whose violent simulated games turn out to be actual warfare, had frighteningly come to pass.[38]

Some morbid humor circulating in the Obama administration held that the CIA "sees three men doing jumping jacks" and "thinks it is a terrorist camp."[39] Hardly funny if we consider the human costs. A report by Stanford and NYU law professors called "Living Under Drones" quoted a charity director who stated that an entire region [Waziristan] was being terrorized by "the constant threat of death from the skies... kids are too terrified to go to school, adults are afraid to attend weddings, funerals, business meetings or anything that involves gathering in groups. [Many] wake up screaming in the middle of the night because they are hallucinating about drones."[40] Michael Kugelman of the Woodrow Wilson International Center for Scholars said that he frequently "heard Pakistanis speak about children in the tribal areas who became hysterical when they hear the characteristic buzz of a drone... Imagine the effect this has on psyches and particularly on young ones scarred by war and displacement."[41]

Targeting "Wild Men" Living in a "Wild Country"

A Pew Research poll found that only 17 percent of Pakistanis favored the drone strikes and that 94 percent believed it "killed too many innocents."[42] A lawyer in Yemen tweeted: "Dear Obama, when a drone missile kills a child in Yemen, the father will go to war with you guaranteed. Nothing to do with Al Qaeda." Mohammed Al-Ahmadi, the legal coordinator of a human rights group in Pakistan, further wrote that drones were "killing Al Qaeda's leaders but they are also turning them into heroes."[43]

As these comments suggest, Obama initiated a strategic catastrophe comparable to Richard Nixon and Henry Kissinger's massive carpet bombing of Cambodia in the early 1970s, which fueled the rise of a radicalized communist Khmer Rouge.[44] A senior U.S. military official called the drone operations a "recruiting windfall for the Pakistani Taliban" while Pakistan's major spy agency reported that "homegrown Islamist militants had overtaken the Indian army as the greatest threat to national security ... for the first time in 63 years."[45] Perhaps this was all by design and the U.S. aim was to destabilize and weaken Pakistan and prevent the development of an independent Waziristan.

Some of the air strikes were diverted by Pakistani intelligence against tribal Islamic groups in the northwest who long opposed governmental intrusions and attempts to control their resources. The same groups had been bombed in the 1920s by the British who considered airpower innovations "admirably suited" for use against these "wild men [living]" in a "wild country," a mentality continuously adopted by the U.S. in the 21st century.[46]

Killing a U.S. Citizen and His Son

The victims of the drone war included U.S. citizen, Anwar Al-Awlaki and his son Abdulrahman who were both killed in Yemen. Obama claimed that "when a U.S. citizen goes abroad to wage war against America…citizenship should no more serve as a shield than a sniper shooting down on an innocent crowd should be protected from a SWAT team. That's who Anwar Awlaki was—he was continuously trying to kill people."[47] This logic is problematic because al-Awlaki was a radical cleric who incited people to violent acts in response to other violent acts (U.S. wars in the Middle East) and, as another main justification for his killing, was accused of planning an attack on a Northwest airlines flight over Detroit in December 2009, which failed.[48] Police forces furthermore have to obtain a warrant from a judge before deploying a SWAT team and arresting someone, which Obama never did. The 5th amendment of the U.S. constitution requires due process for U.S. citizens accused of capital crimes, and conviction on the charge of treason requires at least two witnesses.[49]

After 9/11, al-Awlaki had ironically been depicted in *The New York Times* as part of a "new generation of Muslim leader[s] capable of merging East and West."[50] Radicalized by the wars in Afghanistan and Iraq, he began to give speeches that encouraged jihad and allegedly became an operational planner for Al Qaeda. Al-Awlaki was also found to have exchanged e-mails with Major Nidal Malik Hasan before he killed thirteen U.S. soldiers at Ft. Hood military base in Texas. Proof of al-Awlaki's guilt of criminal acts was never publicly established before his killing, and an FBI inquiry into al-Awlaki's communications with Hasan, who had worshipped at his mosque in suburban Virginia, was dropped.[51]

Al-Awlaki's father appealed to Obama to take his son off the kill-list and the American Civil Liberties Union (ACLU) filed a lawsuit challenging the government's authority to carry out targeted killings, but lost.[52] One September 30, 2011 after an earlier assassination attempt had failed, the CIA succeeded in blowing al-Awlaki apart by hellfire missiles, which also took out Samir Khan, a Pakistani-American propagandist whose killing was not approved by the Justice Department, but who was considered "acceptable collateral damage."[53] A month later, al-Awlaki's teenage son Abdulrahman was struck and killed by a drone strike while lunching with cousins. A letter justifying Anwar's killing by Attorney General Eric Holder evaded mention of Abdulrahman. Obama's former Press Secretary told a reporter that Abdulrahman should have had a "more responsible father."[54] This statement would not provide for a good line of defense at the International Criminal Court (ICC).

Making a Game of the Grim Work

Drone pilots dressed in green flight suits in a nod to military decorum. They worked out of the air-conditioned Creech Air Force base and sent their commands via transatlantic fiber optic cables to a satellite relay station in Ramstein, Germany, which bounced the signal to a satellite connecting the drones over the target regions. Video produced by a geo-locating device affixed to the drone was in turn routed back through Ramstein. The device operated as a fake cell phone tower that forced the mobile phones of targeted individuals to connect to it.[55]

Computer software providing "collateral damage" assessments helped to foster the illusion of surgical precision, which Brennan and Obama extolled. The "powerful machines that collected extraordinary amounts of data" gave operators a feeling of "god-like powers," as one put it. However, according to a drone sensor operator, pilots had little idea where the intelligence was coming from and the wrong people were often killed because of metadata errors, false tips and the switching of cell phones or SIM cards. Most of the targets were referred to as "selectors" and not by their actual name, contributing to a "dehumanizing of the people before you've even encountered the question of whether killing was legitimate or not." Successful strikes were referred to as "touchdowns" as the military developed baseball cards of jihadists and scorecards of those killed or captured in trying to make a game of the grim work they were doing.[56] This was all too reminiscent of the Vietnam War where soldiers competed for the highest kill-ratios and adopted slogans that captured the lost innocence of their youth. Operation Ranch Hand, for example, which sprayed Agent Orange, had as its slogan "Only We Can Prevent Forests," a play on Smokey the Bear.[57]

Predator drones represent the latest phase of American warfare, which has evolved from massive attacks on civilian populations, infrastructure and the environment rather than specifically military targets such as the firebombing of German and Japanese cities in World War II, the bombing of irrigation dams and napalm strikes during the Korean War, and the use of B-52's, chemical defoliants and cluster bombs in Indochina. But the focus has not been on a more human conduct of war, but rather is due to the fact that American leaders, like their counterparts such as Germany's Frederick the Great, had long dreamed about wars that could be fought by machines in order to save their own soldiers' lives.

The costs on the subject population played little part in their considerations, nor that the ease of killing by remote control would make the decision to go to war, or order the assassination of political rivals, too easy. UN Rapporteur Philip Alston warned about a "play-station mentality" where trigger-happy pilots, cut off from the human consequences of their work, think little about pressing the kill-button.[58] While some of the operators came to assume a heavy psychological burden, the trauma of those on the receiving end was far greater.[59] Only a few "cubicle warriors" have ever dissented against a mode of war which extends the tradition of colonial military technologies being designed to ensure the disproportionate killing of "natives" in an unfair fight.[60]

One strong critic of Obama's drone war was Fred Branfman, a long-time antiwar activist whose 1972 book *Voices from the Plain of Jars* provided an insightful analysis of the evils of modern automated warfare.[61] Branfman had been an International Voluntary Service (IVS) worker who taught agricultural principles in a southern Lao village. Lacking the paternalism and cold warrior mentality of many of his contemporaries, Branfman had integrated well into the culture, learned the Lao language and become particularly close to the village elder, Paw Thou Douang, whom he later discovered was the local representative of the communist Pathet Lao. After coming into contact with refugees in the north, he was shocked to hear their stories of seeing relatives burned and buried alive, their livestock killed, and their homes and pagodas demolished. Many had been bombed for five straight years, and survived by living in caves and holes, farming their fields at night.

Seeking to find out where the bombing was coming from, Branfman infiltrated the top-secret Nakhon Phanom Royal Thai base which housed giant super-computers in a heavily fortified underground bunker that received signals from electronic sensor and radar devices and were used to select the targets for bombing. The atmosphere inside, Branfman said, resembled a stock-market exchange, where self-confidant military officers ordered attacks on Laotian rice farmers without much second thought, never hearing the victims anguish, just like in today's drone war.[62]

"If the Nazi activities represented a kind of apex to an age of inhumanity, American atrocities in Laos are clearly of a different order," Branfman wrote. "Not so much inhuman as a-human. The people of Na Nga and Nong Sa were not the object of anyone's passion. They simply weren't considered. What is most striking about American bombing in Laos is the lack of animosity felt by the killers to their victims. Most of the Americans involved have little if any knowledge of Laos or its people. Those who do rather like them."[63]

Branfman's comments are sadly as apropos in the age of Obama as in that of LBJ and Nixon. The United States in the interim years has perfected a mode of war, which further distanced the perpetrators from the victims, and used the latest sanitized language to make it politically palatable. Most of the drone pilots and other military officers did not have anything against the peoples of Waziristan or other Middle Eastern countries—like the people of Laos—they were simply conditioned to consider them as terrorists and not to think about them. Because few American lives were directly affected, a large-scale resistance movement against the drone war never developed and the drone killings could go on and on. But the wars were not without painful impact on Americans, however unseen they might be. In the eight years of Obama's presidency, many innocent lives were shattered. Team Obama, however, was most concerned about burnishing the president's image as a tough guy and in fending off right wing attacks. In that perverse way, the drone war can be considered a success.

Endnotes

1   Jo Becker and Scott Shane, "Secret Kill Station Proves a Test of Obama's Principles and Will," *New York Times*, May 29, 2012.

2   Cheryl Mills to Hillary Clinton, "WP OP ED – Barack Obama: Drone Warrior," May 30, 2012, Wikileaks, Hillary Clinton Email Archive, http://www.wikileaks.org/clinton-emails/emailid/11539.

3   Becker and Shane, "Secret Kill Station Proves a Test of Obama's Principles and
        Will."
4   Mills to Clinton, "WP OP ED – Barack Obama: Drone Warrior," May 30, 2012,
        Wikileaks, Hillary Clinton Email Archive.
5   Chris Cillizza, "The American Public Loves Drones," *Washington Post*,
        February 6, 2013; Peter Bergen and Megan Braun, "Drone is Obama's Weapon
        of Choice," CNN, September 6, 2012; *Living Under Drones: Death, Injury
        and Trauma to Civilians From U.S. Drone Practices in Pakistan* (Stanford and
        NYU Law Schools, September, 2012), 31.
6   H. Bruce Franklin, *War Stars: The Superweapon in the American Imagination*
        (Amherst, MA: University of Massachusetts Press, 2007); George Patton, *War
        as I Knew It* (Boston: Houghton Mifflin, 1947).
7   Kenneth P. Werrell, *The Evolution of the Cruise Missile* (Maxwell, Air Force
        Base: Air University Press, 1985), 7, 36; Gordon Bruce, "Aerial Torpedo is
        Guided 100 Miles by Gyroscope," *New York Tribune*, October 20, 1915, 1;
        "The 36-Hour War: Arnold Report Hints at the Catastrophe of the Next Great
        Conflict," *Life Magazine*, November 19, 1945, 27.
8   Laurence R. "Nuke" Newcome, *Unmanned Aviation: A Brief History of
        Unmanned Aerial Vehicles* (Reston, VI: American Institute of Aeronautics and
        Astronomics, 2004), 83, 86-87; Kenneth P. Werrell, *Chasing the Silver Bullet:
        U.S. Air Force Weapons Development From Vietnam to Operation Desert
        Storm* (Washington, D.C.: Smithsonian Books, 2003), 33, 34.
9   "Status of the Remotely Piloted Aircraft Programs," Report to the Congress by
        the Comptroller General of the United States, February 18, 1977 (Washington,
        D.C.: U.S. G.P.O., 1977); *Cruise Missiles: Technology, Strategy, Politics*, ed.
        Richard K. Betts (Washington, D.C.: The Brookings Institute, 1981).
10   James W. Canan, *The Superwarriors: The Fantastic World of Pentagon
        Superweapons* (New York: Weybright ad Talley, 1975), 324, 326, 327.
11   Michael G. Vickers, "Revolution Deferred: Kosovo and the Transformation
        of War," in *War Over Kosovo: Politics and Strategy in a Global Age*, ed.
        Andrew Bacevich and Eliot A. Cohen (New York: Columbia University Press,
        2001), 195, 196; Richard Whittle, *Predator: The Secret Origins of the Drone
        Revolution* (New York: Henry Holt, 2014).
12   *Living Under Drones*, 10; Jane Mayer, "The Predator War," *New Yorker*,
        October 26, 2009.
13   *Living Under Drones*, 69-74.
14   "Obama's Covert Drone War in Numbers: Ten Times More Strikes than Bush,"
        Bureau of Investigative Journalism, January 17, 2017; *The Wikileaks Files: The
        World According to U.S. Empire*, ed. Julian Assange (London: Verso, 2015), 89.
15   "Afghanistan – Living Beneath the Drones," *Al Jazeera*, July 23, 2015.
16   Quoted in Scott Shane, "The Moral Case for Drones," *The New York Times*,
        July 15, 2012, SR4.

17   *Living Under Drones*, 58, 59; Mark Landler, *Alter Egos: Hillary Clinton,
      Barack Obama, and the Twilight Struggle Over American Power* (New York:
      Random House, 2016), 118. Administration spokesmen claimed the dead were
      insurgent leaders falsely as a detailed study by the Associated Press confirmed

18   Andrew Cockburn, *Kill Chain: The Rise of the High-Tech Assassins* (New
      York: Henry Holt, 2015).

19   Adam Taylor, "The U.S. Keeps Killing Americans in Drone Strikes, Mostly by
      Accident," *The Washington Post*, April 23, 2015; Lindsay Wise, "Confusion
      Blames in Drone Strikes Killing Two in Houston Unit," *Houston Chronicle*,
      October 15, 2011; Medea Benjamin, *Drone Warfare: Killing by Remote Control*
      (London: Verso, 2013), 28.

20   Andy Greenberg, "A Second Snowden Has Leaked a Mother Lode of Drone
      Docs," *Wired*, October 15, 2015.

21   Mark Halperin and John Heilemann, *Double Down: Game Change 2012* (New
      York: Penguin, 2013).

22   Mark Bowden, *The Finish: The Killing of Osama Bin Laden* (New York:
      Atlantic Monthly Press, 2012), 261, 262; President Barack Obama, Remarks
      by the President at the National Defense University, May 23, 2013,

23   President Barack Obama, Remarks by the President at the National Defense
      University, May 23, 2013.

24   Jane Mayer, "The Predator War," in *Drones and Targeted Killing: Legal, Moral,
      and Geopolitical Issues*, ed. Marjorie Cohn, with foreword by Bishop Desmond
      Tutu (Northampton, MA: Olive Branch Press, 2015), 71. The inclusion of
      Afghan drug lords raised concerns that members of Hamid Karzai's inner circle
      including his brother could wind up on the death list.

25   Tom Engelhardt, "Praying at the Church of St. Drone," *The Huffington Post*,
      June 5, 2012.

26   Dan Klaidman, *Kill or Capture: The War on Terror and the Soul of the Obama
      Presidency* (Boston: Houghton Mifflin, 2012), 201, 219, 220.

27   Charlie Savage, *Power Wars: Inside Obama's Post 9/11 Presidency* (Boston:
      Little Brown & Co., 2015), 244; Paul Starobin, "A Moral Flip Flop? Defining
      a War," *New York Times*, August 6, 2011; Mary Ellen O'Connell, "Drones
      Are Illegal Beyond the Battlefield," *New York Times*, April 24, 2015; Jeanne
      Mirer, "U.S. policy of Targeted Killing with Drones: Illegal at Any Speed,"
      in *Drones and Targeted Killing*, ed. Cohn, 135-154. William McGurn, a Bush
      speechwriter wrote: "Surely killing people is worse than waterboarding."

28   https://www.opensecrets.org/news/2010/11/several-federal-lawmakers-
      invested/

29   Dana Priest and William Arkin, *Top Secret America:* The Rise of the New
      American Security State (Boston: Little & Brown, Co., 2011), 110; "GD
      Awarded UAV Contract," Aviation Week, August 4, 2004; Valerie Insinna,
      "General Dynamics, AeroVironment join forces to give combat vehicles their

own drones," Defense News, October 9, 2018; Defense System Staff, "General Dynamics Demos Tactical UAV Strike Capability," *Defense System News*, November 1, 2012.

30   Klaidman, *Kill or Capture*, 121.

31   Landler, *Alter Egos*.

32   Becker and Shane, "Secret Kill Station Proves a Test of Obama's Principles and Will."

33   Charles Derber, *Welcome to the Revolution: Universalizing Resistance for Social Justice and Democracy in Perilous Times (New York: Routledge, August 2017)*.

34   Max Fisher, "Obama Finds Predator Drones Hilarious," *The Atlantic*, May 3, 2010; Mehdi Hassan, "US Drone Strikes Are No Laughing Matter, Mr. Obama," *The Guardian*, December 28, 2010.

35   Jon Schwarz, "D.C. Elite Hated Larry Wilmore's Drone Joke Last Night, But Loved Obama's in 2010," *The Intercept*, May 1, 2016.

36   Benjamin, *Drone Warfare*, 105, 106.

37   Cockburn, *Kill Chain*, 1-8: In at least one strike, children riding bikes rode into the line of the missile and were killed.

38   Matthew Power, "Confessions of a Drone Warrior," *GQ*, October 23, 2013. See also See Matt J. Martin with Charles Sasser, *Predator: The Remote Control Air War over Iraq and Afghanistan: A Pilot's Story* (Minneapolis, MN: Zenith Press, 2010).

39   Becker and Shane, "Secret Kill Station Proves a Test of Obama's Principles and Will."

40   *Living Under the Drones*, 84.

41   *The Civilian Impact of Drones: Unexamined Costs, Unanswered Questions* (New York: Columbia University Law School, Center for Civilians in Conflict, 2012).

42   *Living Under Drones*, 16.

43   *The Civilian Impact of Drones*, 23.

44   See Benedict Kiernan, *How Pol Pot Came to Power (*New Haven: Yale University Press, 1985).

45   Fred Branfman, "Beyond Madness: Obama's War on Terror Setting Nuclear Armed Pakistan on Fire," *Alternet*, November 3, 2010.

46   Ian Shaw and Majer Akhter, "The Dronification of State Violence," *Critical Asia Studies*," 46, 2 (April 2014), 211-234.

47   Richard Falk, "Why Drones are More Dangerous than Nuclear Weapons," In *Drones and Targeted Killing*, ed. Cohn, 35.

48   Scott Shane, "Inside Al Qaeda's Plot to Blow Up an American Airliner," *New York Times*, February 22, 2017. Communications between the FBI and "underwear bomber," Umar Farouk Abdulmutallab, who pleaded guilty, indicate Al-Awlaki was involved in the plot. These documents were released to

the New York Times in 2017 following a two-year legal battle after the filing of a Freedom of Information Act (FOIA) request.

49   Lloyd C. Gardner, *Killing Machine: The American Presidency in the Age of Drone Warfare* (New York: New Press, 2013), 163.

50   James Taranto, "'Moderate' Meets Maker: Anwar Awlaki Then and Now,*" The Wall Street Journal*, September 30, 2011.

51   David Johnston and Scott Shane, "U.S. Knew of Radical Suspect's Ties to Radical Cleric," *New York Times*, November 9, 2009; Gardner, *Killing Machine*, 168, 169.

52   Suzanne Ito, "ACLU Lens: American Citizen Anwar Al-Aulaqi Killed Without Judicial Process," *ACLU*, September 30, 2011.

53   Klaidman, *Kill or Capture*, 264; Benjamin, *Drone Warfare*, 86. Scott Shane, *Objective Troy: A Terrorist, a President, and the Rise of the Drone* (New York: Tim Duggan Books, 2015).

54   Jeremy Scahill, *The World is a Battlefield* (New York: The Nation Books, 2013), 1, 131-133, 306. Drone operators characterized an attempt to kill Anwar al-Awlaki as a "drive by shooting."

55   Jeremy Scahill, "The Heart of the Drone Maze," In Jeremy Scahill and the staff of the Intercept, *The Assassination Complex: Inside the Government's Secret Drone Warfare Program* (New York: Simon & Schuster, 2016), 70-82.

56   Shaw and Akhter, "The Dronification of State Violence," 226; Jeremy Scahill, "The Drone Papers," *The Intercept*, October 15, 2015; Scahill and the staff of the Intercept, *The Assassination Complex*, 93, 107; Power, "Confessions of a Drone Warrior."

57   See Michael Herr, *Dispatches* (New York: Vintage Books, 1977).

58   Benjamin, *Drone Warfare*, 86.

59   Sarah McCammon, "The Warfare May Be Remote but the Trauma is Real," *National Public Radio*, April 24, 2017.

60   Hugh Gusterson, "Towards an Anthropology of Drones: Remaking Space, Time and Valor in Combat," in *The American Way of Bombing: Changing Ethical and Legal Norms, From Flying Fortresses to Drones,* ed. Matthew Evangelista and Henry Shue (Ithaca: Cornell University Press, 2013), 201.

61   Fred Branfman, *Voices from the Plain of Jars: Life Under an Air War*, rev ed. With new introduction by Alfred W. McCoy (Madison: University of Wisconsin Press, 2013); Fred Branfman, "Beyond Madness: Obama's War on Terror Setting Nuclear Armed Pakistan on Fire," *Alternet*, November 3, 2010.

62   Interview with Fred Branfman, Tulsa, Oklahoma, March 5, 2014.

63   Fred Branfman, "The New Totalitarianism," *Liberation*, February-March-April, 1971, 1-2.

Chapter 6

OBAMA'S VIETNAM
THE SURGE INTO AFGHANISTAN
AND HIS WAR IN IRAQ

On June 30, 2009, President Obama dined in the White House with eight other leading presidential historians. The topic was Afghanistan and how Obama could best burnish his legacy. One of the historians at the table, Northwestern's Gary Wills, grew frustrated: "There has been no follow up on the first dinner and certainly no sign that he learned anything from it. The only thing achieved has been the silencing of the main point the dinner guests tried to make—the pursuit of war in Afghanistan would be for him what Vietnam was for Lyndon Johnson." Wills had told Obama that "a government so corrupt and tribal and drug based as Afghanistan could not be made stable." When Obama replied that "he was not naïve about the difficulties but he thought a realistic solution could be reached," Wills added, "I wanted to add when pigs fly but had to restrain myself."[1]

Obama allegedly came to the decision to send 30,000 more U.S. soldiers into Afghanistan, after an initial surge of 21,000, through methodical calculation, reaching a compromise between the military hawks who wanted an even greater escalation and "doves" like Vice President Joe Biden, who did not oppose the U.S. intervention but wanted a smaller troop increase (ten or fifteen thousand) and more air strikes and drone attacks. Aides told the media that Obama deliberated in solitary for 11 hours over the decision the day after Thanksgiving.[2] Seymour Hersh was told, however, that within three weeks of taking office, Obama informed his senior advisers at a secret National Security Council meeting of a plan to send additional American troops; it was a unilateral decision taken by Obama and his National Security Council adviser, James Jones.[3]

Obama's aggressiveness surprised some of the country's most seasoned diplomats. Careful use of language made it seem like American military actions were defensive and undertaken in collaboration with Afghan "partners." Obama further invoked the myth that the Iraq surge had stabilized the country and drew on a new counterinsurgency manual that was designed to sanitize the war for the public. Taking a page from the Reagan playbook, Obama shamelessly advanced a right-wing betrayal narrative that had falsely blamed antiwar activists for denigrating Vietnam War veterans. The Afghan War was in turn cast as a noble crusade in which America had the opportunity to right a historical wrong and provide the troops with the warm welcoming and hero status they always deserved. The Afghan people were mere sideshows in all this, even though they were the ones to suffer from the destruction of their country.

Into the Big Muddy

With the ominous specter of Vietnam hanging over the White House, Obama's staffers were asked to read Gordon Goldstone's book, *Lessons in Disaster,* on leadership failure in the Johnson White House. Obama, however, concluded that comparisons between Afghanistan and Vietnam reflected "a false reading of history."[4] As if drawing on the script of a Rambo movie, he averred America would win this time and treat its veterans honorably. Susan Rice said of the Obama team that "we just don't have the Vietnam hangover."[5] In short, they were not adverse to the use of force.

During the 2008 election campaign, Obama had told audiences that Afghanistan was the right war, blithely dismissing a 2007 admission by General Stanley McChrystal that there were less than 100 and *probably even less than 10 Al-Qaeda fighters in Afghanistan*. General David McKiernan told Vice President Biden on a pre-inauguration visit that we "haven't really seen an Arab here in a couple of years [reference to Al Qaeda].[6] The Taliban had also primarily given up, meaning the U.S. was engaged mostly in private feuds, arming corrupt warlords who fed intelligence designed to eliminate rivals.[7]

Seen in this context, the Obama troop surge, which cost the lives of 1,906 U.S. soldiers, hundreds of civilian contractors and countless Afghans, was complete and utter folly. Obama told the public that "for the Afghan people, the return to Taliban rule would condemn their country to brutal governance, international isolation, a paralyzed economy and the denial of basic human rights to the Afghan people, especially women and girls." Here was thus another war fought for humanitarian ends which Woodrow Wilson would have approved. Obama talked in another speech about confronting a "ruthless adversary that directly threatens the American people and our allies" and insinuated the U.S. was not actually fighting but "working with partners."[8] Ingeniously, Obama presented himself as both a hawk and a dove, mapping out an exit plan and giving a timetable for withdrawal while ordering the troop escalation. Buying into the trickery, few in Congress opposed the escalation. The *Washington Post* praised Obama for his realism, and the *New York Times* for "taking a good first step toward fixing the dangerous situation that former President George W. Bush created when he abandoned the necessary war in Afghanistan for the ill-conceived war of choice in Iraq."[9]

A Place to Fight

Afghanistan, however, may not have been either a necessary or a just war if we consider that it lacked basis in international law. The Taliban's connection to the 9/11 atrocities remain unclear. The 9/11 report identified Saudis as the main source of Al Qaeda financing, and the FBI at the time "merely believed the 9-11 plot came from Al Qaeda in Afghanistan," as Noam Chomsky wrote, though "plotting and financing also traced to Germany and the United Arab Emirates" as well as Pakistan. According to the official U.S. government position, most of the hijackers came from Saudi Arabia. For the war to have been justified as an act of self-defense as it concerned Afghanistan, it would have to be proven that the Taliban government sent the terrorists. Rather, for the first time, article 51 of the UN Charter was applied to a non-state entity. Disdaining bin Laden, who allegedly masterminded the 9/11 attacks, the Taliban agreed to a Russian brokered deal for his surrender, which the Bush administration scuttled. Taliban leader Mullah Omar at another point agreed to turn bin Laden over to a neutral Muslim country for trial but the Bush administration wanted his extradition to the U.S.[10]

Afghan opinion it appears was divided, with many urging other means than war to facilitate the overthrow of the oppressive Taliban. Opposition leader Abdul Haq said the bombing was a "major setback. The U.S. is trying to show its muscle, score a victory and scare everyone in the world. They don't care about the suffering of the Afghans or how many people we will lose."[11]

The first Prime Minister Hamid Karzai was selected by Western donors at an international conference in Bonn, Germany, and not by Afghans. South Vietnam's leader Ngo Dinh Diem was similarly imposed after sitting out the anti-colonial war against France. Whereas Karzai favored his own ethnic Pashtuns (he was of the Popalzai clan) and sought to diminish the influence of Farsi-speaking Persians, Diem favored Catholics and alienated the majority Buddhists. In both cases, Washington had a falling out with its client over their corruption, ineptitude and moves towards independence. Karzai stated in a December 2010 meeting with General David Petraeus and Ambassador Karl Eikenberry that if he had to choose sides again, he would "choose the Taliban."[12] The incoherence of U.S. policy in Afghanistan was exemplified by its pouring over $2 billion into Pakistan when a wing of its intelligence service financed the Taliban. But the latter's survival gave the U.S. under the rubric of NATO a reason for the ongoing occupation of Afghanistan that enabled them to gain an edge over rivals like Russia and China in competition for control of Central Asia and its oil and gas resources.[13]

As the war dragged on, Afghanistan came to serve like Vietnam as a testing ground for new weapons from which to "project [western] power and influence," as Professor Mark Herold put it, and fulfill Heart of Darkness fantasies. Jim Gant, a Special Forces officer fired for insubordination after going "native" in the attempt to win over tribal leaders, told his platoon mates: "we will never win in Afghanistan but know now and always—that does not matter. That's an irrelevant fact. It gives us a place to go and fight; it gives us a place to go and be warriors, that's it."[14]

Obama's surge eventually did give soldiers a reason to fight. By 2016, the Taliban was much stronger than in 2008, controlling at least a third of the country through shadow governments, resembling those South Vietnam's National Liberation Front (NLF) had also set up. Special Forces raids, bombing, drone attacks, and torture in secret prisons had alienated many Afghans who had a history of fighting foreign invaders since the time of Alexander the Great. Their history was similar to the Vietnamese who fought off the Chinese, Mongols, Japanese and French. In both wars, guerrilla forces used suicide bombing tactics, although the Taliban killed proportionately more civilians than the NLF. Extremist groups like ISIS seized on the chaos and brought in foreign jihadists. A popular proverb in Afghanistan noted that there were "no good men among the living, and no bad ones among the dead."[15]

Vietnam: We've All Been There

One great similarity with Vietnam was that high level policy-makers proceeded with war when they had deep private doubts about whether it could be successful. In a May 1964 conversation with Senator Richard Russell (D-GA), President

Lyndon B. Johnson referred to the situation in Vietnam as "about the biggest damn mess that I ever saw"—but then was more concerned that if he did not escalate the war, the Republicans would depict him as soft on communism and he would lose re-election.[16] A similar political calculation drove Obama who feared being depicted as "soft on terrorism."

General David Petraeus was among those to privately admit that the war in Afghanistan was unwinnable; one we'll be in "for the rest of our lives and probably our kids' lives." Diplomat Richard Holbrooke said the Obama administration's strategy "could not work."[17] Despite this prognosis, neither they nor anyone in the top circles of power had the courage to advocate removing U.S. troops, or resign their position and speak out against the war publicly. The same had been true of Defense Secretary Robert S. McNamara who testified in a 1984 deposition in Washington, D.C. that he had begun to believe that the Vietnam War was unwinnable shortly after the introduction of ground troops in 1965, though he had kept his concerns secret.[18]

The lack of democracy in Afghanistan was apparent on the eve of Obama's troop surge when Hamid Karzai captured an election marred by rampant voter fraud. An aide told a reporter: "Its' hard to say that we are sending your children off to fight and die for a guy who steals elections."[19] Similarly, in Vietnam the U.S. had either blocked or rigged elections to ensure the victory of its favored clients who "failed to win [their] own people" according to a high-ranking army officer, and "lacked a political base."[20]

Kai Eidie, a UN Special Representative to Afghanistan, became disillusioned because of the dominance of the military under Obama's leadership and Washington's propensity to make decisions without consulting the UN or even Afghan authorities who were mostly "spectators to the formation of strategy aimed at solving conflict in their own country." During a visit to Washington after the Obama administration had taken over, one of the senior ministers of Karzai's government sent him a text message with one word that said it all: "neocolonialism."[21]

In 2014 elections, Washington's favored candidate Ashraf

Ghani received only thirty percent of the vote. The one-time Vietnam dissenter John Kerry, now cast in the role of Dean Rusk, brokered a power-sharing arrangement with Abdullah Abdullah, who got 45% of the vote, and gave Ghani the reins of power after it was announced he had won a run-off whose results were never publicized. A Pashtun like Karzai, Ghani had spent years outside the country, leaving in 1977 for over two decades to pursue degrees at American universities and work at the World Bank. His Vice President Rashid Dostum was implicated in the suffocation of hundreds of Taliban prisoners in a ventilation container, burnings and drownings, the beating and rape of political opponents, and murder of his wife.[22] This rap sheet was even worse than American client leaders in Vietnam like Nguyen Cao Ky, a Hitler admirer once taken off a CIA mission in Laos for smuggling drugs.[23]

The frustration of U.S. soldiers fighting for a corrupt, quisling government manifested in ugly incidents like the desecration of dead Afghan fighters and the Quran, shooting rampages, and other criminal atrocities reminiscent of Vietnam.[24] *The Nation* reported that at least 434 civilians were killed by U.S.-NATO forces in the first three quarters of 2011 alone. Right after the surge, an air strike hit a tree grove and two buildings in the village of Granai in the Bala Baluk district of Farah Province, killing as many as 140 Afghan civilians.[25] U.S. Special Forces subsequently killed an Afghan police commander and his cousin and three female family members, two of whom were pregnant, in Gardez in Paktia Province, and then tried to cover it up.[26]

Commanding General Stanley McChrystal conceded: "We've shot an amazing number of people [in Afghanistan] and killed a number, and to my knowledge, none has proven to have been a real threat."[27] These comments echoed military commanders in Vietnam such as Colonel Oran K. Henderson who said that "every unit of brigade size has its My Lai [atrocity where U.S. soldiers killed 504 Vietnamese civilians] hidden someplace."[28] McChrystal sounded very much like Robert S. McNamara further when he acknowledged that "most of us, me included, had a very superficial understanding of the situation and history" and "frighteningly simplistic view of recent history, the last fifty years."[29]

A main beneficiary of Afghanistan's Vietnam-style quagmire was one of Obama's top campaign donors: the Crowns, whose firm supplied troops with wearable computers and radios, and provided combat vehicles, tanks and armored trucks resistant to roadside bombs. In Vietnam, President Johnson's top political donor, Brown & Root, made a fortune by building military bases and constructing the Tiger Cages that were used to keep inmates locked beneath the ground at Con Son prison. In both wars, Crown products cost U.S. soldiers' lives. In Vietnam, the TFX jet (later F-111), was called a "flying Edsel," while in Afghanistan, its Stryker combat vehicles were given the nickname "Kevlar coffin" because of serious design flaws that made its navigators sitting ducks for snipers.[30]

Savage Wars of Peace

Historian Francis Jennings wrote that "all war is cruel, horrible, and socially insane is easy to demonstrate, but the nationalist dwells upon destiny, glory, crusades and other such claptrap to pretend his own kind of war is different from and better than the horrors perpetrated by savages."[31] This maxim applies to the U.S. in Afghanistan which considered itself more civilized than the Taliban but relied on high-tech surveillance and drone technologies, jet bombers and rapid-fire artillery that resulted in barbaric local casualties. On Valentine's day, 2010, twelve civilians, ten of them women and children, were killed when their home in Marja was struck by a high mobility artillery rocket system (HIMARS) produced by Lockheed Martin. U.S. troops who came on the scene witnessed a young mother, with her two legs and arm blown off, crying out for her children before succumbing to her wounds.[32]

Equipped with GPS sensors and guidance systems, the HIMARS was supposed to be a low "collateral damage" weapon, which was true only on the practice range. It and other technological

170 OBAMA'S UNENDING WARS

innovations of its kind could not overcome poor intelligence gathering based on metadata acquired from computers and cellphones, poor communication, and a lack of cultural awareness.[33] Air Force technicians undertook painstaking mathematical calculations of targeted regions in the attempt to mitigate collateral damage; however, there were repeated mistakes such as the Marja incident and bombing of a "Doctors Without Borders" clinic in Kunduz at the end of Obama's presidency which resulted in the deaths of over a dozen civilians.[34]

In the town of Garloch in the Eastern Province of Laghman, American helicopter gunships which generated "cold sweats and prayers" among the locals, killed two hundred sheep, resulting in the loss of livelihood among herdsmen who deposited the carcasses in front of the Governor's house in protest. In Vietnam, it had been the buffalo that were struck. U.S. soldiers came back to massacre a family in Garloch after shooting their dog while on pre-dawn patrol. They then dragged the bodies into a house and set off explosives, killing all eyewitnesses. U.S. officials announced the dead were mostly militants, as they repeatedly did in Vietnam, but villagers showed a journalist the photos of lifeless women and old men. The protest upon the Governor's house was now larger and Obama was burned in effigy. After the U.S. army agreed to pay $2,000 in compensation to each family, Malek Herkat told journalist Anand Gopal: "That's what our lives are worth to you Americans—two thousand dollars? You want to kill us and then pay us to keep quiet?" An old man nearby leaned forward and shouted: "My daughter is buried in the ground! You can give me every dollar on Earth, but I won't touch it. It won't bring her back."[35]

Another Bright Shining Lie

In 2016, Obama was forced to backtrack on his pledge for withdrawal and retained an extra three thousand U.S. troops because the claims about progress were all an illusion. Afghanistan at the time sat on the bottom of the world corruption indexes, with two-thirds of its population suffering from mental illness. A Special Forces captain dismissed for beating a militia commander who had taken boys as sex-slaves told the *New York Times*, "we are here because we heard the terrible things the Taliban were doing to people... But we were putting people into power who would do things that were worse than the Taliban did."[36] If bin Laden's goal in plotting 9/11, assuming he was the culprit, was to facilitate America's imperial decline by drawing it into an endless war, then sadly he had gotten what he wanted. And Obama, the supposed real-politick grandmaster, had played right into his hand.

Bowe Bergdahl was a soldier from Sun Valley, Idaho who was taken prisoner after deserting his unit. A filmmaker captured a conversation between him and another soldier, who stated that the Afghans "had gotten dicked by the Russians for 17 years and now we're here." Before his desertion, Bergdahl wrote to his parents that he went overseas "to help Afghan villagers rebuild their lives and learn to defend themselves," but what he found was "the most conceited country in the world telling the [Afghans] that they are nothing and that they are stupid . . . we make fun of them in front of their faces and laugh at them for not understanding that we are insulting them."[37]

Afghan war vet Spenser Rapone wore a Che Guevara t-shirt to his West Point graduation and revealed a hand-scrawled message which read: "Communism will win." Rapone said that in Afghanistan it felt like "we were the big bully and purveyor of violence using expensive equipment in one of the poorest places on earth to serve the interests of the capitalist class." He added that in his unit he "saw no commitment to learning about the Afghan people or trying to understand them or their culture. It was more about taking pleasure in going out every night and killing people with impunity. We were going into [people's] homes and threatening their villages and were creating nothing but chaos and destruction."[38]

These comments were reminiscent of the Vietnam War, where U.S. soldiers with a conscience came to perceive the war as fundamentally unjust. A main difference now was the absence of the draft, a different kind of enemy, and employment of thousands of private military contractors who were in it solely for the money. Many murdered non-combatant Afghans with total impunity. In March 2012, when the U.S. had 88,000 soldiers deployed in Afghanistan, the Pentagon had 117,227 contractors, only a third of whom were American. Besides guarding convoys, they performed menial work for abysmally low pay, cleaning the bases and cooking food for soldiers. This enabled the Obama administration to cut costs and keep troop levels down, hence undercutting dissent.[39]

As social conditions in Afghanistan deteriorated, lying remained a cottage industry in Washington. Phantom figures were adopted even for the number of Afghan girls going to school.[40] British ambassador Sherrod Cowper-Cowley said that many people had become disillusioned about the war, it was "all one bright shining lie."[41] This was the same phrase uttered by John Paul Vann, the director of pacification in Vietnam and title of one of the epic books about the war by Neil Sheehan.[42]

The Myth of the Successful Surge in Iraq

Obama's surge was based on several great myths including that of the Iraq War surge that had been crafted by General David Petraeus and his publicists. When things began to go sour in Iraq starting in 2004, the Bush administration and its neoconservative backers had been forced to concede a series of mistakes but still cast Petraeus, a veteran of the U.S. dirty war in El Salvador, as a knight in shining armor. According to their narrative, the U.S. troop increase in 2006/7, combined with Petraeus' ability to cultivate alliances with Sunni leaders, turned the tide in the Iraq War and reduced the sectarian violence. The country became more stable and the U.S. could gradually prepare its exit.

The problem with this story is that it was not true. The troop surge policy resulted in a five-fold increase in air and gunship strikes and artillery in urban areas and more assassination and night raids by Special Forces. Sectarian violence began to die down only after General Petraeus paid off Sunni tribal groups exhausted by the fighting. These groups had developed a disdain for Al Qaeda, a militant Sunni organization which had come into Iraq only after the Bush invasion and turned against local Sunni leaders, carrying out terrorist bombings that took too many innocent lives such as the bombing of the al-Askari shrine, a Shia holy place. Journalists Michael Weiss and Hassan Hassan note that "the Sunni tribes didn't have to be persuaded that hunting AGI [Al Qaeda] was in their interest – they were already doing so more bravely and ably than most of the Iraqi army."[43]

The Sunni who fought Al Qaeda later felt that they had been abandoned by their government and the Americans. Having "killed its way into power," the Shiite- dominated Nouri al-Maliki government detained thousands unlawfully, prompting thousands to march in Arab Spring demonstrations, which state security forces armed by Obama crushed. Nationalist Shia cleric Muqtada al-Sadr, who had led his Mahdi army against U.S. forces, characterized the country under al-Maliki as a prison "run by wolves.... blinded with wealth, houses, palaces, and aeroplanes.... who shut out the voices [of the people], kill the opposition, force them into exile, and fill prisons with them, and with everyone who resisted and tried to free his country from the tanks and aeroplanes of the occupation."[44]

These comments belie the triumphalist narrative about the surge promoted by Petraeus and then by Obama to support his own troop surge in Afghanistan. Sectarian violence had only been reduced temporarily because of internal political factors and Iraq had never been stabilized. George W. Bush was such a hated figure that during his final news conference, an Iraqi journalist, Muntadhar al-Zaidi, threw his shoe at him on behalf of "the widows, the orphans and those who were killed in Iraq."[45] Al-Zaidi in turn became a national hero. A poll found that 90 percent of young Iraqis considered the United States as an "enemy" of their country.[46]

The Myth of Successful Counterinsurgency

Counterinsurgency in Iraq met with no greater success than had the troop surge. In 2007, with chaos mounting in Iraq, President Bush called on Petraeus to bring back counterinsurgency from the ashes of Vietnam. As head of the army's command and staff college in Fort Leavenworth, Petraeus had directed the writing of the U.S. Army/Marine Counterinsurgency [COIN] Field Manual (FM 3-24), which came to hold a spot in Amazon's Top 100 list. It announced the arrival of an age of "internal" or "irregular wars" in which success would not be determined by military might alone but instead by winning the hearts and minds of the people. To achieve this, COIN had to focus on the needs and interests of the civilian population by providing effective security and other services like electricity, irrigation, health care, schooling and roads. Counterinsurgency forces role was to "protect the people" from terrorists and function as "goodwill ambassadors."[47]

This kind of rhetoric was perfect for the age of humanitarian intervention, which helped advance the illusion that American diplomacy was purer morally than that of previous invaders—the Russians, British, Mongols and Greeks. With Petraeus appointed by Obama to command U.S. forces, counterinsurgency became the guiding doctrine of war, and unofficial state religion of the U.S. military. In a nod to Obama's late mother, funding was increased for human terrain teams, which embedded anthropologists and social scientists with ground troops to help them understand Afghanistan's tribal culture. The smart cards they issued, however, were often superficial.[48] Humanitarian aid programs were considered as fronts for intelligence operations. The COIN manual further rationalized paramilitary police operations, drone strikes and the assassination of insurgent leaders who did not respond to American goodwill overtures. General McChrystal, who headed these operations, was chillingly described by a senior Defense intelligence Agency (DIA) official as an "expert killer."[49] He held much in common with Edward G. Lansdale, a COIN guru of the Cold War era who was known for macabre tactics in the Philippines and Vietnam such as the vampire trick in which his country team would capture a guerrilla commander, drain his body of blood and then string him up on a hook in the town village as an act of intimidation.[50]

Historian Hannah Gurman points out that the contradictions

of COIN played out in the much-publicized counterinsurgency campaigns in Marjah and Kandahar in southern Afghanistan in 2010, which had been advertised as models of "population-centric" or people-centered COIN. These, however, produced only limited security gains but a wide range of grievances resulting from the razing of villages and displacement of thousands of people, including an estimated 3,461 families around Marjah.[51]

Playing the Vietnam Card

To legitimate a permanent war footing in Afghanistan, Obama even resorted to the myth of the spat-upon Vietnam veteran. In his 2012 Memorial Day speech, delivered in front of the Vietnam Memorial Wall with Vietnam veteran Chuck Hagel at his side, Obama vowed that veterans of the wars in Iraq and Afghanistan would not be denigrated like Vietnam veterans allegedly were, but would be warmly welcomed on their homecoming. The main lesson learned from that war, he averred, was the need to treat veterans better. Referring to the Vietnam vets, Obama said:

> You were often blamed for a war you didn't start, when you should have been commended for serving your country with valor. You were sometimes blamed for misdeeds of a few, when the honorable service of the many should have been praised. You came home and sometimes were denigrated, when you should have been celebrated. It was a national shame, a disgrace that should have never happened.[52]

But in fact, as sociologist Jerry Lembcke has shown, returning Vietnam veterans were never actually denigrated or spat upon when they returned home. This myth had long been advanced to malign antiwar activists who were accused of it to displace memory of political activism by antiwar GIs.[53] Barack Obama's sense of the myths power may have come from Jonathan Favreau, the head of his speechwriting department because Favreau had read Lembcke's book *The Spitting Image: Myth, Memory and the Legacy of Vietnam* in a class he took from Lembcke at Holy Cross University.[54] If that's the case, then Favreau had disingenuously appropriated the myth to advance Barack Obama's agenda and to help sell yet more war.

Besides the heavily reliance on subcontractors and drones, the absence of an antiwar movement had much to do with the crafty rhetoric and personality of the commander-in-chief, whose speeches conveyed eternal American confidence about defeating "barbaric terrorist groups," notably the Taliban and ISIS, which emerged in Afghanistan at the end of Obama's tenure, and the need to stand up for veterans. In one speech given before the Disabled Veterans of America, Obama said he was "tired of some folks trash-talking America's military and troops."[55] This was a veiled jab at the antiwar movement that drew upon the myth of the spat upon Vietnam veteran and helped reinforce the equation of antiwar activism with treason. A Bush or a Trump might directly attack antiwar activists, but Obama's subtler approach was more effective, especially since it came from a Nobel Prize winner.

"So Full of Lies": Operation Geronimo and the Killing of Bin Laden

On the night of May 1, 2011, Obama gave a carefully choreographed speech announcing the crowning achievement of his presidency: the killing of Osama bin Laden. Speaking with his usual poise, Obama threw a bone to American liberals by emphasizing that the U. S. was not engaged in a war against Islam while exciting gung-ho patriots with his description of a daring raid by Navy seals based on secret intelligence that resulted in bin Laden's killing in a firefight.[56]

According to journalist Seymour Hersh, Obama's version of the bin Laden killing was so full of lies, misstatement and betrayals that it might have been written by Lewis Carroll, the author of *Alice in Wonderland*. Rather than being a unilateral operation, Hersh found that the raid led by Navy Seal Team 6 was an assassination mission carried out with Pakistani intelligence, which had tipped off the United States about bin Laden's whereabouts rather than his location having been revealed through interrogation of Al Qaeda operatives. Any attempt to uncover the full truth was prevented by the dumping bin Laden's remains at sea.[57] Bin Laden's body was purportedly identified through facial recognition software which was 90-95 percent accurate and DNA testing, although the failure to engage independent witnesses for verification, or release photos or evidence of his death and the swift disposal of his body left some still convinced that bin Laden had died years earlier from renal failure, for which he was already receiving dialysis.[58]

MIT linguist Noam Chomsky was disturbed by the naming of the assassination mission after the Apache chief Geronimo. He wrote that "the imperial mentality [was] so profound... no one can perceive that they are glorifying bin Laden by identifying him with courageous resistance against genocidal invaders. It's like naming our murder weapons after victims of our crimes: Apache, Tomahawk... It's as if the Luftwaffe were to call its fighter planes 'Jew' and 'Gypsy.'"[59] Those who celebrated bin Laden's killing by implication had not much evolved from their frontier forebearers who cheered the exploits of Indian killers like Andrew Jackson when they avenged the death of white settlers.

"The Least Transparent War in Recent American History": Iraq War Redux

Late in the night of September 20, 2015, Basim Razzo, a fifty-six-year-old account manager at a Chinese telecommunications company and descendent of one of Mosul's grand old families, went to sleep at his home on the eastern side of the city. He soon awoke to find himself drenched in blood, lying in rubble, and staring up at the sky as his roof had been blown off. Rushed to the hospital, he was given the devastating news that his wife Mayad and 21-year old daughter Tuqa had been killed, along with his brother and eighteen-year-old nephew who lived next door. Later the same day, the American-led coalition fighting the Islamic State released a video purporting to show an attack on a car bomb factory—in actuality, Basim and his brothers' homes. This clip was one of hundreds that were released to present evidence of a precise and transparent military campaign against ISIS, which was far more messy in reality. In a study for the *New York Times Magazine*, journalists Azmat Khan and Anand Gopal determined that one in five of the 27,500 coalition air strikes over Iraq had resulted in at least one civilian death, more than 31 times that acknowledged by the coalition. The second war in Iraq, the authors noted, "may be the least transparent war in recent American history."[60]

Obama had opposed the 2003 Iraq War in an attempt to burnish his "peace and change" image. Post election, Senator Obama voted for $300 billion in war appropriations and accepted six donations from disgraced Electricity Minister Aiham Alsammarae, who granted a $150 million contract to Tony Rezko's company to build a power plant in Kurdistan and stole from the Coalition Provisional Authority (CPA). During the 2008 election, presidential candidate Obama pledged to withdraw U.S. troops, though subsequently negotiated to try and extend their stay past the date of withdrawal specified in the status of forces agreement signed by President Bush.[61] After the negotiations failed and U.S. troops were formally withdrawn, Obama maintained over 11,000 private contractors and civilian advisers who continued military and police training operations in Iraq.[62] Many worked out of the gargantuan embassy in Baghdad which took up 104 acres of land and was roughly the size of the Vatican. They helped administer over $1 billion in security assistance in 2012 and broker the estimated 510 arms deals between U.S. defense contractors and the Nouri-al-Maliki government worth nearly $11 billion.[63]

Obama delegated most major decisions on Iraq to Joe Biden, who had voted for Bush's military invasion and penned a 2006 op ed with colonialist undertones calling for the country's break up into distinct Sunni, Shia and Kurdish federations.[64] During the 2010 election, Iraq's Accountability and Justice Commission—the sequel bureaucracy to the CPAs de-Baathification commission—banned more than five hundred candidates running for parliament because of links to the Baath Party.[65] Chris Hill, the new U.S. ambassador, told General Ray Odierno that Iraq wasn't ready for democracy and needed a Shia strongman, a position Obama acquiesced to even though only 14 percent of Iraqis felt that al-Maliki, the winner of the flawed election, should stay in power.[66]

In a November 2013 White House speech, Obama expressed appreciation for Al-Maliki's commitment to "ensuring a strong, prosperous, inclusive and democratic Iraq."[67] Residents of Fallujah and other cities at the time had already began launching Arab-Spring style protests aimed at bringing down the "Shia-Saddam" as locals called al-Maliki.[68] Journalist Patrick Cockburn wrote that the lack of concessions by al-Maliki and massacre at a peace camp at Hawijah in April 2013, which was stormed by the Iraqi army and resulted in the deaths of over fifty protestors, "transmuted peaceful protest into armed resistance."[69] Biden and John Kerry now tried to gently push al-Maliki out of power in favor of Haidar Al-Abadi.[70] An underlying motive was al-Maliki's friendliness with Syrian leader Bashir al-Assad, and support for a pipeline running from Iran to Syria through Iraq. Al-Abadi furthermore was committed to privatizing Iraq's economy in line with the original goals of the 2003 U.S. military invasion.[71]

Brad Sherman (D-CA), a ranking member of the House Terrorism, Nonproliferation, and Trade, told the House Committee on Foreign Affairs that "Maliki is not a good guy just because we installed him. His approach to governing is as responsible as any other factor for the emergence of the [Sunni-led] Islamic State of Iraq and the Levant."[72] By mid-2014, ISIS had seized control of Fallujah, Tikrit (Saddam's hometown) and Mosul, and expanded into Syria. It was led by former Baathist military officers tortured in U.S.-run facilities like Camp Bucca, Al Qaeda remnants who entered Iraq after the Bush administration's invasion, and foreign fighters, some of whose careers dated back to the anti-Soviet mujahidin in the 1980s. Apostates, including Yazdi Christians, were forced to flee or were killed and Shia mosques and Christian churches, including the 1600-year-old Mar Benham monastery which had been built by the Assyrian King Senchareb, were destroyed.[73]

Jessica T. Mathews, president of the Carnegie Endowment for International Peace, characterized the Islamic State as a "melange of Sunni militant groups" that had forged a broad insurgency against the al-Maliki government. ISIS included the Military Council of the Tribes of Iraq, which comprised as many as 80 tribes and Army of the Men of the Naqshbandi Order, an organization founded by Saddam's former Vice President Izzat Ibrahim al-Douri, which claimed to have Shiite and Kurdish members and included many Sunni Baathists once loyal to Saddam.[74]

Per her analysis, the problem at the core was that the U.S. invasion of Iraq had intensified the country's sectarian divisions and helped to reverse power relations from the Saddam era in favor of the Shia whom the U.S. was continuously supporting. U.S. intelligence agencies actually referred to the war as a "Sunni-Shia fight." The Iraq Army carried Shiite flags, which was evidence of its sectarian allegiance.[75]

In June 2014, Obama ordered thousands of U.S. troops back to Iraq without seeking authorization from Congress, and began initiating thousands of air strikes that killed hundreds of civilians.[76] The troops were equipped for combat, though Obama said they would only serve in an advisory capacity. Part of the motive was to protect the Kurdish capital of Erbil, an oil-rush town that had been opened up to Exxon-Mobil and Chevron. Kurdistan was thought capable of selling oil to Europe, hence undermining Russia.[77]

Army Captain Nathan Smith sued Obama, challenging his legal authority to conduct military operations against the Islamic State, which exceeded his commander in chief authority since Congress had never been consulted. Obama claimed he did not need authorization because ISIS was Al-Qaeda, against whom the U.S. had already declared war, though actually the two were not one and the same.[78] After the death of Staff Sergeant Louis F. Cardin, an artillery specialist who was hit by an ISIS fired rocket at an American fire base in April 2016 in Makhmour, Obama was forced to concede that American forces were engaged in combat rather than just in an advisory role.[79]

Obama was playing a delicate balancing act in trying to avoid re-emergence of the antiwar movement while placating neoconservatives who accused him of having "lost Iraq" by having left too soon. Obama showed Wilson-type skill in camouflaging what was essentially a renewed war of aggression by claiming that Iraqis had "reached out for our help" and that military intervention was conditioned on "our work to help in the emergence of a new Iraqi government committed to national unity."[80] More realistically, the U.S. was committed to altering Iraq's foreign investment laws in a manner that benefitted U.S. oil companies, and to securing access to military bases. Its foreign presence furthermore was doing much more to enflame rather than quell sectarian divisions.[81]

In December 2015, *USA Today* reported the incineration of a family's vehicle at a checkpoint in Al-Hatra in northern Iraq by A-10 Warthog planes, resulting in the deaths of three women and two children who were misidentified as potential ISIS supporters. An army investigation acknowledged, in heavily sanitized language, that "the NCV [Non-Combat Victims] = 0 objective was not met."[82] Chris Woods, the director of Project Air War noted that the military had come to "believe their own myth of absolute precision," which he said "lulls Western audiences into feeling more comfortable with our countries being at war because we think we don't kill civilians anymore. I'm afraid the reality is far from that."[83]

In the campaign to retake Mosul, residents were subjected to "relentless and unlawful attacks by Iraqi government forces and members of the U.S.-led coalition," according to Amnesty International, which killed an estimated 5,805 civilians. Over 400 died from rocket assisted munitions and the use of powerful explosive weapons which caused blast-related injuries.[84] The

New York Times described a "panorama of destruction in the neighborhood of Judida so vast one resident compared the destruction to that of Hiroshima, Japan. There was a charred arm, wrapped in a piece of red fabric poking from the rubble, rescue workers in red jumpsuits who came wore face masks to avoid the stench, some with rifles slung over their shoulders, searching the wreckage for bodies."[85]

An Obama administration spokesman had told the media that their decision to bomb Iraq was shaped by "Rwanda and other times when we did not act."[86] This analysis was part of Petraeus' "perception management" designed to package war as humanitarian. It was based on disinformation about the American role in Rwanda and masked the ongoing geopolitical imperatives driving U.S. intervention. But the U.S. did not get its way. In May 2018, a political bloc led by Muqtada al-Sadr, a firebrand Shia cleric who once led the Mahdi Army that had fought against American occupation forces and was tied with Iran, won parliamentary elections. Oil exploration contracts were granted in that year to China and UAE but not to American companies.[87] Though ISIS was eventually driven out, Europe and the U.S. became more susceptible to terrorist attacks. British IS fighter Abu Uthman warned author Charles Lister before Uthman's death that when the U.S. "sends their troops from around the world to fight my brothers, then don't be surprised when they retaliate back in their lands. If someone slaps you across the face for hours, would you just stand there and let it happen?"[88] Another ISIS leader remarked that "the only solution to avoid war with the mujahidin is by lifting your hands from their areas completely... and desist from plundering the wealth of Muslims."[89] The Obamians were not capable of doing so, nor is any other group of Western leaders in this age.

Endnotes

1   Gary Wills, "Obama's Legacy: Afghanistan," *New York Review of Books*, July 27, 2010; Oliver Stone and Peter Kuznick, *The Untold History of the United States* (New York: Hyperion, 2012), 570.

2   Peter Baker, "How Obama Came to Plan for 'Surge' in Afghanistan," *New York Times*, December 5, 2009.

3   Seymour Hersh, *The Killing of Osama Bin Laden* (London: Verso, 2016), 4.

4   Marvin Kalb, "The Other War Haunting Obama," *The New York Times*, October 8, 2011.

5   Rice in James Mann, *The Obamians: The Struggle Inside the White House to Redefine American Power* (New York: Viking, 2012), 139.

6   *The Case For Withdrawal From Afghanistan*, ed. Nick Turse and Tariq Ali (London: Verso, 2010); Bob Woodward, *Obama's Wars* (New York: Simon & Schuster, 2010), 71; Felix Kuehn and Alex Van Linschoten, *An Enemy We Created: The Myth of the Taliban/Al Qaeda Merger in Afghanistan* (New York: Oxford University Press, 2012). Dr. Peter Lavoy, deputy for analysis in the Office of the Director of National Intelligence, estimated there were 20 to 100 Al Qaeda operatives at most.

7   Anand Gopal, *No Good Men Among the Living: America, The Taliban, and the War Through Afghan* Eyes (New York: Metropolitan Books, 2014).

8   Woodward, *Obama's Wars*, 214.

9   Ryan Hendrickson, *Obama at War: Congress and the Imperial Presidency* (University Press of Kentucky, 2015); Woodward, *Obama's Wars*, 113, 335.

10   Noam Chomsky, *Hegemony or Survival: America's Quest for Global Dominance* (New York: Metropolitan Books, 2003), 200; Sonali Kolhkatkar and James Ingalls, *Bleeding Afghanistan: Washington, Warlords, and the Propaganda of Silence* (New York: Seven Stories Press, 2006), 43; Michael Mandel, *How America Gets Away with Murder: Illegal Wars, Collateral Damage, and Crimes Against Humanity* (London: Pluto Press, 2004), 37, 38.

11   Carlotta Gall, *The Wrong Enemy: America in Afghanistan, 2001-2014* (Boston: Houghton Mifflin, 2014), 28.

12   Woodward, *Obama's Wars*, 163, 208; Hamid Karzai, Globalsecurity.org.

13   Douglas Valentine, *The CIA as Organized Crime* (Atlanta: Clarity Press, 2017); John Foster, *Oil and World Politics* (Winnipeg: Lorimer, 2019); Mark Landler and James Risen, "Trump Finds Reason for the U.S. To Remain in Afghanistan: Minerals," *New York Times*, July 25, 2017.

14   Marc W. Herold "Afghanistan as Empty Space: The Perfect Neocolonial State of the 21st Century," http://www.grassrootspeace.org/m_herold_ afghanistan_0406.pdf; Ann Scott Tyson, *American Spartan: The Promise, the Mission, and the Betrayal of Special Forces Major Jim Gant* (New York: William & Morrow, 2014), 109.

15   Gopal, *No Good Men Among the Living*, 2.

16   Telephone Conversation Between President Johnson and the President's Special Assistant for National Security Affairs (Bundy) Washington, May 27, 1964, 11:24 a.m; Source: U.S., Department of State, *Foreign Relations of the United States, 1964-68,* Volume XXVII, Mainland Southeast Asia: Regional Affairs, Washington, DC, Document Number 53; Original Source: Johnson Library, Recordings and Transcripts, Recording of a telephone conversation between the President and McGeorge Bundy, Tape 64.28 PNO 11.

17   Woodward, *Obama's Wars*, 332, 333.

18   Charles Mohr, "McNamara on Record, Reluctantly, on Vietnam," *New York Times*, May 16, 1984.

19   David Sanger, *Confront and Conceal: Obama's Secret Wars and Surprising Use of American Power* (New York: Broadway, 2012), 24, 25.

20   Edward S. Herman and Frank Brodhead, *Demonstration Elections: U.S. Staged Elections in the Dominican Republic, Vietnam and El Salvador* (Boston: South End Press, 1984), 61.

21   Kai Eidie, *Power Struggle Over Afghanistan: An Inside Look at What Went Wrong – And What We Can Do To Repair The Damage* (New York: Skyhorse Publishing, 2012), V1.

22   Rod Nordland, "Polarizing Afghan Leader Emerges from Exile," *The New York Times*, July 23, 218, A1; George Packer, "Afghanistan's Theorist In-Chief," *The New Yorker*, July 4, 2016; Bryan Glyn Williams, *The Last Warlord: The Life and Legend of Dostum, the Afghan Warrior Who Led U.S. Special Forces to Topple the Taliban Regime* (Chicago Review Press, 2013); Interview with Mustafa Araie, Afghan Attorney. A technocrat with a violent temper, Ghani had been a U.S. citizen who taught anthropology at U.C. Berkeley and John Hopkins and wrote a book on fixing failed states. He came from a distinguished Pashtun family and grew up in privilege in Kabul in the 1950s. His father served as Transport Minister under King Zahir. After 9/11, Ghani helped craft the Bonn agreements bringing Karzai to power with CIA-connected academic Barnett Rubin in his home in Washington, D.C. Many Afghans viewed Ghani as a foreigner.

23   See Alfred W. McCoy, *The Politics of Heroin: CIA Complicity in the Global Drugs Trade* (New York: Lawrence Hill Books, 1991).

24   Adam Gabbat, "U.S. Marines Charged Over Urinating on Bodies of Dead Taliban in Afghanistan," *The Guardian*, September 24, 2012; Matthew Rosenberg and William Yardley, "U.S. Sergeant Charged with 17 Counts of Murder in Afghan Killings," *New York Times*, March 23, 2012. Staff Sergeant Robert Bales ransacked homes and murdered 16 civilians in Alkozai and Najiban after sneaking off his base.

25   Bob Dreyfuss and Nick Turse, "America's Afghan Victims: Even the Most Staunchly Antiwar Politicians and Pundits Rarely Mention Their Suffering,"

The Nation Magazine, October 7, 2013, 21, 24.

26   Jeremy Scahill, *Dirty Wars: The World is a Battlefield* (New York: The Nation Books, 2013), 334-337; Valentine, *The CIA as Organized Crime*, 104.

27   Scahill, *Dirty Wars*, 347.

28   Nick Turse, "A My Lai a Month," *The Nation*, November 13, 2008.

29   Montgomery McFate and Janice H. Laurence, "Introduction: Unveiling the Human Terrain System" in *Social Science Goes to War: The Human Terrain System in Iraq and Afghanistan* (New York: Oxford University Press, 2015), 2; James Gibson, *The Perfect War: Technowar in Vietnam* (New York: Atlantic Monthly Press, 2000).

30   Robert Bernier, "Was the Navy's F-111 Really that Bad," *Air and Space Magazine*, September 2018; "General Dynamic Grows Its Military Truck Unit," *Market Watch*, November 7, 2011; Samuel Weigley, "Ten Companies That Profit the Most Off War," *USA Today*, March 10, 2013; "Armored Troop Carriers Called Unsafe for Duty," *The Washington Times*, November 5, 2009; James Carter, "War Profiteering from Vietnam to Iraq," *Counterpunch*, December 11, 2003. A test pilot remembered the F-111 as the worst airplane he had ever flown.

31   Francis Jennings, *The Invasion of America: Indians, Colonialism, and the Cant of Conquest* (New York: Simon & Schuster, 1975), 170.

32   C.J. Chivers, *The Fighters: Americans in Combat in Afghanistan and Iraq* (New York: Simon & Schuster, 2018), xvi.

33   Jeremy Scahill, "The Drone Papers," *The Intercept*, October 15, 2015; Patrick Cockburn, *Kill Chain: The Rise of the High Tech Assassins* (New York: Henry Holt, 2015), 145.

34   Jason Hanna, Ben Brumfield and Steve Almasy, "Air Attacks Kill at Least 19 at Afghanistan Hospital, U.S. Investigating," CNN, October 3, 2015.

35   Gopal, *No Good Men Among the Living*, 220, 221. For comparisons, see Howard Zinn, *Vietnam: The Logic of Withdrawal* (Boston: Beacon Press, 1967).

36   Joseph Goldstein, "U.S. Troops Are Told to Ignore Afghan Allies Abuse of Boys," *New York Times*, September 21, 2015, A1.

37   Michael Hastings, "Bowe Bergdahl: America's Last Prisoner of War," *Rolling Stone*, June 7, 2012.

38   Ryan Smith, "Commie Cadet Spenser Rapone on Why He Left the U.S. Military and Became a Socialist," *In These Times*, August 7, 2018.

39   See Noah Coburn, *Under Contract: The Invisible Workers of America's Global War* (Stanford, CA: Stanford University Press, 2018), 14, 15.

40   Gopal, *No Good Men Among the Living*, 273.

41   Matthew Hoh, "Time for Peace in Afghanistan and an End to the Lies," *Counterpunch*, February 15, 2019.

42   See Neil Sheehan, *A Bright Shining Lie: John Paul Vann and America in Vietnam* (New York: Random House, 1988).

43 See Nicolas Davies, *Blood On Our Hands: The American Invasion and Destruction of Iraq* (Ann Arbor: Nimble Books, 2010); Nir Rosen, *Aftermath: Following the Bloodshed of America's Wars in The Muslim World* (New York: The Nation Books, 2010); Michael Weiss and Hassan Hassan, *ISIS: Inside the Army of Terror* (New York: Regan Arts, 2015), 73.

44 Muqtada al-Sadr, "Iraq is Run by Wolves: The Farewell Speech of Muqtada al-Sadr," *Counterpunch*, February 19, 2014; Amnesty International, *New Order, Same Abuses: Unlawful Detention in Iraq* (London: 2010); Nick Turse, *The Changing Face of Empire* (Haymarket Books, 2012), 39; Patrick Cockburn, "Why the War on Terror Went Wrong: Al Qaeda's 2nd Act," *Counterpunch*, March 18, 2014.

45 Patrick Cockburn, "'Shoe-Thrower of Baghdad Brings Iraqis Into the Streets," *The Independent*, December 16, 2008.

46 Murtaza Hussein, "Young Iraqis Overwhelmingly Consider U.S. Their Enemy, Poll Says," *The Intercept*, April 13, 2016.

47 "Introduction" in *Hearts and Minds: A People's History of Counterinsurgency*, ed. Hannah Gurman (New York: The New Press, 2013), 1.

48 Gall, *The Wrong Enemy*; Rochelle Davis, "Culture as a Weapon System," *Middle East Report*, Summer 2010, 9, 11; Mark Price, *Weaponizing Anthropology: Social Science in Service of a Militarized State* (Oakland, CA: AK Press, 2011).

49 *Hearts and Minds*, ed. Gurman, 5; Phyllis Bennis, "Afghanistan," in *The Wikileaks Files: The World According to U.S. Empire*, ed. Julian Assange (London: Verso, 2016), 384.

50 See Jonathan Nashel, *Edward Lansdale's Cold War* (Amherst, MA: University of Massachusetts Press, 2005).

51 *Hearts and Minds*, ed. Gurman, 4.

52 Michael McGough, "Obama Takes Sides in the 'Spitting Vets' Debate," *Los Angeles Times*, May 30, 2012; "Remarks By the President at the Commemoration Ceremony Of the 50th Anniversary of the Vietnam War," May 28, 2012, https://obamawhitehouse.archives.gov/the-press-office/2012/05/28/remarks-president-commemoration-ceremony-50th-anniversary-vietnam-war. Similar references were made in other speeches.

53 Jerry Lembcke, *The Spitting Image: Myth, Memory and the Legacy of Vietnam* (New York: NYU Press, 1998); S. Brian Willson, *Don't Thank Me For My Service: My Vietnam Awakening to the Long History of U.S. Lies* (Atlanta: Clarity Press, 2018).

54 Email correspondence, Jerry Lembcke, February 11, 2018. The author contacted Favreau twice to try and get a confirmation as to whether he wrote the speech and to get his impressions of it, however, Favreau never responded to these emails.

55 "Text of President Obama's Speech to the Disabled Veterans of America," *Stars and Stripes*, August 1, 2016.

56   "Osama bin Laden Dead," White House, May 2, 2011, https://obamawhitehouse.
        archives.gov/blog/2011/05/02/osama-bin-laden-dead

57   Seymour Hersh, *Reporter: A Memoir* (New York: Alfred A. Knopf, 2018);
        Seymour Hersh, *The Killing of Osama bin Laden* (London: Verso, 2016). Other
        journalists came to similar conclusions as Hersh based on different sources. Jon
        Schwarz and Ryan Devereaux, "Sy Hersh's bin Laden Story First Reported in
        2011 – With Seemingly Different Sources," *The Intercept*, May 11, 2015. See
        also Mark Bowden, *The Finish: The Killing of Osama Bin Laden* (New York:
        Grove Press, 2013).

58   "Death of Osama bin Laden," https://en.wikipedia.org/wiki/Death_of_Osama_
        bin_Laden#Identification_of_the_body; "Osama bin Laden Death Conspiracy
        Theories,"   https://en.wikipedia.org/wiki/Osama_bin_Laden_death_
        conspiracy_theories; David Ray Griffin, *Osama bin Laden: Dead or Alive?*
        (Olive Branch Press, 2011); Paul Craig Roberts, *How America Was Lost: From
        9/11 To the Police/Warfare State* (Atlanta: Clarity Press, 2014). Griffin notes
        that videos featuring bin Laden speaking appeared to be manufactured since he
        looked younger than in earlier ones, with a black rather than grey beard, and no
        longer made any religious references, quoting instead from leftist authors like
        William Blum he may never have actually read.

59   Noam Chomsky, "My Reaction to Osama bin Laden's Death," *Guernica,* May
        6, 2011.

60   See Azmat Khan and Anand Gopal, "The Uncounted: An On-the-Ground
        Investigation Reveals That the U.S. Led Battle Against ISIS – Hailed as the
        Most Precise Air Campaign in History – is Killing Far More Iraqi Civilians
        Than the Coalition Has Acknowledged," *New York Times Magazine*, November
        19, 2017, 43-47.

61   "Against Intervention in Iraq," *The Nation Magazine*, June 18, 2014; Evelyn
        Pringle, "Curtain Time for Barack Obama," *Countercurrents*, May 15, 2008.

62   Andrew Feinstein, *The Shadow World: Inside the Global Arms Trade* (New
        York: Farrar, Straus & Giroux, 2011), 404.

63   James Denselow, "The U.S. Departure from Iraq is an Illusion," *The Guardian*,
        October 25, 2011; Michael E. Schmidt and Eric Schmitt, "Weapons Sales to
        Iraq Move Ahead Despite U.S. Worries," *New York Times*, December 28, 2011;
        Security Assistance Monitor, Iraq, https://securityassistance.org/data/program/
        military/Iraq/2009/2016/all/Global//

64   Evan Osnos, "Breaking Up: Maliki and Biden," *The New Yorker*, August 12,
        2014.

65   Weiss & Hassan, *ISIS*, 92, 93, 96.

66   Emma Sky, *The Unraveling: High Hopes and Missed Opportunities in Iraq*
        (New York: Public Affairs, 2015), 322.

67   Sky, *The Unraveling*, 360.

68   Liz Sly, "Arab Spring Style Protests Take Hold in Iraq," *Washington Post*,

February 8, 2013; Valentine, *The CIA as Organized Crime*, 152.

69   Patrick Cockburn, *The Rise of Islamic State: ISIS and the New Sunni Revolution* (London: Verso, 2014), 47.

70   John Kerry, *Every Day is Extra* (New York: Simon & Schuster, 2018), 543, 544; Osnos, "Breaking Up."

71   Michael S. Schmidt and Yasir Ghazi, "Iraqi Leader Backs Syria, with a Nudge from Iran," *New York Times*, August 12, 2011; "Haider al-Abadi: My Country Needs More Help from the U.S.," *Washington Post*, March 23, 2017; Naomi Klein, *The Shock Doctrine: The Rise of Disaster Capitalism* (New York: The Nation Books, 2007).

72   "Terrorist March in Iraq: The U.S. Response," Hearing Before the Committee on Foreign Affairs, House of Representatives, 113th Congress, 2nd Session, July 23, 2014 (Washington: G.P.O., 2014).

73   Cockburn, *The Rise of Islamic State*, x, xi; Weiss & Hassan, *ISIS*, 22, 24, 38; Washington's Blog and Wayne Madsen, *Unmasking ISIS: The Shocking Truth* (San Diego, CA: Progressive Press, 2016), 76, 143.

74   Jessica T. Matthews, "Iraq Ilusions," *New York Review of Books*, August 14, 2014. Kurdish peshmerga armed by the U.S. carried out their own atrocities.

75   Charles J. Lister, *The Syrian Jihad: Al-Qaeda, the Islamic State and the Evolution of an Insurgency* (New York: Oxford University Press, 2015), 290; Michael E. Schmidt and Eric Schmitt, "Weapons Sales to Iraq Move Ahead Despite U.S. Worries," *New York Times*, December 28, 2011.

76   Paul Szoldra, "U.S. Troops Have Fought ISIS in Direct Ground Combat More Than You Think," *Task & Purpose*, April 10, 2018. Paul Szoldra, "The Untold Stories of Marine Special Ops 'Getting Some' Against ISIS," *Task & Purpose*, May 11, 2018.

77   Steve Coll, "Oil and Erbil," *The New Yorker*, August 10, 2014.

78   Michael Savage, *Power Wars: Inside Obama's Post 9-11 Presidency* (Boston: Little & Brown, 2015), 685, 686.

79   Michael S. Schmidt, "Marine's Death in a Secret Iraqi Base Reflects a Quietly Expanding U.S. Role," *New York Times*, April 11, 2016. Assistant Defense Secretary Elissa Slotkin, later elected to Congress under the 2018 Blue Wave lied to Congress in claiming that U.S. Special Forces were not engaging in offensive operations.

80   "Barack Obama, "Remarks by the President on the Administration's Approach to Counter-Terrorism," MacDill Air Force Base, Tampa, Florida, December 06, 2016, https://obamawhitehouse.archives.gov/the-press-office/2016/12/06/remarks-president-administrations-approach-counterterrorism

81   See Gregg Muttit, *Fuel on the Fire: Oil and Politics in Occupied Iraq* (New York: The New Press, 2012); Gary Vogler, *Iraq and the Politics of Oil: An Insider's Perspective* (Lawrence: University Press of Kansas, 2018).

82   Paul Wood and Richard Hall, "U.S. Killing More Civilians in Iraq, Syria than it

Acknowledges," *USA Today*, February 2, 2016.

83   Quoted in Wood and Hall, "U.S. Killing More Civilians in Iraq, Syria than it Acknowledges."

84   Amnesty International, "At Any Cost: The Civilian Catastrophe in West Mosul," London, 2016.

85   Ralph Schoenman, "Shifting the Blame: The Cover-Up of U.S. War Crimes in Mosul," *Socialist Action*, June 8, 2017.

86   Anonymous Obama official quoted in Carol E. Lee and Julian E. Barnes, "Air Attacks in Iraq: Decision Driven by Extreme Turn of Events," *Wall Street Journal*, August 9, 2014, A7.

87   Nicole Gaouette, "Iraqi Election Makes U.S. Foe al Sadr a Potential Kingmaker," *CNN*, May 16, 2018.

88   Lister, T*he Syrian Jihad*, 389.

89   Lister, *The Syrian Jihad*, 293.

Chapter 7

SHADOWING DOUGLAS McARTHUR

OBAMA'S DANGEROUS PIVOT TO ASIA

Every morning for over eight years at 7 A.M, activists in Gangjeong Village on South Korea's Jeju-do island crafted 100 bows conveying their desire for a more peaceful world. One of them stated: "As I hold in my heart that possessions create other possessions and wars only give birth to other wars and cannot solve problem, I make my seventh bow." And another: "As I resolve to let go of chauvinistic nationalism which makes other countries insecure, I make my fifty fifth bow."[1]

The activists were protesting the construction of a giant naval base on a pristine World Heritage site by the South Korean military, which was to function as a key nexus in the Obama administration's military pivot to Asia. This policy sought to increase the U.S. naval presence in the South China Sea from 50 to 67 ships by 2020, extend U.S. defense ties to regional allies and upgrade base facilities. Threatening locals' livelihood as fishermen, the Jeju-do base was designed to house 8,000 Marines and 20 warships, including nuclear submarines, giant aircraft carriers, and destroyers equipped with cruise missiles as well as

Aegis missile destroyers made by General Dynamics, and long-range ballistic missile capability for targeting southeast China.[2]

Located in a strategic location in the Yellow Sea, through which China imported 80 percent of its oil, Jeju had been designated as a peace island after President Roo Moon-Hyun apologized for a horrendous massacre carried by the South Korean army and U.S. on the eve of the Korean War. The U.S., however, strong-armed local politicians into purchasing the land for the base, which had been a breeding ground for over 500 species of seaweed and 86 species of unusual shellfish, as well as three endangered species: the red-footed crab, freshwater shrimp, and boreal digging frog.

In August 2011, riot police broke up a nonviolent rally with water cannons and tear gas and arrested more than three dozen activists, including the mayor of Gangjeong. Film-maker Oliver Stone was among those to travel to Jeju in solidarity with the protestors who were backed by 97 percent of islanders. Stone said that the threat from China had been manufactured, as it had with the Russians and Chinese during the Cold War. "China spends about one tenth of the United States on its military."[3] Obama, however, provided an effective spin by invoking China's human rights abuses towards dissidents and the threat represented by a nuclear armed North Korea, claiming in Wilsonian parlance that America's enduring presence in the region was needed to "deter threats to peace."[4]

Reinvigorating the Open Door: Clinton's Pacific Century

The official impetus behind the Pivot to Asia was articulated by Secretary of State Hillary Clinton in an October 2011 article in *Foreign Affairs* entitled "The Pacific Century," which called for the reassertion of American influence and power in a region that was a source of over $300 billion in annual American exports. According to Clinton, the U.S. had effectively underwritten regional security for decades—patrolling Asia's sea lanes and preserving stability, which helped to create the conditions for remarkable economic growth. Obama's visionary policy would in turn enable the U.S. to continuously champion open markets and free trade along with human rights, backed up by military force.[5]

Clinton's emphasis on open markets harkened back to the famous "Open Door Notes" issued by her predecessor, John Hay, in the late 19th century, which promoted the opening of the China market to U.S. investors. Her blueprint was only slightly more sophisticated than pro-imperialist Senator Albert Beveridge (R-IN) who asked whether "the natives of the Philippines prefer the just, humane, civilizing government of this Republic to the savage, bloody rule of pillage and extortion from which we have rescued them?"[6] and Mark Hanna, William McKinley's top campaign adviser who advocated for a strong foothold in the Philippines, for then "we can and will take a large slice of the commerce of Asia."[7]

The Asia Pivot was adopted in Beveridge and Hanna's spirit and that of the famed Far Eastern General Douglas MacArthur who sought to transform Southeast Asia into an "American Lake" after America's victory in the Pacific War by consolidating a network of military bases from the Ryukyu Islands through South Korea, Taiwan (Formosa) and the Philippines. Japan was built up at this time as a key strategic counterweight to Communist China, whose leaders helped restore the country from the perennial "sick man of Asia" following its 1949 revolution to its traditional stature as a regional hegemon, particularly after its economy boomed following reforms initiated by Deng Xiaoping.[8]

After years of cordial diplomatic relations in the wake of Richard Nixon's 1972 opening, the U.S. perception of China began to shift in the mid-2000s from a useful source of cheap labor for American multinationals like Walmart on whose board Clinton had sat, to a mounting threat to U.S. global hegemony.[9] In January 2005, the Pentagon's Office of Net Assessment issued a classified report to Defense Secretary Donald Rumsfeld prepared by Booz Allen Hamilton, which advocated for a robust response to China's "string of Pearls" strategy that strove to acquire new military bases, warning that China would use its growing economic and military power to project force and undermine U.S. interests and regional security.[10]

Championed by Obama's backers on Wall Street, the Pivot followed from these recommendations, and from the logic of Admiral Robert Willard, head of the Pacific Command, who labeled the Asia Pacific region a "commons to be protected by the United States."[11] Obama proved to be an effective frontman who could invoke his own personal ties to the region, and convey the image of a man of the people - as when he was featured strolling shoeless under the sloped roofs of a Buddhist monastery in Luang Prabang, Laos, shopping for paper lanterns on a side street, and sipping coconut juice while peering at boats along the Mekong River.[12] Though acknowledging the U.S. bombing of Laos during the Indochina War and pledging $60 million for the removal of undetonated ordinance[13], Obama would not meet with the Bishop of Jeju Island who helped construct a peace center in Gangjeong nor Okinawans and others whose lives were adversely affected by his military buildup. He was operating in the tradition of empire builders who embraced human rights as a political tool and required a progressive spokesman to mask the reality of what they were doing.

A Useable Past

The Asia Pivot was symbolically introduced by Hillary Clinton on a U.S. naval destroyer in Manila Bay, the location for America's original pivot in the 1898 Spanish-American Philippines War.[14] The carefully choreographed event implied a proud continuity from an era most historians consider to be shameful since U.S. soldiers committed heinous atrocities, and at least 200,000 Filipinos were killed.[15] Obama and his advisers generally promoted a useable history that erased the violence of America's Asian Wars and economic pitfalls associated with the importation of neoliberalism. Kurt Campbell, the Assistant Secretary of State for East Asian and Pacific Affairs from 2009 to 2013 claimed that America's bloody intervention in the Philippines "stood in stark relief to that of other imperial powers" as America effectively "taught the Filipinos how to pursue democratic rule in the future."[16] Alfred W. McCoy's study, *Policing America's Empire*, shows just the opposite – the U.S. built Filipino constabulary created a police state and warped democratic development for decades.[17]

On the 60th anniversary of the Korean War armistice, Obama waxed nostalgic about the gallantry of U.S. soldiers in that war without mentioning the vast civilian suffering including from intensive U.S. bombardment. Echoing a speech made by George H.W. Bush twenty-five years earlier, he stated: "we can say with confidence that war was no tie. Korea was a victory. When 50 million South Koreans live in freedom—a vibrant democracy, one of the world's most dynamic economies, in stark contrast to the repression and poverty of the North—that's a victory." Furthermore, he claimed melodramatically: "For generations to come, history will recall how free nations banded together in a long Cold War, and how we won that war, let it be said that Korea was the first battle."[18]

Obama's histrionic remarks would have come as a surprise to readers of the now-defunct *Look Magazine* which in February 1951 characterized the U.S. retreat from North Korea as the military's most "shameful disgrace" since northern troops had "cut and run at the first Battle of Bull Run in 1861."[19] The Korean War resulted in continuous waves of social protest in South Korea itself and skewed political and economic development in both North and South.[20]

Obama's revisionism extended to the Vietnam War. He falsely claimed that American troops won every major battle they fought (Khe Sanh was a North Vietnamese victory likened by historians to an American Dien Bien Phu) and insinuated that "misdeeds" (atrocities) were only committed "by a few" when they were in fact systematic. Evading mention of the CIA's torture of Vietnamese prisoners at the Con Son "Tiger Cages" and program of civilian assassinations under the Phoenix program, Obama asserted that "[American] POWs—in those hellholes like... the Hanoi Hilton—didn't simply endure; you wrote one of the most extraordinary stories of bravery and integrity in the annals of military history."[21] Why mention, since it was counterproductive, that some of these POWs were captured while bombing innocent Vietnamese peasants and that many turned against the war?[22] Obama called Vietnam "one of the most painful chapters in our history" because of "how we treated our troops who served there," repeating the demonized Vietnam veteran myth long used to shame antiwar activists and deflect attention from what Noam Chomsky called the "crucifixion" of Indochina.[23]

The implications of Obama's mythmaking are considerable. A revamped, sanitized version of America's conduct in Vietnam was a prerequisite to his renewed military buildup, which extended the standoff in the Koreas and sadly led to deepened military ties with the new generation of Vietnamese who now had to contend with the peacetime onslaught of global neoliberalism. During his second term, the Obama administration lifted its embargo on the sale of lethal weapons to Vietnam, pursued a military base at Cam Ranh Bay, and carried out joint naval exercises with America's former communist adversary. Obama told the public that the access to Vietnam's port facilities was necessary so the United States could better "respond to humanitarian disasters," though the real reason was to further Washington's strategy of containing China.[24] Historical revisionism was an important precondition for carrying out this latter policy since it defused critical questioning of the original containment policy and dangers of history repeating itself, and sought to restore the image of America the Good, where the shining house on the hill was now inhabited by a man of color who surely had the interests of his colored brethren in the rest of the world at heart.

A Return to the Tributary System?

While countries like Vietnam had historical grievances against China, interstate relations in Southeast Asia were more stable in the years before Western colonialism when China's cultural influences and leadership was accepted under the tributary system in which rulers were left to govern their own affairs after paying tribute. David Kang wrote a well received 2009 book *China Rising*, which suggested that East Asian nations were content to return to a similar pattern of relations, a trend accentuated as China began to outpace the U.S. economically.[25]

In *The Second World*, Parag Khanna argued that while the U.S. was mired in quagmires in the Middle East, China began binding Asia together into a Greater East Asia Co-Prosperity Sphere, a reference to Japan's 1930 project for an Asian economic bloc, through the force of its economy and attraction of its culture. He quoted a Malaysian diplomat who stated that: "creating a community is easy among the yellow and brown—but not the white."[26]

In 2012, the Asean+3 nations, including Singapore and Malaysia, established a border equity exchange and compact with China to settle bilateral trade in mutual currency accounts, thus bypassing the U.S. dollar as a medium of exchange.[27] Indonesia at this time began developing anti-ship missiles with China as Xi Jinping became the first foreign leader to address its parliament. A military coup in Thailand in 2014 unseating the Shinawatra dynasty and a corruption scandal in Malaysia led to similar shifts away from the U.S. that threatened American access to air bases. South Korean leader Moon Jae-In tilted to China after the impeachment of Park-Geun-hye, and in 2016 Filipinos elected pro-Chinese nationalist Rodrigo Duterte who announced his "separation from the United States," after confronting Obama with a photograph of Filipinos slain by U.S. forces a century ago.[28] Slowly but surely, the yellow and brown were indeed forging a greater community that excluded the whites from across the sea, although this solidarity was fragile because those whites were more insidious than in the classic age of colonialism, American capital was still seductive and nationalist rivalries were rife.

The Role of Special Interests

At the time Obama's pivot was announced, bookstores

were filled with alarmist accounts of China's rise, such as Martin Jacques' *When China Rules the World*. Orientalist stereotypes about the Chinese "penchant for deceptiveness" were being re-invoked even among Ivy League academics.[29] Obama's Assistant Secretary of Defense, Wallace Gregson, claimed the pivot was "not warmongering [but] deterrence."[30] But since the Asia Pacific was still an American lake, and U.S. power unchecked, as historian Bruce Cumings asked, why pivot at all?[31]

The answer had much to do with the special interests who owned the politicians. The district of Randy J. Forbes (R-VI), chair of the House Armed Services Committee Sea Power and Force Projection Subcommittee and pro-Pivot House China Caucus, happened to encompass Newport News shipbuilding, the only shipyard in the U.S. which built aircraft carriers. His campaigns were financed by Huntington Ingalls Industry, America's largest shipbuilding company, and BAE Systems, which produced cruise missiles and naval ships.[32] General Dynamics got a $1.99 billion contract for submarine construction in December 2012 at its electric boat division in Groton, Connecticut and its Marine Division grew by building more Arleigh Burke and Zumwalt naval destroyers.[33] This despite the fact that, as Defense Secretary Robert Gates noted in a 2010 speech at the Eisenhower library, the U.S. battle fleet was larger than the next 13 navies combined, 11 of which belong[ed] to allies and partners. Gates asked "is it a dire threat that by 2020, the U.S. will have only twenty more advanced stealth fighters than China?"[34]

Private equity firms with close ties to Obama benefited significantly from the pivot. Warburg Pincus, for example, headed by former Treasury Secretary Timothy Geithner, secured 5 new deals in 2015 in Indonesia, Vietnam and Singapore after giving Obama $100,000 for his presidential campaigns and raising at least $200,000 more. KKR & Co., another leading private equity firm secured eight new deals in Southeast Asia after giving Obama over $75,000.[35] Chaired by David Petraeus as of 2013, it exemplified the "revolving door" in which military officers and government officials parlay their political connections into lucrative careers in private industry, and in turn help sway public policy in favor of their new employers.

Obama and Clinton were treading on difficult ground with the Pivot because of a growing economic interdependence with China, which held $1 trillion in U.S. treasury bonds. Two-way trade approached $600 billion in 2012.[36] Underpinning their risky gambit was the growing interest of U.S. energy companies in the extraction of oil and natural gas from the South China Sea. According to a Department of Energy report, major firms such as Chevron, ConocoPhillips and ExxonMobil were partnering with the state-owned oil companies of Malaysia, Vietnam and the Philippines to develop promising reserves in maritime territories. The South China Sea was estimated to contain as much as 213 billion barrels of oil and 190 trillion cubicle feet of natural gas.[37]

The pivot policy was designed to keep these treasures in American rather than Chinese hands and protect the $5 trillion in trade estimated to pass through the South China Seas every year. U.S. arms manufacturers who had donated generously to Obama were also left salivating at the "growing opportunities for our industry to help equip our friends," and the prospect of rising defense budgets that would accompany an increasing crisis environment.[38] *Bloomberg News* reported that defense spending by China, India, Japan, South Korea, and Taiwan accelerated sharply in the second half of the last decade, and at $225 billion in 2012 was almost double the amount of a decade to earlier.[39] Obama as an effective front-man made no mention of these statistics, instead suggesting a military buildup was necessary for "regional and maritime security," to "counter terrorism and violent extremism," and to enhance trading ties and cooperation in tackling global health problems and climate change.[40]

Reinvigorating Dollar Diplomacy

Obama put on his usual charm in promoting the Trans-Pacific Partnership (TPP), a free-trade agreement excluding China, which he claimed had the "strongest environmental protection and anticorruption standards" of any trade agreement in history.[41]

Likened by Defense Secretary Ash Carter to" another aircraft carrier in the Pacific,"[42] this agreement had many of Obama's top donors thrilled by a promised reduction of export tariffs. Commerce Secretary Penny Pritzker, who retained her stock in Hyatt Corporation, which owned twelve luxury hotels across Southeast Asia and opened a resort in Phuket, Thailand in 2016, framed it as crucial to maintaining American leadership in the global economy.[43] South Korea, Indonesia and Thailand dropped out of the TPP, however, because of its dismantling public health safeguards enshrined in international law, obstruction of price-lowering competition for medicines, and an "investor's rights" clause that granted private companies the right to sue governments in special courts if they thought their laws could limit their expected future profits.[44]

Documents obtained through the Freedom of Information Act (FOIA) disclosed collusion between Obama's trade representative, Michael Froman, a former Citibank executive who was instrumental in the 1999 repeal of the Glass-Steagall Act barring banks' ability to speculate with depositors' money, and Wall Street lobbyists. The latter succeeded in pushing Froman to deliver an expansion in corporations' ability to challenge government regulations, and unprecedented legal rights that could render governments impotent in their ability to protect workers' rights and the environment, and would represent a new phase in the subordination of the state to corporate power. Froman assigned a member of his staff to be in close contact with Goldman Sachs' lobbyists who considered the "power to challenge regulations" as critical in "making the TPP a meaningful agreement for our industry."[45] These comments exemplify the major corporate influence on the TPP and Obama's foreign policies in Southeast Asia, which reinvigorated an era of dollar diplomacy associated in history textbooks with the William H. Taft and Theodore Roosevelt administrations.[46]

Disputed Islands

China not surprisingly was disdainful of the TPP and had

come to feel encircled by the United States. The country's top foreign policy adviser told Ms. Clinton point blank: "why don't you pivot out of here?"[47] To protect itself, China intensified efforts to develop anti-ship ballistic missiles and space based satellites. It also became more aggressive in pursuing claims over disputed territory in the South China Sea such as the Spratley and Paracel Islands, which surrounded as much as 105 billion barrels of oil, as well as the Diaoyou islands (the Senkakus to the Japanese), which the U.S. claimed the right to defend under the U.S.-Japan Treaty of Mutual Cooperation. Besides their strategic and economic value, these islands were symbolic of China's humiliating 19th Century when they had been annexed (Japanese government documents show that the Diaoyou island were effectively stolen from China as a booty of their victory in the 1895 Sino-Japanese war). South China Sea specialist Leszek Buszynsky wrote that "China's desire to counter U.S. regional dominance and U.S. insistence on retaining that dominance has transformed the disputes in the South China Sea into a competition between major powers"— with potentially dangerous consequence.[48]

From March 2015 to 2016, the Obama administration sent over 700 naval patrols through the disputed island passages.[49] After China declared a special air defense zone over a contested territory near Vietnam in 2013, and Obama sent B-52 bombers, Chinese naval ships cut in front of the U.S.S. Cooper almost causing a collision. Michael T. Klare wrote in Foreign Affairs that the "Asia pivot surely increased the chances that rash and potentially incendiary behavior by any one of the countries hashing it out in the South and East China seas could lead to war."[50]

Peaceful Alternatives Not Pursued

Obama's negative view of China dated at least from his time in the Illinois Senate when he viewed the Chinese primarily as a threat to mid-western manufacturing. As president, Obama continued Bush's efforts to devalue China's currency and promote trade sanctions and tariffs, though did engage China fairly effectively on climate change.[51] Obama could have pursued an alternative path of diplomatic engagement overall, as China's official position on foreign affairs emphasized dialogue, negotiation, peaceful resolution of conflict and respect for territorial integrity. Chinese leader Xi Jinping explained in a speech at the 2015 Boao forum that "the old mindset of zero-sum game should give way to a new approach of win-win and all-win cooperation. The interests of others must be accommodated while pursuing one's own interests and common development must be promoted."[52]

Former Secretary of State Madeleine Albright admitted that Obama's refusal to accept China's invitation to join the Asian Infrastructure Investment Bank (AIIB), an alternative to the IMF which almost every U.S. ally joined, including Israel, was a mistake.[53] Alleged grandmasters of real-politick, Henry Kissinger and Zbigniew Brzezinski and senior diplomat Richard Holbrook all warned that a confrontational approach to China would backfire.[54] A big problem was the absence of genuine China experts in the Obama administration. Ambassador Max Baucus, a champion of free-trade agreements who served on the CIA's external advisory board, admitted to the Senate Foreign Relations Committee that he was "no real expert on China." Chas Freeman Jr., a thirty-year veteran of the diplomatic corps, noted that for the relationship [between the U.S. and China] to be functional "you need people within the administration who are seen by the Chinese as people they can talk with…staff turnover left Chinese officials with nobody."[55]

Freeman, who served as the principal interpreter for Nixon's historic delegation to China in 1972, told me that Obama's pivot policy was misdirected because it "provided a military response to an economic problem." The People's Liberation Army (PLA) was focused on internal security, the defense of the Chinese homeland against neighbors with a history of invading it, and on countering the powerful U.S. naval and air forces constantly mapping and probing its coastal defenses. A "better response to China's economic rise would have been to try to leverage China's prosperity to our own" and "build better supply chains" which, he said, "corporate America was already attempting to do." The Obama administration could also have "worked to settle competing claims to islands on the South China seas and negotiated on a united basis with China." Instead, "it undertook provocative measures" that were extended by Trump. These included "mock attack runs on Chinese installations," which were "not much appreciated by the Chinese, and led to Chinese counter-measures that included sending ships off the coast of Hawaii and Guam."[56]

Rerun of Cold War Style Containment

As bad relations worsened, China accused the Obama administration of covertly backing Uyghur Islamic terrorists through the National Endowment for Democracy (NED) in Xinjiang where critical oil and gas pipelines passed through as well as Occupy protests in Hong Kong. China further accused the CIA of inciting separatists in Southern Mongolia and Baluchistan to disrupt a new Chinese port and pipeline and machete-wielding supporters of Aung San Suu Kyi—who included an anti-Muslim monk known as the "Buddhist bin Laden"—in Myanmar's Rhakine state, where China hoped to establish a logistical hub.[57] Myanmar was an oil and natural gas producer whose coastline provided naval access off a strategic shipping lane, the Strait of Malacca. The CIA had long backed ethnic minorities linked to the opium trade as part of a campaign to undermine the pro-Chinese military junta. The latter was forced to concede to elections in 2015 which Kyi won, in a major victory for U.S. foreign policy.[58]

By 2015, 29 states and territories in Southeast Asia were hosting U.S. military capabilities, up from 12 in 2011.[59] Subsea and surveillance drones were deployed for intelligence gathering, and America's three main stealth radar-evading warplanes were sent to bases near China.[60] Journalist John Pilger told *Al Jazeera* that American military bases, numbering over 200 (compared to zero for China), "formed a giant noose encircling China with missiles, bombers and warships, all the way from Australia through the Pacific."[61]

America's aggressiveness was further epitomized by its new Air-Sea battle strategy, developed by long-time Pentagon strategist Andrew Marshall, which envisioned a pre-emptive strike in which stealth bombers and submarines would first knock out China's long-range surveillance radar and precision missiles, then carry out a large air and naval attack. Defense Advanced Research Projects Agency (DARPA) assisted the new strategy by developing a missile capable of penetrating Beijing's air defense at 3,300 miles per hour.[62]

Australia's former Prime Minister Malcolm Fraser (1975-1983) denounced the U.S. approach to China as a rerun of Cold War style containment, ruing Australia's treatment as a "strategic colony."[63] Much to his chagrin, the Obama administration reached a deal with Australia's right-leaning Prime Minister Julia Gillard in November 2011 to add 2,500 Marines to the Darwin military base, increase U.S. naval operations off the Australian coasts, expand the drone base at Cocos Island and place a special radar earmarked for tracking Chinese polar satellites in Western Australia along with a space surveillance telescope capable of monitoring China and the entire Southern hemisphere.[64]

Obama emphasized the humanitarian imperative under-lying the expanded military cooperation between the two countries, which dated to the sinking of the U.S.S. Peary by the Japanese in 1942 ("Australia's Pearl Harbor"). His remarks to Australian troops left out their involvement in dirty wars together like Vietnam and the 1965 genocide in Indonesia. When addressing the Australian parliament, Obama said that history was "on the side of the free – free societies, free governments, free economies, free people. And the future belongs to those who stand firm for those ideals, in this region and around the world."[65]

However, numerous countries supported by the U.S. were not free, including Vietnam and Singapore, which was rated only "partially free" by Freedom House because of its harsh criminal justice system, limits on academic freedom, banning of public sector unions and domination by Lee Kuan Yew's People's Action Party (PAP).[66] The Obama administration stationed littoral combat ships built by General Dynamics at a naval base in Singapore off the Strait of Malacca, where 90 percent of China's seaborne energy was shipped. Five out of the eight ships costing taxpayers $478 million were crippled by construction defects, design errors or crew mistakes, and found to be "not operationally suitable in war" by auditors or capable of completing a thirty-day mission.[67]

At Clark Air Force base in the Philippines, American P-3 Orion aircraft were sent to conduct patrol missions over Ayungin Reef as access to four strategic air and military bases was expanded following an agreement with Benigno Aquino III, Duterte's predecessor. The U.S.-Philippines relationship became frayed in January 2015 when the U.S. Joint Special Operations Task Force-Philippines led a bungled raid targeting two terror suspects in Mindanao which left forty-four Philippines army troops and 17 Muslim Moro fighters dead. Historian Alfred W. McCoy noted that "American war fighters trapped inside their hermetic technology and mesmerized by their video screens, proved incapable of grasping the realities of local conditions.....the asymmetry of power between nominal allies accentuated American arrogance and contributed to their damaging debacles."[68]

The looming threat of war with China was accentuated by Obama's approval of a $1.83 billion arms sale package to Taiwan that included two frigates, anti-tank missiles, amphibious assault vehicles and other equipment.[69] China had been hostile to the Taiwanese government ever since its' split under deposed nationalist leader Jieng Jieshi following the 1949 Chinese revolution. Obama further antagonized China by deepening ties with India, a country led by a right-wing Hindu nationalist, Narendra Modi that had gone to war with China before. India became the second largest market for the U.S. arms industry after Saudi Arabia, providing America access to the Trivandrum air base in return.[70]

Australian Prime Minister, Kevin Rudd (2007-2010; 2013), felt that the Asia Pacific at this time had come to resemble "a 21st-century maritime redux of the Balkans a century ago—a tinderbox on water. Nationalist sentiment is surging across the region, reducing the domestic political space for less confrontational approaches....In security terms, the region is more brittle than at any time since the fall of Saigon in 1975."[71] Obama's policies had contributed to this dangerous situation by fomenting rivalry with China and forcing countries to pick sides and by arming belligerents who could one day use the weapons on each other.

"Cleaning Dirt from the Indonesian Military"

In a speech before the G20 Summit in Australia, President Obama claimed that "generations of Americans" had "served and died here so that the people of the Asia Pacific might live free,"[72] though in reality the United States had supported many dictatorships, including that of Mohammed Suharto in Indonesia whose Special Forces, Kopassus, compiled a long record of atrocities. In March 2010, Obama lifted a Clinton-era ban on training Kopassus after Indonesian president Susilo Bambang Yudhoyono, a former Suharto General, threatened that he would explore ties with the Chinese military if the ban continued.[73] Indonesia was coveted strategically because it was surrounded by straits that linked the Indian Ocean and South China seas. The families of people killed by Kopassus organised a demonstration to protest Obama's decision. Maria Catarina Sumarsih of the Commission for Missing Persons and Victims of Violence feared that nobody would ever be held accountable for her son's death during a demonstration against Suharto in 1998. She stated that the U.S. was "acting like a washing machine by cleaning the dirt from the Indonesian military."[74]

These words appeared prophetic when, in March 2013, a dozen Kopassus officers stormed a jail in Yogyakarta and executed four prisoners. Indonesian security forces were also accused of excessive violence in counter-terror operations and in the suppression of the separatist movement in West Papua, where mining giants like Rio Tinto had lucrative operations.[75] In February 2016, when Obama met with Yudhoyono's successor,

Joko Widodo (Jokowi) at the ASEAN summit in Sunnylands California, he did not press him on human rights issues, according to available records, perhaps fearing a tit-for–tat exchange regarding the 1965-1967 genocide, the subject of a recently released documentary film in which Jokowi manifested interest. Obama's reasons may have been as much personal as geo-strategic due to the possibility of light being shed on the role his step-father and mother may have played in one of the great crimes of the 20th century.[76]

"U.S. Military Get the Hell Out": Hawaii and Guam

Like with Indonesia, Obama's family history was deeply intertwined with American policies in Hawaii, which had always served as a key location for the projection of U.S. power into the Asia-Pacific. Coming out on the side of expanding the military-CIA presence, Obama restored $16.7 million in funding for the University of Hawaii's East-West Center, his mother's alma mater. He also bolstered the Navy Special Forces and Command Center at Pearl Harbor, sanctioned funding for a $358 million National Security Agency (NSA) listening post for Asia and the Pacific in Oahu, constructed a missile range facility on Kaua'I for missile launch sites, provisioned $52 million for new housing, a command facility and parking for an increased troop presence, and expanded a range complex over 2.1 million square miles.[77] When Obama gave a speech at the East-West Center, he was greeted with a throng of protestors who chanted: "the military needs to leave Hawaii, people of the world scream and shout, U.S. military get the hell out."[78]

The U.S. controlled territory of Guam was another key launching off point for American power projection into the Asia Pacific. In 2010, the Obama administration announced a proposed $23 billion Pentagon plan to relocate 8,600 Marines from Okinawa that would include the building of live fire training sites, and expanded Andersen Air Force Base to include stationing of B-52 and B-2 stealth bombers and drones. In addition, the plan sought to expand a U.S. naval base for submarines, create berthing for a nuclear aircraft carrier and erect a missile defense system produced by Lockheed Martin, which was made permanent in 2015. Despite economic dependence on the U.S. and high rates of military service, many locals opposed what the Pentagon billed as among "the largest projects [it had] ever attempted." An environmental draft study warned about the effects on already substandard drinking water and wastewater infrastructure that could lead to "significant adverse public health impacts" and "unacceptable impacts to 71 acres of high-quality coral reef ecosystems in [Apra harbor]." A firing range was to be built on an indigenous burial site, and residents conveyed disdain for "apartheid" type segregation that came with a heavy military presence, including private military beaches that denied Chamorrans access to their ancestral heritage.[79]

Turning Back the Clock

Obama's Guam policy displayed stark continuity from the Cold War where Asia Pacific islands were used as launching pads for military operations and testing grounds for new weapons systems at the expense of indigenous peoples. On World Peace Day on September 21, 2011, the Nobel Peace Laureate as a message to those foreign governments who were surely paying attention sanctioned the firing of an intercontinental ballistic missile from Vandenberg Air Force Base, California into the Pacific Ocean. It crashed near the Marshall Islands, which still suffered from the adverse effects of nuclear and hydrogen bomb tests undertaken in the 1950s.[80]

The Obama administration further turned back the clock in its efforts to undermine the democratic left in Seoul and Tokyo and elevate conservative, pro-American, militaristic parties. Obama forged particularly close ties with South Korean Premier Lee Myung Bak, a conservative Hyundai executive who pursued development of a long-range missile in violation of an arms control agreement. He was also close with Lee's successor, Park Geun-

Hye, the daughter of an American Cold War client who further reversed the "sunshine" policy instituted by Prime-Minister Kim Dae-Jung in the early 2000s calling for rapprochement between North-and South.

The Obama years saw little progress on that front. Tensions were enflamed by Obama's increased troop deployments, provision of a sophisticated missile defense system, and selling of a $1.2 billion spy drone and F-35 fighter jets to South Korea after a North Korean missile test.[81] In 2013 war games, a B-2A stealth bomber flew from the U.S. mainland into the sky above South Korea for the first time in history to stage a mock drill for dropping nuclear bombs on North Korea as two nuclear flotillas were deployed in the waters off the Korean peninsula.[82]

Once again, Obama turned to human rights, disregarded elsewhere, to justify these provocative maneuvers, reminiscent of the 1951 Operation Hudson Harbor in which B-29s from Okinawa dropped dummy atomic bombs. North Korea was "the most isolated, the most sanctioned, the most cut-off nation on earth," Obama told a reporter. "The kind of authoritarianism that exists there, you almost can't duplicate anywhere else. It's brutal and it's oppressive and as a consequence, the country can't really even feed its own people.... Over time you will see a regime like this collapse."[83] But the regime had survived for over seventy years by mobilizing its people against a threatened invasion, drawing on memories of the barbarism of the Korean War. That reality was oblivious to Obama, and indeed the mainstream media which swallowed his every bellicose word.

Igniting Resistance: Obama and Japan

Obama's historic visit to Hiroshima, Japan in May 2016 was colored not just by an ongoing failure to take responsibility for the dropping of the atomic bomb, but by a clever eclipsing of that reality. Though conveying sympathy for the bomb's living victims (known as the *hibakusha*), Obama told a rapt audience that "death fell from the sky" and the world changed on a "bright, cloudless morning."[84] In reality, death did not just fall from the sky, but was delivered by the most diabolical weapon in human history to date that was intentionally dropped by the American Enola Gay bombardiers on a civilian population.[85]

The U.S. military at the time of Obama's speech was rebuilding the airfields at Tinian, in the Northern Marianas islands 1500 km from Tokyo, where the Enola Gay had taken off on its mission to destroy Hiroshima.[86] An additional irony was that Obama gave the Hiroshima speech at the side of Japanese Prime Minister Shinzo Abe, an apologist for Japanese war crimes in World War II who was trying to revive Japan's military power in violation of its pacifist constitution and reaffirm its status as a surrogate of U.S. power.[87] These actions were favored and indeed encouraged by the United States, which had posted over 40,000 U.S. military personnel in Japan. Abe's maternal grandfather, Kishi Nobusuke, Prime Minister in the 1950s, had signed a U.S. Japan Mutual Security Treaty allowing U.S. bases. A Class A war criminal in World War II, Kishi had been released from Sugamo Prison by U.S. occupational authorities because of his utility in opposing the Socialists.

In 2010, Obama had helped force the resignation of Japanese Prime Minister Hatoyama Yukio when he opposed an agreement that had been illegally rammed through the Japanese diet by his predecessor mandating the relocation of a Marine Corps Air Station at Henoko in Okinawa, an island occupied since World War II. The proposed building site was a fishing port, with coral and dugong graze on sea grasses in its waters, and protected birds, insects and animals which were threatened by the base. According to historian Gavan McCormack, Hatoyama's capitulation was considered a "day of humiliation" for the Ryukyus' "akin to that of April 1952 when the islands were offered to the U.S. as part of the deal for restoration of Japanese sovereignty." A *Ryukyu Shimpo* survey found opposition to the new base running at 84 percent.[88]

Hatoyama and his Democratic Party (PDJ), which broke more than a half century of Liberal Democratic Party (LDP) dominance in Japan, had striven for the creation of an autonomous

East Asian community based on fraternity, and a more equal relationship with Washington. Hatoyama also wanted the U.S. to reveal its secret agreements with past conservative governments which brought nuclear weapons into Japan and proposed ending the Japanese Navy's mission of refueling U.S. ships in the Gulf.[89] Hatoyama's successor, Naoto Kan, cooperated more closely with the U.S., purchasing Lockheed F-35s stealth fighters at a cost of $6-$8 billion despite the desperate need to rebuild Japan after a devastating earthquake and tsunami.[90] In February 2009, Ryukyu community leaders had sent an Open Letter to Ms. Clinton: "Okinawa, a small island, has lived under great stress for over sixty years. The presence of U.S. military bases has distorted not only the politics and economy of Okinawa, but also its society and people's minds and pride. We do not need to remind you that Okinawa is not your territory. Your 50,000 military members act freely as if this is their land, but of course, it is not."[91]

This letter went ignored and the Obama administration sent only a low-level delegate from the State Department's Japan desk to meet with the elected mayor of Nago City and a delegation of lawmakers and activists who came to Washington to plead for a change in policy.[92] In 2013, Governor Onaga Takeshi gave formal notice of intent to revoke the license for reclamation issued in December 2013 by his predecessor, Nakaima Hirokazu, though suddenly died before he could take action.[93] Sit-ins and other forms of protest continued and another anti-base governor was elected in 2018, an expression of popular resistance similar to that in Jeju-do where Obama's pivot had brought back memories of the darkest chapter in the island's modern history: the killing and displacement of tens of thousands by the South Korean Army and its American advisers on the eve of the Korean War.

Koh Kwon-Il, a member of the Association of Gangjeong Villagers Against the Jeju Naval Base, told a reporter: "The U.S. military killed Jeju residents back then, this is why we don't want a naval base [they can use]. Everyone knows this navy base was made for the U.S., even though the government insists it isn't.... We want to hear an apology from the U.S. for the murder of innocents."[94] Rather than offering an apology, President Obama sought to recast memory of the Korean War as a great American victory, and reinvigorate the foreign policy of Douglas McArthur, all while projecting a liberal image.

Strategic Disappointment

The strategic disappointment of Obama's pivot was evident with the failure to pass the TPP, China's bold construction of a "Great Wall of Sand" in the South China Seas and its ability to win over supporters as a result of its "one belt, one road initiative," a massive infrastructural development project aiming to connect the Pacific and Baltic Seas.[95] As the United States and Western Europe were mired in growing debt, corruption, and economic and moral decline, China was gradually forging an effective counter-pole to Washington's New World (dis-)order in conjunction with Putin's Russia.[96] In April 2015, China took a major step in their campaign to supplant the dollar as the world's dominant reserve currency when European members of the IMF embraced China's demand to include the yuan as a unit of IMF currency.[97]

Former Assistant Secretary of Defense Graham Allison wrote that China's new arsenal of one thousand anti-ship missiles, submarine destroyers, ballistic and cruise missiles and anti-satellite weapons had "degraded the position of Pacific military dominance to which the U.S. had become accustomed since the Battle of Midway in 1942."[98] In December 2013, for the first time, the Chinese Navy openly confronted a U.S. Navy combatant ship, the *U.S.S. Cowpens,* on the high seas prior to its attempted interception of the Chinese navy carrier, *Liaoning,* forcing it to back down.[99] South Korea, Malaysia, Thailand, Indonesia, and the Philippines realigned with China at this time. After promising to end military exercises and joint-sea patrols of disputed water, Filipino President Rodrigo Duterte characterized Washington as a "has-been power." Historian James Petras pointed out that "without total U.S. control over the Philippines, Washington's strategic arc of encirclement against China is broken."[100] The big winners of the pivot appear to be the elites in Japan, Vietnam, and Singapore, which received greater foreign aid, along with the arms manufacturers and other military profiteers. The losers included most of the U.S. public because of all the resources squandered, and a majority of people of the Asia Pacific for whom a looming threat of war was a price they had to pay for living under the boot of the world's "indispensable nation."

Endnotes

1   Ann Wright, "South Korean Villagers Sued for Anti-Base Protests," *Consortium News*, June 10, 2016.

2   Koohan Paik, "'Pacific Pivot: The Obama Administration's 'Pacific Pivot' is Wreaking Environmental Havoc on the Pristine Ecosystems of the Asia Pacific Region," *Foreign Policy in Focus*, January 27, 2014; Gwisook Gwon, "Protests Challenge Naval Base Construction on Jeju Island, South Korea," *The Asia Pacific Journal*, 9, 28, July 11, 2011; Ann Wright, "Jeju Island, South Korea," in *The Military-Industrial Complex at 50*, ed. David Swanson (David Swanson, 2011), 55-58; Vince Scappatura, "The U.S. Pivot to Asia, the China Spectre, and the Australian-American Alliance," *The Asia Pacific Journal*, September 6, 2014.

3   Darren Southcott, "Jeju, Obama's 'Pivot to Asia,' Says Oliver Stone: U.S. Director Warns of Jeju's Becoming a Site of War, Pollution and Crime," *Jeju News*, August 12, 2013, http://www.jejuweekly.com/news/articleView.html?idxno=3454; Noam Chomsky, "The Threat of Warships on an Island of World Peace," in *Making the Future: Occupation, Intervention, Empire and Resistance* (San Francisco: City Lights Books, 2012), 297-300; Michael T. Klare, *The Race for What's Left: The Global Scramble for the World's Last Resources* (New York: Picador, 2012); Joseph P. Gerson, "Countering Washington's Pivot and the New Asia-Pacific Arms Race," *Z Magazine*, January 27, 2013.

4   Mark Landler, *Alter Egos: Hillary Clinton, Barack Obama, and the Twilight Struggle Over American Power* (New York: Random House, 2016), 299; Lenore Taylor, "G20: Barack Obama Uses Visit to Reassert U.S. Influence in the Asia Pacific," *The Guardian*, November 15, 2014; Remarks by President Obama to U.S. Troops and Personnel at U.S. Army Garrison Yongsan," The White House, April 26, 2014.

5   Hillary Clinton, "America's Pacific Century," *Foreign Affairs*, October 11, 2011.

6   Albert Beveridge, "March of the Flag," September 16, 1898, http://voicesofdemocracy.umd.edu/beveridge-march-of-the-flag-speech-text/.

7   Walter LaFeber, *The New Empire: An Interpretation of American Expansion 1860-1898* (Ithaca: Cornell University Press, 1963), 410.

8   See Bruce Cumings, *Dominion From Sea to Sea: Pacific Ascendancy and American Power* (New Haven: Yale University Press, 2010); *America's Asia: Dissenting Essays on Asian-American Relations,* ed. Mark Selden and Edward Friedman (New York: Pantheon, 1971); James Peck, *Washington's China* (Amherst, MA: University of Massachusetts Press, 2007).

9   F. William Engdahl, *Target China: How Washington and Wall Street Plan to Cage the Asian Dragon* (San Diego: Progressive Press, 2014), 7.

10   Engdahl, *Target China*, 149-151; "China Builds Up Strategic Sea Lanes," *Washington Times*, January 17, 2005.

11   Koohan Paik and Jerry Mander, "On the Front Lines of a New Pacific War," *The Nation*, December 14, 2012.

12   Mark Landler, "Obama Takes a Detour to Reconnect with Southeast Asia," *The New York Times*, September 7, 2016.

13   Mark Landler, "Obama Acknowledges Scars of America's Shadow Wars in Laos," *New York Times*, September 6, 2016.

14   Floyd Whaley, "Clinton Reaffirms Military Ties with the Philippines," *The New York Times*, November 16, 2011.

15   See for example Paul Kramer, *The Blood of Government* (Chapel Hill: The University of North Carolina Press, 2004).

16   Kurt Campbell, *The Pivot: The Future of American Statecraft in Asia* (New York: Twelve, 2016).

17   Alfred W. McCoy, *Policing America's Empire: The U.S., the Philippines, and the Rise of the Surveillance State* (Madison, WI: University of Wisconsin Press, 2009).

18   The White House, "Remarks by the President at 60th Anniversary of the Korean War Armistice," July 27, 2013.

19   Garrett Underhill and Ronald Schiller, "The Tragedy of the U.S. Army," *Look Magazine*, February 13, 1951, 27.

20   See George Katsiaficas, *Asia's Unknown Uprisings: South Korea's Social Movements in the 20th Century* (PM Press, 2012).

21   "Remarks by the President at the Commemoration Ceremony of the 50th Anniversary of the Vietnam War," May 28, 2012, https://obamawhitehouse.archives.gov/the-press-office/2012/05/28/remarks-president-commemoration-ceremony-50th-anniversary-vietnam-war.

22   Bruce Franklin, *Vietnam and Other American Fantasies* (Amherst, MA: University of Massachusetts Press, 2000); Jerry Lembcke, "GI, Veteran, and POW Voices of Conscience: Recovering the Voices of GI Resistance to the War in Vietnam," *Asia Pacific Journal*, February 1, 2019.

23   "Remarks by the President at the Commemoration Ceremony of the 50th Anniversary of the Vietnam War;" Jerry Lembcke, *The Spitting Image: Myth, Memory and the Legacy of Vietnam* (New York: NYU Press, 1998); Paul Street, "The Chomsky Challenge for Americans," *Truthdig*, June 13, 2018.

24   Prashanth Parameswaran, "U.S. Vietnam Defense Relations: Problems and Prospects," *The Diplomat*, May 27, 2016; Jane Perlez, "Why Might Vietnam Let U.S. Military Return? China," *New York Times*, May 19, 2016; Daniel B. Larter, "U.S. Deepens Military Ties with Former Foe, Vietnam," *Navy Times*, May 23, 2016.

25   Geoff Dyer, *The Contest of the Century: The New Era of Competition with China – And How America Can Win* (New York: Alfred A. Knopf, 2014), 78; David Kang, *China Rising: Peace, Power and Order in East Asia* (New York: Columbia University Press, 2009).

26   Dyer, *The Contest of the Century*, 78; Parag Khanna, *The Second World: How Emerging Powers Are Redefining Global Competition in the Twenty First Century* (New York: Random House, 2009).

27   Engdahl, *Target China*, 12.

28   Richard McGregor, *Asia's Reckoning: China, Japan, and the Fate of U.S. Power in the Asia Pacific* (New York: Viking, 2017), 350; Jude Woodward, *The US vs China: Asia's New Cold War?* (Manchester: Manchester University Press, 2017), 163; Engdahl, *Target China*, 153; Mark Landler, "Philippines 'Separation' From U.S. Jilts Hillary Clinton, Too," *New York Times*, October 21, 2016; David Feith, "Checking Manila's anti-American Pivot," *The Wall Street Journal*, October 27, 2016. Duterte told Obama that Philippines had long ceased to be a U.S. colony.

29   Woodward: *The US vs China*, 65; Peter Navarro, *Crouching Tiger: What China's Militarism Means For the World* (New York: Prometheus Books, 2015). The deceptiveness stereotype was promoted by Princeton Professor Aaron L. Friedberg, a former assistant to Dick Cheney.

30   Gregson quoted in Yuka Hayashi, "U.S. Builds Up Marines in Asia, Amphibian Push is Meant to Ease Doubts About Asia Pivot," *Wall Street Journal*, April 2, 2014.

31   Bruce Cumings, "The Obama 'Pivot' to Asia in a Historical Context of American Hegemony," in *Asia Pacific Countries and the U.S. Rebalancing Strategy*, ed. David Huang (New York: Palgrave McMillan, 2016), 24.

32   Michael Fabey, *Crashback: The Power Clash Between the U.S. and China in the Pacific* (New York: Scribner, 2017), 178, 179; https://www.opensecrets.org/members-of-congress/summary?cid=N00013799. BAE Systems, a British aerospace company, was also a major donor to the Democratic Party.

33   Andrea Shallal Esa, "General Dynamics, Huntington Ingalls Win Huge Submarine Orders," *Reuters*, December 27, 2012.

34   Cumings, "The Obama 'Pivot' to Asia in a Historical Context of American

Hegemony," in *Asia Pacific Countries and the U.S. Rebalancing Strategy*, ed. Huang, 24.

35 www.opensecrets.org; "This U.S. Based Private Equity Investor is on a Tear in Southeast Asia," September 6, 2017, https://www.cbinsights.com/research/warburg-pincus-asia/; http://www.kkr.com/our-firm/leadership/david-h-petraeus. Warburg Pincus owned one of the leading providers of avionics and electronics for the aerospace and defense industries. According to Open Secrets, Barbara Vogelstein was a key bundler at Warburg Pincus raising large sums for Obama's campaigns. Petraeus had had to resign from the military after sharing classified secrets with his lover, Paula Broadwell.

36 Chas Freeman Jr., *Interesting Times: China, America, and the Shifting Balance of Prestige* (Charlottesville, VI: Just World Books, 2012), 15; Peter Kuznick and Oliver Stone, *The Untold History of the United States* (New York: Hyperion, 2012).

37 Michael T. Klare, "The United States Heads to the South China Sea: Why American Involvement Will Mean Mere Friction – Not Less," *Foreign Affairs*, February 21, 2013; Campbell, *The Pivot*, 175; Engdahl, *Target China*, 158.

38 Jim Wolf, "Analysis: U.S. Arms Sales to Asia Set to Boom on Pacific 'Pivot,'" *Reuters*, January 1, 2013.

39 "Obama's Pivot Depends on What He Can Deliver at Home," *Bloomberg News*, November 16, 2012.

40 "Advancing the Rebalance to Asia and the Pacific," The White House, Office of the Press Secretary, November 16, 2015.

41 "Remarks by President Obama in Address to the People of Vietnam," Hanoi, May 24, 2016.

42 Prasanth Parames, "TPP as Important as another Aircraft Carrier: US Defense Secretary," *The Diplomat*, April 18, 2015.

43 "U.S. Secretary of Commerce Penny Pritzker Highlights TPP Benefits for Small Businesses at Progressive Policy Institute Event," September 16, 2016. Pritzker claimed that "since the end of World War II, U.S. leadership in international trade has helped usher in an era of peace and prosperity." This was not true if we consider the huge number of proxy wars in the Cold War.

44 Woodward, *The U.S. vs. China*, 156, 161.

45 Nadia Propis, "Emails Show TPP Collusion Between Big Banks and Obama Administration," *Common Dreams*, May 27, 2016; Zach Carter, "Why Goldman Sachs Likes Obama's Trade Agenda," *Huffington Post*, May 26, 2016. The TPP also promoted the export of natural gas to the benefit of the fracking industry which Obama was favorable towards.

46 See Scott Nearing and Joseph Freeman's classic, *Dollar Diplomacy: A Study in American Imperialism* (New York: The Viking Press, 1926).

47 In McGregor, *Asia's Reckoning*, 7.

48 Leszek Buszynski, 'The South China Sea: Oil, Maritime Claims, and US-

China Strategic Rivalry," *The Washington Quarterly*, 35, 2 (2012), 144; Navarro, *Crouching Tiger*, 56, 58, 68; "Chinese Naval Strategy, the United States, ASEAN and the South China Sea," *Security Challenges*, vol. 8, no. 2, 19-32, cited in Scappatura, "The U.S. Pivot to Asia, the China Spectre, and the Australian-American alliance;" Malcolm Fraser, *Dangerous Allies* (Melbourne: Melbourne University Press, 2014), 233, 262.

49   Helene Cooper, "Patrolling Disputed Waters, U.S. and China Jockey for Dominance," *New York Times*, March 30, 2016.

50   Michael T. Klare, "The United States Heads to the South China Sea: Why American Involvement Will Mean More Friction – Not Less," *Foreign Affairs*, February 21, 2013; Cumings, "The Obama 'Pivot' to Asia' in Historical Context," 25.

51   Engdahl, *Target China*, 12, 141,167; Landler, *Alter Egos*, 290, 297.

52   Woodward, *The US vs China*, 55, 56.

53   John Ford, "The Pivot to Asia Was Obama's Biggest Mistake," *The Diplomat*, January 21, 2017; Glenn Diesen, *Russia's Geoeconomic Strategy for Greater Eurasia* (New York Routeledge, 2018), 43. Obama took up petty complaints against China before the World Trade Organization (WTO) which could have been resolved in bilateral negotiations.

54   Henry Kissinger, "China: Containment Won't Work," *The Washington Post*, June 13, 2005; Zbigniew Brzezinski, "Towards a Global Realignment," *The American Interest*, 11, 6 (2016), 7-11; Landler, *Alter Egos*, 299.

55   Chi Wang, *Obama's Challenge to China* (London: Ashgate, 2015), 82, 149; Matt Margolis, *The Worst President in History: The Legacy of Barack Obama* (New York: Victory Books, 2016), 45.

56   Author telephone interview Chas Freeman Jr., February 18, 2019; Freeman Jr., *Interesting Times*, 13.

57   Woodward, *The US vs. China*, 16; Tony Cartalucci, "Turmoil on Hong Kong, Terrorism in Xinjiang: America's Covert War on China," *New Eastern Outlook*, October 21, 2014; Wayne Madsen, *Soros: Quantum of Chaos* (WayneMadsenReport.com, 2015), 53-57; Engdahl, *Target China*. The CIA and George Soros Open Society allegedly attempted to infiltrate the Chinese Communist Party Politburo through appointment of Bo Xilai who promoted the privatization of Chinese state assets though this plan was squelched when Bo was indicted for corruption.

58   Engdahl, *Target China*; Julie Hirschfield Davis, "Obama Pledges to Lift All Sanctions Against Myanmar," *New York Times*, September 14, 2016; Webster Griffin Tarpley, *Obama: The Post-Modern Coup* (Joshua Tree, CA: Progressive Press, 2008), 280-284. Kyi's victory however intensified pogroms in the Rhakine state against the Rohingya Muslims.

59   Engdahl, *Target China*; Michael Foulon, "Trade and Security in U.S. Grand Strategy," in *American Hegemony and the Rise of Emerging Powers:*

Cooperation or Conflict, ed. Salvador Regelme Jr. and James Poigot (New York: Routeledge, 2018), 52.

60   Klare, "The United States Heads to the South China Sea;" David Axe, "Pentagon Preps Stealth Strike Force to Counter China," *Wired Magazine*, December 26, 2012; Fabey, *Cashback*.

61   "John Pilger Q & A: U.S. Missiles are pointed at China," *Al Jazeera*, December 06, 2017.

62   Aaron L. Friedberg, *Beyond Air-Sea Battle* (The International Institute for Strategic Studies, 2014); Alfred W. McCoy, *In the Shadows of the American Century: The Rise and Decline of US Global Power* (Chicago: Haymarket Books, 2017), 186.

63   Dyer, *The Contest of the Century*, 101; Fraser, *Dangerous Allies*. Fraser once had supported the Vietnam War.

64   Richard Tanter, "The U.S. Military Presence in Australia," *The Asia Pacific Journal*, November 11, 2013; McCoy, *In the Shadows of the American Century*, 188. Australia housed a secret military facility at Pine Gap that transmitted cell phone and other signals used in drone strikes.

65   "Remarks by President Obama to the Australian Parliament," The White House, Office of the Press Secretary, November 17, 2011; Jennifer Epstein, "In Australia, Obama Thanks Troops," *Politico*, November 17, 2011.

66   Singapore, Freedom House, https://freedomhouse.org/report/freedom-world/2012/singapore; Sally Andrews, "'Soft Repression': The Struggle for Democracy in Singapore," *The Diplomat*, February 16, 2015. Opposition candidates broke through in the 2011 by winning 6 seats in the parliament. The PAP held over 90 percent of them still.

67   Jonathan Marshall, "New Navy Ships Leaking Tax Dollars," *Consortium News*, December 5, 2016.

68   McCoy, *In the Shadows of the American Century*, 181. The operation was led by an American nicknamed Alan Kurtz.

69   Kuznick and Stone, *The Untold History of the United States*; David Brunnstrom, "Obama Administration Authorized $1.83 Billion Arms Sale to Taiwan," *Reuters*, December 17, 2015.

70   Shivaji Kumar, "How Obama Revived U.S. Indian Relations," *The National Interest*, June 6, 2016; Sunny Hundal, "Trump is Tame Compared to India's Newly Strengthened Prime Minister Narendra Modi," *The Independent*, March 17, 2017; "USA Force to Get Military Airbase in Thiruvanthapuram, India," *Financial Express*, August 23, 2013. Boeing netted a $5.8 billion deal to sell transport aircraft, which was the sixth largest arms deal in U.S. history.

71   Kevin Rudd, "A Maritime Balkans for the 21st Century," *Foreign Policy*, January 30, 2013.

72   Carol E. Lee, "Obama Seeks to Reassure Asia Allies on Pivot," *The Wall Street Journal*, November 4, 2014.

73   Philip Darling and Nick McKenzie, "Obama Caved in on Kopassus," *Sydney Times*, December 12, 2010; "Indonesia: U.S. Resumes Military Assistance to Abusive Force," *Human Rights Watch*, July 2, 2010; Joshua Kurlantzick, "Keeping the U.S.-Indonesian Relationship Moving Forward," February 2018, Council on Foreign Relations Special Report No. 81, 2018, 6.

74   John Braddock, "U.S. Ends Ban on Indonesian Kopassus Commandos," *World Socialist Web Site*, August 6, 2010.

75   Indonesia 2013 Human Rights Report, U.S. Department of State, https://www.state.gov/documents/organization/220408.pdf

76   "President Obama at U.S.-ASEAN Summit Press Conference," https://id.usembassy.gov/remarks-by-president-obama-at-u-s-asean-summit-press-conference/; Wayne Madsen, "Obama's Family Role in Indonesian Genocide Protected by Muslim Radicals," *Strategic Culture Foundation*, June 25, 2016.

77   Kyle Kajihiro, "Moannanuiakea or 'American Lake'? Contested Histories of the US 'Pacific Pivot'" in *Under Occupation: Resistance and Struggle in a Militarized Asia-Pacific*, ed. Daniel Broudy, Peter Simpson and Makoto Arakaki (UK: Cambridge Scholars Publishing, 2013), 128, 129; Wayne Madsen, *The Manufacturing of a President* (Self-Published, 2012), 317, 318; McCoy, *In the Shadows of the American Century*, 132.

78   Sophie Cooke, "Obama Talks of Hawaiian Ties, Climate Change at East-West Center Speech," *The Hawaii Star Advertiser*, August 30, 2016.

79   Lisa Linda Natividad and Gwyn Kirk, "Fortress Guam: Resistance to U.S. Mega-Buildup," *The Asia Pacific Journal*, 8, 19, 1 May 10, 2010; Seth Kershner, "Resisting the Guam Military Build-Up," *Z Magazine*, September 2010, 16, 17; Leevin Camacho, "Poison in Our Waters," *The Asia Pacific Journal,* December 22, 2013. After a lawsuit was threatened over the firing range, Major General David Price, Director of the Joint Guam Program Office pointed at several members of the National Trust for Historic Preservation and told them that "unless the Department of Defense got its way, your children will die."

80   Ann Wright, "An ICBM Launch on World Peace Day," in *The Military Industrial Complex at Fifty*, ed. David Swanson (David Swanson, 2011), 50; David Vine, *Base Nation: How U.S. Military Bases Abroad Harm America and the World* (New York: Metropolitan Books, 2015).

81   Ashley Smith, 'U.S. Imperialism's Pivot to Asia,' *International Socialist Review*, April 201; Campbell, *The Pivot,* 234; James Petras, "Washington's 'Pivot to Asia,': A Debacle Unfolding," *Global Research*, October 25, 2016; Wolf, "U.S. Arms Sales to Asia Set to Boom on Pacific Pivot."

82   Bruce Cumings, "Getting North Korea Wrong," *Bulletin of the Atomic Scientists*, July 1, 2015.

83   Cumings, "Getting North Korea Wrong."

84   "Text of President Obama's Speech in Hiroshima, Japan," *New York Times*,

May 27, 2016.

85   See Robert Jay Lifton and Gregory Mitchell, *Hiroshima and America: Fifty Years of Denial* (New York: Harperennial, 1996).

86   John Reed, "Surrounded: How the U.S. is Encircling China with Military Bases," *Foreign Policy*, August 20, 2013.

87   Tim Shorrock, "East Asia" in *The Wikileaks Files: The World According to U.S. Empire*, ed. Julian Assange (London: Verso, 2015), 395-432; Engdahl, *Target China*, 156.

88   Gavan McCormack, "Obama vs. Okinawa" *New Left Review*, 64, July-August 2010, 12.

89   McCormack, "Obama vs. Okinawa;" McGregor, *Asia's Reckoning*, 223; Gavan McCormack and Satoko Oka Norimatsu, *Resistant Islands* (Lanham, Boulder, Rowman and Littlefield, 2012).

90   Kuznick and Stone, *The Untold History of the United States.*

91   McCormack, "Obama vs. Okinawa," 13.

92   Shorrock, "East Asia," in *The Wikileaks Files*, ed. Assange, 429.

93   "Over One Hundred International Scholars, Peace Advocates and Artists Support Local Residents' Decision to Refuse New Military Base Construction in Okinawa," http://peacephilosophy.blogspot.com/2014/01/johan-galtung-david-suzuki-helen.html

94   Crystal Tai, "Jeju Jittery as US warship Visit Reminds Islanders of Dark Chapter in South Korea's History," *South China Morning Post*, October 13, 2018; Hu Joon Kim, *The Massacre at Mt. Halla: Sixty Years of Truth Seeking in South Korea* (Ithaca: Cornell University Press, 2015).

95   Alfred W. McCoy, "Beijing's Bid for Global Power in the Age of Trump: "America First Versus China's Strategy of the Four Continents," Tomdispatch. com, August 21, 2018.

96   Engdahl, *Target China*, 219, 220.

97   Ian Talley and Lingling Wei, "Momentum Builds to Label Chinese Yan a Reserve Currency," *Wall Street Journal*, April 1, 2015.

98   Graham Allison, *Destined For War: Can America and China Escape Thucydides' Trap?* (Boston: Houghton Mifflin Harcourt, 2017), 131.

99   Fabey, *Crashback*, 139, 149.

100   Petras, "Washington's 'Pivot to Asia.'"

Chapter 8

TOO MANY LIES
IGNITING A NEW COLD WAR
WITH RUSSIA

In February 2017, Russian Television America aired a documentary, "Trapped. Life on the Donetsk Frontline Through the Eyes of a Little Girl," which spotlighted the travails of the Ryzhkova family, including seven-year old Masha, as they tried to carry on with life inside the grey zone in the small town of Zaitzevo, located on the demarcation line between the Donetsk rebel forces and Ukrainian military. The film included footage of bombed out buildings like Masha's school, and recorded Masha's fears about being struck by bombs in the night. Masha's grandmother Svetlana stated in an interview that "they call us separatists. But what is a separatist? Someone who wants to live a quiet life in peace?"[1]

The RT network featured many other documentaries which spotlighted the viewpoint of the Donetsk fighters and Russian-speaking Eastern Ukrainian people who were at war with Ukrainian government backed by the U.S. Their view was absent in the American media. One film spotlighted a female commander, Veselina, whose main wish was to survive with her life and that of her comrades intact, and featured footage of the Donetsk city theatre and airport which had been destroyed. Local residents said they had become "trapped like rats" living in a hole in the ground [bomb shelter]" and that "millions of people had cursed at Ukrainian leader Pyotr Poroshenko."[2] Another documentary featured the anguish of internally displaced refugees, some of whom had fought the Nazis in World War II, who said that they never thought the Nazis would come back. A young man who had to walk with a cane said he had been badly tortured in Ukrainian military custody, a fact corroborated by two Ukrainian military officers who expressed a change of heart about their involvement in the war.[3]

The United States involvement in this dirty war in Ukraine was an important manifestation of a new Cold War with Russia that unfolded in the Obama years. In 2010, U.S. Ambassador to Russia, Michael McFaul had promoted a reset policy that resulted in joint commercial ventures and the New Strategic Arms Reduction Treaty (New START) limiting, albeit only marginally, the number of nuclear and ballistic missile launchers and nuclear warheads deployed by each side.[4] During the 2012 presidential debates, Obama depicted his opponent Mitt Romney as a relic of the 1980s when he suggested Russia had come to supersede Al Qaeda as the greatest national security threat, telling Romney that the Cold War had ended twenty years ago.[5]

When Vladimir Putin won a third term, again switching positions with now Prime Minister Dmitry Medvedev, U.S.-Russian relations began to deteriorate, however. The Obama administration sparked a coup in Ukraine, then expanded sanctions against Russia after the accession of Crimea to Russia following a referendum, and continued its intervention in the civil war that followed.[6] Former Defense Secretary William J. Perry was among those to believe that the danger of nuclear catastrophe was now "even greater than during the Cold War."[7]

While Putin was branded as a menace to world peace, his policies were mostly reactive and driven by a determination to restore Russia as a great power.[8] The Obama administration continued expanding NATO to Russia's door, while stationing missiles in Eastern Europe. Guiding Obama's hand was geopolitical strategist Zbigniew Brzezinski whose life's goal was to emasculate and balkanize Russia in order to secure America's indefinite global domination. When the Democrats lost the 2016 election, Obama and his supporters reactivated Americans' deep-rooted Russophobia remnant from the Cold War to scapegoat Russia and falsely accuse the new president, Donald J. Trump, of being a Manchurian candidate. Obama's Wilsonian instincts were displayed in his presentation of a confrontational policy as a moral crusade directed against an authoritarian regime that had allegedly attacked American democracy.

Obama's Views on the First Cold War

Obama's support for a new Cold War was shaped in part by his family history and a triumphalist understanding of the first Cold War. Obama's grandfather, grandmother, alleged father, mother and stepfather were all Cold Warriors who served in one capacity or another in the fight against communism. Obama followed in his family's footsteps and embraced the same political outlook, claiming at a press conference that the United States was on the "right side of history in the Cold War" and justified in opposing an "expansionist and very aggressive communism."[9] In *The Audacity of Hope*, Obama or his ghost-writer wrote with pride that the U.S. won [the Cold War] "not simply because it outgunned the Soviet Union, but because American values held sway in the court of international public opinion, which included those who live within communist regimes." As a classic Wilsonian, Obama went on to praise the postwar leadership of President Harry S. Truman, Secretaries of State Dean Acheson and George Marshall, and State Department diplomat George Kennan for responding to the Soviet threat and "crafting the architecture of a new postwar order that married [Woodrow] Wilson's idealism to hard-headed realism."

This, Obama says, led to a "successful outcome to the Cold War": an avoidance of nuclear catastrophe, the effective end of conflict between the world's great military powers, and an "era of unprecedented economic growth at home and abroad." While acknowledging some excesses including the toleration and even aid to "thieves like Mobutu and Noriega so long as they opposed communism," Obama went on to praise Ronald Reagan's arms buildup in the 1980s during his own coming of political age. He wrote that "given the Soviet invasion of Afghanistan [which, per Brzezinski, the U.S. actually helped to precipitate by arming jihadists], staying ahead of the Soviets militarily seemed a sensible thing to do. Pride in our country, respect for our armed services, a healthy appreciation for the dangers beyond our borders, an insistence that there was no easy equivalence between East and West—in all this I had no quarrel with Reagan....when the Berlin Wall came tumbling down, I had to give the old man his due, even if I never gave him the vote."[10]

Staking out a position in sympathy with the right as one who is "responsible" rather than "anti-American," or "radical," Obama took pains to distance himself from leftist friends who "were more concerned about brutality in Chile than about oppression behind the Iron Curtain" and "gave a pass to Third World leaders who stole from their people."[11] Obama never named these leaders, just as he left out how U.S. policy-makers constantly exaggerated the Soviet threat to justify expanding the U.S. overseas network of military bases.

The implications of Obama's triumphalist account of the Cold War are considerable; he played a major role in igniting Cold War 2.0. If fighting and winning the first Cold War was a noble cause, why not go for a second round—even if Russia was no longer communist? The payoff would be big profits for the arms merchants who financed his campaign and the mobilization of the population against a phantom enemy, curtailing any possibility of progressive social transformation domestically. And in the new Russia, there was again and at last a credible enemy—if Putin would only agree to be so, and stop referring to the West as "our partners."

The Demonization of Putin

A key feature of the new Cold War has been the incessant demonization of Russian President Vladimir Putin and depiction of Russia as a neo-Soviet autocracy. Obama said that the main goal of U.S. policy was "to put him [Putin] in a box to stop making mischief."[12] Such comments were part of Obama's efforts to cast the new Cold War as a moral crusade against an evil dictator. While all propaganda usually has some elements of truth, Putin was accused of every crime imaginable, including assassinating his opponents, without hard evidence to back up the charges. British diplomat Alastair Cook observed that "the compulsive hatred of President Putin in elite western circles has surpassed anything witnessed during the cold war." Canada's former ambassador, Christopher Westdal, stated that the "standard portrait of Putin [was] so wrong that it's hard to keep one's balance taking swings at such a straw man."[13]

Mr. Putin was appointed Deputy Prime Minister and then acting Prime Minister by Boris Yeltsin, who designated him as his successor, and then was elected as Russia's President in 2000, winning elections in 2004, 2012, and 2018. He is a conservative nationalist bent on restoring Russia's economy and global stature following the failed neoliberal "shock therapy" policies promoted by Harvard University advisers in the 1990s. Their policies had resulted in "the largest giveaway of a nation's wealth in history," according to Mortimer Zuckerman, owner of the *U.S. World & Report*. Russia's gold reserves were looted and its wealth taken by predatory financial interests and mafia-connected oligarchs, some with connection to the Bush I administration and the CIA. Over $150 billion left the country in just six years, much of it to be stored in Western or off-shore banks. Russian poverty and inequality rose dramatically in that time with the decline of their social safety net. Desperate Russians sold off privatization vouchers to avert starvation. Millions lost their life savings after Russia defaulted on its debt and devalued its currency, and life expectancy plummeted by over seven years for men.[14]

Famed Russian author Alexander Solzhenitsyn stated that "Putin inherited a ransacked and bewildered country. And he started to do with it what was possible—a slow and gradual restoration."[15] This was in part achieved by ordering oligarchs to pay taxes, by regaining national control over oil and gas deposits sold off to Exxon Mobil and other Western oil companies under Yeltsin, and implementing policies that improved infrastructure, living standards, and led to a decrease in corruption and crime. Inflation, joblessness, and poverty rates subsequently declined while wages improved and the economy grew tenfold. Putin cut Russia's national debt, stymied the exodus of Russian wealth abroad and put in place a successful pension system.[16]

Former U.S. Ambassador Jack Matlock asserted that Putin's power was based on balancing various patronage networks, some of which were criminal.[17] He presided over a "soft authoritarian state" where opponents could be jailed and the climate for investigative journalism was poor, though improved from the Yeltsin era. Political life to an extent opened up, with anti-Putin candidates winning 266 city council seats in Moscow in 2016. Closed judicial proceedings and pretrial detention were eliminated as part of a new code of criminal procedures and 24,000 free legal aid centers were created. Putin overcame Western sanctions by improving Russia's trade relations with China and other so-called BRIC nations (Brazil, South Africa, India and China), and imposing tariffs that raised competitiveness in key industries, leading to diversification away from primary commodities. He also advanced his vision of a Eurasian Union uniting Kazakhstan and Belarus in a regional trading bloc.[18]

Following the Russian Communist Party's success in the December 1995 Duma elections, the International Monetary Fund (IMF) in Washington—de-facto controlled by the U.S. Treasury—had made an extraordinary $10.2 billion loan to the Yeltsin government, $1 billion of which was secretly intended for the campaign to keep Yeltsin president in the 1996 elections. Tape recordings of conversations between President Bill Clinton and Yeltsin showed that in return for the U.S. support, Yeltsin would exempt longtime Clinton supporter, Arkansas-based Tyson Chicken, from a threatened 20 percent import tariff increase on exports to Russia valued at $700 million.[19] When Yeltsin shelled the Russian parliament during a constitutional crisis, killing dozens, Clinton praised him over the telephone and Secretary of State Warren Christopher told Yeltsin his blatant assault on Russian democracy was a "superb handling" of the situation.[20] If Putin had done the same thing, the reaction would have been far different.

In June 2012, after Putin had taken over from Medvedev as President, Secretary Clinton sent a memo to Obama advocating a hard-line stance. Clinton wrote that "Putin was deeply resentful of the U.S. and suspicious of our actions. [He was] intent on reclaiming lost Russian influence in its neighborhood, from Eastern Europe to Central Asia. He might call this project 'regional integration' but it was a code for rebuilding a lost empire."[21] Clinton ignored the fact that Putin might have had a legitimate reason for being suspicious, given that the United States had made a promise to Gorbachev in 1990 not to expand NATO towards Russia's borders, when that is exactly what they did. Furthermore, if Putin was really intent on re-establishing a Russian empire, what about the United States, which at the time Clinton wrote the memo, had well over 800 overseas military bases when Russia had only 13?

The Magnitsky Act: U.S. Sanctions Driven by a Billionaire?

During his first term, George W. Bush enjoyed positive relations with Putin, who was among the first to express Russian sympathy for America after 9/11 and had provided arms to the U.S.-allied Northern Alliance in Afghanistan while acquiescing to U.S. plans to establish bases in Central Asia. Relations began to breakdown, however, when Putin opposed U.S. intervention in Iraq, prosecuted Russian oligarchs and when the U.S. supported Georgia and its neoconservative president, Mikheil Saakashvili, in a 2008 war with Russia over South Ossetia, and agreed to admit both Georgia and Ukraine into NATO. In August 2012, Putin also allowed NSA whistleblower Edward Snowden to stay in Russia.[22]

In December 2012, Congress passed and Obama signed into law the Magnitsky Act, a bill first promoted by Senator Ben Cardin (D-MD), which instituted economic sanctions on Russian individuals and companies associated with the Putin regime. It was designed to punish those responsible for the death of alleged whistleblower Sergey Magnitsky, though only seven of the sixty targeted individuals had anything to do with Magnitsky, suggesting Magnitsky was but a pretext.[23]

According to William F. Browder, a billionaire Hedge Fund manager and lobbyist behind the bill who happened to be the grandson of Communist Party leader Earl Browder, Magnitsky died in prison in 2009 after he had exposed a $230 million Russian government scam which followed the seizure of Browder's company, Hermitage Capital. A film by Andrei Nekrasov and written by Torstein Grude, *The Magnitsky Act: Behind the Scenes* that has been barred from commercial distribution in the United States and a book by Alex Krainer, revealed serious inconsistencies in Browder's story, however. Notable among these was the fact that Magnitsky was not actually a lawyer, as Browder had claimed, but a tax accountant, and that he had been hired years earlier to set up an offshore structure that Russian investigators would later say was used for tax evasion and illegal share purchases by Hermitage.

According to Nekrasov's investigation, Magnitsky was an expert in "circumventing the laws and regulations" which required foreigners like Browder to pay more for business and stock shares. Furthermore, he had never actually accused anyone of malfeasance but was himself questioned by police as a suspect in the scheme. The evidence also shows that Magnitsky was never tortured in prison but died likely of a heart condition and the negligence of prison staff, not murder. The U.S. embassy had never raised any outcry in the period that Magnitsky was in prison, raising further questions.[24]

A protégé of Edmond Safra, whose Republic Bank of New York had joined in the looting of Russia in the 1990s,

Browder repeatedly contradicted his own statements. He had a history of corporate crime including involvement in a scam where Hermitage relocated its entities to the Republic of Kalmykia in southern Russia, which offered low tax rates and incentives for hiring disabled employees. Hermitage did the latter but only on paper.[25] Browder was prosecuted and convicted in absentia for tax evasion after fleeing Russia. Could his private vendetta have fueled the economic sanctions policy that was ultimately extended into the second of such laws, the Global Magnitsky Act of 2016, which allows the U.S. Government to sanction foreign government officials implicated in human rights abuses anywhere in the world? Or were there even wealthier and more powerful people, perhaps connected with HSBC Bank, Hermitage's parent company and a financial partner of billionaire George Soros, who lost even greater sums when Putin took control over Russia's Central Bank and economy, who used Browder as their front-man?

In 2016, a leaked cable by a high-ranking State Department official read, "I am beginning to feel we are all just part of the Browder P.R. machine."[26] Told by his mentor Safra "not to shy away from kicking up a scandal to protect his interests," Browder had a connection to Ben Cardin (D-MD), a key engine behind the Magnitsky Act. A long-time supporter of the Democratic Party, Browder provided financial support to Cardin's campaign through Ziff Brothers, a firm associated with Hermitage, which gave over $1 million to Democratic Party candidates in the 2016 election (Browder had made stock trades for Ziff in Moscow and was using it to try to purchase shares of Gazprom). From 2013-2018, Mr. Cardin also received $33,7000 from Lockheed Martin, $20,005 from Northrop Grumman and $22,500 in 2012 from the Carlyle Group. The source of his funding would plausibly explain his support for the Magnitsky bill, and a biased Senate study promoting Russophobia and hawkish measures.[27]

According to Alex Krainer, the sanctions policy under the Magnitsky Act was supposed to weaken certain segments of the Russian elite supportive of Putin's agenda. It created barriers for Russians seeking to come to the West to investigate and build a legal case, and barriers in the judicial system and courts for prosecution of Western financiers who evaded taxes and committed corporate crime. At the same time, it helped to create a public relations platform to demonize Russia for its alleged abuse of human rights. Krainer stated that "Russia was supposed to have continued the course initiated by Boris Yeltsin in the 1990s in turning over its industry and resources to key Western interests and joining the New World Order. Putin has done the opposite. He has asserted Russia's sovereignty, blocked the theft of Russia's resources including oil and asserted control over the Russian Central Bank."[28]

The implication is that the entire sanctions policy and new Cold War is a fraud. A direct historical parallel occurred during the first Cold War when the Justice Department had begun to investigate treasonous activities on the part of Wall Street executives who had helped finance the Nazi war machine. These executives responded by accusing their enemies of communist subversion and supporting politicians who whipped up anti-Russian sentiment in order to bury the investigations and as a means of bolstering the political fortunes of the Republican Party, and undermining New Deal regulations.[29] This strategy appears to have been replicated in a different context by big businessmen who financed the Democratic Party, and by the Obamians who sought to exploit Russo-phobia in U.S. society to help cover up their own failings, and forestall the re-emergence of Russia as a superpower, thereby intensifying in the process the danger of nuclear war.

Ukraine and Crimea

A key trigger underlying the new Cold War has been the war in Ukraine which broke out following a coup d'état backed by the Obama administration and its European Union (EU) allies in February 2014. The coup resulted from large-scale protests, which erupted the previous November in Kiev's Maidan Square. They were directed against Ukraine's democratically elected pro-Russian leader Viktor Yanukovych, whose corruption had been symbolized by a giant palace in which he lived. While there were legitimate grievances against the regime, many of the protestors were paid. They included phalanxes of black masked right wingers who worshipped Stephen Bandera, a Nazi collaborator in the Second World War. Financing came from pro-western oligarchs like Ihor Kolomoisky, who later offered bounties for the heads of Russians killed in the East.[30]

Yanukovych had spurned an IMF-led proposal that would have pushed austerity measures and contracted Ukraine's economy, instead reaffirming the more advantageous economic ties to Russia. The country was divided between those who saw Ukraine's future as being with the EU, and those attached to Russia, with the division playing out along ethnic and regional lines. By early February 2014, the festive atmosphere at the protests had been replaced by the specter of violence, with security forces opening fire on demonstrators and snipers firing on both sides, killing not only dozens of protestors but also 17 police. Russia alleged that the snipers were among the insurgents. Many of the shots came from the Philharmonic Hall and Ukraine Hotel, which was under insurgent control, and the post office, headquarters of the right sector, which was thought to be behind the beating and slaying of protestors as part of black flag operations or acts of intimidation.[31] On February 20, snipers killed at least 50 people. Three Georgian veterans of Mikheil Saakashvili's security services confessed in Italy to being paid $5,000 to carry out the attack. They said they were operating under the command of American Iraq war veteran Brian Boyenger, a sniper from the elite 101st airborne division from Winston-Salem, North Carolina who took a Ukrainian bride.[32]

On May 2, 2014, far-right activists forced Yanukovych supporters into a trade union building in Odessa and burned it to the ground, clubbing to death those who survived by jumping out the window. Forty-six Yanukovych supporters were killed, many of them burned alive.[33] Just hours after the bloodbath took place, President Obama in a joint-press conference with German Chancellor Angela Merkel, blamed Russia and announced that "the Ukrainian government [led by Poroshenko] has the right and responsibility to uphold law and order within its territory."[34]

For his part, Yanukovych was willing to accept a deal that would have restored the 2005 constitution and a power-sharing arrangement and set up elections for December. The Maidan protestors rejected the White House-backed compromise, believing the election would be rigged. They did not amass enough signatures, however, for impeachment. Yanukovych subsequently fled to Russia, fearing his life, allegedly bringing with him $32 billion which was used to finance resistance in Donbas. Coup leaders seized his administration building and his residence.[35]

In May, a majority of voters elected as his successor Petro Poroshenko, CEO of a chocolate conglomerate with a net worth of $1.3 billion who stored much of his wealth in tax shelters in the British Virgin Islands. He had already discussed extending NATO membership to Ukraine with Hillary Clinton. Members of Yanukovych's party were shot and harassed, and churches and synagogues were ransacked by neo-Nazi thugs. The climate was so bad that Rabbi Moshe Reuven Azman called on Kiev's Jews to flee. Penny Pritzker was among those pushing for austerity policies in Ukraine, which wound up cutting social services and pensions so Western bankers could be repaid at the expense of Ukraine's poor. Ukraine's new finance minister promoting neoliberal policies, Natalie Jaresko, had worked for the U.S. State Department and made an immediate bid to take over one of Ukraine's largest telecom companies.[36]

The U.S. and EU had fanned the flames of the Maidan protests along with investors like George Soros, a sponsor of previous "color revolutions" who gave $250,000 to Obama's inaugural. Economic pressures were applied through the Federal Reserve.[37] Ukraine was considered an important bridge between Eastern and Western Europe and held lucrative oil and gas deposits. Carl Gershman, president of the National Endowment for Democracy (NED), called Ukraine "the biggest prize" and an important interim step towards toppling Putin who "may find himself on the losing end not just in the near abroad but within Russia itself."[38]

Victoria Nuland, the head of the State Department's European desk, traveled to Ukraine three times during the protests, handing out cookies to demonstrators. John McCain (R-AZ) spoke alongside the pro-fascist Bandera-loving Svoboda party co-leader, Oleh Tyahnyna, at a coup rally, accompanied by Chris Murphy (D-CT). Nuland named Tyahnyna to be part of the upcoming coup government. She told U.S. Ambassador Geoffrey Pyatt in a telephone conversation that was tapped and later leaked that his neoliberal colleague, Arseniy Yatsenyuk, head of the "Fatherland" Party, should be Prime Minister as he was thought to have the "economic" and "governing experience." Nuland further revealed that the U.S. had invested over $5 billion in "democracy promotion" in Ukraine since 1991 through the NED, which was carrying on the kind of work previously undertaken by the CIA during the Cold War.[39]

Chas Freeman Jr., a thirty-year veteran of the diplomatic service, believes that the Obama administration should have pursued a treaty for Ukraine modeled after the 1955/1956 Austria State Treaty, which produced a neutral Austria and ensured fair treatment of ethnic minorities.[40] Instead, Obama legitimized the coup as a "constitutional process" and invited Yatseniuk to the White House. His administration further pledged $1 billion in loan guarantees to the new regime, which Putin considered as the "ideological heirs of Bandera, Hitler's accomplice in World War II."[41] In March 2014, Putin supported a referendum in Crimea that led to its rejoining Russia. He stated that the Americans "have lied to us many times, made decisions behind our backs...but there is a limit to everything. And with Ukraine, our Western partners had crossed a line.... Are we ready to consistently defend our national interests, or will we forever give in, retreat to who knows where?"[42]

Crimea had been transferred to Ukrainian jurisdiction in 1954 and had a naval base stationed in Sevastapol. In 1854, Franklin Pierce sent a military mission and enthusiastically supported Russia's defense of Crimea from the British, French and Turks, in a history that had been long forgotten in the U.S.[43]

Crimeans, especially the majority ethnic Russians, were uneasy about the Maidan "revolution" and new regime in Kiev and had long resented the authorities there for neglecting their economic development. In a vote in Crimea, 96% backed reunification with Russia. Without independent observers to confirm this result, a Russian Human Rights Council estimated the vote at 50-60 percent in favor of reunification, still a majority. Even the minority Tatars appeared to support rejoining Russia. The Western media nevertheless accused Putin of a major land grab, and the Obama administration ratcheted up sanctions. Secretary of State John Kerry claimed that "you just don't in the 21st century behave in 19th century fashion by invading another country on completely trumped up pretext."[44] This is, however, actually what the United States had done in Iraq and Libya.

Journalist Ron Ridenour points out that any alleged Russian "invasion" of Crimea involved Russia sending over six helicopters and two small boats with 500 Special Forces acting as police to protect ethnic Russians from ongoing threats and attacks. Senior officers in the Ukrainian garrison defected to Russia, and the rest went home. Six people were killed, including a Russian soldier by a Ukrainian Right sector militant, but none by Russians. *Forbes Magazine* wrote: "The U.S. and European Union may want to save Crimeans from themselves. But the Crimeans are happy right where they are. One year after the annexation of the Ukrainian peninsula in the Black Sea, poll after poll shows that the locals there—be they Ukrainians, ethnic Russians or Tatars, are mostly all in agreement: life with Russia is better than life with Ukraine."[45]

On March 1, just before the Crimea referendum, a large crowd gathered in the capital of the Eastern Ukrainian province of Donetsk, the industrial heartland of the country, carrying Russian flags and the flag of the Donetsk republic. Similar protests also broke out in Luhansk. In a referendum, 89% in Donetsk and 96% in Luhansk voted for independence, which the Poroshenko government did not accept. Counterinsurgency operations were initiated to try to suppress the rebellion, with the Ukrainian military sending in jet fighters and tanks. Civilian homes were shelled, and thousands were forced to live in bomb shelters "like rats" or flee their homes as refugees.

The anti-Maidan movement in Eastern Ukraine was accused of being driven by Russia but had deep popular roots. The people of the region looked to Russia for support after years of economic neglect by Ukraine and because of deep grievances against its government. A key commander, Igor Girkin, was a former Colonel in the Russian army who had fought in Chechnya and Transinistra (a breakaway republic in Moldova) but was not a Russian puppet.[46] The head of the republic, Aleksandr Zakhrchenko, was a local mine electrician who was gunned down while eating at a restaurant.[47] Per the ongoing accusations of Russian support for the movement, he had pointed out to reporters before his death that if Russia was really sending its regular troops, we wouldn't be "talking about the battle of Elenovka [but] about the battle of Kiev or a possible capture of Lvov [on Western border of Poland]."[48]

The first evidence of any direct Russian troop involvement was confirmed in July 2014, well after the war had broken out, meaning it was predominantly reactive. Researcher Serhiy Kudelin reported that "Despite Western accusations that the uprising was provoked and sponsored by Russia, it was in fact primarily a home-grown phenomenon.... Political fragmentation, violent regime change...combined with emotion and fear played a crucial role in launching the armed rebellion."[49] Historian Stephen Cohen added that while Russia no doubt provided some assistance, "calling [the rebels] self-defense fighters is not wrong; they did not begin the combat; their land is being invaded and assaulted by a government [lacking] political legitimacy, two of their regions having voted overwhelmingly for autonomy referenda."[50]

Swayed by a slick lobbying campaign backed by supporters of the Afghan mujahidin in the 1980s looking for a new cause and by the Senate's Ukraine Caucus, the Obama administration provided nearly $600 million in security assistance to the Ukrainian military, supplying it with counter-artillery radars, anti-tank systems, armored vehicles and drones.[51] A back

door arms pipeline was set up through the United Arab Emirates
and Blackwater mercenaries were also allegedly deployed. Before
and after the Ukrainian military's campaign began, Secretary
of State John Kerry, CIA Director John Brennan, and Vice
President Joe Biden visited Kiev, followed by a flow of senior
Pentagon officials. American military advisers, including from
the Oklahoma and New York National Guards, were embedded in
the Ukrainian Defense Ministry. They provided rocket propelled
grenades, carried out training exercises and planned military
operations including with members of the fascist Azov battalion,
which had Nazi-inspired Wolfsangel patches emblazoned on their
sleeves.[52]

In a speech at West Point on May 28th, Obama claimed
that "in Ukraine, Russia's recent actions recall the days when
Soviet tanks rolled into Eastern Europe," which really was not
true.[53] Stephen Cohen pointed out how on May 2nd, at the UN
Security Council, U.S. Ambassador Samantha Power suspended
her revered Responsibility to Protect Doctrine that had been
deployed against Qaddafi, giving Kiev's leaders an international
intervention-free license to kill. Lauding their "remarkable,
almost unimaginable restraint," as Obama had done after the
Odessa massacre, she claimed that the [Ukrainian] governments
"response [was] reasonable, it is proportional, and frankly it is
what any of our countries would have done."[54]

The Ukrainian military and allied warlord and neo-Nazi
militias were not acting reasonably or proportionally, however,
when they carried out artillery and air attacks on cities and struck
residential buildings, shopping malls, parks, schools, hospitals
and orphanages in eastern Ukraine, and tortured and executed
POWs in what amounted to clear war crimes. Cohen notes that
even the *New York Times*, which mainly deleted atrocities from
its coverage, described survivors in Slovyansk living "as if in
the Middle Ages."[55] Conveying his "unwavering support for
Ukraine," Obama blamed Russian backed separatists for all the
destruction and for causing Ukrainian civilians to "needlessly die
every day."[56] John Kerry compared Yanukovych to "a heavyweight

boxer" with a "violent reputation," leaving out how Poroshenko had rewarded the neo-Nazi Svoboda Party and right sector with five to eight minister-ships in his government, incited violence by calling resisters in the bombarded cities "gangs of animals," and ordered his troops to "take hundreds of their lives for each life of our servicemen."[57]

Historian Paul Robinson argues that the reckless damaging of civilian infrastructure and killing civilians alienated the local populace and fueled greater support for the Donetsk People's Army, which was able to overcome a 10-1 advantage in heavy equipment. After the rebels smashed through Ukrainian military lines in the town of Ilovansk in August 2014, the entire 5th battalion of the Ukrainian military deserted. High rebel morale combined with tactical errors on the part of the Ukrainian military contributed to the latter's defeat. None of this was ever reported in Western media.[58]

The Biden family was one of the major beneficiaries of America's interference in Ukraine. While the Vice-President was overseeing U.S. policy toward Ukraine, his son, Hunter joined the board of one of Ukraine's most profitable and corrupt energy companies, Burisma, which gave the potential to the Bidens of becoming billionaires. Journalist Peter Schweizer points out that Biden regularly consulted with Poroshenko by telephone and made five trips to the Ukraine between 2014 and 2017 while his son's business partners prepared to strike a profitable deal with controversial and reportedly violent oligarchs Kolomoisky and Zlochevsky, who would benefit from his actions. Schweizer's investigation further pointed to the disappearance of $1.8 billion in U.S. taxpayer guaranteed money to Ukraine. The IMF loans disappeared after going through Kolomoisky's private bank.[59]

At the UN, Samantha Power was reported to have choked up as she spoke of infants who had died in the crash of a Malaysian Airliner jet over Ukraine in July 2014, which she blamed on Russia even though Senator Saxby Chambliss who headed an investigating body admitted there was no "smoking gun."[60] Obama blamed Russian backed separatists for blocking the investigation and removing evidence from the crash site and dead bodies, though the State Department refused to make public radar information that Kerry said pointed to the location of the offending missile.[61] The *New York Times* further reported on a Ukrainian military assault that touched off a fire near the crash site that consumed plane debris that could have helped identify the reasons for the disaster, and destroyed fuselage fragments with shrapnel holes cited by investigators as possible evidence of an attack by Ukrainian jetfighters.[62]

U.S. policy in Ukraine generally helped empower a violent government that continued to rank near bottom on the world's corruption indexes, and had a popularity rating below 15 percent. After the February 2014 coup, it closed TV stations broadcasting in Russian, supported attacks against the Orthodox Church because of its association with Russia and the word Moscow in its name, and deemed opposition to IMF-EU austerity policies criminal and separatist.[63] Kiev resident, Mihailo Strashok, 72, reflected popular sentiment when he said "we won't sacrifice our bodies and souls for these bandits in power."[64] Samantha Power and other Obamians, however, had long dropped their concern about human rights, since now Ukraine was in the Western camp.

A New Arms Race

As the Ukraine debacle unfolded, tensions with Russia reached an all-time high. New Cold War ideologues grew louder and louder in their hate Putin campaign, which came to resemble the anti-Kaiser sentiment that had been whipped up on the eve of the First World War.[65]

Abandoning diplomatic niceties, Obama insulted Putin. He bashed Putin's view on gays, boasted about crippling Russia's economy through sanctions, and listed Russia as number two of the three main threats to the world—in between the Ebola virus and Islamic State.[66] It was the U.S., however, which had colonized the world with military bases and, in violation of an earlier promise, expanded NATO membership to countries bordering Russia, notably Albania, Croatia, and even, with much celebration, tiny Montenegro, whose leader Milo Djukanovic was thought to be in league with organized crime.[67]

Obama further back-tracked on a pledge to cut back on nuclear weapons. Shaped by the lobbying influence of Bechtel Corporation of San Francisco, which took over many of the nation's nuclear weapons laboratories after they were privatized by Bush, Obama initiated a $1 trillion nuclear weapons modernization program that readied hundreds of B-61 nuclear bombs and provided well over $1 billion for the development of new nuclear long-range bombers and nuclear-armed submarines, as well as nuclear-tipped weapons that gave the illusion of being less dangerous and therefore less unthinkable.[68]

Following Crimea's reincorporation into Russia, American newspapers had begun to reinvoke Cold War imagery by showing photos of Russian military exercises. They left out American incitements such as the Obama administration's quadrupling of military spending in Western Europe, stationing missile launchers in Romania that appeared to violate the Intermediate-Range Nuclear Forces (INF) Treaty, carrying out training exercises in Poland which bought Raytheon's Patriot missile defense system, and the deployment of Aegis destroyers built by General Dynamics in the Black Sea that could reach Moscow with cruise missiles.[69] The Obama administration in addition provided troops for training missions in Georgia to protect the Baku-Tbilisi Ceyhan pipeline, introduced three hundred troops in Norway, and was accused by the Kremlin of funnelling money to ethnic minorities in Russia promoting secession, including to Circassians, Chechens, Ingushetians, Balkars, Kabardins, Abaza, Tatars, Talysh, and Kumyks.[70]

Under the direction of Ambassador Michael McFaul, a Stanford professor with a worldview straight out of the *Quiet American*, the State Department covertly backed Russian dissidents like Pussy Riot, a group of young women who disrupted an Orthodox Church service, and financed NGOs lending support to opposition politicians like Alexi Navalny and Boris Nemtsov.

The latter was a deputy prime minister under Yeltsin who urged the expansion of the Magnitsky Act, served as an adviser to pro-Western Ukrainian leader Viktor Yushchenko, and allegedly outlined plans to overthrow Putin before he was murdered in February 2015.[71]

In 2016, Defense Secretary Ash Carter pushed for increases in the Pentagon's space budget out of concern that Russia and China had developed advanced directed-energy capabilities that could be "used to track or blind satellites and disrupt key operations."[72] A provision in the National Defense Authorization Act of 2016 signed by Obama called for "research, development, test and evaluation" of space-based systems for missile defense. This harkened back to Ronald Reagan's $30 billion Star Wars program, which young Obama had opposed, and set the groundwork for Donald Trump's space command. It aimed to create a missile defense shield to refract Soviet nuclear attacks with lasers. L. David Montague, retired president of missile systems for Lockheed Martin and co-chair of the National Academy of Sciences Panel that studied missile defense, called the attempts to revive Star Wars as "insanity, pure and simple." Philip Coyle III, the former assistant Secretary of Defense, said the idea of a space based nuclear shield was a "sham" that would cost "gazillions and gazillions of dollars" when "the technology was not at hand," and "would only be used by Russia and China to do what they want to do."[73]

The myopia of U.S. military strategy under Obama was further epitomized by investment in billion-dollar boondoggles like Lockheed Martin's F-35 fighter jet, which had serious design flaws, and futuristic weapons with limited practical utility. These weapons included insect-sized drones, stealth jets that could fly above the stratosphere, a laser weapon that could strike earth from space (known as rods from god), a high-tech body armor suit modeled after the one featured in Robert Heinlein's science fiction thriller Starship Troopers, and a cheetah robot that could run 28 miles per hour and jump over obstacles with four hundred pounds of military equipment.[74]

Russian military investments appeared to be more efficacious. Though spending less than a tenth of the U.S., it could deploy command, control, communications, and computer surveillance and reconnaissance capabilities equal to or better than those of the U.S. and air defense and electronic war systems, which an American commander in Ukraine described as "eye watering."[75] Russia was also in the process of adding fifty new warships and twenty new submarines, about forty percent of which would have nuclear strike capability, and long-range subsonic, supersonic and hypersonic cruise missiles that could potentially threaten the U.S. Empire of Bases. According to military analyst Andrei Martyanov, Putin's talk of a growing multilateral world order and tightening alliance with Chinese Premier Xi Jinping had exposed the worst Zbigniew "Grand Chessboard" Brzezinski nightmare of the "two most powerful Eurasian nations declaring full independence from the American vision of the world."[76] This nightmare, which included efforts to decouple from the U.S. dollar, undergirded the anti-Russia, anti-Putin hysteria gripping the U.S.

Russia-Gate Hysteria

The advent of a new McCarthyism was evident in vicious attacks directed against film-maker Oliver Stone in the "liberal media" (*New York Times*) when he produced a documentary, "The Putin Interviews," and by the labeling of critics of U.S. foreign policy as "Putin stooges."[77] The political climate only grew worse after the 2016 election when the defeated Democrats tried to scapegoat Russia for the election of Donald Trump, accusing it of hacking into the Democratic National Committee (DNC) computer servers and leaking emails that made them look bad, planting fake news on social media and colluding with the Trump campaign.

According to Swiss journalist Guy Mettan, Russia-Gate fit with a longstanding tendency in the West to mount accusations against Russia as a means of justifying military mobilization.[78] A Facebook executive testified before Congress that the number of fake news stories reaching Facebook members was vastly less than the government and media were reporting. In July 2018, Special Investigating Council Robert S. Mueller III indicted twelve Russian intelligence agents for phishing attacks to gain access to Democratic Party operatives, money laundering, E-mail hacking and trying to break into election boards, though it was unlikely the case would ever be prosecuted since the U.S. and Russia don't have an extradition treaty. Mueller additionally indicted Trump administration officials for violating the Logan Act and lying to Congress about covert meetings with Russian officials, some of which had been set up by Russian lobbyists seeking the removal of sanctions.[79]

The main substantive charges that Mueller's inquiry uncovered—bribery by Trump's campaign manager Paul Manafort and hush money payments to porn star Stormy Daniels—had nothing to do with Russia. The evidence of collusion came from a salacious dossier produced by Christopher Steele, an ex-British spy who was in contact with an associate Deputy Attorney General in the Obama Justice Department and was financed by the Democratic National Committee. A main source for the allegation of an email hack came from a cybersecurity firm, CrowdStrike, whose chief risk officer worked for the Obama administration.[80]

Obama's own role in the whole affair appears to be considerable since he appointed the Director of National Intelligence James Clapper – who openly espoused Russophobic views - to investigate Russian interference in the elections and asked to be apprised of the FBI's investigations and possible behind the scenes machinations.[81] When Veteran Intelligence Professionals for Sanity (VIPS), headed by CIA veteran Ray McGovern, independently investigated the email hacking, they found, based on assessment of the speed of the communications by an IBM computer expert, that the emails must rather have been downloaded, indicating their source was an inside leak. (The FBI suspiciously never itself examined the servers—but then, it had never examined the emails whose storage on Hillary Clinton's private server was "careless" not "negligent," a felony, either, relying on information on their content from, again, CrowdStrike.) The VIPS sent an open letter calling on Obama to release the evidence that proved Russia aided the Trump campaign, which he never did. Indeed, perhaps because there was none, as the much-bruited Mueller investigation at last released its report with no indictments germane to Trump-Russian collusion whatsoever.[82]

By this time, seasoned political observers had already come to suspect that Team Obama had concocted or exaggerated the story of Russian election meddling not so much with regard to DNC election loss, as in order to justify a new Cold War. John Brennan, whose views were described as resembling "Joseph McCarthy and J. Edgar Hoover in their prime," appeared on Fox News with the message that "Mr. Trump has to understand that absolving Russia of various actions that it's taken in the past number of years is a road that he, I think, needs to be very, very careful about moving down."[83] These comments suggest a deep state operation, supported by Obama, directed not so much against Trump as against Russia, to impede the moves towards détente pressed for by Russia, and indeed, to prepare for the further expansion of the U.S. military budget, as the Pentagon grappled with America's increasingly evident loss of military supremacy and global influence.

By 2015, polls showed that only 13 percent of American citizens had a favorable opinion of Putin and 24 percent a favorable opinion about Russia, an all-time low. A 2017 poll found that 42 percent viewed Russia as a critical threat, up from 23 percent in 2003, while 53 percent thought the United States should work to limit Russia's international influence rather than cooperate. Fifty two percent would support using U.S. troops to defend a Baltic NATO member if attacked; the same total that in a 2019 poll considered Russia as a "critical threat." In a stark reflection of the partisan divide, 61 percent of Democrats viewed Russia as a major threat compared to only 36 percent of Republicans.[84] These figures, worse than even during the first Cold War years, exemplify the institutionalization of anti-Russian sentiment and deterioration of U.S.-Russian relations under Obama, a major failing of his presidency.

Endnotes

1   "Trapped: Life on the Donetsk Frontline Through the Eyes of a Little Girl,"
    RT News America, February 6, 2017, https://www.youtube.com/watch?v=-
    6rX1dc3ti4

2   "Donetsk: An American Glance. A first-hand account of the situation in
    Donbass," November 12, 2014, *RT News America*, https://www.youtube.com/
    watch?v=oV1dHMEft8k.

3   Russian TV, Seen by the author on visit to Moscow, Russia, May 6, 2018.

4   See Michael McFaul, *From Cold War to Hot Peace* (Boston: Houghton Mifflin,
    2018); Andrew Cockburn, "The New Red Scare: Reviving the Art of Threat
    Inflation," *Harper's Magazine*, December 2016, 29.

5   Jillian Rayfield, "Obama: The 1980s Called, They Want Their Foreign Policy
    Back," *Salon*, October 23, 2012.

6   "Ukraine," Security Assistance Monitor, https://securityassistance.org/
    data/program/military/Ukraine/2013/2016/all/Global//; Ivan Medyinsky,
    "U.S. Military Assistance to Ukraine Under Obama and Beyond," *Institute of
    World Policy*, http://kennankyiv.org/wp-content/uploads/2016/04/Medynskyi_
    Agora_V16_final-2.pdf

7   Jerry Brown, "A Stark Nuclear Warning," *New York Review of Books*, July 14,
    2016.

8   Robert H. Donaldson and Vidya Nadkarni, *The Foreign Policy of Russia:
    Changing Systems, Enduring Interests* (New York: Routeledge, 2019), 13.

9   The White House, "Press Conference of the President After ASEAN Summit,"
    Office of the Press Secretary, September 8, 2016, https://obamawhitehouse.
    archives.gov/the-press-office/2016/09/08/press-conference-president-obama-
    after-asean-summit

10 Barack Obama, *The Audacity of Hope: Thoughts on Reclaiming the American
    Dream* (New York: Crown Publishers, 2006), 285, 289, 307.

11 Obama, *The Audacity of Hope*, 289.

12 Derek Chollet, "Obama and Putin," *Diplomatic History*, 42, 4 (2018).

13 Nicolai N. Petro, "Are We Reading Russia Right?" *The Fletcher Forum of
    World Affairs*, 42, 2 (Summer 2018), 3.

14 Stephen Cohen, *Failed Crusade: America and the Tragedy of Post-Communist
    Russia* (New York: W.W. Norton, 2001; F. William Engdahl, *Manifest Destiny:
    Democracy as Cognitive Dissonance* (Wiesbaden: Mine Books, 2018), 29-69;
    I. Marshall Goldman, *The Privatization of Russia: Russian Reform Goes Awry*
    (New York: Routeledge, 2003).

15 Ben Judah, *Fragile Empire: How Russia Fell in and Out of Love with Vladimir
    Putin* (New Haven: Yale University Press, 2013), 57.

16 Anne Garrels, *Putin Country: A Journey Into the Real Russia* (London: Picador,
    2017), 11, 12, 19; Chris Miller, *Putinomics: Power and Money in Resurgent*

Russia (Chapel Hill: University of North Carolina Press, 2018); Andrey P. Tsygankov, "The Dark Double: The American Media Perception of Russia as a Neo-Soviet Autocracy, 2008-2014," *Politics*, April 2016, Stephen Cohen, *War With Russia* (New York: Hot Books, 2019), 4. A former IMF director said that Putin's economic team does "not tolerate corruption" and that Russia now ranks 35th out of 190 in the World Bank's Doing Business Ratings." Miller found that Putin "skillfully managed Russia's economic fortunes."

17   Stephen F. Cohen, "Who Putin is Not," *The Nation*, September 30, 2018.

18   See Natylie Baldwin and Kermit Heartstrong, *Ukraine: Zbig's Grand Chessboard & How the West Was Checkmated* (San Francisco: Next Revelation Press, 2015), 130-132, 305, 332; Alexander Dugin, *Putin v. Putin: Putin Viewed From the Right* (Arktos Media, 2012), 31, 168, 188, 189; Alex Krainer, *The Killing of William Browder: Deconstructing Bill Browder's Dangerous Deception* (Monaco: Equilibrium, 2017), 98-102; Petro, "Are We Reading Russia Right?" 4; Anatoly Kurmasaev, "Putin's Secret Weapon: His Central Banker," *Wall Street Journal*, August 21, 2018, 1; Ron Ridenour, *The Russian Peace Threat: Pentagon on Alert* (New York: Punto Press, 2018); Glen Diesen, *Russia's Geoeconomic Strategy for a Greater Eurasia* (New York: Routeledge, 2018), 58.

19   Ann Williamson, Testimony Before the Committee on Banking and Financial Services of the United States House of Representatives, September 21, 1999; Engdahl, *Manifest Destiny*, 63.

20   Svetlana Savranskya and Tom Blanton, "Yeltsin Shelled Russian Parliament 25 Years Ago, U.S. Praised "Ssuperb Handling"" National Security Archive, October 4, 2018, https://nsarchive.gwu.edu/briefing-book/russia-programs/2018-10-04/yeltsin-shelled-russian-parliament-25-years-ago-us-praised-superb-handling.

21   Hillary Clinton, *Hard Choices* (New York: Simon & Schuster, 2014), 236.

22   McFaul, *From Cold War to Hot Peace*.

23   Ellen Barry, "Kremlin Says New Evidence Ties Lawyer Who Died in Jail to Theft of $230 Million," *New York Times*, November 16, 2010, A12.

24   Andrei Nekrasov and Torstein Grude, *The Magnitsky Act: Behind the Scenes* (Piraya Films, 2016); Krainer, *The Killing of Bill Browder*. See also Luci Komisar, "The Man Behind the Magnitsky Act: Did William Browder Tax Troubles in Russia Color Push for Sanctions," *100 Reporters*, October 20, 2017.

25   Krainer, *The Killing of William Browder*.

26   Clara Weiss, "Yet Another Murder That Wasn't: The Perepilichny Case and the Anti-Russian Campaign," *World Socialist Web*, December 24, 2018.

27   http://www.opensecrets.org/orgs/summary.php?id=D000000624. The Ziff Brothers gave $17,000 directly to Hillary Clinton.

28   Personal Interview, Alex Krainer, November 2017.

29   See Joan Brady, *America's Dreyfuss: The Case Nixon Rigged* (New York:

Skyscraper, 2015); Peter Dale Scott, "The Dulles Brothers, Harry Dexter White, Alger Hiss and the Fate of the Private Pre-War Banking System," *Asia Pacific Journal*, April 20, 2014; John Loftus and Mark Aarons, *The Secret War Against the Jews: How Western Espionage Betrayed the Jewish People* (New York: St. Martin's, 1997)

30   See Robert Parry, "Ukraine's Inconvenient Neo-Nazis," *Consortium News*, March 30, 2014; Paul Craig Roberts, *The Neoconservative Threat to World Order: Washington's Perilous War for Hegemony* (Atlanta: Clarity Press Inc., 2018), 15.

31   Richard Sakwa, *Frontline Ukraine: Crisis in the Borderlands* (London: I.B. Tauris, 2015), 92; Nicole Duran, "Pritzker Practices Commercial Diplomacy in Ukraine, Turkey," *Foreign Policy*, October 9, 2014; Ridenour, *The Russian Peace Threat*; Ivan Katchanovski, "The Maidan Massacre in Ukraine – A Summary of Analysis, Evidence and Findings," in *The Return of the Cold War: Ukraine, the West and Russia*, ed. J.L. Black et al. (London: Routeledge, 2016), 223.

32   Michel Chossudovsky, "Snipers Kill Demonstrators, Italian Documentary Bombshell Evidence," *Global Research*, November 24, 2017, Betran M. Gutierrez, "Winston Salem Vet, Fiancée Run Into Immigration Barriers," *Winston Salem Journal*, June 5, 2017.

33   Barry Grey, "New York Times Covers up Fascist Atrocity in Odessa," *World Socialist Web Site*, May 5, 2014.

34   Mike Whitney, "Obama's Bloodbath in Odessa," *Counterpunch*, May 5, 2014.

35   Sakwa, *Frontline Ukraine*; Ridenour, *The Russian Peace Threat*; author interview with Andrei Nekrasov, Maidan protestor, September 2017; Marci Shore, *The Ukrainian Night: An Intimate History of Revolution* (New Haven: Yale University Press, 2017).

36   Roberts, *The Neoconservative Threat to World Order*, 28, 33; Diesen, *Russia's Geoeconomic Strategy for a Greater Eurasia*, 41; Ridenour, *The Russian Peace Threat*, ch. 16.

37   Robert D. Blackwill and Jennifer M. Harris, *War By Other Means: Geoeconomics and Statecraft* (Cambridge, MA: Harvard University Press, 2016), 21. On Soros, see Wayne Madsen, *Soros: Quantum of Chaos* (Waynemadsenreport. com, 2015). Soros had long violated the 1799 Logan Act which made it a felony for an American citizen to conduct foreign policy without authority.

38   Robert Parry, "The Mess That Nuland Made," *Consortium News*, July 13, 2015.

39   Sakwa *Frontline Ukraine*, 87, 88; Diana Johnstone, *Queen of Chaos: The Misadventures of Hillary Clinton* (Oakland: Counterpunch Books, 2015), 151, 152; Ridenour, *The Russian Peace Threat*; "Ukraine Crisis: Transcript of Leaked Nuland-Pyatt Call," *BBC*, February 7, 2014.

40   Author telephone interview, Chas Freeman Jr., February 18, 2019.

41   Bill Powell, "Vladimir Putin's Truth Problem," *Newsweek*, July 23, 2014.

42 Diesen, *Russia's Geoeconomic Strategy for a Greater Eurasia*, 61.

43 Andrei Martyanov, *Losing Military Supremacy: The Myopia of American Strategic Planning* (Atlanta: Clarity Press Inc., 2018), 54, 55.

44 Sakwa, *Frontline Ukraine*, 119.

45 Ridenour, *The Russian Peace Threat*.

46 Sakwa, *Frontline Ukraine*, 150.

47 Sakwa, *Frontline Ukraine*, 150; Andrew E. Kramer, "Leader of Ukrainian Separatists is Killed in Bombing," *New York Times*, September 1, 2018, A5.

48 Roberts, *The Neoconservative Threat to World Order*.

49 Sakwa, *Frontline Ukraine*, 154. See also Chris Kaspar de Ploeg, *Ukraine in the Crossfire* (Atlanta: Clarity Press, 2017).

50 Stephen F. Cohen, "The Silence of American Hawks About Kiev's Atrocities," *The Nation*, July 1, 2014.

51 "Ukraine," Security Assistance Monitor, https://securityassistance.org/data/program/military/Ukraine/2013/2016/all/Global//; Ivan Medyinsky, "U.S. Military Assistance to Ukraine Under Obama and Beyond," *Institute of World Policy*, http://kennankyiv.org/wp-content/uploads/2016/04/Medynskyi_Agora_V16_final-2.pdf; Adam Entous, "Ukraine's U.S. Backers Use Cold War Playbook: Pair Who Helped Arm Afghanistan Against Soviets Finds New Cause," *Wall Street Journal*, May 7, 2015. Some of the chief lobbyists were Michael Pillsbury, a Pentagon consultant, Gordon Humphrey, a former Republican Senator, Philip Karber and Michael Vickers, Undersecretary for Intelligence who visited Ukraine at least twice. The Senate's Ukraine Caucus was headed by Rob Portman (R-OH).

52 Cohen, "The Silence of American Hawks About Kiev's Atrocities;" Will Cathcart, Joseph Epstein, "How Many Neo-Nazis is the U.S. Backing in Ukraine?" *The Daily Beast*, June 9, 2015; Will Cathcart, Joseph Epstein, "Is America Training Neo-Nazis in Ukraine?" *The Daily Beast*, July 4, 2015; Max Blumenthal, "The U.S. is Arming and Assisting Neo-Nazis in Ukraine, While Congress Debates Prohibition," *Grayzone Project*, April 7, 2018. White Supremacists who rallied in Charlottesville had traveled to Ukraine to train with the Azov. Sgt. Ivan Kharkiv, a commander of the Azov battalion whose goal was to "lead the white races of the world in a struggle for their survival," worked directly with U.S. trainers and volunteers including technical engineers and medics. Congress eventually barred direct aid.

53 Sakwa, *Frontline Ukraine*, 160.

54 Cohen, "The Silence of American Hawks About Kiev's Atrocities."

55 Cohen, "The Silence of American Hawks About Kiev's Atrocities."

56 "Statement by the President on Ukraine," The White House, Office of the Press Secretary, March 17, 2014; Robert Parry, "Flight 17 Shoot-Down Scenario Shifts," *Consortium News*, August 3, 2014.

57 'You Don't Exist:' Arbitrary Detentions, Enforced Disappearances and Torture

in Eastern Ukraine," Human Rights Watch, 2016; Justin Raimondo, "Monsters of Ukraine: Made in the USA," *Ron Paul Institute*, July 31, 2015; John Kerry, *Every Day is Extra* (New York: Simon & Schuster, 2018), 436.

58   Paul Robinson, "Explaining the Ukrainian Army's Defeat in Donbas in 2014," In *The Return of the Cold War*, ed. Black et al., 111-116. The sorry Western reporting is detailed in Oliver Boyd-Barrett, *Western Mainstream Media and the Ukraine Crisis: A Study in Conflict Propaganda* (New York: Routledge, 2017).

59   Peter Schweizer, *Secret Empires: How the American Political Class Hides Corruption and Enriches Family and Friends* (New York: Harper Collins, 2018), 55-65. The New York Times reported that Biden threatened to withhold a $1 billion loan if Ukraine did not fire its top prosecutor who was mounting a case against Zlochevsky, the owner of Burisma. Kenneth P. Vogel and Iulia Mendel, "Biden Faces Conflict of Interest Questions That Are Being Promoted by Trump and Allies," The New York Times, May 1, 2019, A1.

60   Jeremy Kuzmarov and John Marciano, *The Russians are Coming, Again: The First Cold War as Tragedy, the Second as Farce* (New York: Monthly Review Press, 2018); 12; Noam Chomsky, *Who Rules the World?* (New York: Metropolitan Books, 2016), 165; Robert Parry, "Do We Really Want a Nuclear War with Russia?" *Consortium News*, October 3, 2016.

61   "Statement by the President on the Situation in Ukraine and Gaza, " The White House, Office of the Press Secretary, July 21, 2014; Robert Parry. "Fake Evidence Blaming Russia for MH-17," *Consortium News*, May 18, 2015; Robert Parry, "MH-17 Case Slips Into Propaganda Fog," *Consortium News*, July 9, 2015.

62   Parry, "Flight 17 Shoot-Down Scenarios." American intelligence agents told journalist Robert Parry they believed that a rogue faction of the Ukrainian military may have been behind it.

63   Michael Hudson, "The New Cold War and Ukraine Gambit," in *Flashpoint Ukraine: How the U.S. Drive for Hegemony Risks World War III* (Atlanta: Clarity Press, 2014), 34.

64   Dmitry Babich, "Religious Divisions Threaten to Further Inflame Ukrainian Civil War," *Consortium News*, August 19, 2018; Madsen, *Soros*, 22; Andrew E. Kramer, "War Looms Over Vote for Ukrainian Leader, 5 years After Uprising," *New York Times*, March 31, 2019. Poroshenko's unpopularity was reflected in his losing the 2019 election to a comedian with no previous political experience.

65   Sakwa, *Frontline Ukraine*, 113. For the Kaiser precedent, see Roger Peace, Jeremy Kuzmarov and Charles Howlett, "United States Participation in World War I," http://peacehistory-usfp.org/united-states-participation-in-world-war-one/.

66   Eg. "Russia Tops ISIS Threat, Ebola Worst of All? Lavrov Puzzled by Obama's UN Speech," *RT News*, September 24, 2014; "Obama Continues Chiding

Russia on Gay Rights," *CNN,* March 26, 2014.

67   Sinisa Jakov Marusic, "Djukanovic Named 'Criminal of the Year' in Poll," *Balkan Insight,* December 31, 2015. Djukanovic beat out another U.S.-backed client, Ilham Aliyev of Azerbaiajan for the claim of criminal of the year in 2015. The U.S. provided over $27 million in military assistance to his regime.

68   Sally Denton, *The Profiteers: Bechtel and the Men Who Built the World* (New York: Simon & Schuster, 2016), 283; Darwin Bond-Graham, "Obama's Nuclear Weapon Surge," and Karl Grossman, "Obama and the Nuclear Rocket,"in *Hopeless: Barack Obama and the Politics of Illusion,* ed. Jeffrey St. Clair and Joshua Frank (Oakland: AK Press, 2012). Obama further called for the revived production of plutonium 238 for use in space devices and for more research into nuclear thermal propulsion. His choice to head NASA, Charles Bolden, favored nuclear powered rockets which he told the Council on Foreign Relations could be launched from space.

69   Kimberley Marten, "Reducing Tensions between Russia and NATO," *Council on Foreign Relations,* Report No. 79, March 2017, 26; Jonathan Marshall, "Pushing NATO to Russia's Southern Flank," *Consortium News,* September 12, 2016; Cockburn, "The New Red Scare," 31.

70   Engdahl, *Manifest Destiny.*

71   Kuzmarov and Marciano, *The Russians are Coming, Again* 10, 11; Wayne Madsen, "The Ties That Bind Washington to Chechen Terrorists," *Global Research,* April 26, 2013; Daniel Esturlin, *Shadow Masters* (Trine Day, 2010), 27; Ridenour, *The Russian Peace Threat.*

72   Louis A. Del Monte, *Genius Weapons: Artificial Intelligence, Autonomous Weaponry, And the Future of Warfare* (New York: Prometheus Books, 2018), 65; David Price, "Militarizing Space: Starship Troopers, Same as It Ever Was," *Counterpunch,* August10, 2018.

73   "Star Wars II? Obama signs defense bill calling for space-based missile systems," *South China Morning Post,* December 24, 2016.

74   Department of Defense, Unmanned Systems Integration Roadmap, FY 2013-2038, http://www.defense.gov/pubs/DOD-USRM-2013.pdf; Annie Jacobsen, *The Pentagon's Brain: An Uncensored History of DARPA, America's Top Secret Military Research Agency* (Boston: Little & Brown, 2015), 406, 410, 414, 416; "Will Robot Mules Reach the Battlefield?" *Popular Science,* Summer 2017, 18; Vinod Yalburgi, "MITs New Iron Man Suit to Give U.S. Soldiers Super Strength, Night Vision and Liquid Armor," *International Business Times,* October 10, 2013; Dan Grazier, "F-35: Is America's Most Expensive Weapon of War the Ultimate Failure?" *The National Interest,* March 19, 2018.

75   Joe Gould, "Electronic Warfare: What the U.S. Army Can Learn from Ukraine," *Defense News,* August 2, 2015.

76   Andrei Martyanov, *Losing Military Supremacy: The Myopia of American Strategic Planning* (Atlanta: Clarity Press, 2018); Mahdi D. Nazemroaya,

"Military Encirclement and Global Domination: Russia Counters U.S. Missile Shield from the Sea," *Global Research*, November 4, 2012.

77   Jeremy Kuzmarov, "Spirit of McCarthyism Seen in Attacks on Oliver Stone," *The Huffington Post*, June 25, 2018.

78   See Guy Mettan, *Creating Russophobia: From the Great religious Schism to Anti-Putin Hysteria* (Atlanta: Clarity Press, 2017).

79   Mark Mazetti and Katie Benner, "12 Russian Agents Indicted in Mueller Investigation," *New York Times*, July 13, 2018; Joe Lauria, "Clinging to Collusion: Why Evidence Will Probably Never Be Produced in the Indictment of Russian Agents," *Consortium News*, July 14, 2018; Aaron Maté, "New Studies Show Pundits Are Wrong About Russian Social-Media Involvement in U.S. Politics," *The Nation*, December 28, 2018. Only 10 percent of Facebook stories promoted by the Russian Internet Research Agency (IRA) were political and they may have been part of a bait and switch commercial operation.

80   Matt Margolis, *The Scandalous Presidency of Barack Obama* (New York: Bombardier Books, 2018), 137; Dan Bonigno, with D.L. McAllister, *Spygate: The Attempted Sabotage of Donald J. Trump* (New York: Post Hill Press, 2018). Obama allegedly placed a spy in the Trump camp, Cambridge University Professor, Stefan Halper, and the deep state used surveillance and other forms of manipulation to try and entrap Trump officials including George Papadopolous.

81   Ray McGovern, "Unaccountable Media Faced with Dilemma in Next Phase of Deep State-gate," *Consortium News*, April 9, 2018.

82   "US Intel Vets Dispute Russia Hacking Claims," *Consortium News*, December 12, 2016; Mark Mazetti and Katie Benner, "Mueller Finds No Trump-Russia Conspiracy, But Stops Short of Exonerating the President on Obstruction," *The New York Times*, March 24, 2019.

83   Kuzmarov and Marciano, *The Russians are Coming, Again*; Dan Kovalik, *The Plot to Scapegoat Russia* (New York: Skyhorse Press, 2017); Gareth Porter, "How the Department of Homeland Security Created a Deceptive Tale of Russia Hacking U.S. Voter Cites," *Consortium News*, August 28, 2018; Gareth Porter, "The Shaky Case That Russia Manipulated Social Media to Tip the 2016 Election," *Consortium News*, October 11, 2018; Cohen, *War With Russia?*.

84   Cited in Kuzmarov and Marciano, *The Russians are Coming, Again*, 39, 40; Alexa Lardieri, "Americans Say Russia Poses 'Critical Threat; is Country's Greatest Enemy," *U.S. News & World Report*, February 27. 2019.

Chapter 9

OBAMA'S BETRAYAL OF HIS CAIRO VISION

On June 4th, 2009, Barack Obama gave a moving address to a massive crowd at Cairo University in which he called for a "new beginning" in American relations with the Muslim world that would be based on "mutual interest and respect" and "upon the truth that America and Islam.... need not be in competition." Obama in the speech quoted from biblical verses and the Quran, and acknowledged the oppression of the Palestinians and history of colonial intervention by the West, including the U.S. role in the "overthrow of the democratically elected government in Iran." Whereas America in the past had focused on "oil and gas when it comes to this part of the world," he said that "we now seek a broader engagement" that would include an "emphasis on promoting technological development and science and women's rights, along with a more genuine support for human rights and democracy."[1]

Obama's speech gave hope that a new era in American-Middle Eastern relations was possible. Unfortunately, his words didn't match his deeds. At the time of his speech, his administration was providing $1.3 billion in security assistance to the Egyptian government of Hosni Mubarak, who would be ousted a year later in the Arab Spring protests, and was selling weapons to dictatorships like that of Zine el Abadin ben Ali of Tunisia who received $13.7 million in military aid in 2010.[2] These policies exemplify the betrayal of Obama's Cairo vision and his blatant double standard on human rights. Part of the problem was structural and connected to the insatiable U.S. drive for oil and influence of the Israeli, Saudi and Emirati lobbies and right-wing pressure groups. Bill Clinton called Obama a "wuss" for not intervening more aggressively in Syria. The end result was growing distrust for the U.S., and emergence of Russia as a go to country for Middle Eastern leaders who realized they could not trust the U.S. and needed to diversify their international relations.[3]

Playing Both Sides in the Arab Spring: Egypt and Tunisia

The Arab Spring protests, or uprisings, broke out in winter 2011 after a Tunisian street vendor, Tarek Mohamed Bouazizi, set himself on fire to protest high unemployment and abuse of power. The Obama administration predictably sided with the tyrants initially. After throngs of protestors began camping out in Cairo's Tahrir Square to force dictator Hosni Mubarak's removal, Obama gave a statement insinuating Mubarak still had years ahead of him in office. Wanting to appear hip, a few days later, he changed his tune and leaked to the press that he "wanted the kids in the street to win, and for the google guy [Wael Ghonem] to become president."[4]

Behind the scenes, the Obama administration cultivated support for Mubarak's brutal intelligence chief Omar Suleiman and military chief of staff Sami Anan as Egypt's next ruler, who failed his test run before the Egyptian masses, before settling on support for the Muslim Brotherhood. In Tunisia, Obama favored General Rachid Ammar who was given instructions by the U.S.

embassy to take charge if "things got out of control."[5] Meaning: if popular forces took over who would institute radical economic reforms and side with the Palestinians. In December 2011, Moncef Marzouki was named as Tunisia's interim president to replace ben Ali. He was a handpicked Washington choice whose organization, the Tunisian League for Human Rights was part of a front group funded by the National Endowment for Democracy (NED), an organization founded in 1983 to carry on CIA regime change activities, and by George Soros' Open Society Foundation.[6]

The NED sponsored leadership conferences that brought together opposition leaders and provided grants to youth and trade union activists as well as members of the Muslim Brotherhood who took power in both Egypt and Tunisia. Most of the grants were used for training in organizational and leadership skills that included the use of new social media such as Facebook which was used as a platform to broadcast anti-regime messages and to coordinate "Days of Rage" protests; a slogan that came ironically from the Weather Underground [a 1960s radical anti-Vietnam War group headed by Obama's friend, William Ayers]. Activists were further introduced to the writings of Gene Sharp, a University of Massachusetts professor who developed methods for destabilizing governments through nonviolent means that had previously proved useful for advancing U.S. interests elsewhere.[7] Some of the training was carried out through liaison with the Optor resistance youth movement that spearheaded a color revolution against socialist strongman Slobodan Milosovic in Serbia in October 2000, and were involved in training Georgian and Ukrainian youth groups which helped destabilize their pro-Russian governments.[8]

The *Washington Post* estimated that 10,000 Egyptians took part in NED and USAID training in social media and nonviolent organizing techniques. Ron Nixon of the *New York Times* noted that "as American officials and others look back at the uprisings of the Arab Spring, they are seeing that the United States' democracy-building campaigns played a bigger role in fomenting protests than was previously known, with key leaders of the movements having been trained by the Americans in campaigning, organizing through new media tools."[9]

Obama's favorite, Wael Ghonem, was given a paid leave from his job as a Google executive to participate in the protests, exemplifying the foreign corporate support for Egypt's "revolution."[10] Afterwards, Tharwat Al-Kharabawy, a former Muslim Brotherhood member said the Obama administration played a decisive role in the election of Mohammed Morsi, who was forced to upgrade security cooperation with Israel and caved to prodding by Secretary of State John Kerry to continue the neoliberal economic policies of Mubarak, including cutting back food and fuel subsidies and reducing public payrolls to the benefit of Egypt's business elite and Western capital primarily.[11] However, Morsi was ultimately considered to be too independent as he rejected pressure to join in invading Syria, made overtures towards Iran, forged relations with Hamas and refused an IMF loan, which would require further public sector cuts and privatization. As such, the Obama administration backed the counter-revolutionary General Fatah al-Sisi, whom it provided over $1 billion, including a shipment of Apache helicopters used in an onslaught against the city of Rafah and to tighten the siege on Gaza.[12]

Washington was conscious of the fact that both Mubarak and ben Ali, once trained at the U.S. Army School at Fort Bliss Texas and in intelligence at Ft. Holabird in Maryland, had been planning with Libyan ruler Muammar Qaddafi to create an Islamic currency union based on the gold dinar, independent of oil sales denominated in U.S. dollars. They were beginning to divest their oil profits from U.S. banks because of their disgust with the War on Terror and setting up a fund to buy foreign assets and stocks.[13] The way to remove them was not through military intervention, which failed in Iraq and Afghanistan, but covert means. According to Peter Hoekstra, former chair of the House Intelligence Committee, this strategy backfired as the U.S. lost its human intelligence sources in Egypt with Mubarak's ouster like in Libya and saw destabilized countries grow closer to Russia or China.[14]

Responding to a Manufactured Crisis

Iran was long a major target for regime change. The national security establishment never got over its successful defiance during the 1979 Islamic revolution, which ousted Shah Mohammed Reza Pahlevi who came to power in a 1953 CIA-backed coup against the democratically elected Mohammad Mosaddegh. The latter's sin was to nationalize the country's oil industry. During the Shah's rule from 1953-1979, Iran compiled among the world's worst human rights records as the CIA and Mossad trained its secret police, and even helped in the development of a nuclear enrichment program.[15]

In 2004, the CIA purported to have acquired documents and drawings showing Iran's development of a compact warhead to fit atop the Shahab missile. Supreme leader Ayatollah Ali Khameini had invoked Islamic principles, however, in enforcing a ban on work relating to nuclear weapons and the CIA never established the authenticity of the documents. They were found to have originated with a dissident Iranian group, Mujahidin e-Khalq (MEK), which had carried out terrorist acts including the assassination of Iranian scientists in collaboration with Israeli intelligence and were suspected of cooperating with ISIS fighters on joint missions. According to Seymour Hersh, its members had been trained at a remote base in Nevada by U.S. Joint Special Operations Command for covert operations intended to topple the Iranian government.[16]

During the 2008 presidential campaign, Obama had made diplomatic engagement with Iran a priority and in the first weeks of his presidency taped a video greeting for the Persian New Year and then ordered the CIA to sever its contacts with supporters of the Green revolution attempting to topple Iranian president Mahmoud Ahmadinejad.[17] However, Obama soon faced pressure to adopt a more bellicose stance. Israeli Prime Minister Benjamin Netanyahu allegedly applied hidden pressure through "Chicago," meaning Lester Crown, who met with Valerie Jarrett to relay the message of an Israeli military envoy who wanted the U.S. to attack Iran.[18]

Obama, to his credit, did not cave to the demand though he subsequently approved and was intimately involved in planning a cyberattack on Iran's nuclear enrichment facility at Natanz in collaboration with Israeli intelligence.[19] Echoing the Israeli Likud Party line, Obama promoted alarmist claims about Iran's nuclear weapons program and warned of a potential missile attack on Europe despite the National Intelligence Estimate having confirmed that Iran's nuclear program had been halted in 2003. By adopting a hard-line on Iran, Obama hoped to appease Israeli Prime Minister Benjamin Netanyahu and get him to agree to a settlement freeze in the Palestinian occupied territory.[20] The Obama administration advanced a containment strategy, encircling Iran with Raytheon Patriot and Lockheed Martin Aegis missiles equipped with advanced radars placed in Qatar, Bahrain, Kuwait and the United Arab Emirates (UAE). It further waged economic war by pushing Saudi Arabia to raise its oil production to drive prices down (Russia was also a target) and strengthened Bush's economic sanctions, which contributed to a halving of Iran's oil revenue and precipitous decline of the rial.[21]

In 2012, Clinton's State Department removed the MEK from its list of terrorist groups, which left the cult-like organization free to raise funds and plot sabotage operations against the regime.[22] American-Iranian relations improved with the election of Hassan Rouhani as president of Iran in June 2013 to replace the hardliner Ahmadinejad. After a preliminary agreement in November 2013, John Kerry signed the Joint Comprehensive nuclear agreement in July 2015, in which Iran agreed to redesign and convert any nuclear weapon production facilities, allow for inspections and restrict stockpiles and mining of enriched uranium in return for the lifting of all nuclear related sanctions. As part of the quid pro quo, the Obama administration secretly flew into Iran $400 million in cash as the first installment of a $1.7 billion settlement resolving claims at an international tribunal over a failed-arms deal under the Shah. Four Americans were also released from Iranian jails, among them a *Washington Post* journalist, Jason Rezaian, and six Iranians were granted clemency in U.S. courts.[23]

Russian leader Vladimir Putin was instrumental in convincing Iran to sign the deal as a means of averting a world war. Obama was criticized from the right and the Trump administration subsequently withdrew from the deal. While seeming to defuse prospects of war, the prolonged negotiation of the agreement had promoted a false and alarmist narrative about Iran that enabled punitive economic sanctions to degrade the economy of that country for over a decade. Obama in a speech announcing the deal made a point of denouncing Iran's "destabilizing behavior" across the Middle East and support for violent proxies in Syria and Yemen.[24] The neoconservative dream of regime change was shelved only temporarily—and made easier with the elimination of Iran's potential nuclear deterrent.

Underwriting the 51-Day War: "Baruch" Obama and Israel

Obama's betrayal of the Cairo vision was acute in his policy towards Israel. Secretary of State John Kerry (2012-2016) wrote in his memoirs that Obama did as much or more than any other president in history to support Israel[25]—though this would pale compared to the actions of Donald Trump. From December 27th, 2008 to January 22nd, 2009, just after Obama's election to the presidency, the Israeli Defense Forces (IDF) launched Operation Cast Lead, an attack on Gaza that resulted in an estimated 1,400 Palestinian deaths compared to thirteen Israelis. A UN special mission, headed by the South African Justice Richard Goldstone, produced a report accusing the IDF of war crimes and possible crimes against humanity. Nonetheless, Obama lined up in support of Israeli policy. Speaking on CBS's Face the Nation, his chief adviser, David Axelrod, recalled comments that Obama made in a speech the previous July in Sderot, the Israeli town that was the target of rocket attacks from Palestinian militants. Obama said: "If somebody was sending rockets into my house where my two daughters sleep at night, I'm going to do everything in my power to stop that. I would expect Israelis to do the same thing."[26]

These comments provided an important signal to the

Israeli lobby. How Obama would have felt if his daughters were subjected to the indiscriminate white phosphorus, mortar and flechette attacks, hellfire missiles, and anti-tank projectiles used by the Israelis against Palestinian civilians, he never said.[27] Yet unlike his predecessor, Obama was conscious of the Palestinian plight. He had taken a literature class with Palestinian dissident Edward Said at Columbia, attended a fund-raiser for the Arab American Action network in Chicago and claimed to have read critical Israeli authors David Grossman and Amos Oz. Obama's connection to Chicago high society, Betty Lu Saltzman, helped found Peace Now and was on the advisory council of J Street, an alternative Zionist lobby to the American-Israel Public Affairs Committee (AIPAC), one which acknowledged Palestinian rights.

During his time in the State Senate, Obama lived next to a synagogue run by Rabbi Arnold Jacob Wolf who had had launched one of the first Jewish organizations supporting creation of a Palestinian state. Through him, he developed a friendship with Palestinian historian Rashid Khalidi, whose wife Mona noted that when conversing with Obama about Palestine, "you felt that he understood [and] was not taking an opposite position," but he "always seemed very, very careful about what he said." When the issue of Israel was raised with a conservative neighbor, Harry Gendler, Obama would "turn poker face, turn ice cold" and told him that we needed "a more balanced approach." Harry said that "Barack did not want to have an exchange of ideas or thoughts on that topic" and indeed "walked away."[28]

These recollections exemplify Obama as the consummate politician afraid to express himself candidly, which disappointed Wolf. His pro-Israel policies are not too surprising if we consider that "Jews made Obama," as a Jewish observer of the political scene in Chicago put it.[29] His major campaign strategist, David Axelrod, was a New York-raised Jew who had previous success positioning minority candidates to appeal to Jewish voters. Obama told the Jewish *Forward* in 2003 that he was trying to reconstitute the black-Jewish civil rights coalition, which he considered natural because "blacks and Jews... share a set of core values about the need for government to address injustice."[30]

258 | OBAMA'S UNENDING WARS

During the 2008 election, 78 percent of Jews voted for Obama. One of his foreign policy advisers, Lee Rosenberg, a venture capitalist, was AIPAC's Treasurer. Many top donors and bundlers were ardent Zionists like the Pritzkers, whose family patriarch, Abe, received the Israeli Prime Minister's medal and built a Hyatt hotel on occupied land in East Jerusalem. Insiders credit Obama's shift to a pro-Israeli stance to Penny's influence. Jeffrey Katzenberg, who co-owned Dreamworks with Stephen Spielberg, gave huge amounts to the Simon Wiesenthal Center, Spielberg's Shoa Foundation and Anti-Defamation League, and took celebrities like Jerry Seinfeld and Chris Rock on tours of the Holy Land, which Katzenberg considers a "jewel."[31] With donors like these, Obama's priorities in office were clearly set.

Philip Klutznick, Jimmy Carter's commerce secretary and co-owner of the Chicago Bulls, was another early Obama supporter who has since passed away. President of B'nai B'rith and the Jewish World Congress, Klutznick had played a leading role in financing Israel's creation. A business partner of Lester Crown and old friend of Jerusalem's first mayor, Teddy Kollek, who smuggled weapons during the 1948 independence war, Klutznick had vast real estate holdings in Israel and held ties to Israeli intelligence and almost every Prime Minister and President. Eclipsing Jay and Robert Pritzker as the wealthiest Illinoisan in 1983, Crown provided Israel with an aircraft manufacturing plant that laid the basis for the Israeli Aircraft Industries and allegedly assisted in the development of Israel's nuclear program.[32]

James Crown told the *New York Times* that his father was "fairly hawkish about Israel's security," and felt Obama was "terrific on Israel."[33] Lester Crown in turn told the *Chicago Jewish News* that Obama was an "ardent backer of Israel's defense" and supported a two-state solution, but only on the "hopes that you will have a demilitarized, peaceful Palestinian entity which you do not have now."[34] This implied a state lacking capability for self-defense, with Crown unable to say the word state.

As State Senator, while failing to show up at any black rallies against police brutality, Obama participated in a walk along

Lake Michigan on Israel Solidarity Day and also co-sponsored an amendment to the Illinois pension code allowing the state to make loans to Israel and purchase Israeli bonds.[35] He joked to his friend Abner Mikva that his real name was Baruch Obama. When running for the U.S. Senate, Obama apologized to Palestinian activist Ali Abuminah for "not saying more about Palestinian rights" but he said, "we are in a tough primary race. I'm hoping when things calm down, I can be more upfront."[36] Obama's first chief of Staff and chief adviser on Israel, Rahm Emmanuel, had served as a volunteer in the Israeli Defense Force (IDF), and his father in the Irgun Zvi Leumi, which bombed the King David hotel in Jerusalem and murdered a UN envoy (Count Bernadotte) on the eve of Israel's independence.[37]

Backtracking on demands for a temporary halt on illegal settlements, "Baruch" and his administration continued to serve as "Israel's lawyer" in fleeting negotiations, perpetuated joint military and cyber-security training exercises, and approved nearly $24 billion in military assistance to Israel. $3.8 billion was provided in 2016 alone, the largest military aid package in history. Israel got F-16 fighter jets, Apache helicopters and $504 million to develop the Iron Dome missile defense system designed to knock Hamas-fired rockets from the sky.[38] Despite all this support, the Israeli right-wing loathed Obama for being not being hardline enough. Prime Minister Benjamin Netanyahu had the effrontery to address the U.S. Congress to protest the Iran nuclear deal without Obama's support and received a standing ovation from the Republican dominated body. This was pure political theatrics.[39] More privately, Netanyahu along with former Israeli Defense Minister Moshe Ya'alon expressed satisfaction with U.S.-Israeli security collaboration under Obama. Long-time senior U.S. official Dennis Ross—who helped design that collaboration in the Ronald Reagan administration—acknowledged that it went "beyond what any previous administration has put in place."[40]

These comments say a great deal about where Obama's political calculations led. The Palestinian Occupied Territories in his presidency evolved into "ground zero for Israel's drone revolution" to the further benefit of General Dynamics which had forged a joint venture partnership with Israeli Aircraft Industries to develop unmanned surveillance drones. A British surgeon characterized Gaza as a laboratory for testing "high tech weapons from hell." Among them were shells containing white phosphorus manufactured in the U.S. that caused horrific burns, dense inert metal explosives, foul-smelling "skunk water," a Kamikaze drone, a remote-controlled machine gun and Joint Direct Attack Munition tail kits which convert free-fall bombs into satellite guided ordinance.[41]

During the 2014 Operation Protective Edge, the Obama administration provided Israel with hellfire missiles, emergency aid for its Iron Dome anti-missile system, Mark 82 dumb bombs, 155 mm howitzers with a kill radius of 164 feet and General Dynamics' bunker buster bombs capable of penetrating six meters of reinforced concrete known as "Saddamizers." They were used to pummel Gaza's high rise towers and wipe out entire families as they sought shelter in their homes.[42] 2,200 Gazans were killed by the Israelis in the war, 70 percent of them civilians, and 10,000 more were wounded. 120 business and shops were destroyed along with the Al-Omani mosque in Jabalia which had been built in 647 A.D.[43]

Though conveying "distress" at the suffering of Gaza's civilians in Protective Edge, Obama suggested that Israel had "a right to defend itself" and do "what it feels it needs to do" in the face of Hamas' irresponsible "taunts against Israel and its placement of rocket launchers in civilian areas during conflict with the Jewish state."[44] Obama's trick was to appear like he was balanced and humane by acknowledging the Palestinians plight, while giving credence to Israeli propaganda claims such as regarding the alleged placement of rocket launchers in civilian areas that justified its destruction of Gaza. Early in the war, president Obama claimed that he tried to compel Netanyahu to "minimize civilian casualties," though again underscored his recognition of the Israeli right to "self-defence."[45] The latter was an Orwellian phrase given that Protective Edge followed from a long Israeli siege after Gazans voted the wrong way in 2006 elections, and was in essence a revenge operation for the murder of three Israeli teens by a rogue clan in Hebron, the Qawasmeh, that was a thorn in the side of Hamas.[46]

Obama's complicity with Israeli state atrocity undercut the credibility of his 2009 Cairo speech and its declaration that freedom, democracy and the rule of law "are not just American ideas; they are human rights. And that is why we will support them everywhere." Everywhere clearly did not include Gaza, which had come to resemble an open-air prison in which 400,000 children grew up traumatized from witnessing friends, neighbors and families blown apart by high explosives.[47]

Obama and Saudi Arabia

In *Kings and Presidents*, former CIA officer Bruce Riedel wrote that "no president since Franklin Roosevelt courted Saudi Arabia as zealously as did Obama."[48] Over eight years, he sanctioned a record $115 billion in arms sales to the Saudis in 42 separate deals and protected the kingdom by refusing to declassify 28 pages from the 9/11 report on Saudi Arabia, which could possibly detail their role in the terrorist attacks. Obama also vetoed legislation allowing 9/11 victims' families to sue the Saudi government.[49] And for all that, when Obama and Michelle visited with the new King Salman, they were left standing by themselves as Salman and his entourage went to pray.[50]

The Saudis were valued as a main hedge against Iran. They provided the U.S. with a secret drone base in a remote stretch of the desert along with cheap oil and sold their oil in U.S. dollars, a key bulwark sustaining the Petro dollar. The Pritzkers and other political donors also did major business there. Hyatt had three major hotels. McKinsey & Co. provided economic advice and may have aided in the crackdown on dissidents, according to a *New York Times* report.[51]

Obama's CIA Director John Brennan was a Saudiphile who developed valuable relationships with the security services from his time as CIA station chief. The Clinton Foundation received $10 to $25 million from the Kingdom, though Hillary averred in a memo leaked by Wikileaks that Saudi Arabia was a "leading sponsor of Sunni Islamic terrorism in the Middle East."[52] Saudi workers also suffered "slavery like conditions," according to Human Rights Watch. King Abdullah ordered the public crucifixion of children who supported the Arab Spring, and beheaded Shia cleric Nimr al-Nimr and his nephew.[53]

These and other atrocities evoked no tears or calls for humanitarian intervention from Samantha Power. Obama personally met the Saudi interior chief who had orchestrated a wave of repression, and cut short a trip to India to travel to Saudi Arabia and pay tribute to the just-deceased King Abdullah, whom he lavished with a glowing eulogy.[54] During the Arab Spring, Obama gave full backing to Saudi Arabia as it sent troops to crush a predominantly Shia pro-democracy demonstrators seeking to overthrow the Sunni al-Khalifa dynasty in Bahrain, home of the U.S. fifth fleet.[55] Hundreds of Bahraini Shiites were beaten, tortured or disappeared and forty mosques were desecrated. The Obama administration not only boosted arms sales to Saudi Arabia during the crackdown but also hired American police sergeants to train Bahrain's internal security forces in riot control. Among those sent was John Timoney, the former police chief in Miami who was the target of an ACLU civil rights lawsuit for promoting tactics designed to intimidate demonstrators and silence dissent during protests directed against a free-trade agreement.[56]

In a speech before the UN heralding America's championing of pro-democracy movements in the Arab Spring, Obama reiterated America's close friendship with Bahrain and stated that "the patriotism that binds Bahrainis together must be more powerful than the sectarian forces that would tear them apart."[57] The implication was that both Sunni and Shia were responsible for the violence. The U.S. and Saudi involvement was in turn airbrushed from history.

Secret Teams in another Secret War

In his last year in office, Obama spoke eloquently about the dangers of proxy wars before the United Nations and told *Atlantic*

Magazine reporter Jeffrey Goldberg that the Saudis and Iranians "needed to find an effective way to share the neighborhood."[58] These words rang hollow since the Obama administration had played a vital role in supporting the Saudi invasion of Yemen, which caused a biblical type humanitarian crisis, and sowed greater tension with Iran, which backed the anti-Saudi Houthi rebels.

Obama's claim that American forces were not directly participating in the Yemeni conflict was another of his poker-faced lies: the *New York Times* reported in May 2018 on the presence of secret teams of American Green Berets on the Saudi Arabian border. They were involved with training Saudi ground forces, providing intelligence for bomb targeting, assisting in aerial refueling and helped to locate and destroy caches of ballistic missiles at a launch site that Houthi rebels were using to attack Riyadh and other Saudi cities from Yemen.[59]

The Obama administration further provided over $20 billion in new weapons transfers to Saudi Arabia after the Yemen war broke out and forty million pounds worth of jet fuel. Weapons included Apache and Black Hawk helicopters, F-15 jet fighters, cruise missiles, "smart bombs," white phosphorus, an incendiary that burns through the skin to the bone, and a $1.5 billion shipment of 152 Abrams battle tanks made by General Dynamics, twenty of which were destined to replenish vehicles from Yemen.[60] Previously, the Obama administration sold cluster bombs to Saudi Arabia made by the Rhode Island Company, Textron, whose shell-casings were recovered at the site in Western Yemen where a thirty-four-year old fisherman, Ali Mohammed Medarij, was struck and killed while sleeping on his boat.[61] Mark-84 bombs manufactured by General Dynamics were further used in a marketplace bombing in Mastaba that killed 97 civilians.

The roots of the Saudi war in Yemen lay with the Arab Spring of 2011, when Yemenis dislodged longstanding ruler Ali Abdullah Saleh, a former tank commander who first took power in North Yemen in 1978 and unified the two Yemens after the implosion of the southern socialist regime in the 1990s.[62] The Obama administration at this time helped secure an agreement by which power was handed over to Abdy Rabu Mansour Hadi, Saleh's Vice-President for twenty years, whom one Middle East expert referred to as "empire's man."[63] Praising him for his work combatting terrorism, Obama provided Hadi's regime with $346 million in military and economic aid in 2012 alone, the largest in the history of U.S. foreign aid to Yemen. When a counter-terrorism force was deployed to protect the American embassy against protests, Jamal Jubran, a Yemeni analyst, described the U.S. Ambassador, Gerald M. Feierstein, as "The New Dictator of Yemen," arguing the country had fallen under U.S. trusteeship.[64]

The Houthis took their name from Hussein Badr al-Din al-Houthi, a charismatic leader burned alive in a cave in 2004 who had opposed Saleh's kleptocratic ways and fealty to Saudi Arabia and the U.S. Led subsequently by Hussein's son, Abdel-Malek al-Houthi, whom the government accused of trying to set up a Shiite theocracy, the Houthis wanted to restore the traditional supremacy of the Zaydeh clan, who had ruled North Yemen prior to the outbreak of civil war in the 1960s. The clan's founder, Zayd bin Ali, had led an uprising against the Umayyad Empire in 740 A.D., the first dynastic empire in Islamic history.[65] Supporting the Arab Spring protests against Saleh, the Houthis disdained Hadi, who was backed by Yemen's Muslim Brotherhood, and took as his Vice president, Ali Mohsen al-Ahmar, who was accused of enlisting jihadis to fight the Houthi.[66]

Though the U.S. and Saudis played up Iranian backing of the Houthi, Zaydism was doctrinally distinct from the mainstream Shite Islam practiced in Iran. Isa Blumi points out in his book, *Destroying Yemen: What Chaos in Arabia Tells Us About the World,* that the Houthi by 2013 were part of a larger coalition that included Saleh and his loyalists, various tribal militias, and a major swath of the military and public sector workers who felt aggrieved by the corruption and poor living standards that existed under Hadi's government and by years of neoliberalism that had resulted in Yemen's impoverishment following a period of successful local development initiatives in the 1970s under Ibrahim Al-Hamdi.[67]

During Hadi's rule, the number of assassinations and bombings of mosques frequented by Zaydi Muslims increased, while poverty, unemployment and property confiscations grew to epidemic proportions. With no parliamentary oversight, Hadi had put many of Yemen's public assets up for sale and slashed public services. Blumi writes that a broad coalition backed by the Houthi "threw out the corrupt foreign imposed government filled with crooks and Islamist bigots [and] reversed the selling of Yemen's economic future."[68] This is not the way the rebellion or war was presented by the Obama administration or mainstream media, which condemned the Houthi for destabilizing Yemen.[69]

In a May 2013 speech on national security at the National Defense University, Obama claimed that the United States supported security forces that reclaimed territory from al-Qaeda in Yemen, though actually backed security forces that allied with it. Undersecretary of Defense Michael Vickers expressed disappointment that the productive informal intelligence relationship America had developed with the Houthis against al-Qaeda, who allied with Sunni tribes fighting the Houthi, did not endure.[70] An Associated Press investigation found that the U.S.-led Saudi coalition cut secret deals with al-Qaeda, paying them to leave cities, and recruited known al Qaeda operatives to fight the Houthi; U.S. drone strikes targeting al-Qaeda in Yemen then stopped. Khaled Baterfi, a senior military commander, stated that al-Qaeda militants were present on all major front lines of the fighting. Video footage showed that a coalition backed unit advancing on Mocha were openly al-Qaeda, wearing Afghan style garb and carrying weapons with the group's logo. When an adviser to Taiz's Governor told military commanders not to recruit al Qaeda, the response was, "we will unite with the devil in the face of the Houthis."[71]

The U.S. valued Yemen strategically because of its port facilities and access to the Bab al-Mandab straits connecting the Red Sea and Gulf of Aden. The country also possessed mineral wealth, including copper, nickel, lead and petroleum reserves, which American companies like Hunt Oil and Conoco Phillips and other foreign interests from Saudi Arabia, UAE and Qatar, have sought to exploit. An ancillary hidden motive was control of the coveted strategic island of Socotra, a wildlife preserve and world heritage site with 50,000 inhabitants located 380 kilometers off the coast of Yemen, 80 kilometers off the Horn of Africa and 3,000 kilometers from the U.S. naval base at Diego Garcia, one of America's largest overseas military facilities in the Indian Ocean. Socotra's strategic waterway serves as a major transit point for the shipment of oil as well as China's exports to Western Europe. Control over it could thus enable the denial of oil to China (which had become dependent on oil imports) or any country opposing the U.S.[72]

In 2010, David Petraeus, then head of the U.S. Central Command, held a secret meeting with then-President Saleh in which Saleh allegedly allowed the U.S. to set up a military base on Socotra from which to launch seaborne missiles and possibly drone strikes to counter "pirates and Al Qaeda." The U.S. in turn agreed to double security assistance to over $150 million. Since that time, a new civilian airport was built on Socotra in accordance with U.S. military specifications. Then in February 2016, acting Yemeni President Hadi, after passing a decree rewriting Yemen's internal boundaries, leased Socotra to the United Arab Emirates (UAE) for 99 years. The UAE in turn installed a pliable governor with whom it could negotiate independently and began to use the island for military training while promoting economic development and tourism.[73] The situation appeared to bear parallels to American plans in Panama in the early 19th century when the U.S. supported Panama's secession from Colombia and then pushed through an agreement that prompted Panama to cede its sovereignty.[74] This is how many Yemenis viewed it.

Private military contractors played a vital role in camouflaging the U.S. role in Yemen. Obama extended a $4 billion effort by Vinnell Corporation, a subsidiary of the defense contractor Northrop Grumman that once ran black operations in Vietnam, to train and equip the Saudi National Guard, which was key in the invasion of Yemen.[75] The Obama administration also contracted with DynCorp through the United Arab Emirates (UAE); allowed the awarding of a $95 million contract to train the Saudi Air Force to L-3 Communications, whose board of directors included a former chairman of the Army's Joint Chief of Staff (Hugh Shelton); and arranged a deal in which Booz Allen Hamilton, which gave $199,061 to Obama's 2012 campaign, trained the Saudi Navy as it ran a devastating blockade on Yemen.[76]

The Obama administration waged war on Yemen extensively through the UAE, home of the al-Dhafra air base, whose ruling al-Nahyan dynasty trained, paid and equipped more than 25,000 Yemeni soldiers, and sent at least 1,500 Special Forces into Yemen, along with hundreds of Colombian mercenaries and Sudanese, who included Janjaweed militiamen under U.S. sanctions for human rights abuses in Darfur.[77] The U.S. made offers to sell the UAE $27 billion worth of arms, including Paveway and Joint Direct Attack Munitions (JDAM) and tactical missiles such as the hellfire already used in the war in Yemen, and trained UAE troops. Prior to his appointment as Secretary of Defense under Trump, General James "Mad Dog" Mattis, a General Dynamics Board member, served as an unpaid adviser to the UAE military, starting this arrangement when the intervention in Yemen was already underway.[78]

The UAE's Joint Aviation Command, whose arsenal included Apache, Chinook and Black Hawk helicopters and converted crop dusters, was headed by another American General, Stephen Toumajan, who was employed by a private contractor, Knowledge International, whose board included Stanley McChrystal. According to a retired CIA agent, Toumajan and an Australian who headed the presidential guard (Mike Hindmarsh) were essentially "commanding the war [in Yemen]." A military officer told *Buzz Feed* that Toumajan's role was "bizarre. We would call him Little Napoleon." Another colleague said that "he sees himself as the white 'bwana' who can lead them to the promised land."[79] Just like in colonial days.

Obama's outsourcing strategy helped to effectively minimize public attention that was devoted to the war in Yemen and public dissent. Obama himself said little about Yemen, believing that the Houthis were a "nasty militia" and that the country was a "shit show" before the war, and would be a "shit show" whatever the United States did. According to his analysis, which was not far removed from Trump's labeling foreign countries as "sh*tholes," the United States "should not jeopardize its sometimes-unpleasant, but necessary relationship with the Saudis to produce the same end result."[80] CIA analyst Bruce Riedel stated in April 2016, however, that "if the United States and the United Kingdom, tonight, told King Salman [of Saudi Arabia] 'this war has to end,' it would end tomorrow. The Royal Saudi Air Force cannot operate without American and British support."[81] But Obama, like Trump, had no interest in ending a war whose humanitarian toll was devastating.

Timber Sycamore and a Failed Regime Change Effort in Syria

In an interview with journalist Amy Goodman, General Wesley Clark stated that prior to the U.S. invasion of Iraq in 2003, he had met with a high level Pentagon General who showed him a memo from the Secretary of Defense, Donald Rumsfeld, which described how "we're going to take out seven countries in five years, starting with Iraq, and then Syria, Lebanon, Libya, Somalia, Sudan, and finishing off, Iran."[82] This blueprint provides a pivotal backdrop in understanding the Obama administration's policy in Syria, which continued the program for regime change by funding anti-Assad propaganda outlets and backing Islamic and other rebel forces that triggered the uprising and fought against Syrian President Bashir-al Assad.

Obama was following the precedent not only of Bush, but another great patron of the CIA, Dwight Eisenhower. In 1957, under Operation Wappen, Eisenhower's CIA Director Allen Dulles sent in coup wizards Kermit Roosevelt and Rocky Stone to arm and incite Islamic militants and bribe Syrian military officers in a failed attempt to overthrow the secular nationalist regime of Shukri al-Quwatli, which went on to support merger with Egypt as part of an effort to cultivate Pan-Arab unity. Similar in outlook to Iranian Prime Minister Mohammad Mosaddegh and Egyptian President Gamal Abdel Nasser, who were also victims of CIA machinations, Quwatli had hesitated to approve the Trans Arabian pipeline connecting Saudi Arabia and Lebanon through Syria and had been overthrown once before in a CIA-backed operation in 1949.[83]

Bashir al-Assad was a nationalist like Quwatli who allied with Iran, stood up to Israel, and earned the enmity of the U.S. by rejecting a pipeline project passing through it from Qatar to Turkey to be financed by Qatar, host of the U.S. Middle East Central Command and a fundraising headquarter for Al Qaeda. Along with other Sunni kingdoms, Qatar stood to gain decisive domination of the world's natural gas markets at the expense of Russia and Iran. "Secret cables and reports by the U.S., Saudi and Israeli intelligence agencies indicate that the moment Assad rejected the Qatari pipeline, military and intelligence planners quickly arrived at the consensus that fomenting a Sunni uprising in Syria to overthrow the uncooperative Bashar Assad was a feasible path to achieving the shared objective of completing the Qatar/Turkey gas link," wrote Senator Robert Kennedy's son, Bobby Kennedy Jr. "In 2009, according to WikiLeaks, soon after Bashar Assad rejected the Qatar pipeline, the CIA began funding opposition groups in Syria," well before the Arab Spring began.[84]

The Arab Spring in Syria originated in Dara'a, a medium sized town adversely affected by drought near the Jordan border after teenagers were caught spraying anti-government graffiti in March, 2011.[85] A month earlier, Hasan Ali Akleh had set himself on fire in the spirit of Tunisian vendor Mohamed Bouazizi in the small northeastern city of Al-Hasakah. Many Syrians were disaffected with Assad's harsh rule, the parasitical corruption of the ruling elite and inequality bred by a turn towards neoliberalism. However, the rebel groups lacked cohesive political or military leadership or alternative governing vision, and were often sectarian. The army and intelligence agencies stayed loyal to Assad unlike in Tunisia and Egypt. Islamists seized on the crisis to press for regime change, aiming to establish a Salafist principality, an Islamic state in Eastern Syria.[86] (Salafism is promoted by Sunnis connected to Saudi Arabia's Wahhabism)

British commentator Patrick Seale pointed out that "the Syrian uprising should be seen as only the latest, if by far the most violent, episode in the long war between Islamists and Baathists which dates back to the founding of the secular Baath Party in the 1940s. The struggle between them is by now little short of a death feud."[87] In the early 1980s, the Islamists had risen up in Homs and were violently suppressed by Hafez Assad, Bashir's father, who ruled Syria from 1970-2000, in what many analysts saw as a prelude to 2011. In both cases, a considerable portion of the population sided with the government: a 2012 Qatari poll found that 55 percent of Syrians living inside the country wanted Assad to stay.[88] Assad's political base included his own Alawite community and other Shiite groups, most of Syria's Christians and parts of the merchant classes as well as the business elite including rich Sunni industrialists, and religious minorities like the Druze who had done well under his and his father's rule.[89]

Father Frans van der Lugt, a priest who lived in Homs for 48 years and was murdered by Jabat al Nusra, noted before his death that:

> most citizens in Syria do not support the [armed] opposition...you cannot say that this is a popular uprising...From the beginning the protest movements have not merely been peaceful. I have seen from the beginning armed protestors in those demonstrations walking around, they were the first to fire on the police. Very often the violence of the security forces comes in response to the brutal violence of the armed insurgents... Most Christian leaders stand behind [Bashar] because they are convinced that they would be worse with any alternative.[90]

U.S. intelligence concurred with this analysis, noting that "the Syrians are pragmatists who do not want a Muslim Brotherhood government."[91] Researcher Tim Anderson points out that the main rebel group touted by the West as freedom fighters, the Free Syrian Army (FSA), was two-thirds dominated by the Muslim Brotherhood. Another U.S. intelligence report affirmed that "the Salafist, the Muslim Brotherhood and AQI [Al-Qaeda in Iraq, later ISIS] are the major forces driving the insurgency in Syria... AQI supported the Syrian opposition from the beginning, both ideologically and through the media."[92] Obama effectively disguised the truth by referring to the rebels as "moderates" and "former farmers or teachers or pharmacists" though Vice President Joe Biden acknowledged that many were extremists in a speech at Harvard University.[93]

By late 2012, the Obama administration had launched Operation Timber Sycamore, a covert twelve-billion-dollar weapons supply program to arm and train "moderate" rebels based in Jordan and Turkey. Under the direction of the "grim Irishman," John Brennan, the rebels were provided with Kalashnikov assault rifles, mortars, rocket propelled grenades, anti-tank guided missiles, and night vision goggles. Similar to Afghanistan in the 1980s, additional financing and weapons came from Saudi Arabia, Qatar, Turkey, Jordan, Libya, the UAE, as well as Israel and the UK.[94] One group directly armed by the CIA, Nourredine al Zinki, formed a coalition with an outfit called "the bin Laden front." It was singled out by Amnesty International for carrying out gruesome atrocities in rebel-held Eastern Aleppo.[95]

To distance the dirty war from the public, the Pentagon hired private contractors who carried out military operations alongside Special Forces. Six 3 Intelligence Solutions, a private intelligence company acquired by CACI International, the firm implicated in the Abu Ghraib torture scandal, won a $10 million no-bid army contract to provide "intelligence analysis services" in Syria.[96] *The Daily Beast* wrote about a conflict between the Pentagon which focused on defeating Daesh (ISIS) and the CIA whose main goal was to topple Assad. The two were funding different groups which regularly clashed on the ground. In February 2016, a CIA-armed militia was run out of the town of Morea, about 20 miles north of

Aleppo by Pentagon-backed Syrian Democratic Forces who were 80 percent Kurdish.[97]

In late Summer 2013, President Obama promoted air strikes designed to eradicate any military capabilities that Assad had after rejecting a plan of the Joint Chiefs for being "insufficiently painful." Obama's push for war was based on reports from U.S. intelligence agencies which claimed high confidence but not certainty that Assad had deployed chemical weapons and poisoned over 1,000 men, women and children, some in their sleep, as Samantha Power put it before the UN.[98] Human rights agencies, however, placed the death toll at about one half of what Power and Obama suggested. Obama went on TV to proclaim: "We are prepared to strike whenever we choose. What message will we send if a dictator can gas hundreds of children to death in plain sight and pay no price?"[99]

When British intelligence obtained a sample of Sarin gas used in the August 21st attack, analysis demonstrated that the gas used hadn't matched the batches known to exist in the Syrian army's chemical weapons arsenal. Actual exposure to Sarin appears to have been minimal or non-existent for thirty-one of the thirty-six people sampled (88%) in a UN probe. According to journalist Seymour Hersh, President Obama "ignored the data regarding al-Nusra and their ability to use Sarin and continue[d] to claim only the Assad government has chemical weapons."[100] A former senior intelligence official told Hersh that Obama's altering of intelligence and distortions "reminded him of the 1964 Gulf of Tonkin incident, when the Johnson administration reversed the sequence of National Security intercepts to justify one of the early bombings of North Vietnam [and sending of U.S. ground forces]."[101]

This time the public, however, was weary of another war on a Muslim country. Forced to seek a Congressional resolution, Obama recognized he did not have the votes (phone calls to Congress numbered 499-1 opposing the war) and concluded an agreement with the Russians to bring Syrian chemical weapons stockpiles under international control and have them destroyed.[102]

In an early 2018 news conference at the Pentagon, Defense Secretary James Mattis diverted from the previously stated American position on nerve gas use by Assad and said: "we do not have evidence of it." "Fighters on the ground said that sarin had been used so we were *looking for evidence*, credible or uncredible."[103] The U.S. was thus still looking for evidence of his pretext, five years after its Nobel peace prize winning president had tried to use its reported occurrence to sell a full-out war on Syria.

In 2016, the Obama administration launched four-dozen tomahawk cruise missiles and dropped 12,192 tons of bombs on Syria even though this was illegal under international law and the American public had repudiated air strikes.[104] A single attack in July struck a cluster of houses in Tokkhar near Manbij, killing at least 73 civilians including 35 children and 20 women.[105] Another caché of rockets fired from Apache helicopters killed 47 civilians in the tiny village of al-Khan, whose residents had actually mobilized to fight ISIS.[106] True to his Wilsonian roots, Obama kept emphasizing the humanitarian imperative, telling the UN General Assembly that "there can be no reasoning, no negotiation, with this brand of evil [represented by Assad]. The only language understood by killers like this is the language of force."[107] To sustain the illusion of humanitarian intervention further, the Obama administration provided $23 million to white helmeted aid workers who helped clean up what were purported to be Assad's chemical bombing sites. The leader of the white helmets, Raed Saleh, was thought to have extremist connections, however, and its members were implicated in public executions, lobbied for more air strikes, and helped jihadists dispose of beheaded corpses.[108]

The war in Syria was never a morality play between good and evil, as the Obama administration depicted it, but rather a brutal competition for power, which the U.S. was trying to exploit for its own benefit. As for Russia, Alexey Pushkov, a Russian Senator and former head of the foreign affairs committee in the state Duma, told me in an interview that Russia felt it had to become more involved in Syria [beginning in October 2015] to prevent further chaos. Russia was intent that the country would not become another failed state and haven for jihadism like Libya.[109] Their gamble appears to have paid off as Vladimir Putin, checkmating Obama, secured a 49-year base rights agreement with the Assad government, which emerged as the winner in Syria's civil war.[110] While the U.S. may have lost, Lockheed Martin was nonetheless another of the war's winners; its CEO Marilyn Hewson enthused that the continued volatility in the Middle East and Asia would make them "growth areas for the foreseeable future."[111] By the end, only seven percent of Syrians believed that the U.S. government was a "friend of the Syrian people."[112] 82 percent also blamed America for the rise of ISIS, which eighty percent of the people opposed.[113]

In his Cairo speech, Obama had outlined a progressive approach capable of potentially defusing conflict. Unfortunately, his words had little meaning. The Arab Spring quickly turned into a long and dark winter, first in Libya, then in Bahrain, Yemen and Syria where America, promoting regime change, allied with jihadists who corrupted any hope of positive democratic transformation. Little progress was made in the Israeli-Palestine conflict as Obama increased arms shipments even as Israel pulverized Gaza in a murderous 51-day war. The double standards of U.S. foreign policy were vividly apparent in Obama's copious arms sales to Saudi Arabia as it assaulted Yemen, and Obama's support for other state sponsors of terrorism like Pakistan and Turkey under strongman Recep Tayyip Erdogan, which no longer required a State Department license to import American weapons.[114] A member of the Muslim Brotherhood locked-up in General al-Sisi's gulag told an interviewer that "the one thing everyone [in the prison] had in common—the ISIS group, the Muslim Brotherhood group, the liberals, the guards, the officers— is they all hate America."[115] What a testament to the failings of Obama's foreign policies in the Middle-East.

Endnotes

1   "The President's Speech in Cairo: A New Beginning," June 4, 2009, The White House, https://obamawhitehouse.archives.gov/the-press-office/remarks-president-cairo-university-6-04-09.

2   "Tunisia: The Fall of the West's Little Dictator," in *Africa Awakening: The Emerging Revolution*, ed. Sakari Ekine, Firoze Manji (Pambazuka Press, 2011), 47. In 2010, Obama wrote a letter asking Congress to approve $282 million on the sale of military equipment to ben Ali's security forces.

3   Author telephone interview with Chas Freeman Jr., February 18, 2019; Josh Rogin, "Bill Clinton: Obama May Look Like a 'Wuss' Over Syria," *The Daily Beast*, June 13, 2013.

4   David D. Kirkpatrick, *Into The Hands of the Soldiers: Freedom and Chaos in Egypt and the Middle East* (New York: Viking, 2018), 41.

5   F. William Engdahl, *Manifest Destiny: Democracy as Cognitive Dissonance* (Wiesbaden: Mine Books, 2018), 181; Gamal M. Selim, "The U.S. and the Arab Spring: The Dynamics of Political Engineering," *Arab Studies Quarterly* (Summer 2013), 255-272; Kirkpatrick, *Into the Hands of the Soldiers*, 60. Anan was considered the Pentagon's man in Egypt.

6   Engdahl, *Manifest Destiny*, 181, 182.

7   Engdahl, *Manifest Destiny*, 179-187; Ahmed Bensaada, *Arabesque Americaine* (Montreal: Michel Brulé, 2011); Patrick Hawley, "Hillary Clinton Sponsored Secretive Arab Spring Program That Destabilized Middle East," *Breitbart News*, September 23, 2016; Galina Saphznikova, *The Lithuanian Conspiracy and the Soviet Collapse: Investigation into a Political Demolition* (Atlanta: Clarity, 2018). In Tunisia, the Muslim Brotherhood won the first post-revolution elections, though were defeated in 2014 elections which Habiba Bourguiba's former Interior Minister, 87-year old Beji Caid Essebsi won.

8   John Foran, "Global Affinities: The New Cultures of Resistance Behind the Arab Spring," in *Beyond the Arab Spring: The Evolving Ruling Bargain in the Middle East*, ed. Mehran Kamrava (New York: Oxford University Press, 2014), 64.

9   Ron Nixon, "U.S. Groups Helped Nurture Arab Uprisings," *New York Times*, April 14, 2011.

10 Bensaada, *Arabesque Americaine*; Stuart Bramhall, "The Arab Spring: Made in the USA," *Global Research*, October 2015.

11 Selim, "The U.S. and Arab Spring," 263; Kirkpatrick, *Into the Hands of Soldiers*, 212. Kerry oddly considered the $80 billion in U.S. aid to the Egyptian military over the previous decades the "best investment America had made for years in the region."

12 Max Blumenthal, *The 51-Day War: Ruin and Resistance in Gaza* (New York: The Nation Books, 2015), 195-200; Nick Turse, *The Changing Face of Empire*

(Chicago: Haymarket Books, 2012), 35; Security Assistance Monitor, Egypt, https://securityassistance.org/data/country/military/country/2009/2016/ all/Middle%20East%20and%20North%20Africa//; Eric Walberg, *Islamic Resistance to Imperialism* (Atlanta: Clarity Press Inc., 2017), 229; Glenn Greenwald, "After Feigning Love for Egypt's Democracy, U.S. Back to Open Support for Tyranny," *The Intercept*, October 2, 2014. Sisi was trained at the U.S. Army War College.

13   Engdahl, *Manifest Destiny*, 167, 189.

14   Peter Hoekstra, "U.S. Intel is Fighting Blind Against ISIS," *Newsmax*, February 5, 2019; Peter Hoekstra, *Architects of Disaster: The Destruction of Libya* (The Calamo Press, 2015).

15   See Stephen Kinzer, *All the Shah's Men: An American Coup and the Roots of Middle Eastern Terror* (New York: Wiley, 2008).

16   Gareth Porter, *Manufactured Crisis: The Untold Story of the Iran Nuclear Scare* (Charlottesville, VI: Just World Books, 2014); Gareth Porter, "Was There Ever an Iranian Nuclear Weapons Program?" *The American Conservative*, May 14, 2018; Seymour Hersh, "Our Men in Iran," *New Yorker*, April 5, 2012; Wayne Madsen, *Unmasking ISIS: The Shocking Truth* (Progressive Press, 2016), 96. Rudolph Giuliani, Howard Dean, Ed Rendell, James Jones, former CIA Directors James Woolsey and Porter Goss, John Bolton and Alan Dershowitz all openly supported MEK.

17   Jay Solomon, *The Iran Wars: Spy Games, Bank Battles, and the Secret Deals That Reshaped the Middle East* (New York: Random House, 2016), 181.

18   Margaret Kimberley, "Israel, Big Money and Obama," *Counterpunch*, August 20, 2010.

19   David E. Sanger, *Confront and Conceal: Obama's Secret Wars and Surprising Use of American Power* (New York: Broadway, 2012), xii.

20   "Statement by the President on Iran," Office of the Press Secretary, January 17, 2016; Joshua Rovner, "Why U.S. Intelligence is Right about Iran," *Washington Post*, April 13, 2015; Porter, *Manufactured Crisis*, 284, 285. The NIE suggested that Iran would have sufficient material for a bomb by 2015 if it chose to enrich its uranium stockpile to weapons grade, however, there is no evidence it chose to do so. Israeli intelligence later concluded that the program never took root.

21   Sanger, *Confront and Conceal*, 178, 179; Porter, *Manufactured Crisis*, 296, 299.

22   Porter, *Manufactured Crisis*, 276; Gareth Porter, "Iran" in *The Wikileaks Files: The World According to U.S. Empire*, ed. Julian Assange (London: Verso, 2015), 295; Dan Kovalik, *The Plot to Attack Iran* (New York: Skyhorse, 2018), 11, 12; Spencer Ackerman, "Iranian Cult is no Longer Officially a Terrorist Group," *Wired Magazine*, September 21, 2012.

23   John Kerry, *Every Day is Extra* (New York: Simon & Schuster, 2018), 523; Elise Labott, Nicole Gaouette and Kevin Liptak, "U.S. Sent Plane With $400

Million in Cash to Iran," *CNN*, August 4, 2016.

24   "Statement by the President on Iran," Office of the Press Secretary, January 17, 2016.

25   Kerry, *Every Day is Extra.*

26   Ewen Macaskill, "Obama Adviser Aligns with White House in Criticism of Rocket Attacks on Israel," *The Guardian*, December 29, 2008; "Obama's Speech in Sderot Israel," *New York Times*, July 23, 2008.

27   See *Israel/Gaza: Operation Cast Lead, 22 Days of Death and Destruction* (London: Amnesty International, 2009).

28   David J. Garrow, *Rising Star: The Making of Barack Obama* (New York: William Morrow, 2017), 632; Richard Miniter, *Leading From Behind: The Reluctant President and the Advisors Who Decide for Him* (New York: St. Martin's Press, 2012), 177. 178.

29   Pauline Dubkin Yearwood, "Obama and the Jews," *Chicago Jewish News*, October 24, 2008. Peter Beinart, "The Jewish President," in *The Crisis of American Zionism* (New York: Henry Holt, 2012), ch. 5.

30   E.J. Kessler, "Illinois Senate Candidates Eying State's Jewish Voters," *Jewish Forward*, May 9, 2003.

31   Irving Cutler, *The Jews of Chicago: From Shtetl to Suburb* (Urbana: University of Illinois Press, 1976), 176-178, 181; Danielle Berin, "Jeffrey Katzenberg: Mogul on a Mission," *Hollywood*, July 17, 2003; Jerome Corsi, *The Obama Nation* (New York: Threshold, 2008), 144. A non-observant Jew, Katzenberg and his partner Andy Spann raised over $6.5 million for Obama from 2007 through 2012. "Obama's Top Fundraisers," *New York Times*, September 13, 2012.

32   "Lester Crown's Story: A True American Tale," *Weizmann Magazine*, September 28, 2014; "GD Awarded UAV Contract," *Aviation Week*, August 4, 2004; Louise Daly, "Crowns," Crain's Chicago Business, October 17, 2005; Jane Ammeson, "The Busy Life of Billionaire Lester Crown," *Chicago Life Magazine*, February 7, 2008; Cutler, *The Jews of Chicago* 176-178. Klutznick was Betty Lu Saltzman's father. The Crowns ties to Israel dated to the 1930s, with Lester's mother serving in the Hadassah. They were major donors to Jewish philanthropy. Alan Solow was chairman of the Israeli Policy Forum, which sought to advance the vision of slain Israeli Prime Minister Yitzhak Rabin, and a Jewish community leader in Chicago who chaired the Obama-Biden reelection campaign.

33   Jo Becker and Christopher Drew, "Pragmatic Politics, Forged on the South Side," *New York Times*, May 11, 2008.

34   Yearwood, "Obama and the Jews."

35   Ibid., David Remnick, *The Bridge: The Life and Rise of Barack Obama* (New York: Alfred A. Knopf, 2010), 224.

36   Garrow, *Rising Star*, 875.

37   On the latter incidents, see Mike Davis, *Budda's Wagon: A Brief History of the Car Bomb*, rev ed. (London: Verso, 2017).

38   Mark Perry, "Israel's Lawyer, Revisited," *Al Jazeera*, January 24, 2011; Ken Klippenstein and Paul Gottinger, "U.S. Provides Israel the Weapons Used on Gaza," *Truthout*, July 23, 2013; Juan R.I. Cole, "Top 5 Ways the U.S. is Israel's Accomplice in War Crimes in Gaza," *Informed Comment*, August 4, 2014; Ali Abunimah, *The Battle for Justice in Palestine* (Chicago: Haymarket Books, 2012), 26. The Obama administration sold Israel F-35 Joint Strike Fighters and approved unprecedented release of military capabilities including the V-22 Osprey aircraft, K-35 tankers, electronically scanned radars and anti-radiation missiles.

39   See eg. Bernard Avishai, "Netanyahu's Speech," *New Yorker*, March 3, 2015.

40   Dennis Ross, *Doomed to Succeed: The U.S.-Israel Relationship from Truman to Obama* (New York: Farrar Strauss and Giroux, 2015), 350; Robert D. Blackwill and Philip H. Gordon, "Repairing the U.S.-Israel Relationship," Council on Foreign Relations, Special Report No. 76, November 2016, 6.

41   "A Whiff from Hell," *The Economist*, June 4, 2015; Yaakov Katz and Amir Bohbot, "How I Took a Toy and Made it a High-Tech Weapon," *Commentary*, December 14, 2016; Kyle Mizokami, "Israel Made a Kamikaze Quadcopter from Hell: The ROTEM-L will hunt you down and blow you up," *Popular Mechanics*, February 22, 2016. Laser weapons supplied by the U.S. may have also been tested.

42   Rania Khalek, "Obama Gives $1.9 Billion in Weapons as Welcome Gift to Israel," *Electronic Intifada*, May 22, 2015; Blumenthal, *The 51 Day War*, 49, 135, 163.

43   Blumenthal, *The 51-Day War*; Norman Finkelstein, *Gaza: An Inquest Into Martyrdom* (Berkeley: University of California Press, 2017).

44   Michael Wilner, "'I Have No Sympathy with Hamas,' Obama Says," *The Jerusalem Post*, August 7, 2014.

45   Jack Simpson, "Israeli-Gaza Conflict: Barack Obama Warns Benjamin Netanyahu Against Escalating Civilian Deaths in Gaza," *The Independent*, July 19, 2014.

46   "A Hideous Atrocity": Noam Chomsky on Israel's Assault on Gaza & U.S. Support for the Occupation," *Democracy Now*, August 7, 2014; Noam Chomsky, "Nightmare in Gaza," *Truthout*, August 3, 2014.

47   Blumenthal, *The 51-Day War*.

48   Bruce Riedel, *Kings and Presidents: Saudi Arabia and the United States Since FDR* (Washington, D.C.: Brookings Institution Press, 2017), 177.

49   Branco Marcetic, "Obama Didn't Coddle the Saudis? Yes, He Did," *Jacobin*, October 23, 2018.

50   George E. Condon Jr. "What King Salman's Snub Means for Barack Obama," *The Atlantic*, May 11, 2015.

51   Peter Schweizer, *Secret Empires: How the American Political Class Hides Corruption and Enriches Family and Friends* (New York: Harper Collins, 2018), 193; Michael Forsyth, Mark Mazetti, Ben Hubbard and Walt Bogdanovich, "Advisory Firms Cultivate Role as Saudi Ally," *New York Times*, November 4, 2018, A1.

52   Daniel Klaidman, *Kill or Capture: The War on Terror and the Soul of the Obama Presidency* (Boston: Houghton Mifflin, 2012), 22; Michelle Malkin, *Culture of Corruption: Obama and His Team of Tax Cheats, Crooks and Cronies* (Washington, D.C.: Regnery, 2010), 261.

53   See Stephen Gowens, *Washington's Long War on Syria* (Montreal: Baraka Books, 2017).

54   Marcetic, "Obama Didn't Coddle the Saudis? Yes, He Did."

55   Larry Diamond, "Forsaken by the West: Obama and the Betrayal of Democracy in Bahrain," *The Atlantic*, January 9, 2013.

56   John Glaser, "Why Obama Supports Tyranny Over Democracy in Bahrain," *The Huffington Post*, September 02, 2013; *Dispatches From the Arab Spring*, ed. Paul Amar and Vijay Prashad (Minneapolis: University of Minnesota Press, 2013), 64; Selim, "The U.S. and the Arab Spring," 268; Kyle Munzenreider, "John Timoney, Former Miami Police Chief to Train Police in Middle East Kingdom of Bahrain," *Miami New Times*, December 11, 2011; "Police Trampled Civil Rights during 2003 Free Trade Protests in Florida, ACLU Charges," *ACLU Press Release*, November 17, 2005, https://www.aclu.org/news/police-trampled-civil-rights-during-2003-free-trade-protests-florida-aclu-charges. Timoney promoted "the 'Miami Model,' a police tactic designed to intimidate political demonstrators, silence dissent, and criminalize protest against the government policies," said ACLU Greater Miami Chapter President Terry Coble, referring to the City of Miami's law enforcement strategy during 2003 protests directed against the signing of a free-trade agreement.

57   Max Fisher, "Obama's UN Address and the Bahrain Exception," *The Atlantic*, September 21, 2011.

58   Samuel Oakford and Peter Salisbury, "Yemen: The Graveyard of the Obama Doctrine," *The Atlantic*, September 23, 2016.

59   Helen Cooper, Thomas Gibbons-Neff, Eric Schmitt, "Green Berets Quietly Aid War on Yemen Rebels," *New York Times*, May 4, 2018, A1; Ginny Hill, *Yemen Endures: Civil War, Saudi Adventurism and the Future of Arabia* (New York: Oxford University Press, 2017), 282.

60   Isa Blumi, *Destroying Yemen: What Chaos in Arabia Tells Us About the World* (Berkeley: University of California Press, 2018), 215; Ben Norton, "America's Deadly Gift: The U.S. Gave Saudi Arabia Skin Burning White Phosphorus," *Salon*, September 30, 2016; William D. Hartung, "U.S. Arms Transfers to Saudi Arabia and the War in Yemen," *Center for International Policy*, December 1, 2016.

61   Alex Emmons, "Banned by 119 Countries, U.S. Cluster Bombs Continue to Orphan Yemeni Children," *The Intercept*, December 14, 2016. Alex Kane, "Here's Exactly Who's Profiting from the War in Yemen," *In These Times*, May 20, 2019.

62   Hill, *Yemen Endures*. Saleh was a protégé of Col. Ahmed Husayn al-Ghashmi suspected of involvement in the assassination of Ibrahim Al-Hamdi, North Yemen's leader from 1974-1977. He built his military base through a controlling stake in the army's trade in bootleg alcohol. He opened the country up to foreign exploitation including U.S. oil interests and was skilled at manipulating the country's mixture of tribes, religious groups, and interested foreign parties—a feat he called "dancing on the heads of snakes."

63   Blumi, *Destroying Yemen*, 189.

64   Selim, "The U.S. and the Arab Spring," 265, 266, 267.

65   Bruce Riedel, "Who are the Houthis and Why Are We at War with Them?" *Brookings Institute*, December 18, 2017; Tom Finn, "Abdel-Malek al-Houthi: From Shadow Rebel Leader to Kingmaker," *Middle East Eye*, September 26, 2014; Mohamed Vall, "The Rise of Yemen's Houthi," *Al Jazeera*, March 26, 2014. Later the Zaydeh fought the Ottomans and Wahhabists.

66   Maggie Michael, Trish Wilson and Lee Keath, "AP Investigation: U.S. Allies, al-Qaeda Battle Rebels in Yemen," *Associated Press*, August 6, 2018.

67   Blumi, *Destroying Yemen*.

68   Blumi, *Destroying Yemen*.

69   "Statement by NSC Spokesperson Bernadette Meehan on the Situation in Yemen," The White House, Office of the Press Secretary, March 25, 2015.

70   Riedel, "Who are the Houthis and Why Are We at War with Them?" President Barack Obama, Remarks by the President at the National Defense University, May 23, 2013. On Houthi opposition to Al Qaeda, see also Safa al-Ahmad, "Meeting the Houthis – and Their Enemies," *BBC*, March 17, 2015.

71   Maggie Michael, Trish Wilson and Lee Keath, "AP Investigation: U.S. Allies, al-Qaeda Battle Rebels in Yemen," *Associated Press*, August 6, 2018.

72   F. William Engdahl, *Target China: How Washington and Wall Street Plan to Cage the Asian Dragon* (San Diego: Progressive Press, 2014), 33, 34; Blumi, *Destroying Yemen*.

73   See Michael Chossudovsky, "Yemen and the Militarization of Strategic Waterways," *Global Research*, April 4, 2015. The mainstream U.S. media acknowledged the Petraeus-Saleh meeting but said its focus was on the shoe bomber who had tried to bomb a flight landing in Detroit. "UAE Seeking to Establish Dominance Over Yemen's Strategic Socotra Island," *Press TV*, April 24, 2017; Blumi, *Destroying Yemen*, 182, 258.

74   Ovidio Espino, *How Wall Street Created a Nation: J.P. Morgan, Teddy Roosevelt, and the Panama Canal* (New York: Basic Books, 2003).

75   Hartung, "U.S. Arms Transfers to Saudi Arabia and the War in Yemen."

76   Michael Forsythe, Mark Mazetti, Ben Hubbard and Walt Bogdanovich, "Advisory Firms Cultivate Role as Saudis Ally," *New York Times*, November 4, 2018, A1, 15; "New American Private Military Contractors Arrive in Yemen," *Press TV*, March 7, 2016; Company Overview of DynCorp, LLC, https://www.bloomberg.com/research/stocks/private/people.asp?privcapId=13154196.

77   Emily B. Hager and Mark Mazetti, "Emirates Secretly Sends Colombian Mercenaries to Yemen Fight," *New York Times*, November 25, 2015.

78   William Hartung, "U.S. Arms Transfers to the UAE and the War in Yemen," Center for International Policy, September 27, 2017.

79   Hartung, "U.S. Arms Transfers to the UAE and the War in Yemen;" Rajiv Chandasekaran, "In the UAE, the U.S. Has a Quiet, Potent Ally Nicknamed Little Sparta,*"* *Washington Post*, November 9, 2014; Aram Rostom, "This American is a General For a Foreign Army Accused of War Crimes in Yemen," *Buzz Feed News*, May 7, 2018. A veteran of the 1st Persian Gulf War who received a medal following his service in a covert aviation regiment known as the night stalkers, Toumajan served under McChrystal in Afghanistan and won a Bronze Star in Iraq while on the side running a breast enhancement company in Tennessee called Breast Wishes.

80   Samuel Oakford and Peter Salisbury, "Yemen: The Graveyard of the Obama Doctrine," *The Atlantic*, September 23, 2016.

81   Emmons, "Banned by 119 Countries, U.S. Cluster Bombs Continue to Orphan Yemeni Children."

82   Gowens, *Washington's Long War on Syria*, 113; Robert Naiman,"Syria" in *The Wikileaks Files, ed. Assange, 272-321. The World According to U.S. Empire, ed.* Julian Assange (London: Verso, 2015), 272-321.

83   Robert F. Kennedy Jr. "Why the Arabs Don't Want Us in Syria," *Politico*, February 23, 2016; Tim Weiner, *Legacy of Ashes: A History of the CIA* (New York: Doubleday, 2007); Ron Ridenour, *The Russian Peace Threat: Pentagon on Alert* (New York: Punto Press, 2018). Stone was taken prisoner in the failed coup against Quwatli and gave a televised confession. In 1949, Quwatli had been overthrown by the brutal and inept General Husmi al-Zaim but won election in 1955.

84   Kennedy Jr. "Why the Arabs Don't Want Us in Syria;" Seymour Hersh, *The Killing of Osama Bin Laden* (London: Verso, 2016), 103.

85   Michael Slackman, "Syrian Troops Open Fire on Protestors in Several Cities," *New York Times*, March 25, 2011.

86   Reese Erlich, *Inside Syria: The Backstory of Their Civil War and What the World Can Expect*, with foreword by Noam Chomsky (Amherst, NY: Prometheus Books, 2016), 16, 123; Paulo Gabriel and Hilu Pinto, "Syria" in *Dispatches from the Arab Spring*, ed. Amar and Prashad, 215, 228, 229.

87   Patrick Seale, "Islamist-Baath Divide Still Torments Syria," *Gulf News*, September 28, 2012.

88   Max Blumenthal, *The Management of Savagery: How America's National Security State Fueled the Rise of Al Qaeda, ISIS, and Donald Trump* (London: Verso, 2019), 160.

89   Charles Glass, *Syria Burning: ISIS and the Death of the Arab Spring* (London: OR Books, 2015), 22; Anthony Shadid, "Thousands Turn Out for Assad," *New York Times*, June 22, 2011, A9; Kourash Ziaberi, "Sharmine Narwine: Syrian Opposition is Not United and Cohesive Force," *Fox News*, December 9, 2013; Erlich, *Inside Syria*, 123.

90   Tim Anderson, *The Dirty War in Syria: Regime Change and Resistance* (Global Research Publishers, 2016), 23.

91   Anderson, *The Dirty War in Syria*. British journalist Robert Fisk reported on a pro-Assad rally that reached 200,000 by mid-day, in which he said that "there was no Saddam style trucking of the people to Omayad Square (Damascus)... There were veiled women, old men, thousands of children...were they coerced? I don't think so." Later he reported that anti-regime protests dwindled because of Salafi attacks.

92   DIA report cited in Blumenthal, *The Management of Savagery*, 171, 172.

93   "Press Conference and Transcript: President Obama's June 19 Remarks on Iraq," June 19, 2014; Adam Taylor, "Behind Biden's Gaffe Lie Real Concerns About Allies Role in the Rise of the Islamic State," *The Washington Post*, October 6, 2014.

94   Gareth Porter, "How America Armed Terrorists in Syria," *The American Conservative*, June 22, 2017; Madsen, *Unmasking ISIS*, 54, 85. Chechen terrorists and Chinese Uighur were among those to join the fight.

95   Daveed Gartenstein Ross and Nathaniel Barr, "The CIAs Syria Program and the Peril of Proxies," *The Daily Beast*, January 19, 2016; Max Blumenthal, "How Critics of Trump's Syria Withdrawal Fueled the Rise of ISIS," *The Mint Press*, December 28, 2018; Blumenthal, *The Management of Savagery*, 193, 194.

96   Jeremy Kuzmarov, "The New Merchants of Death," *Roar Magazine*, https://roarmag.org/magazine/the-new-merchants-of-death/

97   Nancy A. Youssef, "CIA and Pentagon Bicker While Russia Wipes Out U.S. Backed Rebels," *Daily Beast*, June 9, 2016; W.J. Hennigan, Brian Bennett and Nabih Boles, "In Syria, Militias Armed By the Pentagon Fight Those Armed By the CIA," *Los Angeles Times*, March 27, 2016."

98   "Statement by Ambassador Samantha Power: U.S. Permanent Representative to the United Nations, U.S. Mission to the United Nations," New York, NY, September 11, 2013.

99   Robert Rampton, Jeff Mason, "Obama Delays Strikes Against Syria to Seek Congress Approval," *Reuters*, August 30, 2013; "Syria Chemical Attack: What We Know," *BBC News*, September 24, 2013.

100   Seymour M. Hersh, "The Red Line and the Rat Line," *London Review of Books*, April 17, 2014; D. Gareth Porter, "In Search of Truth: UN Probe Chief Doubtful

on Syria Sarin Exposure Claims," *Counterpunch*, May 7, 2014; Daniele Ganser, "Who Used Poison Gas in Syria," *Free 21*, http://www.free21.org/?p=28190. The chemical weapons were launched from grenade launchers, a weapon used by the insurgents.

101   Hersh, *The Killing of Osama bin Laden*, 79.
102   Hersh, *The Killing of Osama Bin Laden*, 58.
103   Seymour M. Hersh, *Reporter: A Memoir* (New York: Alfred A. Knopf, 2018), 330, 331; Ian Wilkie, "Now Mattis Admits There Was No Evidence Assad Used Poison Gas On His People," *Newsweek*, February 8, 2018.
104   Harriet Agerholm, "Map Shows Where President Barack Obama Dropped His 20,000 Bombs," *The Independent*, January 19, 2017.
105   Emma Graham-Harrison, "U.S. Airstrikes Allegedly Kill at Least 73 Civilians in Northern Syria," *The Guardian*, July 20, 2016.
106   Paul Wood and Richard Hall, "U.S. Killing More Civilians in Iraq, Syria Than It Acknowledges," *USA Today*, February 2, 2016. Yet another bomb killed eighteen civilians including five young sisters between the ages of four and ten after military commanders misspelled the name of a city district and bombed an FSA-affiliated faction.
107   Evan Osnos, "In the Land of the Possible: Samantha Power Has the President's Ear – To What End?" *The New Yorker*, December 22 & 29, 2014.
108   Max Blumenthal, "How the White Helmets Became International Heroes While Pushing U.S. Military Intervention and Regime Change in Syria," *Alternet*, October 2, 2016; Max Blumenthal, "Exclusive Emails Show How White Helmets Tried to Recruit Roger Waters With Saudi Money," *Gray Zone Project*, April 19, 2018.
109   Author interview with Alexey Pushkov, Moscow, Russia, May 7, 2018.
110   Patrick Cockburn, "How Putin Came Out on Top in Syria," *Counterpunch*, September 25, 2018.
111   William Hartung, "The U.S. Government is Literally Arming the World, and Nobody's Even Talking About It," *Mother Jones*, July 30, 2016.
112   Doug Rivers, "Do Ordinary Syrians Want the U.S. To Intervene?" *The Huffington Post*, November 12, 2013.
113   Ridenour, *The Russian Peace Threat*, ch. 15.
114   William Hartung, "The Obama Administration Has Brokered More Weapons Sales Than Any Other Administration Since World War II," *The Nation*, July 26, 2016.
115   Alain Gresh, "Barack Obama Lackey of Egypt and the Muslim Brotherhood," *Orient XXI*, September 13, 2018; Kirkpatrick, *Into the Hands of The Soldiers*. Obama made sure to restore military funding to al-Sisi even after the massacre of 1,000 civilians at Rabaa in August 2013.

Chapter 10

BAD NEIGHBOR POLICY
BEATING BACK THE LEFT
IN LATIN AMERICA

In December 2009, Venezuela's leftist President Hugo Chavez gave a speech at the Copenhagen climate summit mocking President Obama, whom he referred to as having won "the Nobel Prize of War." Chavez considered Obama a phony who had won the peace prize "almost the same time as he sent 30,000 soldiers off to kill innocent people in Afghanistan." Referencing his famous 2006 speech at the UN when he had held up Noam Chomsky's book *Hegemony or Survival* and referred to George W. Bush as the "devil," Chavez said he "still smelled sulfur" coming from Obama as he was perpetuating many of the same inhuman policies.[1] Evo Morales, the first indigenous leader in Bolivia's history, followed Chavez by excoriating Obama for being the only leader to leave the summit's stage from a concealed door. If Obama genuinely wanted to promote positive social change, Morales said that he should "use the money you are spending for wars against the peoples of Afghanistan and Iraq, for militarizing Colombia with seven military bases to save lives, to save the planet, our Mother Earth."[2]

Chavez and Morales understood Obama's true character

better than most Americans and the good cop, bad cop routine in which he played a part. Despite putting on a "charm offensive" directed against leftist Latin American leaders in his debut at the Summit of the Americas in Trinidad and Tobago, Obama tried to undermine both Morales and Chavez along with Nicaraguan president Daniel Ortega, a hero of the 1979 Sandinista revolution and old foil of Ronald Reagan. Obama additionally signed a new agreement in Colombia that gave the U.S. access to seven military bases and an unlimited number of unspecified "facilities and locations," and tacitly supported a military coup in Honduras that resulted in the consolidation of an oppressive right-wing regime.[3]

During his second term, Obama orchestrated a major historic breakthrough by opening up ties to Castroist Cuba. Nevertheless, Obama did not live up to the progressive model of FDR's Good Neighbor Policy. He appointed as his point man on Latin America, Mark Feierstein, who had supported regime change operations since the 1980s, and hired other old Latin American hands like Jeffrey Davidow who served in the U.S. embassy in Chile in the early 1970s when the Nixon administration had launched a fascist coup against democratically elected socialist leader Salvadore Allende.[4]

At the 2015 Summit of the Americas in Panama, Obama claimed that America's "days of meddling" in Latin America were over. As Journalist Wayne Madsen noted, these remarks would "come as a surprise to Suriname, Venezuela, Ecuador, Bolivia, Paraguay, Honduras, Haiti, Brazil, Argentina, Guatemala, El Salvador, Costa Rica, Colombia, and Nicaragua, all of which have seen more than their fair share of meddling from the CIA, the DEA, and the Pentagon during the Obama administration"[5]—the extent of which we will probably not know for a long time.

The Attack on Venezuela

A progressive attorney got a preview of Obama's policy at a dinner in 2003 when Obama turned to him and said: "it's really troubling what's happening down there with all these anti-American politicians being elected." When the attorney objected, Obama shifted to a different line of analysis but the cat had slipped out of the bag.[6] The anti-American leaders which Obama was referring were those who broke with the so-called Washington Consensus, the neoliberal free-trade orthodoxy that emphasized deregulation, privatization, fiscal austerity and trade liberalization, and instead promoted social democratic policies. The rise of Latin America's New Left had begun with Chavez' 1998 election in Venezuela following protests (the Caracazo) that had culminated in a massacre by the regime of Carlos Andrés Perez. Repudiating the neoliberalism of his predecessor, Chavez forced foreign companies to pay greater taxes and used revenues from Venezuela's state-owned oil company, Petroleos de Venezuela Sociedad Anonima (pdVSA) to fund public education, health care and other social welfare programs.[7]

Under his rule, over 1.4 million new homes were built, poverty rates were cut in half and extreme poverty by three quarters, and illiteracy was ended. The economy also grew, unemployment was halved, and inflation was brought under control, though violent crime increased.[8] Drawing closer to Cuba, Chavez passed a law against racial discrimination and established an Afro-Venezuelan holiday honoring José Leonardo Chirino, a black revolutionary who led an insurrection against the Spanish in 1795. In addition, he was a strong proponent of MERCOSUR, a trading alliance and common market between Latin American nations, and the Bolivarian Alliance for the Peoples of the Americas (ALBA), an intergovernmental organization that was initiated by Chavez and Cuban leader Fidel Castro under the premise that Hispanic America should be united as a single great nation.[9]

The U.S. not surprisingly responded to the Bolivarian revolution in a hostile manner. The Bush administration supported a right-wing coup against Chavez in 2002 backed by former PdVSA oil executives opposed to his reforms, and shored up alliance with the right-wing Columbian government of Alvaro Uribé Velez (2002-2010).[10] Representing continuity more than change, Obama referred to Chavez on the campaign trail as a "demagogue" adopting a "predictable yet perilous mix of anti-American rhetoric, authoritarian government and check-book diplomacy that....offers the same false promise as the tried and failed ideology of the past."[11] Obama's first CIA director Leon Panetta acknowledged a policy of stepped-up surveillance of Venezuela's "brusque and combative leader [Chavez]... and those [leaders] in Nicaragua and Ecuador who were following Chavez' lead."[12]

In 2015, Obama issued an executive order classifying Venezuela as an extraordinary national security threat and slapped sanctions on the Socialist regime of Nicolás Maduro, who succeeded Chavez after his death from cancer in March 2013. Maduro was a former bus driver and trade union leader considered "the most capable administrator in Chavez' inner circle."[13] The U.S. at this time sustained a $5 million annual budget for backing opposition candidates and strove to undermine Petrocaribe, a state-owned agency which provided oil to member countries on a concessionary basis through low interest loans.[14] Obama's aggressive policies were a consequence of the shale gas or fracking boom, which gave America the latitude to crush a petrostate such as Venezuela, a top five U.S. oil supplier, without damaging the U.S. economy because of growing energy independence.[15]

A coalition of twelve South American nations stood together in condemning Obama's sanctions as a "threat to Venezuela's sovereignty and the principle of non-interference in the internal affairs of other countries." Uruguayan leader José Mujica told a crowd of protestors that "to say that Venezuela is a threat to U.S. security, you need to have a screw loose."[16] Washington stood isolated when it refused to recognize the legitimacy of the April 2013 election which Maduro won after backing Henrique Capriles. When right-wing protests erupted in 2014, the Obama administration imposed a crippling deflation on the Venezuela currency, intensified by U.S. corporate hoarding of commodities in Venezuela leading to shortages while its economy suffered from low oil prices.[17] Secretary of State John Kerry alleged at the time that Maduro was waging a "terror campaign;" however, *Guardian* journalist Seamus Milne reported that most of the 39 killed were by anti-Maduro *Guarimba*. Several Chavistas were assassinated and two were beheaded.[18]

A key *Guarimba* leader, Leopoldo López, a mentor of Juan Guiadó, the right wing firebrand recognized by Donald Trump as Venezuela's leader in 2019, was part of one of three families that had orchestrated the 2002 coup attempt against Chavez. He was put under arrest in his home in a wealthy district of Caracas after being accused of playing a key role in the death of 13 people during the 2014 uprising. Groups aligned with him received millions of dollars from U.S. organizations which promoted tactics designed for regime change.[19] This contradicted Vice-President Biden's claim that U.S. support for the anti-Maduro *Guarimbas* was a "conspiracy theory." Leaked cables cite an employee of Development Alternatives Inc. (Ann Dunham's old employer) referring to anti-regime protestors as "our grantees." American funding for USAID and the National Endowment for Democracy (NED) in Venezuela increased by 80 percent from 2012-2014 as a plan was developed to "penetrate," "isolate," and "divide" the socialist government. In 2015, an American citizen, Todd Michael Leininger, believed to be CIA, was arrested with an arms caché and two U.S. military attachés were expelled after they were caught trying to recruit Venezuelan military officers. The U.S. was also accused of supporting secessionists in the oil rich Zulia State and promoting military provocations from its bases in Columbia.[20]

Maduro further alleged that the Obama administration was behind a failed coup attempt launched in February 2015 by the Mayor of Caracas and Congresswomen, Corina Machado, who had been invited to the White House. In response to Obama's comments that the U.S. was considering "tools to better steer the Venezuelan government," Maduro told a crowd that "for a long time in Latin America, we have stripped away American imperialist aggression...I feel sorry for President Obama because he is trapped in an alley without an exit, and he now thinks the way out is to attack Venezuela."[21] Similar and increased machinations against the Venezuelan government would leave the Trump administration in the same position.

Obama and the Honduras Coup

The first strike in the war against Latin America's left had been Obama's support for the June 28, 2009 coup d'état that ousted Honduran leader José Manuel Zelaya, another benefactor of blacks and the poor. Hugo Chavez characterized the coup as being part of "a retrograde and anti-historic counteroffensive" by "the U.S. Empire," whose aim was to "roll back the union, sovereignty, and democracy of our continent."[22] The coup was carried out at 4 A.M. on June 28, when a battalion of 150 masked Honduran soldiers under orders from U.S. trained General Romeo Vásquez Velásquez initiated a shootout with the Presidential Honor Guard and dragged President Zelaya in his pajamas onto a plane at gunpoint, flying him to San José, Costa Rica. Foreign Minister Patricia Rodas was also seized by Honduran soldiers and flown out in an aircraft belonging to one of Honduras's wealthiest billionaires, Miguel Facussé. Power, cell-phone service, and broadcast facilities were cut throughout the capital city, Tegucigalpa, followed by a weeklong curfew enforced by tanks in the streets.[23]

A mustachioed rancher with a signature Stetson hat, Zelaya, though running as a conservative law and order candidate, had raised Honduras' paltry minimum wage, increased teacher pay and joined with the Chavez-led Bolivarian Alliance for the Americas. Just a month before his overthrow, Zelaya had responded to an investigation that charged a Vancouver-based company (Goldcorp) with contaminating Honduras's Siria Valley by introducing a law that would have required community approval before new mining concessions were granted. His government also nationalized the telecommunications industry and was trying to break the dependent relationship whereby the region was exporting oil to U.S. refineries only to buy back gasoline at monopolistic prices. Even "worse," he was vowing to convert the Soto Cano Air Force base, which housed U.S. troops, into a civilian airport.[24]

Within days of the coup, which was condemned by the Organization of the Americas (OAS), Honduras reverted to a narco-state as it had been after coups in 1978 and 1987. Public death lists began to circulate. The coup plotters pretext was that Zelaya had violated Honduras' constitution when he attempted to organize a nonbinding referendum that would have changed the constitution and allowed an extension of presidential term limits. However, it was not clear who had the authority to enforce the edict, and under the new proposed law, Zelaya could only have run for the presidency again in four years.[25]

In November 2009, Porfirio Lobo Sosa won an election marred by forced disappearances of political activists and attacks on opposition candidates like Carlos H. Reyes who withdrew after his wrist was broken by a police attack. Pulling out of the Bolivarian alliance, the Lobo regime promoted the interests of the businesses who had been behind the coup, and hired a PR firm run by Clinton-family fixer Lanny Davis to gloss over its significant human rights abuses.[26] In a sign of continuity with Reagan's Contra War, Lobo appointed as a special security adviser Fernando Joya, a former member of battalion 316, a paramilitary death squad financed by the U.S. and its ambassador, John Negroponte, who had run the Contra war against Nicaragua during the 1980s.[27] Serving subsequently as the U.S. ambassador to Iraq during the peak period of Shiite death squad operations, Negroponte was appointed as an unofficial adviser to the *golpistas* by Secretary of State Hillary Clinton.[28]

Obama ironically on June 29th told the media that the coup was not legal, that Zelaya was still the legitimate president of Honduras, and that "it would be a terrible precedent if we start moving backwards into the era in which we are seeing military coups as a means of political transition rather than democratic elections. The region has made enormous progress over the last 20 years in establishing democratic tradition…. We don't want to go back to a dark past."[29] However, like in other cases, Obama's deeds didn't match his words. He alienated other Latin American countries in doing nothing to try and help restore a constitutional government and recognized Lobo's November 2009 election victory as Hillary Clinton used the powers of her office to block Zelaya's return.[30] One of Zelaya's aides told the press that his plane had stopped at the Palmerola airbase, home to 600 U.S. troops, on its way out of the country. This would indicate a more direct U.S. involvement, which Obama's progressive-sounding rhetoric helped provide a cover for.[31]

Obama's ambassador, Hugo Llorens, director of Andean Affairs at the National Security Council during the failed attempt to overthrow Chavez, called the November 2009 elections a "great celebration of democracy."[32] Leaked emails showed that beforehand, Hillary "the hawk" signed off on the flow of $11 million to the putsch regime even as the White House told the world aid had been suspended. State Department lawyer Harold "Killer" Koh concluded this was a legal since the transition to power did not fit the legal category of a coup because the military had not acted on its own or installed a General in power.[33] Further contradicting some of Obama's rhetoric, the Obama administration later doubled funding to Lobo and poured over $50 million into expanding the Soto Cano base.[34]

Overall, the Obama administration provided $95,871,801 in security assistance, including $22.5 million alone in 2015 to Honduras' post-coup regime.[35] This was in violation of the 1997 Leahy Amendment forbidding military assistance to governments violating human rights. Honduran military officers were continuously trained at the Western Hemisphere for Security Cooperation (formerly the U.S. Army School of the Americas) at Ft. Benning Georgia, which had a history of training human rights abusers to suppress popular insurgencies. The Inter-American Development Bank lent $60 million to the police with U.S. approval despite the conclusion of a government commission that nearly three-quarters of the force—headed by an alleged death squad leader—were "beyond saving."[36]

The destabilizing effects of the coup were manifested in refugees fleeing Honduras in numbers not seen since Ronald Reagan's dirty wars in the 1980s. Al Jazeera reported a whopping 1,272 percent increase in the number of Honduras children apprehended by the U.S. Border patrol between 2009 and 2014.[37] Rather than being a deft manager of empire, the Obama administration as these numbers show helped exacerbate a regional crisis in an effort to "muscle out" the political left.

Colombia and the Expansion of the U.S. Military Base Network

The Obama administration again violated the Leahy Amendment by giving $2.5 billion in security assistance to Colombia, the most oppressive government on the continent. U.S. Southern Command formed two elite battalions that led the fight against the leftist Fuerzas Armasas Revolucionario de Colombia (FARC) who were eventually forced into peace negotiations.[38] Robert Gates called President Uribé a "great hero" and Obama said he had "performed admirably on a range of fronts" and "with diligence" and "courage" despite a UN report concluding that his security forces had killed over 1,400 civilians in the war against FARC.[39] Obama's Attorney General Eric H. Holder Jr. had worked on the legal defense team of Chiquita Banana in 2004 when it was accused of funneling money and weapons to paramilitaries in Colombia, which were responsible for hundreds of massacres against unarmed peasants, including in the banana growing region of Urabá where it is believed that at least 4,000 people were killed. Thanks to Holder, not one Chiquita executive served any time in prison.[40]

As in Honduras, U.S. military assistance was justified as part of the War on Drugs, whose contradictions were evident in President Uribé's ties to drug cartels and DEA agents being caught attending cartel-affiliated sex parties.[41] Half of the $520 million intended for counter-narcotics operations in Obama's first year went to private military contractors such as Lockheed Martin, DynCorp, the Rendon Group and Oakley Network which provided high tech equipment, training and surveillance technologies to the national police.[42] The real purpose underlying the military aid was to help defeat the FARC "terrorists," and guarantee the safety of over $7 billion in foreign direct investment, including over $3 billion in the petroleum sector.[43] In October 2011, Obama signed a free trade agreement that benefited wealthy investors like Clinton Foundation donor, Frank Giustra, whose company Pacific Rubiales had received a $280 million U.S. Export-Import Bank loan for construction of a liquefied natural gas barge despite repeated complaints over labor conditions and environmental violations in its lumber mills.[44]

The other main purpose of the military aid was to secure access to seven military bases, which could accommodate up to 800 military and 600 civilian contractors, allowing the military to "conduct full spectrum operations throughout South America" and expand its "expeditionary warfare capability."[45] Colombia was envisioned as a major intelligence hub, and source for training officers for conflicts as far away as Yemen. Enrique Daza, Secretary of the Hemispheric Social Alliance, stated that the base agreement "generated great national indignation. [It] constituted a concession without precedent, since [in doing so] the Colombian government formally ceded the monopoly of force, increasing the risk of violations of human rights and heightening tensions in the region."[46]

The Obama administration had concluded the base deal after Ecuador's leftist president Rafael Correa closed a U.S. military base at Manta. Correa subsequently survived a failed police coup backed by "foreign actors" believed by local investigators to be the State Department and CIA.[47] Obama announced plans for two additional new bases in Panama, concluded a $465 million agreement with Chile's right-wing leader Sebastian Piñera to establish military operations at the Fort Aguayo naval base, and funded a new naval base and dock on the Sanoa Island, a protected nature reserve off the Dominican Republic, which raised local fears of renewed colonization (U.S. Marines had invaded the country in 1917 and 1965). A new base in the Chaco region of northern Argentina was additionally established, and forward operating facilities in Aruba and Curacao, off Venezuela, were expanded.[48]

These facilities helped enable major surveillance operations which extended across the continent.[49] Obama reactivated the Second World War's 4th Fleet to patrol the Caribbean and northern South America even though several presidents, including Lula of Brazil, asked for a reconsideration of the decision.[50] A leaked briefing showed that the 7th Special Forces group had missions in almost every Latin American country.[51] With barely a whisper of protest from the American liberal community, Obama was quietly expanding the U.S. military footprint in Latin America with the primary goal of destroying the Bolivarian revolution.

Keeping Latin America's Veins Open

During the April 2009 meeting of the Summit of the Americas in Trinidad, on the slim chance that Obama would read it, Hugo Chavez gave him Uruguayan writer Eduardo Galeano's book *Open Veins of Latin America*, which analyzes five centuries of foreign exploitation of Latin America and plunder of its resources.[52] Even if he had, he ignored its message. His military buildup and Alliance for Prosperity represented a stark continuity from the Open Door imperialism that Galeano linked to the continent's underdevelopment. The Alliance for Prosperity provided tax breaks for corporate investors in Central America and money for new pipelines, highways and power lines to speed up resource extraction and streamline the process of import and export at low wage maquiladoras. It was modeled after John Kennedy's Alliance for Progress, which had been designed to "lessen internal dissent in Latin American countries by making minor concessions to the people," according to 1960s icon Ernesto Che Guevara, "on condition that these countries surrender their interests completely and renounce their own development."[53]

Like Kennedy, Obama favored moderate liberal leaders who opened their countries to foreign exploitation—Mexico's Enrique Peña Nieto, who privatized the jewel of Mexico's economy, PEMEX, the giant oil company which had been nationalized in 1938 after the Mexican revolution; Peru's Ollante Humala, who sold out his leftist base by granting millions of acres to giant mining companies, cooperating with U.S. anti-narcotics units and privatizing even Peru's prisons; and Columbia's Juan

Manuel Dos Santos, Uribé's successor, who signed a peace deal with FARC but ignited protests by giving sweetheart deals to foreign mining companies, and supporting the free-trade deals that undermined local farmers.[54]

In December 2010, Arturo Valenzuela, Obama's assistant secretary of state for the Western Hemisphere, caused a scandal in Argentina when he urged a return to the investment climate of 1996, just before the country was plunged into depression![55] The Obama administration withheld loans to left-leaning President Cristina Férnandez de Kirchner, which contributed to the 2015 election of right-winger Mauricio Macri. During Obama's visit in March 2016, on the 40th anniversary of Argentina's last military coup, the American Chamber of Commerce announced that U.S. firms would invest $2.3 billion over the next 18 months, including $100 million from General Motors, Dow Chemical Company, AES and Ford as Obama proposed a new free trade deal.[56] Alluding to the 1998-2001 financial crisis that plunged millions into poverty, Rosario dos Santos, a 21-year old economics student told *Fortune Magazine*: "every time we implemented policies like these, it has had an unhappy ending."[57]

Obama ensured further unhappy endings by telephoning South African president Jacob Zuma to prevent the return of Haiti's deposed president Jean Bertrand-Aristide, a populist who had aroused hope in Haiti's poor. No similar call was put into Nicholas Sarkozy in January 2011 when former right-wing dictator Jean Claude "Baby" Doc DuValier returned to Haiti from France.[58] Following a devastating 2010 earthquake, Hillary Clinton set up a business racket that enabled Clinton Foundation donors and cronies like her brother Tony Rodham to reap enormous profits from the reconstruction "gold rush," as a cable from the U.S. ambassador Kenneth Merten described it. The Obama administration's deployment of aid relied too heavily on the military, leaving Haitians with the feeling of being occupied as a cholera epidemic broke out. An underlying goal, as a Wikileaks cable explained, was to "realize core [U.S. government] policy interests" centered on "managing resurgent populist and anti-market economy political forces [in the country]."[59]

In the 2011 Haitian election, the Obama administration took the unprecedented step of using the OAS to change the vote count in order to disqualify the left-leaning candidate Jude Célestin from the run-off, and threatened to bar earthquake aid and deport Célestin's mentor, Rene Préval, who had fallen out of favor with Washington.[60] The consequence was the election of the Miami lobby candidate Michel Martelly, a musician whose conservative economic policies and ties to criminal gangsters aroused protests that were met with police repression.[61] Obama appeared as the reincarnation of Woodrow Wilson also in Puerto Rico when he signed a bill that placed an unelected seven member board in charge of the country's finances in order to help pay down a $73 billion debt. The board consisted of Wall Street financiers whose plan was to convert much of Puerto Rico's beautiful coastline into tourist spots or homes for wealthy North Americans; close schools to "save money," despite the protests of teachers, students, and parents; and charge high interest rates, which meant more capital flowing out of Puerto Rico to the United States. Puerto Ricans took to the streets and to Twitter to denounce Obama for selling them out in this way and reminding them of their colonial status.[62]

Plan Mérida and Obama's War on Drugs

Obama's admission that he had engaged in recreational drug use while in college and his claim that drugs should be treated as a public health issue, prompted hope that he would end the War on Drugs. Instead, he expanded it, spending on average $9 billion per year on narcotics law enforcement, which was triple the total spent by the drug war guru, Ronald Reagan.[63] The Obama administration continued aerial fumigation operations in Latin America that resulted in major health and environmental problems and renewed a Bush-era program that sent Special Forces to work with local police units in countries besotted with transnational drug cartels. The Obama administration also beefed up border security, contracting with Elbit Systems of America through a $600 million supplement to a border security bill to build a "virtual wall" in Arizona to try to stop drug smuggling. Surveillance balloons were further deployed with high-powered cameras made by Lockheed and long-range radar surveillance developed for tracking insurgents in Afghanistan, which fed real-time pictures to command posts in Tucson.[64]

The War on Drugs provided a pretext for the construction of new military bases in the Caribbean after the signing of the Caribbean Security Basin Initiative, a $70 million annual initiative to fight drugs. In Central America, the FBI assisted the DEA in developing fingerprint and biometric capabilities and implemented a gun-tracing system called e-Trace. The Obama administration also financed construction of new facilities for wiretapping and installed an 85-camera surveillance system in Guatemala City, reviving training of the Kaibiles Special Forces, which had carried out gross human rights violations in the 1980s.[65]

The showcase for Obama's War on Drugs was the Plan Mérida, a $1.7 billion program in Mexico that was modeled after Bill Clinton's Plan Colombia, a drug war operation which had failed to reduce coca production and caused the displacement of millions of campesinos. With drones guiding military-police raids, the U.S. under Mérida supplied Mexican law enforcement agencies with electronic signals technology, ground censors, voice recognition gear, night-vision goggles, cell-phone tracking devices, data analysis tools, computer hacking kits, and airborne cameras that could read license plates from miles away.[66] This in addition to surveillance aircraft satellites, ion scanners, ballistic and biometric identification systems and over a dozen Black Hawk helicopters that were deployed in a 2010 operation that supposedly killed drug kingpin Nazario Moreno Gonzalez (AKA "El Chayo"), though Nazario was reported to have been killed again in March 2014.[67]

Despite much rhetoric about good governance, only a small percentage of the money in Plan Mérida was devoted to anti-poverty programs capable of providing opportunities for impoverished Mexican youth, who see joining a criminal gang as the road to wealth and status, or for other crime prevention measures. While judicial and criminal justice reform was prioritized, at least in the abstract, Congress first threatened to cut off only a small percentage of the aid if human rights requirements were not met and then did away with this standard entirely.[68] Plan Mérida also failed to seriously address the problem of corruption on either side of the U.S.-Mexican border.

Obama's betrayal of his promise to renegotiate the North American Free Trade Agreement (NAFTA) was further significant as it had made drug smuggling easier across the border and helped undermine local agricultural production, fueling the rise of urban slums and growth of drug production among farmers who see growing drug crops as the best means of escaping poverty. Drug enforcement efforts were additionally undermined because of the Obama administration's unwillingness to prosecute executives working for money laundering banks which enabled the drug cartels' smuggling operations. In 2012, Obama's Justice Department refused to pursue a criminal indictment against HSBC which laundered money for the Mexican cartels and the CIA, and had ties with a Saudi Bank described by the CIA as a conduit for extremist finance. Obama had also bailed out banks like Wachovia, Well Fargo and others that had been investigated by the DEA and IRS.[69]

Attorney General Eric Holder lied to Congress in an attempt to cover-up a scandalous Bureau of Alcohol, Tobacco, Firearms and Explosives (ATF) sting operation, Fast and the Furious, which promoted the sale of 2,500 guns and ten thousand rounds of ammunition to drug cartel operatives, who could then be tracked. Sinaola cartel kingpin Juaquin "el Chapo" Guzman, was found with a .50 caliber rifle sold through the program. An investigation by Charles Grassley (R-IA) found that straw purchasers being tracked by the ATF were allowed to continue purchasing weapons even after they were identified. Weapons resold on the black market were used to shoot down government helicopters and kill an estimated 300 people. They included the brother of Mexico's Attorney General, a group of high school and college students in Ciudad Juarez, an Immigration and

Customs Enforcement Agent (Jaime Zapata), and an American Border Patrol agent (Brian Terry) who was shot with a rifle that investigators tracked to Fast and the Furious.[70]

Latin American leaders conveyed their discontent with the War on Drugs at the Summit of the Americas in April 2011, linking it to corruption and savage violence among the drug cartels. Colombian President Juan Manuel Santos asserted that after forty years of fighting, his country was no closer to victory, while Guatemala's President, General Otto Perez Molina, called on the U.S. to pay countries for the drugs that they bust. The Obama administration, however, stubbornly reaffirmed a commitment to punitive law enforcement despite UN studies and academic work showing this to be a clear failure.[71]

To coordinate military operations under the Plan Mérida, the CIA ran a fusion center in Monterrey consisting of "Star-Wars" like screens and computer terminals, which was reminiscent of similar high-tech facilities in the War on Terror. Drone missions were undertaken deep into the interior and CIA and civilian operatives were dispatched to Mexican military bases for counterdrug operations. Sophisticated biometric and police telecommunications systems were imported. Much of the vital intelligence and police training functions were performed by private companies, including DynCorp and L-3 Communications (an outgrowth of Military Professional Resources Inc.). Videos surfaced showing private contractors employed by Risks Inc. training an elite police unit in what appeared to be torture techniques. Mexican security forces routinely carried out forced disappearances and torture constituting crimes against humanity according to a report by the Open Society Justice Initiative.[72]

Clinton was a major proponent of Mérida while several of the contractors profiting from U.S. security assistance, including General Electric, Lockheed, and United Technologies which owns Sikorsky, contributed to the Clinton Foundation.[73] Many of the weapons bolstered the arsenal of the cartels who recruited their enforcers from among police and military officers trained by the U.S. They were also used by the Mexican army and police to kill unarmed civilians, including recovering drug addicts; to suppress peasant uprisings in Chiapas and Oaxaca provinces driven by rampant inequalities, and to force the displacement of peasants to make way for megaprojects by mining corporations.[74] Abel Barren, director of a human rights group in Mexico's Guerrero Province, commented that "the War on Drugs is no less than continuing to use military force to contain nonconformist, disruptive movements, groups in resistance, and collectives who raise their voices."[75]

The DEA started recruiting "cold blooded killers" as informants to infiltrate the Mexican drug cartels. A few killed law enforcement officers while on the DEA or related government agencies payroll.[76] Of the 53,174 people detained under President Felipe Calderon's crackdown, only 941 belonged to the favored Sinaola cartel. Journalist Anabel Hernandez wrote that "what Mexico experienced in the last decade is not a war on drug traffickers, but a war between drug traffickers" with the government taking the side of Sinaola. One of Calderon's drug czars, Noé Ramirez, accepted $450,000 in bribes each month. Secretary of Public Security Genaro Garcia Luna acquired sudden personal wealth and threatened to kill journalists.[77] An associate testified at El Chapo's 2019 trial that he had given a $100 million bribe to President-elect Enrique Peña Nieto in October 2012.[78]

In May 2011, a caravan of protestors led by poet Javier Sicilia, whose son Juan Francisco was murdered with six others by drug traffickers, marched from Cuernavaca to Ciudad Juarez chanting slogans like "We Have Had It" and "No More Blood." The protestors denounced the War on Drugs as a principal factor underlying the violence that had left 39,274 dead since Felipe Calderon had taken over the presidency in 2006. Sicilia stated that for him, with the death of his son, "the world is no longer worthy of the word. Poetry no longer exists in me."[79]

Sicilia's anguish never captured the attention of Samantha Power or other Obamians who lacked the vision to consider alternatives to the War on Drugs, a policy that failed to curb drug supply. Despite advances in sensors designed to locate speed boats, the Coast Guard only had money to go after 39 percent of drug vessels. Cartels developed underground tunnels and high-speed submarines ("narco-subs") that traveled 80 to 90 percent below the sea's surface and could go 2,500 miles without refueling. The cartels also concealed drugs in jalapeno peppers, watermelons, and fish imports, garnering over $3 billion in profits per year. When the electronic fence was built in Arizona along the border, the Sinaola cartel used catapults to launch drugs over the fence. Michael Braun, DEA. chief of operations, told a reporter: "We've got the best fence money can buy, and they counter us with a 2,500-year-old technology."[80]

In Honduras in May 2012, DEA-trained security forces opened fire on a group traveling up-river by canoe in the northeast Mosquitia region, killing two pregnant women and a schoolboy. A scathing report by the Inspector Generals of the Department of Justice and State found no evidence that there was any gunfire from the taxi-boat at any time, nor that there was any narcotics on board. It also determined that DEA agents observed the massacre from a helicopter above and directed a Honduran door gunner to fire his machine gun on the boat. The DEA and their local counterparts subsequently failed to conduct a search and rescue mission to assist the Honduran victims and instead focused solely on recovering law enforcement officers stranded on their own broken-down vessel.

The Inspector General reports and spied on her pointed to further abusive action in a neighboring village, where Honduran police beat civilians at gunpoint after accusing them of drug trafficking. In Brug Laguna, American-trained agents also shot suspects who allegedly refused to comply with their oral demands and killed a pilot from a downed plane allegedly carrying drugs whom they claimed was attempting to reenter the plane to obtain a weapon.

The police report in the latter incident made no mention of the use of deadly force by Honduran police and claimed the man had died in the plane crash. A second report claimed the pilot had aimed a hand gun at officers, though no gun was ever found on the scene; one was only planted later in evidence but reported as a weapon found at the scene. Senator Patrick Leahy of Vermont (D) called the Inspector Generals' report "an indictment of the DEA," that unmasked "egregious events and conduct and a cover up that demeaned the lives of the victims and the reputation of the United States."[81]

The United States all the while was helping to arm and protect biofuel magnate Miguel Facussé, a leading importer of cocaine to the U.S., and the engine behind Honduras' 2009 coup.[82] A former police commissioner declared that one out of every ten members of the post-coup Congress was a drug trafficker and that "major national and political figures" were involved in drug trafficking.[83] These facts raise questions as to the actual intent and beneficiaries of Obama's drug war, which rendered the Plan Mérida and other efforts to fight the drug trade a destructive waste of tax payer dollars.

Opening to Cuba While Widening War on Latin America's Left

Obama's diplomatic recognition of Cuba at the end of his term, after years of backchannel diplomacy, ended over a half century of subversion and resulted in the freeing of the Cuban Five intelligence agents who had been sent to monitor and infiltrate right-wing Cuban terrorist networks in Miami. Cuban leader Fidel Castro took the rare step of praising a U.S. president because of his desire for friendship. On his 90th birthday, Castro expressed concern, however, that Obama in his speech in Havana glossed over the history of Yankee subversion in Cuba and its mercenary attacks—let alone the repeated assassination attempts on Castro himself—and failed to credit the positive achievements of the Cuban revolution such as its abolishing of segregation, contribution to the defeat of apartheid in Southern Africa and major gains in health care and education. Ending on a note of defiance, Castro stated that Cubans were "capable of producing the food and material riches we need with the efforts and intelligence of our people. We do not need the empire to give us anything. Our efforts will be legal and peaceful, as this is our commitment to peace and fraternity among all human beings who live on this planet."[84]

Like Nixon's opening to China in 1972, Obama's policy had been driven by real-politick. U.S. capitalists sought an end to the blockade to gain access to new markets and avoid further embarrassment at the UN whose member states overwhelmingly supported lifting it, and America's ruling class saw an opportunity to exert greater influence with the Castros aging out of power. The long-term goal is likely to avenge the Bay of Pigs, the humiliating military operation directed by the Kennedy Brothers against Castro in 1961. Obama said he was "convinced through a policy of engagement we can more effectively stand up for our values and help the Cuba people help themselves as they move into the 21st century."[85] Clearly this meant, he was implying, movement away from state socialism.

If Obama's opening to Cuba might be represented as the belated fulfilment of his pledge for hope and change, his policies towards much of the rest of the continent reflected business as usual. In Paraguay, the Obama administration supported a coup in 2012 that ousted leftist Francisco Lugo, a liberation theologian known to his constituents as "the bishop of the poor" who had canceled joint exercises with U.S. troops.[86] When black trade unionists called on Obama to condemn the illegitimate impeachment of leftist Dilma Rousseff in Brazil that was tantamount to a coup, he did no such thing.[87] Having given Rousseff the cold shoulder and spied on her, Obama established normal diplomatic relations with her successor Michel Temer, a U.S. government informant expected to pass laws beneficial to foreign investors like Goldman Sachs, one of Obama's top campaign donors.[88] The day after Rousseff's impeachment, the leader of Brazil's Senate Foreign Relations Committee, Aloysio Nunes, came to the U.S. and met with Thomas Shannon, the Under-Secretary of State for Political Affairs. This signalled American backing of Temer's coup, which brought an end to what the World Bank called the "golden decade" of rule by Brazil's Workers Party in which millions were lifted out of poverty and the country emerged as a voice of the Global South.[89]

Many of Latin America's progressive leaders made their countries more vulnerable to Yankee subversion through their failure to truly move forward to implement a socialist economy based upon putting greater power into the hands of the producers, that is, the working classes. They also failed to diversify their economies, sustaining dependence on major commodities subject to world-price fluctuations and extractive industries that despoiled the environment. Corruption remained a problem and many responded to outside subversion following the trajectory of the Castros by becoming more authoritarian, which was part of the regime change playbook.[90]

Bolivian president Evo Morales took to the Jon Stewart show to convey his discontent that a "black president could hold so much vengeance against an Indian president."[91] The Obama administration tried to undermine him by financing opposition movements, including in the Santa Cruz Province which held strong separatist leanings, and spearheading a rumor campaign. Morales expelled the U.S.-based Chemonics International Inc. after their US$2.7 million USAID-funded "Strengthening Democracy" program was accused of financing destabilization attempts against the government. Later Chemonics turned up in Ecuador.[92]

In Nicaragua, the Obama administration ceded to pressure from the Miami lobby of right-wing Cuban, Venezuelan and Nicaraguan exiles and imposed sanctions on the government of Daniel Ortega, a leader of the 1979 Sandinista revolution and target of the Reagan administration's Contra War in the 1980s. After coming back to power in 2006, Ortega had improved road infrastructure and literacy levels, expanded access to health care and cut poverty by 30 percent and malnutrition rates in half. The economy at the same time grew by an average of five percent per annum, well above the regional average.[93] Most damning from the American viewpoint was Ortega's signing a $50 billion deal with Chinese telecommunications mogul Wang Jing to build an interoceanic canal, which Ortega believed would lift Nicaraguans out of poverty and offer an alternative to the American dominated Panama Canal that effectively controlled access to South America.[94]

Retaining as ambassador an old CIA-hand, Robert Callahan, who had served as John Negroponte's speechwriter as he directed the Contra war in the 1980s, the Obama administration continued financing opposition candidates like Eduardo Montealegre Rivas, who lived in exile during the period of Sandinista rule, and the right-leaning Nicaraguan Liberal Alliance (ALN), and tried to split the Sandinistas between pro and anti-Ortega factions.[95] A NED publication bluntly acknowledged spending $4.1 million dollars between 2014 and 2017 laying the "groundwork for insurrection." This strategy replicated that of the 1980s when the NED poured $15.8 million into Nicaraguan civil society groups and political parties who opposed Ortega's Sandinista government.[96]

Prior to 2011 elections which he won legitimately with over 60% of the vote, Ortega had reinstated a constitutional provision that permitted judges and other government officials to stay in office beyond their terms until replacements could be appointed and dismissed some MPs under questionable circumstances. In an act of intimidation, the Obama administration landed 7,000 U.S. Marines and 200 helicopters in Costa Rica, and is rumored to have used DynCorp to train ex-Contra commanders who vowed to "remove Ortega from office by bullets" in Honduras, where Dyncorp had a $22 million contract for air base support.

Adopting the old Reagan playbook, the former ambassador to Costa Rica stressed in Congressional testimony Ortega's close ties with Muammar Qaddafi and fact that his personal secretary was Qaddafi's nephew.[97] Two Western media outlets later reported that Russia was building a signals intelligence (SIGINT) base in Nicaragua as "part of a recent deal between Moscow and Managua involving the sale of 50 T-72 Russian tanks." The reports came after the 14 June 2016 expulsion of some U.S. Homeland Defense personnel by the Nicaraguan government.[98] The era of the Cold War had indeed come back.

While it is difficult for any president to confront the structural imperatives underlying American imperialism in Latin America, including the lobbying power of multi-national corporations and the military, a genuine progressive could realistically attempt to replicate the model of FDR's Good Neighbor Policy. FDR surrounded himself with a diverse array of advisers, some of whom had left wing sensibilities and genuinely cared about the region's peoples. While sustaining support for dictators like Anastasio Somoza, whom FDR famously referred to as "our son of a bitch," the Good Neighbor Policy broke with precedent by limiting the U.S. military presence in Latin America and tolerating leftist factions.[99] Roosevelt's Vice President, Henry Wallace, was particularly enlightened. On a visit to Ecuador, he earned the ire of a British diplomat by skipping a formal state luncheon in order to spend an afternoon with a working-class Indian couple to learn more about the country and its problems from the people themselves, and to see what he could do from his position to help them.[100]

The Obama administration initiated a breakthrough with Cuba but did not live up to FDR's towering legacy nor that of Wallace. There were few if any leftist voices, and none like Wallace who would take the time to listen to Latin American aspirations. If they did, they would have urged Obama to reject the violent post-coup government in Honduras, cut off military aid to Colombia, denounce Temer, stand up to predatory U.S. business interests and adopt alternatives to the militarization of the War on Drugs. The modern-day Wallace would have also understood the historical importance of the Bolivarian revolution and promoted an accommodation with its leaders and not tried to undermine it. He would recognize that if South American economies are not allowed to develop their economies independently to meet domestic needs, there will be no end to the flow of economic and political refugees northward, which would in turn further divisions in America and give fodder to right-wing xenophobes.

Unfortunately, it was not to be. Though less heavy handed than Reagan or Bush, Obama followed a traditional approach not far removed from another liberal icon John F. Kennedy who backed multiple coups and right-wing regimes under the benign sounding Alliance for Progress.[101] Obama like Kennedy provided a liberal front for policies that exacerbated internal inequalities and setback movements for progressive change. The ramping up of police training and other security assistance was found to have had a "disturbingly negative impact on public safety, human rights, violence against women and democratic institutions," to quote from an NGO study.[102] U.S. policy we can see remained locked in the Cold War, whether a black or white was at its helm.

Endnotes

1   "Venezuela's President Still Smells Sulfur after Obama Speech," *Fox News*, December 18, 2009.

2   Interview with Ron Ridenour who served as Morales' public relations man for the conference, January 28, 2019.

3   See Greg Grandin, "Muscling Latin America: The Pentagon Has a New Monroe Doctrine," *The Nation Magazine*, July 21, 2010.

4   Mark Weisbrot, "Obama's Handshake with Latin America," *The Guardian*, April 22, 2009; Sean Nevins, "Coups, Massacres and Contras: The Legacy of Washington's New Point Man in Latin America," May 13, 2015, https://www.mintpressnews.com/coups-massacres-and-contras-the-legacy-of-the-washingtons-new-point-man-in-latin-america/205494/. Feierstein had also been a consultant to Bolivian president Gonzalo Sanchez de Lozada (1993-1997), a multimillionaire mining executive and protégé of Chicago School economist Milton Friedman who caused thousands to lose their jobs through ill-conceived privatization and austerity measures and was indicted for repressing popular protests.

5   Wayne Madsen, "Obama's Diplomacy Masks His Bullying at Jamaica and Panama Summits," *Voltaire Network*, April 17, 2015.

6   David J. Garrow, *Rising Star: The Making of Barack Obama* (New York:

William Morrow, 2017), 801.

7   Richard Gott, *Hugo Chavez and the Bolivarian Revolution* (London: Verso, 2011); Alba Carioso, "From Reliable US Oil Supplier to Extraordinary Threat," in *How the US Creates "Sh*thole" Countries*, ed. Cynthia McKinney (Atlanta: Clarity Press, 2019), 256.

8   Maxim Nikolenko, "Planting Regime Change in Venezuela," *Counterpunch*, June 30, 2017; Alan Macleod, *Bad News From Venezuela: Twenty Years of Fake News and Misreporting* (New York: Routeledge, 2018), 44.

9   See Nikolas Kozloff, *Revolution: South America and the Rise of the New Left* (New York: Palgrave McMillan, 2008); Tonya J. Weathersbee, "Why the Black and Poor Loved Hugo Chavez," *The Root*, March 2013.

10   See Eva Gollinger, *The Chavez Code: Cracking U.S. Intervention in Venezuela* (Olive Branch Press, 2006); Gollinger, *Bush Versus Chavez: Washington's War on Venezuela* (New York: Monthly Review Press, 2007).

11   Benjamin Dangl, "Obama Set for a Summit in the Sun," *The Nation*, April 16, 2009.

12   Leon Panetta, *Worthy Fights: A Memoir of Leadership in War and Peace* (New York: Penguin Press, 2014), 277.

13   José de Córdoba and Kejal Veyas, "Venezuela's Future in Balance" *The Wall Street Journal*, December 9, 2012.

14   Dan Beeton, Jake Johnston, and Alexander Main, "Venezuela," in *The Wikileaks Files: The World According to U.S. Empire*, ed. Julian Assange (London: Verso, 2015), 522, 524,525, 530.

15   "Notes From the Editors," *Monthly Review*, March 2019, 64; Lawrence Schoup, *Wall Street's Think Tank: The Council on Foreign Relations and the Empire of Neoliberal Geopolitics, 1976-2014* (New York: Monthly Review Press, 2015), 198; Robert D. Blackwill and Meghan L. O'Sullivan, "America's Energy Edge: The Geopolitical Consequences of the Shale Revolution," *Foreign Affairs*, March/April 2014.

16   Camillo Osorio Avendano, "The Consequences of Obama's Sanctions Against Venezuela," *Latin America is a Country*, April 9, 2015.

17   James Petras and Henry Veltmeyer, *Extractive Imperialism in the Americas* (Leiden: Brill, 2014), 272, 277.

18   Seamus Milne, "Venezuela Shows That Protest Can be a Defense of Privilege," *The Guardian*, April 9, 2014.

19   Macleod, *Bad News From Venezuela*, 83, 94, 95; Beeton et al., "Venezuela," in *The Wikileaks Files*, 522, 524,525.

20   Richard Walker, "Obama Administration Targets Venezuela for 'Regime Change,'" *American Free Press*, March 14, 2014; David William Pear, "Venezuela Regime Change Project Revealed," *The Real News*, August 4, 2017; Wayne Madsen, "CIA/Obama Versus Latin America," https://www.waynemadsenreport.com/categories/20140526; Petras and Veltmeyer,

Extractive Imperialism in the Americas, 268, 272; James Petras and Henry Veltmeyer, *Power and Resistance: U.S. Imperialism in Latin America* (Netherlands: Brill, 2015), 157, 159. Three U.S. embassy officials were kicked out for their participation in destabilization activity with members of the far-right opposition.

21   Girish Gupta, "Venezuela Mayor is Accused of U.S.-Backed Coup Plot," *New York Times*, February 21, 2015; Petras and Veltmeyer, *Power and Resistance*, 162.

22   Kiraz Janicke, "South American Leaders Concerned over Columbia-U.S. Military Plan," *Venezuela Analysis*, August 11, 2009.

23   Daniel Beckman, "A Labyrinth of Deception: Secretary Clinton and the Honduran Coup," *Council on Hemispheric Affairs*, April 12, 2017.

24   Dan Rosenheck, "Everyone's Wrong About Honduras," *Slate*, July 5, 2009; Grandin, "Muscling Latin America," *The Nation Magazine*, July 21, 2010; Eva Golinger, "Washington Behind the Honduran Coup," *Monthly Review online*, July 9, 2009. Zelaya also signed a competitive contract with Conoco Phillips. This move earned him the ire of Exxon and Chevron, which dominate Central America's fuel market.

25   George Gray Molina, "U.S.-Brazilian relations Behind the Impasse," in *Shifting the Balance: Obama and the Americas*, ed. Abraham J. Lowenthal, Theodore J. Piccone and Laurence Whitehead (Washington, D.C.: Brookings Institute Press, 2011), 115.

26   See Honduras Human Rights Report, 2013, https://www.state.gov/documents/organization/220663.pdf

27   Conn Hallinan, "The Honduran Coup: A U.S. Connection," In *Hopeless: Barack Obama and the Politics of Illusion*, ed. Jeffrey St. Clair and Joshua Frank (Oakland: AK Press, 2012), 65. Davis had previously lobbied on behalf of Laurent Gbagbo (Ivory Coast), Teodoro Obiang Nguema (Equatorial Guinea), and Pervez Musharraf (Pakistan) though still claimed to be a liberal Democrat.

28   Beckman, "A Labyrinth of Deception: Secretary Clinton and the Honduran Coup."

29   "Remarks by President Obama and President Uribe of Colombia in Joint Press Availability," The White House, Office of the Secretary, June 29, 2009.

30   Lowenthal, "The Obama Administration and the Americas," in *Shifting the Balance*, ed. Lowenthal, 13; Hillary Clinton, *Hard Choices* (New York: Simon & Schuster, 2014).

31   Mark Weisbrot, "Obama's Deafening Silence on Honduras," *The Guardian*, August 21, 2009. Dan Kovalik, *"The Plot to Control the World"* (New York: Skyhorse, 2018), 116, 117.

32   Noam Chomsky, *Hopes and Prospects* (Chicago: Haymarket Books, 2015), 67.

33   Charlie Savage, *Power Wars: Inside Obama's Post 9/11 Presidency* (Boston:

Little & Brown, 2015), 675.

34   Dana Frank, "Honduras in Flames," *The Nation Magazine*, February 16, 2012; Bill Conroy, "Emails Show Secretary Clinton Disobeyed Obama Policy and Continued Funding for Honduras Coup Regime," *The Narcosphere*, July 5, 2015; Beckman, "A Labyrinth of Deception."

35   Security Assistance Monitor, Honduras, https://securityassistance.org/data/program/military/Honduras/2009/2016/all/Global//

36   John James Conyers Jr. et al., "America's Funding of Honduras Security Forces Puts Blood on Our Hands," *The Guardian*, July 8, 2016; Dana Frank, "The Thugocracy Next Door," *Politico*, February 27, 2014. On the SOA, see Lesley Gill, *School of the Americas: Military Training and Political Violence in the Americas* (Durham, NC: Duke University Press, 2004). The School of the Americas changed its' name in the 1990s and claimed to introduce a human rights curriculum after many of its graduates were connected with death squad activities, however, independent researchers found that the course was not taken seriously.

37   Nevins, "Coups, Massacres and Contras."

38   Security Assistance Monitor, Colombia, https://securityassistance.org/data/program/military/Colombia/2009/2016/all/Global//; Alfred W. McCoy, *In the Shadows of the American Century: The Rise and Decline of US Global Power* (Chicago: Haymarket Books, 2017), 178; Forrest Hylton, *Evil Hour in Colombia* (London: Verso, 2006).

39   "Brief memo for Cheryl Mills on Colombia - for Secretary Clinton," June 3, 2010, https://wikileaks.org/clinton-emails/emailid/65; "Remarks by President Obama and President Uribe of Colombia in Joint Press Availability," June 29, 2009.

40   Mario Murillo, "Holder, Chiquita and Colombia," *Counterpunch*, November 8, 2008.

41   See Oliver Villar and Drew Cottle, *Cocaine, Death Squads and the War on Terror: U.S. Imperialism and Class Struggle in Colombia*, foreword by Peter Dale Scott (New York: Monthly Review Press, 2011); Tim Dickinson, "Why America Can't Quit the Drug War," *Rolling Stone*, May 5, 2016; Joshua Goodman, "Declassified U.S. Cables Link Uribe to Colombia Drug Cartels," *U.S. News & World Report*, May 28, 2018.

42   Eva Golinger. "U.S. Privatizes Colombian War with its Transnational Mercenaries," *Venezuela Analysis*, August 12, 2009.

43   Bureau of Economic and Business Affairs, 2016 Investment Climate Statements, report, July 5, 2016, https://www.state.gov/e/eb/rls/othr/ics/2016/wha/254517.htm; Bill Van Auten, "U.S. Military Base Plan Fuels Latin American Tensions," *Voltaire Network*, August 5, 2009.

44   Peter Schweizer, *Clinton Cash: The Untold Story of How and Why Foreign Governments and Businesses Helped Make Bill and Hillary Rich* (New York:

Harper, 2015), 155. See also Dan Kovalik, "Obama's War for Oil in Colombia," *Counterpunch*, January 28, 2010. Boeing and Caterpillar were also major beneficiaries of the free-trade agreement which was opposed by Congressional Democrats by a 158-31 vote.

45   John Lindsay Poland, "Retreat to Colombia: The Pentagon Adapts its Latin American Strategy," *North American Congress on Latin America*, January 5, 2010.

46   Van Auten, "U.S. Military Base Plan Fuels Latin American Tensions;" Latin American Peoples Organize to Resist Increased Militarization in the Region, Portland Central America Solidarity Committee, https://www. pcasc.net/2010/11/19/latin-american-peoples-organize-to-resist-increased-militarization-in-the-region/; Rory Carroll, "Outcry in South America Over U.S. Military Base Pact," *The Guardian*, August 27, 2009.

47   Alexander Main et al. "Latin America and the Caribbean," *The Wikileaks Files*, ed. Assange.

48   Main et al., "Latin America and the Caribbean," in *The Wikileaks Files*, ed. Assange, 503; Wayne Madsen, *The Manufacturing of a President* (Self Published, 2012), 315, 316; Colonel Ann Wright, "U.S. Military Bases in the Caribbean, Central and South America," Presentation for the 4th International Seminar for Peace and Abolition of Foreign Military Bases," Guantanamo Bay, Cuba, November 23-24, 2015, https://worldbeyondwar.org/united-states-military-bases-in-the-caribbean-central-and-south-america/; Nikolas Kozloff, "What's Behind Obama's New Military Base in Chile?" *Al Jazeera*, June 2, 2012; Rachel Glickhouse, "U.S. Funded Naval Base Sparks Controversy in the Dominican Republic," *Council of the Americas*, February 27, 2012. Chile's leader Sebastien Piñera was a hedge fund billionaire involved in illegal bank schemes during the Pinochet era.

49   Petras and Veltmeyer, *Extractive Imperialism in the Americas*, 266.

50   "Dangerous Complacencies: Obama, Latin America and the Misconception of Power," *Latin American Perspectives*, 38, 4 (July 2011).

51   Briefing, Congressman Miller and Members of Florida's 31st District, May 14, 2009, www.filewikileaks.org.

52   Andrew Clark, "Chavez Creates Overnight Bestseller with Book Gift to Obama," *The Guardian*, April 19, 2009; Eduardo Galeano, *Open Veins of Latin America: Five Centuries of the Pillage of a Continent*, rev ed. (New York: Monthly Review Press, 1997).

53   Dawn Paley, "The Alliance for Prosperity Will Intensify the Central American Refugee Crisis," *The Nation*, December 21, 2016; "Che Guevara Exposes U.S. Alliance for Progress," *The Militant*, January 20, 2003.

54   Petras and Veltmeyer, *Power and Resistance*; Petras and Veltmeyer, *Extractive Imperialism in the Americas*, 292; Dolio Estevez, "Most Mexicans Oppose President Pena Nieto's Plans to Open Up PEMEX to Private Investment,"

Forbes, June 26, 2013; Sarah Lazare, "Columbia Nationwide Strikes Against Free-Trade, Privatization, Poverty," *Farmlandgrab.org*, August 26, 2013; Colin Post, "Peru to Privatize Prison System" Peru Reports, September 26, 2015. Humala was later jailed for corruption.

55   Grandin, "Muscling Latin America."

56   "The Role the U.S. Played in Reversing Latin America's Pink Tide," *The Real News*, July 29, 2018,; Nick Miroff, "In Argentina, Obama Will Cheer on South America's Shift Away from the Left," *Washington Post*, March 17, 2016; Jeff Mason, Richard Lough, "Obama Praises Argentina's Man in a Hurry Macri for Reforms," *Reuters*, March 22, 2016. The state-owned oil company also signed a venture with Chevron to exploit an enormous gas field. Kirchner promoted protectionist policies, including trade restrictions and currency controls and clashed with a New York Hedge Fund over public debt.

57   Jonathan Gilbert, "President Obama's Argentina Visit is all About Trade," *Fortune*, March 23, 2016. Bill Clinton forged a close relationship with Argentine President Carlos Menem whose neoliberal policies caused the 2001 crisis.

58   Alexander Main et al., "Latin America and the Caribbean," in *The Wikileaks Files*, ed. Assange, 514. For more on Aristide and U.S. opposition to him, see Paul Farmer, with foreword by Noam Chomsky, *The Uses of Haiti* (Monroe, ME: Common Courage Press, 2004).

59   Schweizer, *Clinton Cash*, 169; Antony Lowenstein, *Disaster Capitalism: Making a Killing Out of Catastrophe* (London: Verso, 2015), 107, 108, 115, 116; Jake Johnson, "Outsourcing Haiti: How Disaster Relief Became a Disaster of Its Own," *Boston Review*, January 16, 2014. DynCorp was contracted to train the Haitian police through the UN, raising fear that would evolve as a reincarnation of DuValier's Tonton Macoutes (repressive force). See Dady Chery, "Inside the Occupation of Haiti," *Counterpunch*, December 26, 2014.

60   Mark Weisbrot, "Obama's Latin American Policy: Continuity without Change," *Center for Economic and Policy Research*, September 2013.

61   James North, "Why Haitians are Chanting 'Down with Obama,'" *The Nation*, January 27, 2016; Frances Robles, "Haitian Leaders Power Grows as Scandals Swirl," *New York Times*, March 16, 2015.

62   Yara Simon, "As Soon as Obama Signed PROMESA Budget Bill, Puerto Ricans Hit the Streets to Protest," http://remezcla.com/lists/culture/obama-signed-promesa-into-law/; Ryan Cooper, "Thanks to Obama, Puerto Rico Might Never Recover from Irma," *The Week*, September 19, 2017' "Protests Erupt in San Juan as Obama Forms Unelected Control Board to Run Puerto Rico," *Democracy Now*, September 1, 2016; Margaret Power, "Puerto Rico: A U.S. Colony in the Caribbean," Historians for Peace and Democracy, Broadsides for the Trump Era, April 2019.

63   See eg. "The Federal Drug Control Budget New Rhetoric, Same Failed Drug

War," *Drug Policy Alliance*, February 2015, https://www.drugpolicy.org/sites/default/files/DPA_Fact_sheet_Drug_War_Budget_Feb2015.pdf. In 2015, the Obama administration spent $26 billion on the War on Drugs, 55 percent of which was devoted to interdiction, eradication and law enforcement (nearly $14 billion).

64   Andy Greenberg, "Want to See Domestic Spying's Future? Follow the Drug War," *Wired Magazine*, April 10, 2014; Todd Miller and Gabriel M. Schivone, "Gaza in Arizona: How Israeli High Tech Firms Will Up Armor Along the U.S.-Mexican Border," *Mother Jones*, January 26, 2015; Savage, *Power Wars*, 633; Paul Street, *They Rule: The 1% Vs. Democracy* (Boulder, CO: Paradigm, 2014), 169; William Neuman, "Defying U.S., Colombia Halts Aerial Spraying of Crops Used to Make Cocaine," *New York Times*, May 14, 2015.

65   Robert Beckhusen, "Here's What Your $97 Million Drug War in Central America Actually Bought," *Wired Magazine*, February 1, 2013; John Lindsey Poland, "Pentagon Using Drug War as Excuse to Build Military Bases in Central America," *New American Media*, June 3, 2011.

66   Dana Priest, "U.S. Role at Crossroads in Mexico's Intelligence War on the Cartels," *Washington Post*, April 27, 2013; Andrew Cockburn, *Kill Chain: The Rise of the High-Tech Assassins* (New York: Henry Holt, 2015), 106.

67   Ibid;, Jesse Franzblau, "A Dark Legacy: Hillary Clinton's Role in the Mexican Drug War," *Counterpunch*, March 3, 2016; National Southwest Border, Narcotics Strategy Implementation Update, 2010, (Washington, D.C.: Office of the U.S. President, 2010).

68   Clare Ribando Seelke and Kristin Finklea, "U.S. Mexican Security Cooperation: The Mérida Initiative and Beyond," *Congressional Research Service*, June 29, 2017.

69   Charles Bowden, *Murder City: Ciudad Juarez and the Global Economy's New Killing Fields* (New York: Nation Books, 2010); Anabel Hernandez, *Narcoland: The Mexican Drug Lords and their Godfathers* (London: Verso, 2013), 238-239, 241; "AP Investigation Suggests Border Corruption at All-Time High," *Drug War Chronicle*, http://www.csdp.org/news/news/corruption.htm; Matt Taibbi, "Gangster Bankers, Too Big to Jail: How HSBC Hooked Up With Drug Traffickers and Terrorists and Got Away With It," *Rolling Stone*, February 14, 2013.

70   Katie Pavlich, *Fast and Furious: Barack Obama's Bloodiest Scandal and Its Shameless Cover-Up* (Washington, D.C.: Regnery, 2012); Ian Tuttle, "'El Chapo's Capture Puts Operation Fast and the Furious Back in the Headlines," *National Review*, January 22, 2016. The Justice Department confirmed that at least 11 crimes were committed on American soil with guns traceable to Fast and the Furious.

71   Jackie Calmes, "Obama Says That Legalization is Not the Answer," *New York Times*, April 14, 2012.

72 Counter-Narcotics Contracts in Latin America, Hearings Before the Ad Hoc Subcommittee on Contracting Oversight of the Committee on Homeland Security and Government Affairs, U.S. Senate, 111th Congress, 2nd Session, May 20, 2010; 1; Frank Koughan, "U.S. Trained Death Squads? How America's Latest Drug War Initiative Could Aid the Cartels and Enrich Military Contractors," *Mother Jones*, July-August 2009; Nick Turse, *The Changing Face of Empire: Special Ops, Drones, Spies, Proxy Fighters, Secret Bases, and Cyberwarfare* (Chicago: Haymarket Books, 2012), 6; Dawn Paley *Drug War Capitalism* (Oakland, CA: AK Press, 2014), 114; *Undeniable Atrocities: Confronting Crimes Against Humanity* (Open Society Foundation, 2016).

73 Franzblau, "A Dark Legacy."

74 Counter-Narcotics Contracts in Latin America 1; Franzblau, "Hillary Clinton's Dark Drug War Legacy in Mexico;" Peter Watt and Roberto Zepeda, *Drug War Mexico: Politics, Neo-liberalism and Violence in the New Narco Economy* (London: Zed Books, 2012), 206; Paley, *Drug War Capitalism*, 136; *The Department of Justice's Operation Fast and Furious: Fueling Cartel Violence*, Joint Staff Report, Prepared for Rep. Darrell E. Issa & Senator Charles E. Grassley, 112th Congress, July 26, 2011; *Undeniable Atrocities*.

75 Paley, *Drug War Capitalism*, 133, 134.

76 Pavlich, *Fast and Furious*, 161.

77 Hernandez, *Narcoland*, 238-239, 241; Bowden, *Murder City*.

78 Brandan Pierson, "'El Chapo' Paid Former Mexican President $100 Million: Trial Witness," *Reuters*, January 15, 2019.

79 Watt and Zepeda, *Drug War Mexico*, 1.

80 Brian Anderson, "Catapults and Jalapenos: The Ingenious Smuggling Tech of the World's Top Drug Kingpin," *Motherboard*, June 18, 2012; William Booth and Juan Ferero, "Semi-Subs Stealthily Plying the Pacific," *Washington Post*, June 6, 2009, A1, A7; Rob Nixon, "The Case for Tech War Concrete Along the Border," *New York Times*, June 21, 2017, A9.

81 Jeremy Kuzmarov, "DEA Malfeasance and Trump's Foolish Drug War Escalation," *The Huffington Post*, May 25, 2017.

82 Ginger Thompson and Scott Shane, "Cables Portray Expanded Reach of Drug Agency," In *Open Secrets: Wikileaks, War and American Diplomacy*, ed. Alexander Starr (New York: Grove Press, 2011), 186, 188; Dana Frank, "WikiLeaks Honduras: U.S. Linked to Brutal Businessman," *The Nation*, October 21, 2011; Paley, *Drug War Capitalism*, 212; Bill Conroy, "Emails Show Secretary Clinton Disobeyed Obama Policy and Continued Funding for Honduras Coup Regime," *Narco News*, July 21, 2015,; *The Wikileaks Files, ed. Assange, 71.*

83 Alma Guillermoprieto, "Drugs: The Rebellion in Cartagena," *New York Review of Books*, June 7, 2012; Dana Frank, "WikiLeaks Honduras: U.S. Linked to Brutal Businessman," *The Nation*, October 21, 2011; Paley, *Drug War Capitalism*, 212;

Elyssa Pachico, "Post-2009 Coup, Honduras a 'Narco-Storehouse,'" *InSight Crime,* September 23, 2011, http://www.insightcrime.org/news-analysis/post-2009-coup-honduras-a-narco-storehouse. Jake Johnston, "How Pentagon Officials May Have Encouraged a 2009 Coup in Honduras," *The Intercept,* August 29, 2017. Fabio Lobo, Porfirio's son, was convicted of drug trafficking.

84   "Fidel Castro's Letter to Obama: 'We Don't Need the Empire to Give Us Anything," *Alternet,* March 28, 2016

85   Ron Ridenour, "U.S. Cuba Policy Change: Score 11-1: U.S. Wins," *Ronridenour.com,* December 12, 2014; Paul Craig Roberts, "Regime Change in Cuba," *Dissident Voice,* December 19, 2014.

86   Shamus Cook, "Paraguay: Obama's Second Latin American Coup," *Workers Action,* June 23, 2012; Natalia Viana, "USAID's Dubious Allies in Paraguay," *The Nation Magazine,* April 29, 2013.

87   Brian Finnegan, "Black Trade Unionists Call on Obama to Condemn a Coup and Support Brazil's Democratically Elected Government," *AFL-CIO,* June 6, 2016, https://aflcio.org/2016/6/6/black-trade-unionists-call-obama-condemn-coup-and-support-brazils-democratically-elected; Julien Borger, "Brazilian President: U.S. Surveillance a Breach of International Law," *The Guardian,* September 24, 2013; Nicholas Kozloff, "Is Obama Wary of Brazil and Dilma Rousseff?" *Al Jazeera,* May 5, 2012. Rousseff had also been a target of NSA surveillance.

88   Kit O'Connell, "Wikileaks: Brazil's Acting President Michel Temer is a U.S. Government Informant," *MPN News,* May 13, 2016, Expanding foreign investment was important to gain an edge over the Chinese who invested $46.8 billion in Brazil across 87 projects from 2003-2017.

89   "The Role the U.S. Played in Reversing Latin America's Pink Tide," *The Real News,* July 29, 2018; Ted Snider, "A U.S. Hand in Brazil's Coup?" *Consortium News,* June 1, 2016; Noam Chomsky, "I Just Visited Lula, the World's Most Prominent Political Prisoner," *The Intercept,* October 2, 2018.

90   See *The New Latin American Left: Cracks in The Empire,* ed. Jeffrey Webber and Barry Carr (New York: Rowman & Littlefield, 2012).

91   "Bolivian President Evo Morales on President Obama: 'I Can't Believe a Black President Can Hold So Much Vengeance Against an Indian President'" *Democracy Now,* April 23, 2010.

92   Nil Nikandrov, "The U.S. Is Preparing to Oust President Evo Morales," *Strategic Culture Foundation,* September 6, 2016. In 2013, Morales expelled USAID and DEA.

93   Roger Harris, "Chomsky on Regime Change in Nicaragua," *Counterpunch,* August 3, 2018; Nina Lakhani, "Nicaragua Suppresses Opposition to Ensure One-Party Election, Critics Say," *The Guardian,* June 26, 2018; Tim Rogers, "Why Daniel Ortega Will Go on Ruling Nicaragua," *Time Magazine,* February 9, 2011. Per capita GDP increased under Ortega from $1,204 in 2006 to $1,929

in 2015.

94   Jonathan Watts, "Nicaragua Gives Chinese firm Contract to Build Alternative to Panama Canal," *The Guardian*, June 6, 2013.

95   Max Blumenthal, "An Exclusive Interview with Nicaraguan President Daniel Ortega," *The Grayzone Project*, July 30, 2018; Main, Johnston, and Beeton, "Latin America and the Caribbean," in *The Wikileaks Files*, ed. Assange, 492-497.

96   See Benjamin Waddell, "Laying the Groundwork for Insurrection: A Closer Look at the U.S. Role in Nicaragua's Social Unrest," *Global Americans*, May 1, 2018.

97   Madsen, *The Manufacturing of a President,*, 311-315; Security Assistance Monitor, Costa Rica, https://securityassistance.org/data/program/military/Costa%20Rica/2009/2016/all/Global//; STATEMENT OF THE HONORABLE JAIME DAREMBLUM, FORMER COSTA RICAN AMBASSADOR TO THE UNITED STATES, HUDSON INSTITUTE, HEARING, BEFORE THE COMMITTEE ON FOREIGN AFFAIRs, HOUSE OF REPRESENTATIVES, ONE HUNDRED TWELFTH CONGRESS, FIRST SESSIO, DECEMBER 1, 2011 (Washington, D.C.: U.S. Government Printing Office, 2011). Ortega won the 2016 election with 73 percent of the vote. It was certified by the OAS. Additional support for destabilization operations in Nicaragua was provided by Panamanian president Ricardo Martinelli, one of Israel's few allies in Latin America.

98   John R. Haines, "Everything Old Is New Again: Russia Returns to Nicaragua," *Foreign Policy Research Institute*, July 22, 2016.

99   Greg Grandin, *Empire's Workshop: The U.S., Latin America and the Rise of the New Imperialism* (New York: Metropolitan Books, 2005).

100   See Marc Becker, *The FBI in Latin America: The Ecuador Files* (Durham, NC: Duke University Press, 2017), 51.

101   On Kennedy's Latin American policy, see Stephen G. Rabe, *'The Most Dangerous Place in the World:' John F. Kennedy Confronts Communist Revolution in Latin America* (Chapel Hill: University of North Carolina Press, 1999).

102   "Rethinking the Drug War in Central America and Mexico," Meso America Working Group, November 2013, http://www.ghrc-usa.org/wp-content/uploads/2013/12/Mesoamerica-Working-Group_Rethinking-Drug-War-Web-Version.pdf; Alexander Main, "The Remilitarization of Mexico and Central America," *North American Congress on Latin America*, July 3, 2014.

CONCLUSION
SEEKING A BETTER
WAY TO LIVE

Historian William Appleman Williams ended his classic
essay "Empire as a Way of Life" by urging Americans to turn
away from empire and work towards building a cooperative
commonwealth. Recounting a story of his grandmother forcing
him to return a knife he had stolen as a boy to its rightful owner,
Williams says that "remembering all that, I know why I don't want
the empire. There are better ways to live and better ways to die."[1]

Williams' story and vision resonates with the content
of this book which has recounted in detail the violent practices
promoted by a purportedly liberal U.S. administration. Much like
another liberal icon, Woodrow Wilson, Obama effectively played
his part as commander-in-chief through his slick disguising of wars
by humanitarian rhetoric and through creation of a misleading
autobiography and public image that made him appear as an
icon of multiculturalism and a genuine liberal internationalism.
Obama's presidency in many ways shows how liberal-progressive
politicians can be more dangerous than their conservative

counterparts, who tend to be more truthful in their aspirations to dominate the world and earn profits in whatever ways, thus making them easier to mobilize against.

Journalist Glen Ford aptly described Obama and his wife Michelle as a "two cynical lawyers on hire to the wealthiest and the ghastliest" who are "no nicer or nastier than the Romneys and the Ryans [opponents in 2012 election], although the man of the house bombs babies and keeps a kill list."[2] He also had a Big Brother complex. Every day during Obama's presidency, the NSA intercepted and stored more than 1.7 billion emails, phone calls and other forms of communications.[3] Failing in his efforts to close down Guantanamo Bay, Obama further permitted the military to detain those suspected of aiding terrorists indefinitely without due process, and expanded the Pentagon's 1033 program providing military equipment to local police at levels that eclipsed the peak of the Bush administration by 14 percent. Surely, Obama must have known that this equipment would be used against his own purported community, African Americans.[4]

The consequence was evident in Ferguson, Missouri where following the slaying of an unarmed black teenager in August 2014, police confronted citizen-protestors equipped with Kevlar helmets, gas masks, mine resistant anti-ambush vehicles used in Afghanistan, M4 carbine rifles, pepper spray projectiles, rubber bullets, acoustic devices and military style helicopters.[5] Occupy Wall Street protesters were also teargassed and threatened by masked officers brandishing clubs. Twenty-five-year-old Marine Scott Olsen, on October 25th, 2011, was hit in the head with a beanbag bullet fired by police at Occupy Oakland, causing him to suffer permanent brain damage. The same police then threw a flashbang grenade towards protesters who rushed to aid him. Olsen said his first tour of duty in Iraq had "given him perspective, empathy for people's struggles around the world, against occupiers, against imperialism." He added that: "I think people are getting able to see the way the system works, and I think people see the connecting dots of exploitation around the world that's enabled by the military and keeps our American interests flying."[6]

The late political economist Seymour Melman pointed to a way forward three decades ago in his book *The Demilitarized Society*, which critiqued the peace movement for being primarily reactive to government atrocities and suggested that it should instead develop a long term program for converting the U.S. into an economy of peace. While the popular stereotype holds that large-scale military spending provides jobs, Melman showed that it in fact diverts the productive resources and technical skills of scientists and engineers into parasitic military industries that do not create outlaying industries and operate inefficiently because of guaranteed contracts and lack of competition.

The U.S., according to Melman, had evolved into a second or third-rate industrial power, which produced inferior products, could not compete with foreign competition even in domestic markets, and was experiencing pronounced societal decay as a result of the downgrading of infrastructure and neglect for public education and social services. A militarized state capitalist economy took hold with an unprecedented degree of centralized management which was antithetical to America's libertarian tradition. Democracy was further subverted through lobbying and cronyism, along with the manipulation of public opinion by corporate controlled media.

Melman advocated for development of a program to convert military production facilities and research laboratories into ones that produced civilian goods and made better use of scientific and intellectual brainpower. This would entail a commitment of government resources to retraining programs and capital investment in infrastructure and environmental clean-up and should follow a decentralized democratic model, in which local agencies and employees played a key role in the conversion planning. Melman emphasized that while some might consider this plan to be utopian, the American economy reconverted rapidly from its war-time footing after the Second World War and prior to the outbreak of the Korean War, and that laboratories and companies also did so effectively in the wake of protests during the Vietnam War.[7] The Boeing-Vertol Corporation, for example, which had manufactured helicopters used in the Vietnam War, began to produce subway cars used by the Chicago Transit Authority.[8]

During the late 1980s, Melman found a powerful promoter for his ideas in the Speaker of the House, Jim Wright (D-TX), who ironically had been known during the Vietnam era as "the Congressman from Convair [subsidiary of General Dynamics]."[9] On the first day of the opening of the 101st Congress in January 1989, Speaker Wright convened a meeting of members who had proposed economic conversion legislation and their aides with the goal of ensuring that all proposals be joined into one, and that this legislation be given priority. To dramatize the importance of this bill, it would be given number H.R. 101. Having read Melman's writings, Wright had come to believe that "the arms race had taken on dangerous but also economically damaging characteristics" and that military spending "sapped the strength of the whole society."[10]

Wright was subsequently brought down for financial improprieties in a political witch-hunt led by Newt Gingrich, whose Georgia district served as the headquarters for Lockheed Martin. Congressman Ted Weiss (D-NY), the "conscience of the House" who had called for Reagan's impeachment following the invasion of Grenada, was another powerful sponsor of reconversion legislation. With fifty-four colleagues in the 1980s, he called for a national level commission chaired by the Secretary of Commerce, which would publish a manual on local alternative use planning and would encourage federal, state and local governments to make capital investment plans and provide guaranteed incomes during a period of changeover, allowance for occupational retraining for workers and family relocation.[11]

The timing was very opportune for the proposed peace dividend with the fall of the Soviet Union and end of the Cold War. According to Melman, the media campaign of Gingrich and his counterparts unfortunately "drowned out any further discussion of economic conversion.... A historic opportunity had been destroyed."[12] George H.W. Bush's invasion of Iraq in 1991, which Barack Obama supported, was the nail in the coffin. Local efforts persisted nevertheless such as that of Irvine, California Mayor Larry Agran who in the 1990s planned to make his home town a national model for economic conversion by using "under-worked" defense companies to build a major monorail project. Envisioning a major local mass-transportation industry, his proposed Irvine Institute for Entrepreneurial Development would also look for ways to push local rocket scientists toward environmental cleanup, healthcare, and other such enterprises.[13]

The peace movement today should work in conjunction with progressive Congresspeople and libertarians like Ron and Rand Paul to develop similar programs. Mary Beth Sullivan, a social worker and outreach coordinator for the Global Network Against Weapons and Nuclear Power in Space, points out that Melman and Weiss's legacy lives on through groups like the Peace Economy Project in St. Louis, and the Woodstock, New York peace community which held a conference focused on the conversion of Ametek/Rotron, a Woodstock company that makes parts used in F-16 fighter planes, Apache attack helicopters, tanks, and missile delivery systems.[14]

After the 2008 election, Deepak Chopra, a leader in the field of mind body medicine, sent a letter to the White House titled "Nine Steps to Peace for Obama in the New Year." Asserting that it was an antiwar constituency that elected Obama, Dr. Chopra invoked the spirit of Dwight Eisenhower's farewell address in insisting that Obama move from an economy dependent on war-making to a peace-based economy. He recommended that in every defense contract there should be a requirement for a peacetime project, that tax incentives should be provided to subsidize conversion of military companies to peaceful use, that the government should criminalize arms dealing, convert military bases into houses for the poor, and that there should be a moratorium on future weapons technologies and phasing out of all foreign military bases.[15]

Rather than incorporating these suggestions, Obama did just the opposite, expanding the military base network, easing restrictions on arms sales, promoting confrontation with China and Russia, and investing heavily in new military technologies, including miniaturized drones and robotics. Though packaging himself as a peace candidate, Obama ultimately proved indispensable to the military-industrial complex in his ability to sustain the illusion of humanitarian intervention and defuse anti-war activism. His career exposes deep flaws in the American cultural ethic in its win-at-costs mentality, its prioritization of material accumulation, and its enthralment with military technological gadgets and belief in the redemptive function of violence.[16] A symbol of the Obama era was the "great tower of nothing" being constructed in his honor on 19.3 acres of choice lakefront land in Chicago at major taxpayer expense: a presidential library displacing residents that would not include his actual papers, and a museum that was artifact free.[17]

By looking critically at Obama's time in office and the consequences of his foreign policies, we can see the limitations of the two-party system and the corrupting influence of money in politics. The way forward is to embrace the vision of Chopra, Melman and Weiss and other peace makers around the world, and to articulate a constructive peace agenda capable of mobilizing thousands and thousands of people.

Endnotes

1   William Appleman Williams, *Empire as a Way of Life: An Essay on the Causes and Character of America's Present Predicament Along with a Few Thoughts About an Alternative* (New York: Oxford University Press, 1980), 226.

2   In Michael Eric Dyson, *The Black Presidency: Barack Obama and the Politics of Race in America* (Boston: Houghton Mifflin, 2016), 26.

3   See William Arkin and Dana Priest, *Top Secret America: The Rise of the New American Security State* (Boston: Little & Brown, 2011).

4   Paul Street, *They Rule: The 1% Versus Democracy* (New York: Routeledge, 2014).

5   Sarah Jaffe, *Necessary Trouble: Americans in Revolt* (New York: The Nation Books, 2016).

6   Jaffe, *Necessary Trouble*, 217, 218.

7   See Seymour Melman, *The Demilitarized Society: Disarmament and Conversion* (Montreal: Harvest House, 1988).

8   Jonathan Feldman, "Seymour Melman and the New American Revolution: A Reconstructionist Alternative to a Society Spiraling into the Abyss," *Counterpunch*, December 29, 2017.

9   J. Brooks Flippen, *Speaker Jim Wright: Power, Scandal and the Birth of Modern Politics* (Austin: University of Texas Press, 2018), 219.

10   Mary Beth Sullivan, "Moving from a War Economy to a Peace Economy," *The Humanist*, December 23, 2011.

11   Melman, *The Demilitarized Society*, 60; James Dao, "Rep. Ted Weiss, 64 Dies; Liberal Stalwart in the House," *New York Times*, September 15, 1992.

12   David Swanson, "Moving from a War Economy to a Peace Economy," *warisacrime.org*, October 22, 2011.

13   Mary Beth Sullivan, "Moving from a War Economy to a Peace Economy," in David Swanson, *The Military-Industrial Complex at 50*, ed. David Swanson (David Swanson, 2011).

14   Sullivan, "Moving From a War Economy to a Peace Economy," in *The Military Industrial Complex at 50*, ed. Swanson, 267-279. Sullivan's group in rural Maine promoted converting the General Dynamics plant that builds Aegis destroyers into a manufacturer of wind turbines and other renewable energy projects.

15   Deepak Chopra, "Nine Steps to Peace for Obama in the New Year: Steps the Incoming President Can Take to Build a Peace Based Economy," *Alternet*, December 31, 2008.

16   Some books that provide critical perspectives include: Richard Slotkin, *Gunfighter Nation*, rev ed. (Norman: University of Oklahoma Press, 1998); H. Bruce Franklin, *War Stars: The Superweapon in the American Imagination* (Amherst, MA: University of Massachusetts Press, 2007); Richard Rosenfeld and Stephen Messner, *Crime and the American Dream*, 5th ed. (London: Wadsworth, 2012).

17   Hugh Iglarsh, "Barack Obama's Great Tower of Nothing: Gentrification on a Presidential Level," *Counterpunch*, November 2, 2018.

APPENDIX I

"BREAKING THE WAR MENTALITY"
BY BARACK OBAMA*

Most students at Columbia do not have first hand knowledge of war. Military violence has been a vicarious experience, channeled into our minds through television, film, and print.

The more sensitive among us struggle to extrapolate experiences of war from our everyday experience, discussing the latest mortality statistics from Guatemala, sensitizing ourselves to our parents' wartime memories, or incorporating into our framework of reality as depicted by a Maller [sic] or a Coppola. But the taste of war—the sounds and chill, the dead bodies—are remote and far removed. We know that wars have occurred, will occur, are occurring, but bringing such experience down into our hearts, and taking continual, tangible steps to prevent war, becomes a difficult task.

Two groups on campus, Arms Race Alternatives (ARA) and Students Against Militarism (SAM) work within these mental limits to foster awareness and practical action necessary to counter the growing threat of war. Though the emphasis of the two groups

*Article by Barack Obama circa 1983, published in *Sundial,* Columbia University, October 3, 1983, accessed by Columbia University Archives, http://d.scribd. com/docs/1xm69wn2lozlgbwr5nb0.pdf

differ, they share an aversion to current government policy. These groups, visualizing the possibilities of destruction and grasping the tendencies of distorted national priorities, are throwing their weight into shifting America off the dead-end track.

"Most people my age remember well the air-raid drills in school, under the desk with our heads tucked between our legs. Older people, they remember the Cuban Missile Crisis. I think these kinds of things left an indelible mark on our souls[?], so we're more apt to be concerned," says Don Kent, assistant director of programs and student activities at Earl Hall Center. Along with the community Volunteer Service Center, ARA has been Don's primary concern, coordinating various working groups of faculty, students, and staff members, while simultaneously seeking the ever elusive funding for programs.

"When I first came here two years ago, Earl Hall had been a holding tank for five years. Paul Martin (director of Earl Hall) and I discussed our interests, and decided that ARA would be one of the programs we pushed." Initially, most of the work was done by non-student volunteers and staff. "Hot issues, particularly El Salvador, were occupying students at the time. Consequently, we cosponsored a lot of activities with community organizations like SANE (Students Against Nuclear Energy)."

With the flowering of the nuclear freeze movement, and particularly the June 12 rally in Central Park, however student participation has expanded. One wonders whether this upsurge comes from young people's penchant for the latest 'happenings' or from growing awareness of the consequences of nuclear holocaust. ARA maintains a mailing list of 500 persons and Don Kent estimates that approximately half of the active members are students. Although he feels that continuity is provided by the faculty and staff members, student attendance at ARA sponsored events -- in particular a November 11 convocation on the nuclear threat -- reveals a deep reservoir of concern. "I think students on this campus like to think of themselves a sophisticated, and don't appreciate small vision. So they tend to come out more for the events; they do not want to just fold leaflets."

326 | OBAMA'S UNENDING WARS

Mark Bigelow, a graduate intern from Union Theological Seminary who works with Don to keep ARA running smoothly, agrees. "It seems that students here are fairly aware of the nuclear problem, and it makes for an underlying frustration. We try to talk to that frustration." Consequently, the thrust of ARA is towards generating dialogue which will give people a rational handle on this controversial subject. This includes bringing speakers like Daniel Ellsberg to campus, publishing fact sheets compiled by interested faculty, and investigating the possible development of an interdisciplinary program in the Columbia curriculum dealing with peace, disarmament, and world order.

Tied in with such a thrust is the absence of what Don calls "a party line." By taking an almost apolitical approach to the problem, ARA hopes to get the university to take nuclear arms issues seriously. "People don't like having their intelligence insulted," says Don. "so we try to disseminate information and allow the individual to make his or her own decision."

Generally, the narrow focus of the Freeze movement as well as academic discussions of first versus second strike capabilities, suit the military-industrial interests, as they continue adding to their billion dollar erector sets. When Peter Tosh sings that "everybody's asking for peace, but nobody's asking for justice," one is forced to wonder whether disarmament or arms control ensues, severed from economic and political issues, might be another instance of focusing on the symptoms of a problem instead of the disease itself. Mark Bigelow does not think so. "We do focus primarily on catastrophic weapons. Look, we say, here's the worst part .Let's work on that. You're not going to get rid of the military in the near future, so let's at least work on this."

Mark Bigelow does feel that the links are there, and points to fruitful work being done by other organizations involved with disarmament. "The Freeze is one part of a whole disarmament movement. The lowest common denominator, so to speak. For instance, April 10-16 is Jobs For Peace week, with a bunch of things going on around the city. Also, the New York City Council may pass a resolution in April calling for greater social as opposed to military spending. Things like this may dispel the idea that disarmament is a white issue, because how the government spends its revenue affects everyone."

The very real advantages of concentrating on a single issue is leading the National Freeze movement to challenge individual missile systems, while continuing the broader campaign. This year, Mark Bigelow sees the checking of Pershing II and Cruise missile deployment as crucial. "Because of their small size and mobility, their deployment will make possible arms control verification far more difficult, and will cut down warning time for the Soviets to less than ten minutes. That can only be a destabilizing factor." Additionally, he sees the initiation by the U.S. of the Test Ban Treaty as a powerful first step towards a nuclear free world.

ARA encourages members to join buses to Washington and participate in a March 7-8 rally intended to push through the Freeze resolution which is making its second trip through the House. ARA also will ask United Campuses to Prevent Nuclear War (UCAM), an information and lobbying network based in universities, nationwide, to serve as its advisory board in the near future. Because of its autonomy from Columbia (which does not fund political organizations), UCAM could conceivably become a more active arm of disarmament campaigns on campus, thought the ARA will continue to function solely as a vehicle for information and discussion.

Also operating out of Earl Hall Center, Students Against Militarism was formed in response to the passage of registration laws in 1980. An entirely student-run organization, SAM casts a wider net than ARA, though for the purposes of effectiveness, they have tried to lock in on one issue at a time.

"At the heart of our organization is an anti-war focus," says junior Robert Kahn, one of SAM's fifteen or so active members. "From there, a lot of issues shoot forth -- nukes, racism, the draft, and South Africa. We have been better organized when taking one issue at a time, but we are always cognizant of other things going on, and collaborate frequently with other campus organizations like CISPES and REELPOLITIK."

At this time, the current major issue is the Solomon Bill, the latest legislation from Congress to obtain compliance to registration. The law requires that all male students applying for federal financial aid submit proof of registration, or else the government coffers will close. Yale, Wesleyan, and Swathmore have refused to comply, and plan to offer non-registrants other forms of financial aid. SAM hopes to press Columbia into following suit, though so far President Sovern and company seem prepared to acquiesce to the bill.

Robert believes students tacitly support non-registrants, though the majority did not comply. "Several students have come up to our tables and said that had they known of the ineffectiveness of the prosecution, they would not have registered." A measure of such underlying support is the 400 signatures on a petition protesting the Solomon Bill, which SAM collected the first four hours it appeared. Robert also points out that prior to registration, there were four separate bills circulating in the House proposing a return to the draft, but none ever got out of committees, and there have not been renewed efforts. An estimated half-million non-registrants can definitely be a powerful signal.

Prodding students into participating beyond name signing and attending events is tricky, but SAM members seem undaunted. "A lot of the problem comes not from people's ignorance of the facts, but because the news and statistics are lifeless. That's why we search for campus issues like the Solomon bill that have direct impact on the student body, and effectively link the campus to broader issues." By organizing and educating the Columbia community, such activities lay the foundation for future mobilization against the relentless, often silent spread of militarism in the country. "The time is right to tie together social and military issues," Robert continues, "and the more strident the Administration becomes, the more aware people are of their real interests."

The belief that moribund institutions, rather than the individuals, are at the root of the problem, keep SAM's energies alive. "A prerequisite for members of an organization like ours is the faith that people are fundamentally good, but you need to show them, and when you look at the work people are doing across the country, it makes you optimistic."

Perhaps the essential goodness of humanity is an arguable proposition, but by observing the SAM meeting last Thursday night, with its solid turnout and enthusiasm, one might be persuaded that the manifestations of our better instincts can at least match the bad ones. Regarding Columbia's possible compliance, one comment in particular hit upon an important point with the Solomon bill, "The thing we need to do is expose how Columbia is talking out of two sides of its mouth."

Indeed, the most pervasive malady of the collegiate system specifically, and the American experience generally, is that elaborate patterns of knowledge and theory have been disembodied from individual choices and government policy. What members of ARA and SAM try to do is infuse what they have learned about the current situation, bring the words of that formidable roster on the face of Butler Library, names like Thoreau, Jefferson, and Whitman, to bear on the twisted logic of which we are today a part. By adding their energy and effort in order to enhance the possibility of a decent world, they may help deprive us of a spectacular experience--that of war. But then, there are some things we shouldn't have to live through in order to want to avoid the experience.

APPENDIX 2

BURIED BODIES?

During the 2008 primaries, Lawrence W. Sinclair held a press conference to announce that in November 1999, on a visit to Chicago, he had oral sex and smoked crack cocaine with the then-state Senator in the back seat of a limousine. Sinclair claimed that Obama has three bumps on his uncircumsized penis that could confirm if he was telling the truth about their affair. Sinclair has suggested that Obama or his handlers were behind the December 23, 2007 gangland style murder of Donald Young, the choirmaster at Jeremiah's Wright's Trinity Church and a campaign staffer, whom Obama was alleged to have had a gay affair with. According to Sinclair, Young phoned him and told him not to go public about his encounters with Barry, telling him that Barry was talking with Reverend Wright and would be making a statement. In early November 2007, a worried Donald phoned Larry again and told him that "Barry and Jeremiah lied to me" and that he would be well advised to "get away from all of this as far as possible." Soon after he was found shot to death in his south side Chicago apartment.

Even though they had been friends for twenty years and Young worked on Obama's campaign, Obama never attended his funeral. Two other black members of Jeremiah Wright's choir, Larry Bland and Nate Spencer, were also murdered before the 2008 election. Like Young, their cases were never solved. On January 3, 2008, Delaware County Attorney General Beau Biden, Joe's son, issued a Grand Jury indictment against Larry Sinclair, though charges were eventually dropped.[1] It is easy to dismiss Sinclair because of a criminal past, however, his allegations gain potential plausibility with the revelation in David Garrow's 2017 biography that Obama considered pursuing a homosexual relationship. In a letter to a girlfriend uncovered by Garrow, Obama wrote that "he [had] thought about and considered gayness but ultimately decided that same-sex relationships would be less challenging and demanding than developing one with the opposite sex."[2]

Obama's high school yearbook had paid tribute to a gentleman nicknamed "Gay Ray" who was later killed by a jilted lover, and a poem Obama published while at Occidental College called "Pop" references father and son having a stain on their pants, which had to be from semen.[3] Obama's probable father Frank Marshall Davis was known to be gay, which is considered to be a hereditary condition. A source in the Chicago police department told journalist Wayne Madsen that the Chicago police had maintained an open case in the late 1990s on Obama's activities with drugs and "morals violations."[4] This would be further consistent with Sinclair's allegations. A private investigator connected to the Chicago Police Department told a reporter that "Donald Young was silenced because of something he knew about Obama. Donald was in a position where he heard a lot of things and saw a lot of things concerning Barack."[5]

One theory is that the Sinclair case was processed as a threat to Obama in case of his non-compliance with the dictates of the U.S. power elite or deep state. Larry Sinclair said that the encounter he had with Obama was set up by limousine driver Jagir P. Multani who did not charge him because he said he was "paid on the other end." A theory is that Multani was part of a drugs-sex influence peddling operation run by Tony Rezko, Obama's political patron. Rezko is now in prison and Multani has long since disappeared, allegedly going back to India. Others implicated like Rod Blagojevich are also in prison. He was convicted and given a fourteen-year sentence for trying to sell Obama's old Senate seat. Sylvia and Kimball Ladien who investigated the case, believe that Blagojevich was used as a patsy by Obama and David Axelrod to shield Obama from any true investigation related to what Tony Rezko knew, including pertaining to the murder of Donald Young.[6] Rezko significantly was never asked to testify at Blagojevich's trial, and was placed in solitary confinement during the 2008 election. Blagojevich, who knew many of Obama and Rahm Emmanuel's secrets, was given a very harsh sentence for his transgressions. Sylvia Ladien later died, and her husband Kimball believes there was foul play in her case.[7] A confidante said that Michelle Obama could never push Valerie Jarrett out of Obama's inner orbit because she knows "where all the bodies are buried."[8] Inquiring minds want to know: what bodies was she referring to?

Endnotes

1   See Lawrence W. Sinclair, *Barack Obama & Larry Sinclair: Cocaine, Sex, Lies & Murder?* (Fort Walton Beach Florida: Sinclair Publishing, 2009); Webster G. Tarpley, *Barack H. Obama: The Unauthorized Biography* (Joshua Tree, CA: Progressive Press, 2008), 469, 470; Sylvia D. Ladien and Kimball Ladien, *Obama and the Murder of Don Young: Sylvia's Last Case? Getting Away with Murder?* (self-published).

2   David Garrow, *Rising Star: The Making of Barack Obama* (New York: William Morrow, 2017), 113.

3   Jerome R. Corsi, "Claim: Obama Hid Gay Life to Become President," *World Daily Net*, September 11, 2012; Wayne Madsen Report, May 2010; Wayne Madsen, *The Manufacturing of a President* (self-published, 2012), 292; David Maraniss, *Barack Obama: The Story* (New York: Simon & Schuster, 2013).

4   Ibid. Madsen, *The Manufacturing of a President*, 291, 292; Wayne Madsen Report, May 2010.

5   Victor Thorn, *Frontman: Obama's Darkest Secrets Revealed* (Washington, D.C.: American Free Press, 2010), 19.

6   Ladien and Ladien, *Obama and the Murder of Don Young*.

7   Ladien and Ladien, *Obama and the Murder of Don Young*.

8   Edward Klein, *Blood Feud: The Clintons versus the Obamas* (New York: Pinnacle, 2015), 54.

ACKNOWLEDGMENTS

I would like to thank numerous people for assisting me with this project: Paul McKinley and Dr. Randy Short gave me a real education about the importance of Obama's Chicago roots and failings toward the black community. Dr. Joel Gilbert answered questions about Obama's family background. Chas Freeman Jr., a thirty-year veteran of the diplomatic service, gave his time to provide great insights into U.S. foreign policy. Diana Collier saw the importance of the project and was an excellent editor. Ron Ridenour gave a very thorough review of the manuscript and shared his wisdom, giving many excellent suggestions. John Marciano and Jerry Lembcke did the same and provided invaluable editing, ideas and guidance. Other friends have assisted me in different ways, including: Peter Kuznick, Daniel Kovalik, and Roger Peace. I would also like to thank intellectual influences such as Noam Chomsky, Alfred McCoy and Peter Dale Scott, the guru of deep politics who advised a young graduate student to "read everything" with a critical but open mind no matter what the background or viewpoint of the author. This is the best professional advice I ever received and it has kept the interlibrary loan department at my various colleges very busy. I would like to thank the staff at the Tulsa Community College Northeast Library who have assisted me with many requests. I would also like to

334 | OBAMA'S UNENDING WARS

thank my daughters Olivia and Chanda and family. I dedicate this work to the late Fred Branfman, a true man of peace who was a critic of U.S. foreign policy and Obama. As a young man, Fred helped to expose the U.S. military and CIA atrocities in Laos and torture in USAID-run prisons in South Vietnam. He went on to develop a clean energy plan for the state of California in 1979 while working for Governor Jerry Brown. At the end of his life, Fred studied human psychology in an attempt to understand how humans could be so self-centered and cruel as a species. He sustained his political commitments and compassion for humanity throughout his life, and was a great role model whom I had the pleasure of knowing.

INDEX

Morocco, 106.
Morsi, Mohamed, 253.
Mosul, 181.
Mubarak, Hosni, 251, 253.
Mueller, Robert S., 241.
Mugabe, Robert, 87, 99, 107, 114.
Mujica, José, 287.
Multani, Jagir, 331.
Museveni, Yoweri, 96, 97, 112.
Muslim Brotherhood, 251, 252, 270,
 271, 274, 275.

N

Nagl, John, 23.
National Endowment for Democracy
 (NED), 202, 231, 252, 288, 305.
Navalny, Alexei, 238.
Negroponte, John, 290, 305.
Nekrasov, Andrei, 228.
Nemtsov, Boris, 238.
New START Treaty, 221.
Nicaragua, 304, 305.
Niger, 104.
Nkrumah, Kwame, 107, 122.
North Atlantic Treaty Organization
 (NATO), 120, 124, 128, 129,
 130, 144, 166, 168, 221, 226,
 237, 242.
Northrop Grumman, 149, 266.
Nixon, Richard M. 59, 121, 152,
 157, 192, 201, 303.
North American Free Trade
 Agreement (NAFTA), 298.
Nuland, Victoria, 232.
Nye, Gerald, 40.

O

Obama II, Barack Hussein see full
 manuscript
Obama Sr., Barack, 63, 64, 80.
Obama, Malik, 78, 136.
Obama, Michelle, 27, 75.
Occidental College, 60, 65, 79.
Odinga, Raila, 91.
O'Conner, Mary Ellen, 149.

Ogletree, Charles, 76.
Okinawa, 18, 193, 209, 210.
Olsen, Scott, 318.
Omar, Ilhan, 27.
Ondiba, Bongo, 89.
Operation Timber Sycamore, 271.
Operation Wappen, 268.
Optor resistance youth movement,
 252.
Ortega, Daniel, 285, 304, 305, 316.

P

Pakistan, 19, 152, 153, 165.
Palmer, Alice, 71.
Palmer, Lu, 74.
Panetta, Leon, 21, 121, 127, 287.
Paraguay, 285.
Patton, George, 145.
Paul, Rand, 126, 321.
Peña Nieto, Enrique, 294.
Petraeus, David, 23, 165, 167, 172,
 173, 174, 182, 197, 215, 266.
Pettigrew, Richard, 34.
Perry, William J. 221.
Philippines, 193, 204.
Pierce, Ann, 24.
Pilger, John, 202.
Piñera, Sebastien, 293, 311.
Poe, Tef, 74.
Poroshenko, Petro, 221, 231, 233,
 235.
Post-Traumatic Stress Disorder
 (PTSD), 27.
Power Africa, 92.
Power, Samantha, 22, 53, 79, 96,
 100, 118, 119, 124, 127, 235,
 236, 237, 262, 272, 300.
Pringle, Evelyn, 20.
Pritzker, Penny, 36, 37, 38, 53, 199,
 215, 231, 258, 261.
Puerto Rico, 31, 296.
Pushkov, Alexei, 273.
Pussy Riot, 238.
Putin, Vladimir, 18, 221, 223, 224,
 225, 226, 227, 228, 229, 230,
 231, 232, 237-242, 244, 256,
 274.